The African American EXPERIENCE in a Pluralistic Society

edited by
Leonard Gadzekpo
Southern Illinois University

Kendall Hunt
publishing company

Cover image © Lucian Coman. Used under license from Shutterstock, Inc.

Kendall Hunt
publishing company

www.kendallhunt.com
Send all inquiries to:
4050 Westmark Drive
Dubuque, IA 52004-1840

ISBN 978-0-7575-7943-1

Printed in the United States of America
10 9 8 7 6 5 4 3 2 1

Contents

Preface vi

Part 1 Defining African Americans 1

The Africana Paradigm 5
Leonard Gadzekpo
"What Is Africa to Me?": Language, Ideology, and *African American* 10
Geneva Smitherman
Of Our Spiritual Strivings 26
W. E. B. DuBois
Of the Faith of the Fathers 32
W. E. B. DuBois
The Sorrow Songs 41
W. E. B. DuBois
The Battle for Black Studies 48
Nathan Hare

Part 2 Social Construction of Race and Social Reality 67

Race and Race Theory 70
Howard Winant
Racism and Fascism 88
Toni Morrison
W.E.B. DuBois's Challenge to Scientific Racism 90
Carol M. Taylor
Discrimination and the American Creed 98
Robert K. Merton

Part 3 Sexualization, Gender and Culture 111

Sex and Racism 114
Mary Frances Berry and John W. Blassingame
African Diaspora Women: The Making of Cultural Workers 135
Bernice Johnson Reagon
The Hip Hop Generation: African American Male-Female Relationships in a Nightclub Setting 145
Janis Faye Hutchinson

Part 4 Facing the Present 163

A Profile of Familial Relations among Three-Generation Black Families 166
Robert Joseph Taylor, Linda M. Chatters, James S. Jackson

"The Streets": An Alternative Black Male Socialization Institution 191
William Oliver

... Contemporary Socioeconomic Trends: An Overview of Trends in Social and Economic Well-Being, by Race 205
Rebecca M. Blank

Demand-Side Changes and the Relative Economic Progress of Black Men: 1940–90 219
Elaine Reardon

Part 5 African Americans and Africana in the 21st Century 249

The Black Church, the Civil Rights Movement, and the Future 252
Leonard Gadzekpo

Black versus Black: The Relationships among Africans, African American, and African Caribbean Persons 266
Jennifer V. Jackson, Mary E. Cothran

Africans and Racism in the New Millennium 287
Femi Ojo-Ade

Black Transnationalism, Africana Studies, and the 21st Century 306
Michael George Hanchard

Preface

What is the African American or Black American experience in the United States of America, given the diversity and pluralistic character of the nation? Who is an African American? What makes a person Black and belong to the Black World or Africana? These questions generate discussion and answers that students and anyone interested in understanding and gaining insight into African American life will find elucidated in the selected texts.

The authors present a variety of positions, arguments, and analyses that demand readers question their own knowledge of African American life and become more critical of information concerning the African American experience. Their writings were chosen to awaken further discussion and analysis, so that the reader arrives at an informed and balanced insight not only into the African American experience, but also the American experience and the human condition. Core cultural, social, economic, and political aspects of the African American experience, as well as the undergirding imperative of all human endeavor to have access to resources, are brought to the fore so that, while understanding the control, distribution, and utilization of these resources exposes cultural, socioconomic, and political skeletal structures, the reader also builds a full-bodied nuanced insight.

I wish to acknowledge Amanda Smith and Doug Kovell of Kendall Hunt Publishing Company for their help in seeing this project through. Special thanks go to Rev. Dr. Joseph Brown, SJ, Director of the Black American Studies Program at Southern Illinois University Carbondale for his support of and contribution to this project. I also thank my colleagues in the Black American Studies program. In conclusion, I am grateful to the students, whose interest, inquisitive minds, and questioning inspired this project. Here's to deeper reading and questioning!

Leonard Gadzekpo
Carbondale, IL
April 11, 2010

Introduction

Throughout the essays collected in this book, an underlying question resonates as an often-submerged theme: Who defines the terms by which we all live? In matters of race and ethnicity, this question is central to how we understand all that is implied in the term *pluralistic society. Race* is a fluid term, with little or no basis in biological science, shaped and refined in certain academic disciplines, privileged by various political and economic developments. The attendant term, *racism*, has even more problems in all discussions dealing with people of different ethnic and cultural backgrounds. In the decades since the height of the civil rights movement, *prejudice*, *bigotry*, *bias*, and *racism* have often become interchangeable terms, more frequently approaching the point of total confusion. Attentive reading through this volume of essays may help restore the integrity of the terms and refresh the way we talk about the complexity of all forms of stereotypical judgments made by dominant social groups against less-powerful social groups.

In other contexts, studying the stumbling we can sometimes perform when trying to talk about the most vexing aspect of American society, we can further note that the words that refer to people of African descent are also frequent sources of linguistic problems, in that there is a plurality of terms, each with its own specific nuance and connotation. Are such people—as self-described or outwardly labeled—*colored*, *Negro*, *Black*, *Afro-American*, *African American*, or *Africana*? Each of these terms can be found in the essays of this collection. Some of the terms overlap and can be found near each other in the same selection—as they are often found simultaneously in U.S. cultural discourse.

From William Edward Burghardt (W.E.B.) DuBois, describing the essential dichotomy of the Black experience ("double consciousness"), to Audre Lorde's call to be attentive to issues of gender and sexuality difference (Black, female, lesbian), the notion of *social group* keeps expanding as conversations on cultural identity become increasingly complex and as the participants and the subjects of the conversations continue to refine their own identities—or have identities imposed upon them.

It is a measure of the strength of this collection that it quickly becomes clear to both the novice and the veteran student of cultural studies that inherited terms must be critically examined to find who most benefits by the classifications that permeate the media, politics, education, religion, and economics.

> *There is no single experience that covers the multiplicity of communities to which each of us belongs.*

There are many ways to configure a *selfhood*, each way having implications for the way an individual can choose to live or how the life and well-being of that individual can be either supported or limited by the perceptions and needs of others. One example can represent this sociological puzzle: *Male*—young, middle-aged, old; poor, middle-class, wealthy; unschooled, barely educated, literate; heterosexual, gay, transgendered, bisexual; nonchurched, Protestant, Catholic, Jewish, Islamic, nonbeliever, atheist. These suggested "fields of difference" can be manipulated almost endlessly, before race and ethnicity are even introduced to the discussion. Shift the reflection to other foundational terms and the same lesson is confirmed: we may be who we say we are, but we are also quite often who others say we are; and sometimes the words used as descriptors are as politically and economically motivated as are—for yet another example of information that does not clarify as much it intends to do—the racial categories supplied by the U.S. census forms.

One central focus of the readings in this collection is a study of the "social construction of race." We are challenged, in this section of the book and throughout, to reflect on the value systems that demand that laws be created to privilege one racial group over another, using the less than stringent tools of scientific racism in order to create the classifications of race. These value systems have generally been founded on economic systems derived from capitalism. Seemingly disconnected academic disciplines have often been used to reinforce these easily and often-discredited racial theories, and yet the damage has been done.

The hard work of engaging in the conversations found in this book will repair that intellectual damage by filling in the blanks, connecting the disparate pieces of information into a pattern that can illuminate and explain, and providing the reader/student with the critical skills to challenge all information presented in popular and "pseudo-scientific" discourse that would further diminish the contributions of all historically marginalized and devalued groups found in or affected by the dominant forces that have shaped and continue to sustain U.S. culture.

Powerful voices are found within the covers of this book. Witnesses are found here who have seen oppressed people triumph over massive dislocations and physical, emotional, and psychological traumas. An overview is provided that should easily support the claim that African American culture is not a collection of pathological behaviors that will forever infect the carriers of such a culture; but, rather, that African American culture is the grand story of people who sang, talked, plotted, and organized themselves from enslavement to freedom and who continue to instill great power into the words, "We shall overcome."

Joseph A. Brown, SJ, PhD
Professor and Director, Africana Studies
Southern Illinois University Carbondale

Part 1

Defining African Americans

INTRODUCTION

The African American experience is unequivocally an American experience in which people of African descent have for four hundred years survived, thrived, and flourished under conditions and impositions that for the greater part of the four centuries undermined their humanity and citizenship. At the core of that American experience are a phenomenon and a process involving creation of a new peoplehood within a nation that initially denied individuals and a people rights and full participation in national life as equals, even though it was their labor as slaves upon which the wealth of the nation was predicated and built. Designations given them and they themselves create are indicative of the issues of identity they have had to grapple with and the identity they fashioned from and within the American experience. Identity is important to African Americans because it situates them fully in the American experience and affords them a link to a global peoplehood of Black people, Africana, and to humanity. No other individuals and group in the United States of America had to forge their identity to override denial, rejection, and denigration of their humanity and to overcome political, social, and cultural impositions that systematically denied them full access to all aspects of their heritage, an access readily available to other Americans.

"The Africana Paradigm" deals with aspects of the African American experience, life and identity in which individual, group, national, and global manifestations are interwoven. That race is a social construct and, therefore, not viable in identity formation among African Americans is underscored by Black or Africana socio-cultural value of choosing family, the extended family, over race. For African Americans, biological relatedness, interdependence, and interconnectedness generated by consanguinity, marriage, and parentage are identifiable and concrete as against falsity of race with its proven inexactitude, unattainable practice of race assignment, and accompanying rejection of related people and racism. Leonard Gadzekpo presents in the essay genetic heritage and extended families, culture, awareness of history of struggle and progress, and multiplicity of identities as the Africana Paradigm that are defining aspects of African American identity, life, and experience in America.

In ""What Is Africa to Me?": Language, Ideology and *African American*" by Geneva Smitherman, she uses Countee Cullen's poem, entitled "What is Africa to me?" to launch into a discussion of designations given to people of African descent in America and their own self-designation tracing the changes that occurred over four hundred years. She examines sociolinguistic dimensions of designations given people of African descent and argues self-designation is emblematic of a paradigm shift necessary for the emergence and affirmation of an identity so as "to facilitate the creation of policy, tactics, strategies, and programs to redress"[1] the plight of the African American community.

---

[1] **Geneva Smitherman, ""What Is Africa to Me?": Language, Ideology, and African American", *American Speech*, Vol. 66, No. 2., (Summer, 1991):.129.**

Three essays by W.E.B DuBois from *The Souls of Black Folk* articulate African American ethos. DuBois examines in "Of Our Spiritual Strivings" a central existential condition confronted by African Americans in the first half of the twentieth century that one may project into the twenty-first and onto all Africana. The issue of multiple identities and unifying them positively is a twenty-first century reality for African Americans and all Africana just as it was a twentieth century lived experience. The DuBoisian phenomenology of "double-consciousness" or "twoness" points to dual identity within African Americans being both "Negro", demeaned, and American, creating a "sense of always looking at one's self through the eyes of others" who regard them with "contempt and pity".[2] He encourages African American artists to espouse "soul beauty" that captures "innate love of harmony and beauty" of the people.[3] He sees an urgent need for knowledge in which "the history of the Negro in America and in Africa" is an integral part of interpretation of all history and in understanding of the social development of all mankind through the ages and, thus, generate and affirm self-understanding, self-respect, self-reliance, and self-realization among African Americans.[4]

In "Of the Faith of the Fathers", DuBois looks at African American religious culture and its significance in navigating the gauntlet of slavery, terrorism of racists, and in a society that had "the Negro Problem". The Black Church developed after emancipation into a singular institution addressing the plight of communities. DuBois is, however, critical of well-to-do Black Christians in urban communities who looked down on less fortunate ones, especially from the South, while offering no solutions to their wanton disposition and condition or plight. He concludes the strength of African American spirituality lies in its perseverance in face of inhumanity and its ability to heal the soul of a people so oppressed.

"The Sorrow Songs" bemoans the African American condition, but Dubois also sees spiritual fortitude and emotional strength in Black religious music, the Spirituals. He traces its African roots to plantations in the American South among the enslaved, for example the Sea Islands of Carolina, and to Fisk Jubilee Singers and points to a legacy and a tradition of cultural transmission from generation to generation. The songs heal, but they are also songs of protest that capture the African American experience within the larger American experience. DuBois asks: Would America have been America without her Negro people?[5]

Nathan Hare's "The Battle for Studies" chronicles the emergence of Black Studies as an academic discipline and an intellectual enterprise. Unlike most academic disciplines that have their genesis in efforts of academicians and intellectuals to study and teach

---

[2] W.E.B. DuBois, *The Souls of Black Folk*. Radford, Wilder Publications, LLC, 2008. 6.

[3] Ibid.

[4] Ibid.

[5] Ibid. 114.

areas of human endeavor that they deemed worthy of study, the initial vehicle that brought Black Studies into academia was mass movement and mass struggle among African Americans who saw education as belonging to the people and that it should be relevant to the community and help in transforming it. Strivings of earlier years came to a head in the 1960s during the era of the Civil Rights Movement and affirmation of Black culture when students translated agitation and demand for equality and access to resources America has to offer into intellectual activism on campuses. San Francisco State University was the first to institute Black Studies as an academic discipline after drawn-out agitation and became the epicenter of a wave that reverberated in universities and colleges across America with large enrollments of African American students demanding establishment of Black Studies programs. Hare argues that in their demand for and with establishment of Black Studies programs in academic institutions, the African American students were the vanguard of their generation in the long struggle of Black self-determination and did "activate and energize the black intelligentsia" to the benefit of society

The Africana Paradigm

Leonard Gadzekpo

What makes a person an African American, Black, or belong to Africana? To answer this question and deal with the African American experience and Africana, a paradigm that examines the reality of Africana or Black humanity, culture, history and experience, a paradigm that addresses aspects generated by Africana ethos and essence has to be employed. I term it the Africana Paradigm. Africana means all things and issues dealing with and connected to Africa, especially sub-Saharan Africa or Africa South of the Sahara or Black Africa and her Diaspora. African Americans are part of the African Diaspora and therefore Africana.

While *paradigm* has been used in a variety of disciplines with different meanings and sometimes seen as ambiguous, the working meaning employed in this context is drawn from Thomas Kuhn's definition of *paradigm* he applied to scientific communities as an entire constellation of beliefs, values and techniques, and so on, shared by the members of a given community.[1] The reality lived by Black people, engrained in their values and practices, and expressed in beliefs, concepts and ideas that embody their essence is the Africana Paradigm. To be Black, to belong to Africana involves four aspects of genetic Black African heritage, culture, awareness and a composite multiplicity of identities. These four aspects are not mutually exclusive but overlap often dovetail into each other; in some cases inseparable and

[1] Thomas Kuhn, *The Structure of Scientific Revolutions,* Chicago: The Chicago University Press, 1970

at other times are mutually inclusive and in an ever-expanding permutation affirming and making concrete the concepts of *Africana* or *Blackness*.

1. GENETIC MEMORY OR HERITAGE

The first aspect is biological in that to be Black means one has African ancestry, a direct line of genetic markers even if several generations removed from the original Black African. It means skin color or hair texture or other physical features are not necessarily the most significant markers but rather DNA. To be Black or belong to Africana has nothing to do with race, a socially constructed taxonomy that is given a veneer of biological validation that is false and unscientific and intellectually bankrupt.

It is a historical fact that millions of Africans were brought to the United States and the rest of the Americas against their will; so the genetic diversity in Africa continues to be replicated wherever populations of Black people live outside Africa – in other words, the "Diaspora". The females among these people were the mothers of Blacks against whom laws were made to keep them and their children in perpetual bondage during the long centuries of chattel slavery and the denial of Black humanity. This "sisterhood of women" indicated by mitochondrial DNA (mtDNA) and their motherhood gave birth to all men, hence brotherhood and common humanity.

Genetic analysis, even though limited in ability at the present stage of development, offers remarkable information on origins of descendants of Black Africans in the Diaspora. Henry Louis Gates' statement that "Because a family unit is a bond- and an extended family is a larger bond- and out of such bonds, loyalty and resistance are built", succinctly articulates power and longevity of both genetic and cultural bonds that outlive temporality of oppression and deprivation despite continuing residual effects of such experience in Africana.[2] Physical memory or genetic memory passed on through parents to their children gives the individual a body that carries genetic imprints left over the millennia along with mutations. Herein lies the most basic biological aspect of being African American, being of African-descent or being Black and belonging to Africana, to which community and society give a social defining character imprinted with centuries-old cultural memory bestowed upon individuals and learnt through extended families and communities.

2. CULTURE AND EXTENDED FAMILY

The second aspect involves *cultural values* epitomized by sense of family, the extended family, and cultural norms that have been *transmitted through the centuries* from generation to generation adapting and adopting to serve the needs of the extended

[2] Henry Louis Gates, Jr., "We are all Africans: Genealogical Research and DNA Testing Can Reveal your Ethnic Connection to Africa", *Ebony*, December 2007. 134.

family wherever people of African descent live. The Black child's acculturation starts amidst a host of relatives and other community members. If the genetic aspect of being Black is a given by virtue of parentage, cultural aspects are acquired through learning and the extended family teaches and is the transmitter of African American culture. This aspect involves family traditions that are inherent parts of a larger community of extended families made up of biological and fictive family members and friends. Elmer P. Martin and Joanne Mitchell Martin's definition of African American extended family captures a commonality with the African manifestation and practice evidencing continuity on both sides of the Atlantic:

> When we speak of a black extended family, we mean a multigenerational, interdependent kinship system which is welded together by a sense of obligation to relatives; is organized around a "family base" household; is generally guided by a "dominant family figure", extends across geographical boundaries to connect family units to an extended family network; and has a built-in mutual aid system for the welfare of its members and maintenance of the family as a whole.[3]

Extended families derive their existence neither from skin color nor hair types, nor from putative visible "racial" physical characteristics, nor metaphysical similarities, nor commonalities of members, but from what Kwame Anthony Appiah sees as "brute biological relatedness"[4] that is exponentially populated with members of connected families by virtue of consanguinity and marriages.

Membership of Africana through nuclear and extended families by virtue of birth and marriage does not determine race, neither does genetic heritage, nor socio-cultural connectedness of groups that expands and exponentially augments in complexity through fictive kinship. One may define fictive kinship as a bond formed between individuals, groups, and in communities of those who are not blood relatives but share living environments and experiences and thus develop commonalities including identity, sense of belonging, commitment, and mutual obligations that are found in kinship involving blood relations and marriages. Fictive kinship extrapolates inclusivity not only in extended families but also in Africana communities.

A sense of family and belonging to an extended family generate sustenance, resistance, preservation and growth of community. At the core of African American life and culture is the extended family. Because African Americans, Blacks, Africana, choose family race is of no relevance, not significant, and issues of racial purity or dichotomous fallacy of superiority or inferiority based on race are vacated by inclusiveness of extended families as against exclusivity of race.

---

[3] Elmer P. Martin and Joanne Mitchell Martin, *The Black Extended Family*. Chicago: The University of Chicago Press, 1980. 1.

[4] Kwame Anthony Appiah, "Racisms," in *Anatomy of Racism*, ed. D.T. Goldberg. Minneapolis: University of Minnesota Press, 1990. 15.

3. AWARENESS OF THE HISTORY OF STRUGGLE AND PROGRESS

The third aspect is awareness of *the history of resistance, struggle and progress.* Moral, social and cultural investments in the individual guarantee a committed agent of stability within nuclear and extended families and community. Lived experiences by individuals and communities become integral parts of collective narratives of African Americans and create sense of place in community and history that revere and honor ancestors. These narratives are preserved and transmitted from generation to generations in oral traditions, artifacts and other texts, receptacles of thought and cultural values and repositories of African American collective memory. Collective memory and its power of engendering awareness and sense of place in community and history function at local levels as a source of resistance among African Americans within extended families and communities.

Peoplehood, African American peoplehood, was forged out of individuals, nuclear and extended families and communities thrown together into harsh and deprived conditions through the centuries in which they had to depend on inner strength and common cultural values for their survival. In the African Diaspora, slavery, internal colonization and the struggle for freedom and rights as full citizens generated and perpetuated collective memories in the various communities and countries in which these African-derived people live. An understanding of these experiences and a common cultural denominator of extended families and community building underscore collective memory on a global scale in Africana. Awareness of history of resistance, struggle, and progress brings to the fore a self-reflexive ability to question not only oneself, but more importantly community, society, country, and all humanity.

4. COMPOSITE MULTIPLICITY OF IDENTITIES

The fourth aspect of the African Paradigm is *multiplicity of identities.* In extended families individual and group identities develop simultaneously. Identity formation does not occur in a vacuum nor can the cultural and social parameters within which an individual lives be vacated in affirmation of personhood. Among African Americans and all Africana, identity formation involves reciprocity. Extended families offer a constant source of reciprocity and validation affirming both individual and group or family identities to which other identities are developed and added.

Reciprocity, giving and receiving, starts even before a child of Africana is born. Like their ancestors, Africana asks: If there are no children, how can one be an ancestor? The child, therefore, is central to Africana cycle of life, the past, the present and the future. Ancestors of African Americans chose life faced with horrific conditions on slave ships and on slave plantations or in maroon communities and in so doing procreated generations giving them tools to live their lives. These tools include giving back to their extended families, communities and societies and revering them, roots of family trees that multiply in forests of extended families and communities, African Americans, Africana. The concept of reciprocity is deeply inherent in Africana culture and is a marker in all cultural expressions.

Call and Response, a functional and aesthetic characteristic of music and other performing arts among Black people, epitomize reciprocity permeating all aspects of Black life and culture.[5] Abu Shardow Abarry affirms that callers and responders "simultaneously articulate and reinforce each individual's connections with their social, spiritual and physical worlds. It thereby promotes a sense of security and solidarity among the people."[6] The call and response performance among African Americans, from work songs and ring-shouts to preaching, blues, jazz, soul, and rap, is reciprocity and not a random development but consistent retention and reinterpretation of specific cultural values by descendants of those who forebears developed it for community cohesion and for inter-generational transmission of cultural and social norms.

The presence of extended family in other Africana communities outside Africa brings into focus common identity formation process among Black people. While individuality is important, as clearly evidenced by names given to children, all naming and/or baptismal ceremonies are performed in extended family members' presence, linking an individual child to family and community; thus affirming identity a child acquires is intrinsically connected and drawn from family and community. The child receives a name and group identity from family as he or she gives the family assurance of the future. Reciprocity in Africana is a cycle linking the past, present and future.

The individual affirms identity in "I am." Often it is a name. Interconnectedness and group identity extended families generate are given affirmation with "We are." At the most elemental level, to be human is to be born of a woman and a man, what in Africana makes an individual by default a member of multiplicity of extended families from maternal and paternal relatives, the genesis of the aforementioned interconnectedness. It is in these extended families that "I am" multiplies and the first articulation of group identity emerges as "We are." Identity formation, effective and positive identity formation in Africana, can only be possible when there is validation. Extended families through interconnectedness and interdependence give concrete validation to all who belong to Africana.

While within extended families multiplicity of identities, including gender and age identities, ferment, it is when individual and extended family group identities expand beyond intimacy of family that multiplicity and complexities of a composite identity and its fluidity allow the individual to embrace being African American, peoplehood, and the fullness of Africana to encompass all humanity. It means to be of Africana, to be Black, to be African American is not to have a monolithic identity, but to possess a diversity of identities, incontrovertibly exemplified by the designation African American or Black American, overarched by a sense of peoplehood within a nation that is manifested on a global scale as Africana.

---

[5] Kariamu Welsh-Asante, ed, *The African Aesthetics: Keeper of the Traditions.* New York: Preager, 1994. 28. Robert Farris Thompson, *Flash of the Spirit: African and Afro-American Art and Philosophy*. New York: Vintage Books, 1984.

[6] Abu Shardow Abarry, "Mpai: Libation Oratory" in *The African Aesthetics: Keeper of the Tradition,* ed., Kariamu Welsh-Asante. 86-87.

"What Is Africa to Me?": Language, Ideology, and *African American*

Geneva Smitherman

The relationship of Black Americans to "Mother Africa" is being raised anew and in a broad public forum as the national Black community struggles with the call to move from the racial designation "Black" to "African American." Because of Reverend Jesse Jackson's widespread popularity, many have assumed him to be the catalyst for the current linguistic change. However, it was actually Dr. Ramona H. Edelin, President of the National Urban Coalition, who, in late 1988, proposed that the then upcoming 1989 summit be called the "African American Summit" because the semantics "would establish a cultural context for the new agenda" (quoted in Lacayo and Monroe 1989). Taking up Edelin's call at the December 1988 news conference to announce the Summit, Jackson indicated that "just as we were called colored, but were not that . . . and then Negro, but not that . . . to be called Black is just as baseless," and further, like other groups of Americans, African Americans want to link their heritage to the land of their origin (quoted in Page 1989).

The issue of racial semantics set in motion by Edelin, Jackson, and others has generated far greater national publicity and media attention than the Summit itself. In addition to extensive coverage by *The New York Times*, articles have appeared in *Time*, *The Chicago Tribune*, *The Washington Post*, several metropolitan dailies across the country, and in *Ebony*, *Essence*, and other African American media. CBS "Nightwatch" News hosted an hour-long panel discussion on the issue.[2] Even Ann Landers (1989) devoted attention to the question, publishing responses in one column and indicating in another column that *African American* "seems appropriate because it gets away from color and designates origin instead. I hope it catches on." As recently as 28 October 1990, *The Washington Post National Weekly Edition* featured the issue in a column by Michael Specter headlined "Men and Women of Their Word: But Should that Word be 'Black' or 'African American'?" (10). And in December, 1990, as I was writing this article, Rosemary Bray dealt with this topic in a special section of *Essence*.

Inasmuch as the current linguistic movement is complexified by the dynamics of race, there are bound to be cases of uncertainty as well as confusion. Lexicographers, such

Geneva Smitherman, "What is Africa to Me?: Language, Ideology, and African American," in *American Speech*, Volume 66, No. 2, pp. 115-132.

as those at Random House, and the mainstream press, such as the Associated Press and *The New York Times*, are waiting for a consensus among speakers and writers before establishing a policy decision on *Black* versus *African American*. Although the United States Census Bureau did not use "African American" as a category on the 1990 census form—reportedly because the call for change was issued too late to be included (Wilkerson 1989)—the Bureau DID add special instructions to the form indicating that "Black" or "Negro" includes "African Americans." Humorous instances of linguistic confusion are starting to crop up, as these two examples indicate:

> We, the Black African American people will soon rise to our God-given greatness—if we just hold on to His unchanging hand. [banquet speaker at an African American church, 22 September 1990, Detroit]
>
> An item in Thursday's *Nation Digest* about the Massachusetts budget crisis made reference to new taxes that will help put Massachusetts "back in the African-American." The item should have said "back in the black." [*The Fresno Bee*, 21 July 1990, 12A]

This article seeks to illuminate the age-old question of a name for the enslaved African population of the United States and its emancipated descendants. Two dimensions of the question will be presented: (1) the history of racial labelling from the perspective of the changing material conditions of Blacks; and (2) contemporary opinions about the use of *African American* based on the author's five-city survey of public opinion about language matters.

WHAT'S IN A NAME ?

This study is informed by the paradigm, in linguistics, of "language as social semiotic" (Halliday 1978) and the theoretical framework, in sociology, of the "social construction of reality" (Berger and Luckmann 1966). Following Berger and Luckmann's contention that language constitutes the most important content and instrument of socialization, I will here summarize an argument I've made extensively elsewhere (Smitherman 1980, 1983, 1989): reality is not merely SOCIALLY, but SOCIOLINGUISTICALLY, constructed. Real-world experience and phenomena do not exist in some raw, undifferentiated form. Rather, reality is always filtered, apprehended, encoded, codified, and conveyed via some linguistic shape. This linguistic form exists in a dialectical relationship with social cognition and social behavior. While Humboldtian linguists (and most Whorfians, for that matter) overstate the case for language as THE determiner of thought, consciousness and behavior, nonetheless, language DOES play a dominant role in the formation of ideology, consciousness, and class relations. As Vološinov put it, "ideology is revealed in a word" (1929, 70). Thus my contention is that consciousness and ideology are largely the products of what I call the SOCIOLINGUISTIC CONSTRUCTION OF REALITY.

For African Americans, the semantics of race have been recurring themes in our sociolinguistic constructions of reality since 1619, when the first cargo of African slaves landed at Jamestown. The societal complexity of the Black condition continues to necessitate a self-conscious construction of identity. Notwithstanding historical, cultural, and cosmological linkages with Continental and Diasporic Africans and, further, notwithstanding similarities between American slavery and slavery in other historical epochs, the African American, as James Baldwin once put it, is a unique creation. Whereas other African peoples lay claim to national identity in countries where the population is "Black"—e.g., Jamaicans, Ghanains, Bajans, Nigerians—African Americans claim national identity in a country where most of the population is non-Black. After being emancipated and granted citizenship, there were (and continue to be) profound implications for a group with a lifetime suntan trying to forge an identity and a life in the midst of the European American population which for decades had found them lacking the necessities of intellect and morality.[3]

From 1619, and right up until Emancipation, in fact, the identity question was complexified by the widely divergent statuses of Blacks. Because of the commonality of skin color, it was impossible to distinguish permanent from "temporary" African slaves (i.e., those who, like the European indentured servants, were working to purchase their freedom), or either of these from those Africans freed by their masters or those born to free parents. None of the aforementioned groups, by virtue of "blackness" alone, could be distinguished from escaped/"fugitive" slaves. And what about the products of miscegenation, where one parent was European (and therefore free), the other was an African slave, and the skin color was light black?

AFRICAN. Europeans in Colonial America used racial labels based on what was for them the critical category of enslavement. Thus, depending on status, Africans were referred to as "free" or "slave" (Franklin 1969). Where enslavement status was unknown, or where there was occasion to use a collective term for all Africans, they used "nigger" (not a racial epithet until the late nineteenth century) or "negro" (Portuguese adjective 'black'; used by fifteenth century Portuguese slave traders; lowercased until the 1920s).

Although the small number of "free" Africans tended to refer to themselves as "colored," the most frequently used label, for "free" and "slave" alike, was *African* (Drake 1966). The first church was called the African Episcopal Church. The first formally organized self-help group was designated the Free African Society, followed by the African Educational and Benevolent Society, the Sons of Africa Society, and the African Association for Mutual Relief. The first Masonic Lodge was called African Lodge No. 459. And the writer of one of the first slave narratives referred to himself as "Olaudah Equiano, or Gustavus Vassa, the African" (1789).

The sociolinguistic reality these early Africans constructed reflected a distinct African consciousness. Since the African experience was still very immediate for most Blacks, regardless of their status, the possibility of returning to Africa haunted them constantly. Two years before the signing of the Declaration of Independence, a group of African slaves formally petitioned the British governor of Massachusetts for permission to return to Africa (Drake 1987). The legendary folk hero Solomon (also of Toni Morrison's novel *Song of Solomon*) was believed to have the capacity to fly back to Africa—and hence, freedom. In fact, according to Asante (1988), what some scholars refer to as the African American pre-generic quest myth of freedom speaks originally to escape to Mother Africa out of bondage, with Canada and the northern United States coming in at a later historical stage. In any case, the ideological function of the label *African* served as a logical rallying point, since all Blacks had current or ancestral ties to Africa, whether they were temporary or permanent slaves, free men/women, fugitives, or mixed-bloods (albeit if the mother was a slave—the usual case—the offspring was also classified as a slave). *African* symbolized a common heritage, thus becoming a focal, unifying semantic for socially divergent groups of Africans, both creating and reinforcing the social construction of group solidarity and commonality.

Colored

The Black condition became even more complexified after England's colonies became the United States. For one thing, slavery WAS NOT ABOLISHED, as the enslaved African population had anticipated, and as the free Africans—such as the leader Prince Hall, who fought at Lexington, Concord, and Bunker Hill—had believed. The Black Codes passed in the eighteenth century had abolished temporary slavery and instituted the "slave-for-life" status for all enslaved Africans, including their offspring, thus differentiating African slaves from the European indentured servant population (Franklin 1969). But 1776 brought about neither a repeal of these laws nor universal emancipation. Further, the costly, inefficient method of importing shiploads of human cargo across the abyss of the Middle Passage was gradually supplanted by the greater cost-benefit system of local slave (re)production (enhanced on some plantations by the designation of certain males as breeders).[4] Yet the importation did not cease altogether, even after passage of the 1808 Slave Trade Act outlawing this transportation of human chattel. Then there were the free men/women who, though not slaves, were denied full citizenship and equal rights in the newly formed United States. Finally, the processes of individual manumission and miscegenation continued, each adding another layer of complexity to the status of people of African descent during the era between the Revolutionary and the Civil Wars. Could the same racial label be used for slaves fresh from Africa as for slaves born in the United States, some of whom were fifth and sixth generation descendants of Africans? (In some of the advertisements for runaway slaves, recently captured Africans were referred to as "NEW negroes" [Read 1939].) And if freed men/women of African descent were not full citizens of the newly created American State, what should they be called? (Surely not *African AMERICANS*?!])

In the nineteenth century, the era of *colored* began, and the semantics of *African* declined in use and significance. By this era, several generations of Blacks had been born on American soil, and with fewer arrivals from Africa, there was decreased cultural infusion into the slave community. Further, although colonization societies and movements to resettle the slaves in Africa persisted right up until the Civil War, the huge Black population—well over one million by 1800—made wholesale emigration of Blacks to Africa impractical, if not impossible. Most critically, both the free and the enslaved African populations were developing a new understanding of their role in the making of America (Frazier 1957). They had helped build the country through nearly two hundred years of free labor, and the free Africans had participated both in the Revolutionary War and the War of 1812. The possibility for emancipation and citizenship was being created through their agitation and struggle, as well as through the efforts of European American Abolitionists. The Africans reasoned that the

European American-dominated movements to resettle them in Africa would effectively disinherit them of their share of the American pie whose ingredients included not only their own blood, sweat, and tears, but that of many thousands gone.

Although *colored* had been used in the earlier period by some "free" Africans, it re-emerged in the nineteenth century as a racial referent for the entire Black group, now united in its collective move toward emancipation. There was the formation of the Pennsylvania Augustine Society "for the education of people of colour." There was the publication of David Walker's radical *Appeal* (1829) calling for open rebellion against enslavement, which he addressed to the "Coloured Citizens of the World, but in Particular and very Expressly to Those of the United States of America." Abolitionist leader Frederick Douglass used *colored* (as well as *negro*) in his speeches and writings. Oral histories and folk narratives indicate the widespread use of *colored* among everyday Black people (Bennett 1961). Even into the early twentieth century, *colored* was the preferred racial designation. The oldest civil rights organization, founded in 1909, was (and still is) called the National Association for the Advancement of COLORED People.

Negro

The shift away from *colored* to *negro*, and the subsequent campaign for its capitalization, began at the turn of the century and hit its full stride during the period of the two world wars. The initial signs of linguistic change were the American Negro Academy, founded in 1897, and the National Negro Business League, founded in 1900. Booker T. Washington and other leaders of this period used *negro* frequently in their speeches (Bennett 1967). The ideological vision was that with the spotlight on Europe and global struggles for freedom against fascism, and with "colored" soldiers (albeit in segregated regiments) shedding their blood for America, surely the still-unrealized quest for first-class citizenship and racial equity would at last be fulfilled. The appropriate conceptual label to usher in this new phase was *negro*, which had come into widespread linguistic currency among European Americans, especially those in the North, the seat of capital and political power. The new language was needed to construct a new identity of dignity, respect, and full citizenship, all of which had been lacking in the past.

Negro leaders of the 1920s launched a massive, nation-wide campaign for the capitalization of *negro* in order to elevate the Portuguese slavery-time adjective to the symbolic level of dignity and respect accorded a racial label. The NAACP sent out over 700 letters to European American publishers and editors, Dr. W. E. B. Du Bois wrote numerous editorial "Postscripts" in *Crisis.* Significant efforts were launched on local-community and grass-roots levels (e.g., the biweekly newsletter published by the Paul Laurence Dunbar Apartments in Cincinnati, Ohio). Finally the European American press capitulated: "In our Style Book, *Negro* is now added to the list of words to be capitalized. It is not merely a typographical change, it is an act in recognition of racial self-respect for those who have been for generations in the 'lower case'" (*New York Times*, 7 Mar. 1930, 22). Although some Negroes continued to use *colored*, and although some Negro leaders and intellectuals—Du Bois among them—balanced *Negro* with *Black* (Smitherman 1986), *Negro* became the label of choice, dominating discourse by and about Negroes for over forty years.

Black

In 1966, Negro activist and leader Stokeley Carmichael issued a call for "Black Power," and Negroes began to create a new sociolinguistic construction of reality. Several local and national conferences were held under the rubric of "Black Power" in 1966 and 1967 (Walters forthcoming). Symbolizing a new ideological phase in the Negro Experience, these conferences and their leadership called upon Negroes to abandon the "slavery-imposed name" (Bennett 1967).

The move from *Negro* to *Black* signalled an ideological shift, a repudiation of whiteness and the rejection of assimilation. The failure to embrace Blackness and to capitalize on the strengths of Black Culture and the Black Experience was reasoned to have stagnated the progress of the Civil Rights Movement. Only by being true to themselves and their heritage would Black people be able to harness the necessary power to liberate themselves. Freedom could not be achieved without a healthy racial consciousness, underscored by a strong belief in the collective Black Will to change the conditions of oppression. Thus it was imperative that Blacks eradicate the negativity and self-hatred of the Coloracracy, exemplified in the folk ditty, "If you white, you all right, if you brown, stick around, if you Black, git back."

The choice of a label that had traditionally been a way of calling a Negro "outa they name" now was being employed to purify Negroes of the idealization of white skin, white ideas, and white values. Spreading throughout the national Black community, the newly constructed reality was captured in the popular, best-selling 1968 song by James Brown, "Say it loud: 'I'm Black, and I'm proud.'" It was a profoundly classic case of the semantic inversion characteristic of Black English Vernacular speakers.[5] *Bad* was truly turned on its head and made *good* as the celebration of "Black"—Black Culture, Black skin color, the Black Experience—became a rallying cry for unity, empowerment and self-definition. Negro History Week, in existence since its founding by Dr. Carter G. Woodson in 1926, became BLACK History Week (and eventually Black History Month). The language announced Black people's right to chart their destiny; it conveyed their determined will for freedom and equity on their own terms. Most critically, the new racial semantics served a cathartic function as the national Black community purged itself of age-old scripts of self-hatred and denial. This period of catharsis was necessary, for it enabled African Americans to come to grips with centuries of much ado about the nothingness of skin color.

African American

In 1977 (in the first edition of Smitherman 1986), I stated:

> The semantic designations 'Afro-American' and 'African American' accompanied the 1966 rise of 'Black' but have yet to achieve its widespread general usage in the Black community. . . . The . . . terms denote the reality of the double consciousness and dual cultural heritage of Black folk: part Africa, part America. Perhaps the more frequent use of Afro-American and African American awaits the complete healing of the psychic wounds of the Black past. [41–42]

That healing has now been completed. It is time to evolve to a new ideological plateau.

The call for *African American* is a call for a new paradigm in the unceasing quest for freedom. The hard-won progress of the previous generation of struggle is being eroded by national policies and court decisions that would turn back the hands of time. At the same time, the freedom struggle on the Continent—e.g., South Africa—and in the Diaspora outside of the United States—e.g., Grenada—has taken center stage in the world. It is time to redefine and reconceptualize the identity of the African in North America.

Though minimizing the significance of language, Dr. Manning Marable, prolific African American scholar and newspaper columnist, addresses the domestic issues that have triggered the current call for a new racial semantic:

> The important question, therefore, is not the terminology per se, but why the phrase has emerged now. . . . The decade of the 1980's is . . . bleak: . . . the massive white electoral mandates for the Reagan/Bush administrations, which campaigned successfully on programs of thinly veiled racism; the growth of urban youth violence, Black-on-Black homicides, high unemployment and drug proliferation; and the fragmentation of many Black social institutions such as the Black Church. . . . The combination of destructive socio-economic and political forces from without and the social decay and chaos from within have prompted a looking inward. [1989, 72]

Writer Gloria Naylor, addressing the internationalist domain evoked by the call for *African American*, notes that "to call ourselves that, we would have to forge true ties with other people of color" (quoted in Anon. 1989, 80). Dr. Dorothy I. Height, President of the National Council of Negro Women, makes a similar point when she says, "It is a recognition that we've always been African and American, but we are now going to . . . make a unified effort to identify with our African brothers and sisters" (quoted in Anon. 1989, 80). Perhaps Jesse Jackson made the most eloquent and succinct statement about the international scope of the new label when he said, "Black tells you about skin color and what side of town you live on. *African American* evokes discussion of the world" (quoted in Wilkerson 1989). In this period of reassessment and reevaluation of the rapidly deteriorating Black condition, the new semantic constructs an identity of unified global struggle against race domination, linking Africans in North America with Continental Africans and with other Diasporic African groups. For a people grappling with disempowerment and its tragic effects on entire Black communities across the nation, the term provides the security of "I am somebody" by reaffirming the origin and cultural continuity of our African heritage. At the same time, *African* AMERICAN calls attention to four hundred years of contributions to the making of America and legitimates the political and economic demand for equity. The 'American' identity of African Americans has been sustained and continues to be embraced in the form that Walker articulated over a century and a half ago, stating in his Appeal, "Men who are resolved to keep us in eternal wretchedness are also bent on sending us to Liberia. . . . America is more our country than it is the whites—we have enriched it with our BLOOD AND TEARS" (1829, 65).

The call for *African American* has been issued. What has been the response?

There are several noteworthy institutional examples of its use. Atlanta, Chicago, and Detroit, three urban school districts with predominantly African American student populations, have adopted the term in their curricula and are encouraging teachers to use it. Tennis great Arthur Ashe titled his 1988 book *A Hard Road to Glory: A History of the African American Athlete.* WWRL and WLIB, both large Black-oriented radio stations in New York City, use the term, as well as New York's first African American mayor, David Dinkins. According to Joseph Hollander, Director of Publications for The Modern Language Association, *African American* is used in most cases, but *Black* and other terms are acceptable as long as they are appropriate (personal communication 1991). Three of the largest African American newspapers in the country now use the term: New York's *Amsterdam News*, Chicago's *Daily Defender*, and Detroit's *Michigan Chronicle.* In the November, 1990, Motown television special, in which Motown celebrated its thirty-year history in the recording and entertainment industry, all of the entertainers who participated in the narration used *African American* consistently throughout the entire program (a few did so quite self-consciously).

The NAACP, which was in the forefront of the movement from *colored* to *Negro* in the 1920s, has adopted a wait-and-see posture on the current linguistic movement. According to Dr. Benjamin Hooks, Executive Director, "We will neither oppose nor endorse the use of the term 'African-American.' This does not indicate a lack of concern, but rather an abiding respect for the sound judgment of our people, who, on their own, will reach a consensus, just as they have done in the past" (quoted in Anon. 1989, 78).

THE PEOPLE SPEAK: FIVE-CITY PUBLIC OPINION SURVEY

Sample and method

In an attempt to assess the "sound judgment of our people," I included a question about *African American* in a language attitude instrument designed to elicit opinions about foreign language teaching in the public schools and "English-only" legislation (Smitherman, in preparation). This survey research project involved five cities with large African American populations. It was conducted between May and September, 1989. The cities were Atlanta, Chicago, Cincinnati, Detroit, and Philadelphia. The 667 respondents included both African and European Americans, 512 of whom answered the *African American* question.

In Chicago, Cincinnati, and Philadelphia, the data (hereafter C1) were collected using written questionnaires which the respondents completed themselves. They were selected using a sample-of-convenience approach. Thus while the results are informative, the power of the claims we could make is somewhat limited by the sampling procedures.[6] The Detroit and Atlanta surveys (hereafter C2) were administered to scientifically

TABLE 1 Opinions About Use of *African American* (African Americans only; n = 264)

	C1 Sample	*C2 Sample*
YES	43%	37%
NO	57%	63%

selected samples, using census data, ZIP acodes, and computer-generated telephone numbers. These data were collected through telephone surveys by a staff of interviewers trained in survey research techniques. Thus there is greater confidence in these results.

The *African American* question was posed in the following form: "There is a lot of talk about what different racial and ethnic groups should be called. Do you think the term "African American" should replace the term "Black" as the name for Black people in the United States?" Respondents were then asked to explain their answers.

Results

When all respondents are considered, results show that anywhere from slightly more than one-third to one-halt favor the shift to *African American*. In the C1 sample (n = 210), opinions were split exactly evenly, whereas in the C2 sample, the scientifically selected group (n = 30), only 34.4 percent favored the shift.

When we consider only the African American respondents, results are somewhat, but not significantly, different from results for all respondents. In the C1 group, 43 percent favored the shift, and in the C2 sample, 33 percent favored the shift. (See table 1.)

African Americans gave three broad explanations for APPROVAL of the proposed change: (1) identification with Africa/dual heritage, for example "It tells our origin and cultural identity"; (2) inadequacy of a color label (e.g., "Black is a color, not a race" and "Colors belong in a crayon box"); (3) aesthetic quality of *African American* (e.g., "I can't explain it, it just has a better sound to it").

Three types of explanations were given for DISAPPROVAL of the linguistic shift: (1) lack of identification with Africa (e.g., "Blacks are not African" and "We are more American than African; we have been here too long"); (2) syllabic density of *African American* (e.g., "It takes too long to say it and it's too much trouble"); (3) semantic change unnecessary and irrelevant (e.g., "Every ten to fifteen years it's something new. However you want to say it, we are still Black").

As anticipated, the most frequently given reason in support of *African American* was its reflection of the African past (46.4%). Also as anticipated, the negative version of this same reason was given by a large percentage of those who did not favor the term (26.3%). Typical responses were, "I wasn't born in Africa, I was born in Illinois" and "What do they mean about African American? By now we have no African in us." However, among those who said "No," a far larger number (55.8%) indicated that a name change was insignificant and irrelevant to changing the Black condition. (See table 2.)

TABLE 2 Approval/Disapproval of Linguistic Shift (C2 sample, African Americans only; n = 194)

Reasons for Approval of Shift	
1. Identification with Africa/dual heritage	46.4%
2. Inadequacy of a color label	17.4%
3. Aesthetic quality of *African American*	36.2%
Reasons for Disapproval of Shift	
1. Lack of identification with Africa	26.3%
2. Syllabic density of *African American*	9.5%
3. Semantic change unnecessary and irrelevant	55.8%
4. Other	8.4%

If we look at the results by age and sex, some significant interactions emerge. In the C1 sample, respondents 21 and under were more favorably disposed to the shift than those over 21. (See table 3.) Although age was not significant in the other cities, I think the results are indicative of a trend among African American youth. The semantic movement parallels the re-emerging 1960s-style nationalism and Afrocentric consciousness taking place in youth culture. Witness the Malcolm X revival, the political messages of popular rap groups like Public Enemy, the wearing of medallions embossed with the map of Africa, African-style haircuts, and reinvigorated campus activism.

Sex was also significant, but only in Detroit. In that city, African American women were more overwhelmingly opposed to the semantic shift than African American men. (See table 4.) Although I can offer no definitive explanation to account for this difference, recent scholars in both African American and Women's Studies (e.g., Gates 1988, Spillers 1983) have made a convincing case for the uniqueness of the African American woman's consciousness and experience. They have advanced the need for research to disaggregate what Toni Morrison has called the "invented lives" of African American women from the work done on African Americans and European American women (quoted in Giddings 1984). The finding from this survey lies in this general direction and suggests the need for further study of the views of African American women.

TABLE 3 Opinions About Use of *African American* By Age (C1 sample only; $p < .02$)

	21 & under	*22–30*	*31–40*	*Over 40*
YES	55%	24%	37%	29%
NO	45%	76%	63%	71%

TABLE 4 African American Males and Females on the Linguistic Shift (Detroit only; $p < .01$)

	Females	*Males*	*Total*
YES	19.5%	15.3%	34.8%
NO	50.8%	14.4%	65.2%

TABLE 5 Opinions About Use of *African American* by Race (C2 sample only; p <.05)

	African Americans	*European Americans*	*Total*
YES	36.6%	25.3%	33.0%
NO	63.4%	74.7%	67.0%

Although the focal point of this analysis was to get an index of the "sound judgment of our people" on the semantic issue, race as a significant factor in my results deserves more comment. In the C2 sample, African Americans disapproved of the semantic shift to a significantly greater degree than did European Americans. One explanation for this difference is that African Americans have a lot more at stake in the naming controversy. That the group has the power to define and name itself and gain mainstream acceptance and usage for any label it chooses has been demonstrated both in the shift from *colored* to *Negro* (with the capital, no less) and from *Negro* to *Black*. In fact, the general response to the issue by European Americans in the survey is typified by the following statement from one respondent: "If that's what they want to be called, it's okay with me." However, for African Americans the issue is about the construction of identity through NOMMO, an African concept that has survived in African American culture as a belief in the power of the word—"the awareness that the word alone alters the world (John 1961, 125). Racial group identity, whatever the paradigm that emerges, will dictate strategies, tactics, policies, programs and, in general, shape the direction of the struggle in the twenty-first century. This is no small matter; one does not make such a fundamental shift without internal debate, deliberation, and struggle. Edelin, Jackson, and others in national leadership have sounded the clarion call for the debate to begin.

As far as I was able to ascertain, no other survey of the current naming issue has been reported in the literature to date, although at least three opinion polls have been undertaken by the popular press.[7] *Time* reported that, although its survey was too small to be statistically valid, it did show that the "name change has made some headway," with 26 percent of the Blacks polled favoring *African American* (Lacayo and Monroe 1989). The *Washington Post-ABC News Poll* indicates that only 34 percent of the Blacks surveyed approved of *African American* (Specter 1990). However, Specter also notes "in the late 1960s, a majority of both races also favored *Negro* over *Black*." Finally, the *Michigan Chronicle* reports on a small sample survey of students attending historically Black colleges, indicating that a majority favor the shift from *Black* to *African American* (17 June 1989, 3A). This compares with the results of the present survey in terms of the positive responses from young (age 21 and under) respondents, most of whom were college students.

CONCLUSION

Given the lack of empirical data on African American views on the proposed terminological shift, the results of the five-city survey are a significant beginning. We can conclude that at least one-third of African Americans are in favor of the name change and that such support is seemingly strongest among African American youth, particularly those in college. However, that support is probably weakest among African American women, who continue, as they have historically, to be a potent factor in social change. The obstacles to be overcome to broaden the base of terminological change are the lack of a feeling of connectedness to Africa and the perception that, as one Sistuh put it, "this language thang ain bout too much."

Further empirical studies are warranted to assess the impact of the current linguistic movement and its relationship to the historical semantics of race. African American historians and political theorists contend that, in times of severe racial crisis, the name issue re-emerges as a call for re-examination of the status of African Americans. This reassessment forces a necessary and widespread discussion of the question, "Where do we go from here?" Bennett states, "In periods of reaction and extreme stress, black people usually turn inward. They begin to re-define themselves and they begin to argue seriously about names" (1967, 50). The current period is a singularly dramatic manifestation of this "turning inward," paralleled perhaps only by the post-Reconstruction period, "one of the whitest times in American history" (Bennett 1967, 50). Thus the linguistic debate raised by Edelin, and carried forth into the popular press by Jackson, is an appropriate and historically logical call to action. Baldwin (1981) and others have argued that the semantics of *Black* are a unique—and historically inappropriate—American-style invention. The ethnic identities of Africans in North America were eradicated so that Ibos, Yorubas, Hausas, and other African ethnic groups were robbed of their distinctiveness, and everybody just became "Black." By the same token, all Europeans just became "white." While this analysis fits the Black condition, it fails to recognize that the "white" race created in America retained its European ethnic identity. In fact, "Black" as a name for African Americans is asymmetrical with naming practices for ALL other groups in the United States. For these other groups, the term employed denotes land of origin—Polish Americans, Italian Americans, Hispanic Americans, German Americans, Asian Americans, and so on. *AFRICAN American* brings the "Black" race into semantic line with these other ethnolinguistic traditions.[8]

Our survey results and the press polls, with the promising exceptions of the African American college students in the *Michigan Chronicle* survey, and the 21 and under age group in Philadelphia, Cincinnati, and Chicago, indicate that current leaders have their work cut out for them. As with the shift from *Negro* to *Black*, it is the everyday people who must arise to the semantic challenge and rally around the new paradigmatic shift. Yet as the lexicosemantic history presented here indicates, the current issue of racial labelling is but a variation on a familiar theme: the unfinished business of forging an identity and a life for Africans in North America.

As an African American womanist linguist, it is clear to me that this is not a debate about semantics at the expense of addressing the plight of the community, as some intellectuals fear. Rather, this new racial designation can lead to the construction of an identity to facilitate the creation of policy, tactics, strategies, and programs to redress that plight—that is, the use of language to create a new theory of reality. As Ramona Edelin so eloquently put it (quoted in Anon. 1989, 76):

> It is our obligation to reconstruct our culture at this critical point in history so that we can move forward and not be satisfied with one or two people rising to the surface. . . . Calling ourselves African American is the first step in the cultural offensive. Our cultural renaissance can change our lot in the nation and around the world.

NOTES

Research for this article was made possible by a Research Stimulation Grant from Wayne State University. My thanks to Vice President Garrett Heberlein at Wayne State. I also wish to acknowledge the assistance of Thomas Kochman, Laverne Summerlin, and Ronald Stephens for assistance with data collection; Alida Quick for assistance with research design, instrumentation, and statistical analysis; and Joshua Bagakas, statistician. Any shortcomings are entirely my own.

1. Countee Cullen (1903–1946) was a Harlem Renaissance poet whose "Heritage" is considered "perhaps the finest statement of the then-popular [1920s] alien-and-exile theme in Black writing" (Davis and Redding 1971, 323). Italics appear as in the original poem.
2. The program was aired on 16 Jan. 1989. Panelists were poet Sonia Sanchez, Temple University; political scientist James Turner, Cornell University; and the author.
3. I employ the term *European American* to refer to the "white" population in the United States. Just as Black, an adjective, a color term only, is an inappropriate sociolinguistic construction for Africans in America, so too is the label *white* inappropriate for Europeans in American. Further, shifting from *white* to *European American* resolves the seeming contradiction of capitalizing *Black* with lower-casing *white*, a practice I have used in the past and have defended on the following grounds. First, *Black* as a racial designation replaced *Negro*, and *Negro* was capitalized (at least since 1930), whereas *white* was not. Second, for people of African decent in America, *Black* functions to designate race AND ethnicity because the slave trade and U.S. enslavement practices made it impossible for "Blacks" to trace their ethnic origins in Africa. This has not been the case for Europeans in the U.S., who typically have labelled themselves German, Italian, English, Irish, Polish, etc., according to their European ethnicity. In fact, it was not until the rise of *Black* that European Americans raised questions about the lower-casing of white.
4. While historically women (African American and European American) have been constructed as sex objects, deriving their worth from the number of children they produce, it was only in the slave community that MEN were encouraged to be fruitful and multiply, it being a fairly common practice for masters to designate certain MALES as breeders, nurturing their promiscuity on

the plantation so as to have as many female slaves pregnant as possible. The point is especially significant in light of current discussions about the supposed weakness of the Black family, "fatherless" homes, and the "irresponsibility" of African American men.

5. "Inversion," turning a negative mainstream linguistic or social concept into its opposite—e.g., *bad* = 'good'—was first used to describe the language practices of Black English Vernacular speakers by Holt (1972). "Semantic inversion" (Smitherman 1977) is believed to have its origins in West African language use (Turner 1949; Dalby 1969).
6. Although self-administered questionnaires can be problematic—e.g., low return rate among both African and European Americans—there are often particular problems when racial identification of African Americans is requested. In the C1 sample, 84 of the 210 persons who answered the *African American* question refused to give their race, either implicitly (e.g., through omission) or explicitly (e.g., "Why does it matter?" "What difference does it make?" and similar comments written on several questionnaires). Based on the distribution points for these questionnaires, about 60 of the 84 are believed to be African American.
7. See, however, John Baugh's article in this issue of *American Speech*. On 29 Jan. 1991, while this article was under editorial review, the *New York Times* (A19) published the results of a national poll by the Joint Center for Political and Economic Studies, a research organization specializing in African American political affairs. Based on a survey of 759 African Americans across the country, results indicate that, depending on region, anywhere from 22–28% of African Americans outside the South favor *African American* over *Black*; in the South only 15% favor the term. Among African American intellectuals, the Joint Center has long been lauded for its work in Black politics. Typically, though, as in the case with Gallup and other political pollsters, samples are based on REGISTERED VOTERS, thereby excluding many speakers of what John Baugh calls "Black street speech" (1983), as well as many young adults, among whom "voter apathy" is perhaps strongest. I'm raising a question about a type of class bias in public polls involving African Americans. We tried to control for this with a sampling frame designed to include college students in the C1 group, and in the C2 sample, by targeting areas populated by working, unworking, and under-class African Americans. The success of Jackson's "rainbow coalition" politics in mobilizing large numbers of disempowered and young African Americans demonstrates the latent power of the "root culture" (Pasteur and Toldson 1982) to impact on national politics.
8. Note that I do not hyphenate *African American*. The notion of "hyphenated Americans" is an older expression that most "hyphenated Americans" cringe at because it (the term and the hyphen) suggest a hybrid, lacking in authenticity. Note that I also do not hyphenate *European American*. Of course the only (nationally) authentic, i.e. indigenous, group is the Native American/Indian. By a similar line of reasoning, I no longer advocate *AfroAmerican* (nor its current alternative *AfriAmerican*), with or without the hyphen. Both smack of something hybrid, truncated, cut off—'Afro,' or 'Afri,' but not 'African.'

REFERENCES

Anon. 1989. "African-American or Black: What's in a Name? Prominent Black and/or African-Americans Express Their Views." *Ebony* July: 76–80.

Asante, Molefi Kete. 1988. *Afrocentricity.* Trenton: African World P.

Baldwin, James. 1981. "Black English: A Dishonest Argument." *Black English and the Education of Black Children and Youth: Proceedings of the National Invitational Symposium on the "King" Decision.* Ed. Geneva Smitherman. Detroit: Wayne State Univ. Center for Black Studies, 54–60.

Baugh, John. 1983. *Black Street Speech.* Austin: U of Texas P.

Bennett, Lerone. 1961. *Before the Mayflower.* Chicago: Johnson.

____________. 1967. "What's in a Name?" *Ebony Nov.*: 46–54.

Berger, Peter L., and Thomas Luckmann. 1966. *The Social Construction of Reality: A Treatise in the Sociology of Knowledge.* New York: Doubleday.

Bray, Rosemary. 1990. "Reclaiming our Culture." *Essence.* Dec. 84–86, 116, 119.

Brewer, J. Mason. 1972. *American Negro Folklore.* Chicago: Quadrangle.

Cullen, Countee. 1925. "Heritage." *Cavalcade.* Ed. Arthur P. Davis and Saunders Redding. Boston: Houghton, 1971. 326–27.

Dalby, David. 1969. *Black Through White: Patterns of Communication in Africa and the New World.* Bloomington: Indiana UP.

Davis, Arthur P., and Saunders Redding, eds. 1971. *Calvacade.* Boston: Houghton.

Drake, St. Clair. 1966. "Negro Americans and the Africa Interest." *The American Negro Reference Book.* Ed. John P. Davis, Englewood Cliffs: Prentice, 662–705.

____________. 1987. *Black Folk Here and There: An Essay in History and Anthropology.* Center for Afro-American Studies Monograph Series 17. Los Angeles: Center for Afro-American Studies, U California.

Franklin, John Hope. 1969. *From Slavery to Freedom.* New York: Random.

Gates, Henry L. 1988. *Contending Forces.* New York: Oxford UP.

Giddings, Paula. 1984. *When and Where I Enter: The Impact of Black Women on Race and Sex in America.* New York: Morrow.

Halliday, Michael A. K. 1978. *Language As Social Semiotic: The Social Interpretation of Language and Meaning.* London: Arnold.

Holt, Grace. 1972. "'Inversion' in Black Communication." Ed. Thomas Kochman. 1972. *Rappin and Stylin Out.* Urbana: U Illinois P, 152–59.

Jahn, Janheinz. 1961. *Muntu.* London: Faber.

Lacayo, Richard, and Sylvester Monroe. 1989. "In Search of a Good Name." *Time* 6 Mar.: 32.

Landers, Ann. 1989. "'African American' Label Draws Fire from All Races." *Detroit Free Press* 2 Apr.: 2L.

Marable, Manning. 1989. "African-American or Black? The Politics of Cultural Identity." *Black Issues in Higher Education.* 13 Apr.: 72.

Page, Clarence. 1989. "African American or Black? It's Debatable." *Detroit Free Press* 1 Jan: A1, A12.

Pasteur, Alfred B., and Ivory L. Toldson. 1982. *Roots of Soul.* New York: Doubleday.

Read, Allen Walker. 1939. "The Speech of Negroes in Colonial America." *Journal of Negro History* 24: 247–58.

Smitherman, Geneva. 1980. "Black Language as Power." International Language and Power Conference, Rockefeller Foundation Study and Conference Center, Bellagio, Italy. Rev. version in *Language and Power.* Ed. Chris Kramarae, Muriel Schulz, and William O'Barr. Beverly Hills: Sage, 1984. 101–15.

____________. 1983. "Language and Liberation." *The Journal of Negro Education* 52: 15–23.

____________. 1986. *Talkin and Testifyin: The Language of Black America.* Detroit: Wayne State UP.

____________. 1989. "'A New Way of Talkin': Language, Social Change and Political Theory." *Race Relations Abstracts*, 5–23.

____________. In preparation. "African Americans Speak on English Only."

Specter, Michael. 1990. "Men and Women of Their Word: But Should That Word be 'Black' or 'African-American'?" *The Washington Post National Weekly Edition*, 28 Oct.–4 Nov.: 10.

Spillers, Hortense. 1983. "A Hateful Passion, A Lost Love: Three Women's Fiction." *Feminist Studies*: 9.

Turner, Lorenzo D. 1949. *Africanisms in the Gullah Dialect*, Chicago: U Chicago P.

Vološinov, V. N. 1929. *Marxism and the Philosophy of Language*. Trans. Ladislav Matejka and I. R. Titunik. Cambridge: MIT P, 1973.

Walker, David. 1829. *Appeal, in Four Articles; Together with a Preamble to the Coloured Citizens of the World, but in Particular, and Very Expressly, to those in the United States of America*. Ed. Charles M. Wiltse. New York: Hill and Wang, 1965.

Walters, Ronald. Forthcoming. *Pan Africanism in the African Diaspora: The African American Linkage*. Detroit: Wayne State UP.

Wilkerson, Isabel. 1989. "Many Who are Black Favor New Term fur Who They Are." *New York Times* 31 Jan.: 1, 8.

Of Our Spiritual Strivings

W.E.B. DuBois

O water, voice of my heart crying in the sand,
All night long crying with a mournful cry,
As I lie and listen, and cannot understand
The voice of my heart in my side or the voice of the sea,
O water, crying for rest, is it I, is it I?
All night long the water is crying to me.

Unresting water, there shall never be rest
Till the last moon drop and the last tide fail,
And the tire of the end begin to burn in the west;
And the heart shall be weary and wonder and cry like the sea,
All life long crying without avail,
As the water all night long is crying to me.

ARTHUR SYMONS

BETWEEN me and the other world there is ever an unasked question: unasked by some through feelings of delicacy; by others through the difficulty of rightly framing it. All, nevertheless, flutter round it. They approach me in a half-hesitant sort of way, eye me curiously or compassionately, and then, instead of saying directly, How does it feel to be a problem? they say, I know an excellent colored man in my town; or, I fought at Mechanicsville;[1] or, Do not these Southern outrages make your blood boil? At these I smile, or am interested, or reduce the boiling to a simmer, as the occasion may require. To the real question, How does it feel to be a problem? I answer seldom a word.

And yet, being a problem is a strange experience,—peculiar even for one who has never been anything else, save perhaps in babyhood and in Europe. It is in the early days of rollicking boyhood that the revelation first bursts upon one, all in a day, as it were. I remember well when the shadow swept across me. I was a little thing, away up in the hills of New England, where the dark Housatonic winds between Hoosac and Taghkanic to the sea. In a wee wooden schoolhouse, something put it into the boys' and girls' heads to buy gorgeous visiting-cards—ten cents a package—and exchange. The exchange was merry, till one girl, a tall newcomer, refused my card,—refused it peremptorily, with a glance. Then it dawned upon me with a certain suddenness that I was different from the others; or like, mayhap, in heart and life and longing, but shut out from their world by a vast veil. I had thereafter no desire to tear down that veil, to creep through; I held all beyond it in common contempt, and lived above it in a region of blue sky and great wandering shadows. That sky was bluest when I could beat my mates at examination-time, or beat them at a foot-race, or even beat their stringy heads. Alas, with the years of all this fine contempt began to fade; for the worlds I longed for, and all their dazzling opportunities, were theirs, not mine. But they should not keep these prizes, I said; some, all, I would wrest from them. Just how I would do it I could never decide: by reading law, by healing the sick, by telling the wonderful tales that swam in my head,—some way. With other black boys the strive was not so fiercely sunny: their youth shrunk into tasteless sycophancy, or into silent hatred of the pale world about them and mocking distrust of everything white; or wasted itself in a bitter cry, Why did God make me an outcast and a stranger in mine own house? The shades of the prisonhouse closed round about us all: walls straight and stubborn to the whitest, but relentlessly narrow, tall, and unscalable to sons of night who must plod darkly on in resignation, or beat unavailing palms against the stone, or steadily, half hopelesly, watch the streak of blue above.

After the Egyptian and Indian, the Greek and Roman, the Teuton and Mongolian, the Negro is a sort of seventh son, born with a veil, and gifted with second-sight in this American world,—a world which yields him no true self-consciousness, but only lets him see himself though the revelation of the other world. It is a peculiar sensation, this double-consciousness, this sense of always looking at one's self through the eyes of others, of measuring one's worth by the tape of a world that looks on in amused contempt and pity. One ever feels his twoness,—an American, a Negro; two souls, two thoughts, two unreconciled strivings; two warring ideals in one dark body, whose dogged strength alone keeps it from being torn asunder.

The history of the American Negro is the history of this strife—this longing to attain self-conscious manhood, to merge his double self into a better and truer self. In this merging he wishes neither of the older selves to be lost. He would not Africanize America, for America has too much to teach the world and Africa. He would not bleach his Negro soul in a flood of white Americanism, for he knows that Negro blood has a message for the world. He simply wishes to make it possible for a man to be both a Negro and an American, without being cursed and spit upon by his fellows, without having the doors of Opportunity closed roughly in his face.

This, then, is the end of his striving to be a co-worker in the kingdom of culture, to escape both death and isolation, to husband and use his best powers and his latent genius. These powers of body and mind have in the past been strangely wasted, dispersed, or forgotton. The shadow of a mighty Negro past flits though the tale of Ethiopia the Shadowy and of Egypt the Sphynx. Throughout history, the powers of single black men flash here and there like falling stars, and die sometimes before the world has rightly gauged their brightness. Here in America, in the few days since Emancipation, the black man's turning hither and thither in hesitant and doubtful striving has often made his very strength to lose effectiveness, to seem like absence of power, like weakness. And yet it is not weakness,—it is the contradiction of double aims. The double-aimed struggle of the black artisan—on the one hand to escape the white contempt for a nation of mere hewers of wood and drawers of water, and on the other hand to plough and nail and dig for a poverty-stricken horde—could only result in making him a poor craftsman, for he had but half a heart in either cause. By the poverty and ignorance of his people, the Negro minister or doctor was tempted toward quackery and demagogy; and by the criticism of the other world, toward ideals that made him ashamed of his lowly tasks. The would-be black *savant*[2] was confronted by the paradox that the knowledge his people needed was a thrice-told tale to his white neighbors, while the knowledge which Would teach the white world was Greek to his own flesh and blood. The innate love of harmony and beauty that set the ruder souls of his people a-dancing and a-singing raised but confusion and doubt in the soul of the black artist; for the beauty revealed to him was the soul-beauty of a race which his larger audience despised, and he could not articulate the message of another people. This waste of double aims, this seeking to satisfy two unreconciled ideals, has wrought sad havoc with the courage and faith and deeds of ten thousand thousand people,—has sent them often wooing false gods and invoking false means of salvation, and at times has even seemed about to make them ashamed of themselves.

Away back in the days of bondage they thought to see in one divine event the end of all doubt and disappointment; few men ever worshipped Freedom with half such unquestioning faith as did the American Negro for two centuries. To him, so far as he thought and dreamed, slavery was indeed the sum of all villainies, the cause of all sorrow, the root of all prejudice; Emancipation was the key to a promised land of sweeter beauty than ever stretched before the eyes of wearied Israelites. In song and exhortation swelled one refrain—Liberty; in his tears and curses the God he implored had Freedom in his right hand. At last it came,—suddenly, fearfully, like a dream. With one wild carnival of blood and passion came the message in his own plaintive cadences:—

> "Shout O children!
> Shout you're free!
> For God has bought your liberty!"

Years have passed away since then,—ten, twenty, forty; forty years of national life, forty years of renewal and development, and yet the swarthy spectre sits in its accustomed seat at the Nation's feast. In vain do we cry to this our vastest social problem:—

> "Take any shape but that and my firm nerves Shall never tremble!"

The Nation has not yet found peace from its sins; the freedman has not yet found in freedom his promised land. Whatever of good may have come in these years of change, the shadow of a deep disappointment rests upon the Negro people,—a disappointment all the more bitter because the unattained ideal was unbounded save by the simple ignorance of a lowly people.

The first decade was merely a prolongation of the vain search for freedom, the boon that seemed ever barely to elude their grasp,—like a tantalizing will o'-the-wisp, maddening and misleading the headless host. The holocaust of war, the terrors of the Ku-Klux Klan, the lies of carpet-baggers, the disorganization of industry, and the contradictory advice of friends and foes, left the bewildered serf with no new watch-word beyond the old cry for freedom. As the time flew, however, he began to grasp a new idea. The ideal of liberty demanded for its attainment powerful means, and these the Fifteenth Amendment gave him. The ballot, which before he had looked upon as a visible sign of freedom, he now regarded as the chief means of gaining and perfecting the liberty with which war had partially endowed him. And why not? Had not votes made war and emancipated millions? Had not votes enfranchised the freemen? Was anything impossible to a power that had done all this? A million black men started with renewed zeal to vote themselves into the kingdom. So the decade flew away, the revolution of 1876[3] came, and left the half-free serf weary, wondering, but still inspired. Slowly but steadily, in the following years, a new vision began gradually to replace the dream of political power,—a powerful movement, the rise of another ideal to guide the unguided, another pillar of fire by night after a clouded day. It was the ideal of "book-learning'; the curiosity, born of compulsory ignorance, to know and test the power of cabalistic letters of the white man the longing to know. Here at last seemed to have been discovered the mountain path to Canaan; longer than the highway of Emancipation and law, steep and rugged, but straight, leading to heights high enough to overlook life.

Up the new path the advance guard toiled, slowly, heavily, doggedly; only those who have watched and guided the faltering feet, the misty minds, the dull understandings, of the dark pupils of these schools know how faithfully, how piteously, this people strove to leam. It was weary work. The cold statistician wrote down the inches of progress here and there, noted also where here and there a foot had slipped or some one had fallen. To the tired climbers, the horizon was ever dark, the mists were often cold, the Canaan was always dim and far away. If, however, the vistas disclosed as yet no goal, no resting-place, little but flattery and criticism, the journey at least gave leisure for reflection and self-examination; it changed the child of Emancipation to the youth with dawning consciousness, self-realization, self-respect. In these sombre forests of his striving his own soul rose before him, and he saw himself,—darkly as through a veil; and yet he saw in himself some faint revelatlon of his power, of his mission. He began to have a dim feeling that, to attain his place in the world, he must be himself and not another. For the first time he sought to analyze the burden he bore upon his back, that dead-weight of social degradation partially masked behind a half-named Negro problem. He felt his poverty; without a cent, without a home, without land, tools, or savings, he had entered into competion with rich, landed, skilled neighbors. To be a poor man is hard, but to be a poor race in a land of dollars is the very bottom of hardships. He felt the weight of his ignorance,—not simply of letters, but of life, of business, of the humanities the accumulated sloth and shirking and awkwardness of decades and centuries shackled his hands and feet. Nor was his burden all poverty and ignorance. The red stain of bastardy, which two centuries of systematic legal defilement of Negro women had stamped upon his race, meant not only the loss of ancient African chastity, but also the hereditary weight of a mass of corruption from white adulterers, threatening almost the obliteration of the Negro home.

A people thus handicapped ought not to be asked to race with the world, but rather allowed to give all its time and thought to its own social problems. But alas! while sociologists gleefully count his bastards and his prostitutes, the very soul of the toiling, sweating black man is darkened by the shadow of a vast despair. Men call the shadow prejudice, and learnedly explain it as the natural defense of culture against barbarism, leaning against ignorance, purity against crime, the "higher" against the "lower" races. To which the Negro cries Amen! and swears that to so much of this strange prejudice as is founded on just homage to civilization, culture, righteousness, and progress, he humbly bows and meekly does obeisance. But before that nameless prejudice that leaps beyond all this he stands helpless, dismayed. and well-nigh speechless; before that personal disrespect and mockery, the ridicule and systematic humiliation, the distortion of fact and wanton license of fancy, the cynical ignoring of the better and the boisterous welcoming of the worse, the all pervading desire to inculcate disdain for everything black, from Toussaint[4] to the devil,—before this there rises a sickening despair that would disarm and discourage any nations save that black host to whom "discouragement" is an unwritten word.

But the facing of so vast a prejudice could not but bring the inevitable company repression and breed in an atmosphere of contempt and hate. Whisperings and portents came borne upon the four winds: Lo! we are diseased and dying, cried the dark hosts; we cannot write, our voting is in vain; what need of education, since we must always cook and serve? And the Nation echoed and enforced this self-criticism, saying: Be content to be servants, and nothing more; what need of higher culture for half-men? Away with the black man's ballot, by force or fraud,—and behold the suicide of a race! Nevertheless, out of the evil came something of good,—the more careful adjustment of education to real life, the clearer perception of the Negroes' social responsibilibes, and the sobering realization of the meaning of progress.

So dawned the time of *Sturm und Drang*: storm and stress today rocks our little boat on the mad waters of the world-sea; there is within and without the sound of conflict, the burning of body and rending of soul; inspiration strives with doubt, and faith with vain questionings. The bright ideals of the past,—physical freedom, political power, the training of brains and the training of hands,—all these in turn have waxed and waned, until even the last grows dim and overcast. Are they all wrong,—all false? No, not that, but each alone was oversimple and imcomplete,—the dreams of a credulous childhood, or the fond imaginings of the other world which does not know and does not want to know our power. To be really true, all these ideals must be melted and welded into one. The training of the schools we need to-day more than ever,—the training of deft hands, quick eyes and ears, and above all the broader, deeper, higher culture of gifted minds and pure hearts. The power of the ballot we need in sheer self-defense, —else what shall save us from a second slavery? Freedom, too, the long-sought, we still seek,—the freedom of life and limb, the freedom to work and think, the freedom to love and aspire. Work, culture, liberty, —all these we need, not singly but together, not successively but together, each growing and aiding each, and all striving toward that vaster ideal that swims before the Negro people, the ideal of human brotherhood, gained through the unifying ideal of Race; the ideal of fostering and developing the traits and talents of the Negro, not in opposition to or contempt for other races, but rather in large conformity to the greater ideals of the American Republic, in order that some day on American soil two world-races may give each to each those characteristics both so sadly lack. We the darker ones come even now not altogether empty-handed: there are to-day no truer exponents of the pure human spirit of the Declaration of Independence than the American Negroes; there is no true American music but the wild sweet melodies of the Negro slave; the American fairy tales and folklore are Indian and African; and, all in all, we black men seem the sole oasis of simple faith and reverence in a dusty desert of dollars and smartness. Will America be poorer if she replace her brutal dyspeptic blundering with light-hearted but determined Negro humility? or her coarse and cruel wit with loving jovial good-humor? or her vulgar music with the soul of the Sorrow Songs?

Merely a concrete test of the underlying principles of the great republic is the Negro Problem, and the spiritual striving of the freedmen's sons is the travail of souls whose burden is almost beyond the measure of their strength, but who bear it in the name of an historic race, in the name of this the land of their fathers' fathers, and in the name of human opportunity.

And now what I have briefly sketched in large outline let me on coming pages tell again in many ways, with loving emphasis and deeper detail, that men may listen to the striving in the souls of black folk.

NOTES

1 *Mechanicsville*: Civil War battle (June 26, 1862), in which Union forces threatened Richmond, Virginia (*Ed.*)

2 *savant*: (French) learned person or scholar (*Ed.*)

3 *revolution of 1876*: 1876 marked the ed of the failed effort at "reconstructing" the South after the Civil War, an effert that had established civil and political rights for African Americans and had embittered many white Southerners. After the disputed election of 1876, Rutherford B. Hayes (Republican) withdrew federal troops from the South and with Southern interests returned to dominance. (*Ed.*)

4 *Francois Dominique Toussaint L'Ouverture* (1744–1803): Haitian patriot, leader of slave rebellions and eventual governor of Haiti (1801) until the French captured and imprisoned him (*Ed.*)

Of the Faith of the Fathers

W.E.B. DuBois

Dim face of Beauty haunting all the world,
Fair face of Beauty all too fair to see,
Where the lost stars adown the heavens are hurled,—
There, there alone for thee
May white peace be.

Beauty, sad face of Beauty, Mystery, Wonder,
What are these dreams to foolish babbling men
Who cry with little noises 'neath the thunder
Of Ages ground to sand,
To a little sand.

FIONA MACLEOD.

It was out in the country, far from home, far from my foster home, on a dark Sunday night. The road wandered from our rambling log-house up the stony bed of a creek, past wheat and corn, until we could hear dimly across the fields a rhythmic cadence of song,—soft, thrilling, powerful, that swelled and died sorrowfully in our ears. I was a country school-teacher then, fresh from the East, and had never seen a Southern Negro revival. To be sure, we in Berkshire were note perhaps as stiff and formal as they in Suffolk of olden time; yet we were very quiet and subdued, and I know not what would have happened those clear Sabbath mornings had someone punctuated the sermon with a wild scream, or interrupted the long prayer with a loud Amen! And so most striking to me, as I approached the village and the little plain church perched aloft, was the air of intense excitement that possessed that mass of black folk. A sort of suppressed terror hung in the air and seemed to seize us,—a pythian madness, a demoniac possession, that lent terrible reality to song and word. The black and massive form of the preacher swayed and quivered as the words crowded to his lips and flew at us in singular eloquence. The people moaned and fluttered, and then the gaunt-checked brown woman beside me suddenly leaped straight into the air and shrieked like a lost soul, while round about came wail and groan and outcry, and a scene of human passion such as I had never conceived before.

Those who have not thus witnessed the frenzy of a Negro revival in the untouched backwoods of the South can but dimly realize the religious feeling of the slave; as described, such scenes appear grotesque and funny, but as seen they are awful. Three things characterized this religion of the slave,—the Preacher, the Music, and the Frenzy. The Preacher is the most unique personality developed by the Negro on American soil. A leader, a politician, an orator, a "boss," an intriguer, an idealist,—all these he is, and ever, too, the centre of a group of men, now twenty, now a thousand in number. The combination of a certain adroitness with deep-seated earnestness, of tact with consummate ability, gave him his preëminence, and helps him maintain it. The type, of course, varies according to time and place, from the West Indies in the sixteenth century to New England in the nineteenth, and from the Mississippi bottoms to cities like New Orleans or New York.

The Music of Negro religion is that plaintive rhythmic melody, with its touching minor cadences, which, despite caricature and defilement, still remains the most original and beautiful expression of human life and longing yet born on American soil. Sprung from the African forests, where its counterpart can still be heard, it was adapted, changed, and intensified by the tragic soul-life of the slave, until, under the stress of law and whip, it became the one true expression of a people's sorrow, despair, and hope.

Finally the Frenzy or "Shouting," when the Spirit of the Lord passed by, and, seizing the devotee, made him mad with supernatural joy, was the last essential of Negro religion and the one more devoutly believed in than all the rest. It varied in expression from the silent rapt countenance or the low murmur and moan to the mad abandon of physical fervor,—the stamping, shrieking, and shouting, the rushing to and fro and wild waving of arms, the weeping and laughing, the vision and the trance. All this is nothing new in the world, but old as religion, as Delphi and Endor. And so firm a hold did it have on the Negro, that many generations firmly believed that without this visible manifestation of the God there could be no true communion with the invisible.

These were the characteristics of Negro religious life as developed up to the time of Emancipation. Since under the peculiar circumstances of the black man's environment they were the one expression of his higher life, they are of deep interest to the student of his development, both socially and psychologically. Numerous are the attractive lines of inquiry that here group themselves. What did slavery mean to the African savage? What was his attitude toward the World and Life? What seemed to him good and evil,—God and Devil? Whither went his longings and strivings, and wherefore were his heart-burnings and disappointments? Answers to such questions can come only from a study of Negro religion as a development, through its gradual changes from the heathenism of the Gold Coast to the institutional Negro church of Chicago.

Moreover, the religious growth of millions of men, even though they be slaves, cannot be without potent influence upon their contemporaries. The Methodists and Baptists of America owe much of their condition to the silent but potent influence of their millions of Negro converts. Especially is this noticeable in the South, where theology and religious philosophy are on this account a long way behind the North, and where the religion of the poor whites is a plain copy of Negro thought and methods. The mass of "gospel" hymns which has swept through American churches and well-nigh ruined our sense of song consists largely of debased imitations of Negro melodies made by ears that caught the jingle but not the music, the body but not the soul, of the

Jubilee songs. It is thus clear that the study of Negro religion is not only a vital part of the history of the Negro in America, but no uninteresting part of American history.

The Negro church of to-day is the social centre of Negro life in the United States, and the most characteristic expression of African character. Take a typical church in a small Virginian town: it is the "First Baptist"—a roomy brick edifice seating five hundred or more persons, tastefully finished in Georgia pine, with a carpet, a small organ, and stained-glass windows. Underneath is a large assembly room with benches. This building is the central club-house of a community of a thousand or more Negroes. Various organizations meet here,—the church proper, the Sunday-school, two or three insurance societies, women's societies, secret societies, and mass meetings of various kinds. Entertainments, suppers, and lectures are held beside the five or six regular weekly religious services. Considerable sums of money are collected and expended here, employment is found for the idle, strangers are introduced, news is disseminated and charity distributed. At the same time this social, intellectual, and economic centre is a religious centre of great power. Depravity, Sin, Redemption, Heaven, Hell, and Damnation are preached twice a Sunday with much fervor, and revivals take place every year after the crops are laid by; and few indeed of the community have the hardihood to withstand conversion. Back of this more formal religion, the Church often stands as a real conserver of morals, a strengthener of family life, and the final authority on what is Good and Right.

Thus one can see in the Negro church to-day, reproduced in microcosm, all that great world from which the Negro is cut off by color-prejudice and social condition. In the great city churches the same tendency is noticeable and in many respects emphasized. A great church like the Bethel of Philadelphia has over eleven hundred members, an edifice seating fifteen hundred persons and valued at one hundred thousand dollars, an annual budget of five thousand dollars, and a government consisting of a pastor with several assisting local preachers, an executive and legislative board, financial boards and tax collectors; general church meetings for making laws; subdivided groups led by class leaders, a company of militia, and twenty-four auxiliary societies. The activity of a church like this is immense and far-reaching, and the bishops who preside over these organizations throughout the land are among the most powerful Negro rulers in the world.

Such churches are really governments of men, and consequently a little investigation reveals the curious fact that, in the South, at least, practically every American Negro is a church member. Some, to be sure, are not regularly enrolled, and a few do not habitually attend services, but, practically, a proscribed people must have a social centre, and that centre for this people is the Negro church. The census of 1890 showed nearly twenty-four thousand Negro churches in the country, with a total enrolled membership of over two and a half millions, or ten actual church members to every twenty-eight persons, and in some Southern States one in every two persons. Besides these there is the large number who, while not enrolled as members, attend and take part in many of the activities of the church. There is an organized Negro church for every sixty black families in the nation, and in some States for every forty families, owning, on an average, a thousand dollars' worth of property each, or nearly twenty-six million dollars in all.

Such, then, is the large development of the Negro church since Emancipation. The question now is, What have been the successive steps of this social history and what are the present tendencies? First, we must realize that no such institution as the Negro church could rear itself without definite historical foundations. These foundations we can find if we remember that the social history of the Negro did not start in America. He was brought from a definite social environment,—the polygamous clan life under the headship of the chief and the potent influence of the priest. His religion was nature-worship, with profound belief in invisible surrounding influences, good and bad, and his worship was through incantation and sacrifice. The first rude change in this life was the slave ship and the West Indian sugar-fields. The plantation organization replaced the clan and tribe, and the white master replaced the chief with far greater and more despotic powers. Forced and long-continued toil became the rule of life, the old ties of blood relationship and kinship disappeared, and instead of the family appeared a new polygamy and polyandry, which, in some cases, almost reached promiscuity. It was a terrific social revolution, and yet some traces were retained of the former group life, and the chief remaining institution was the Priest or Medicine-man. He early appeared on the plantation and found his function as the healer of the sick, the interpreter of the Unknown, the comforter of the sorrowing, the supernatural avenger of wrong, and the one who rudely but picturesquely expressed the longing, disappointment, and resentment of a stolen and oppressed people. Thus, as bard, physician, judge, and priest, within the narrow limits allowed by the slave system, rose the Negro preacher, and under him the first Afro-American institution, the Negro church. This church was not at first by any means Christian nor definitely organized; rather it was an adaptation and mingling of heathen rites among the members of each plantation, and roughly designated as Voodooism. Association with the masters, missionary effort and motives of expediency gave these rites an early veneer of Christianity, and after the lapse of many generations the Negro church became Christian.

Two characteristic things must be noticed in regard to this church. First, it became almost entirely Baptist and Methodist in faith; secondly, as a social institution it antedated by many decades the monogamic Negro home. From the very circumstances of its beginning, the church was confined to the plantation, and consisted primarily of a series of disconnected units; although, later on, some freedom of movement was allowed, still this geographical limitation was always important and was one cause of the spread of the decentralized and democratic Baptist faith among the slaves. At the same time, the visible rite of baptism appealed strongly to their mystic temperament. To-day the Baptist Church is still largest in membership among Negroes, and has a million and a half communicants. Next in popularity came the churches organized in connection with the white neighboring churches, chiefly Baptist and Methodist, with a few Episcopalian and others. The Methodists still form the second greatest denomination, with nearly a million members. The faith of these two leading denominations was more suited to the slave church from the prominence they gave to religious feeling and fervor. The Negro membership in other denominations has always been small and relatively unimportant, although the Episcopalians and Presbyterians are gaining among the more intelligent classes to-day, and the Catholic Church is making headway in certain sections. After Emancipation, and still earlier in the North, the Negro churches largely severed such affiliations as they had had with the white churches, either by choice or by compulsion. The Baptist churches became independent, but the Methodists were compelled early to unite for purposes of episcopal government. This gave rise to the great African Methodist Church, the greatest Negro organization in the world, to the Zion Church and the Colored Methodist, and to the black conferences and churches in this and other denominations.

The second fact noted, namely, that the Negro church antedates the Negro home, leads to an explanation of much that is paradoxical in this communistic institution and in the morals of its members. But especially it leads us to regard this institution as peculiarly the expression of the inner ethical life of a people in a sense seldom true elsewhere. Let us turn, then, from the outer physical development of the church to the more important inner ethical life of the people who compose it. The Negro has already been pointed out many times as a religious animal,—a being of that deep emotional nature which turns instinctively toward the supernatural. Endowed with a rich tropical imagination and a keen, delicate appreciation of Nature, the transplanted African lived in a world animate with gods and devils, elves and witches; full of strange influences,—of Good to be implored, of Evil to be propitiated. Slavery, then, was to him the dark triumph of Evil over him. All the hateful powers of the Under-world were striving against him, and a spirit of revolt and revenge filled his heart. He called up all the resources of heathenism to aid,—exorcism and witchcraft, the mysterious Obi worship with its barbarous rites, spells, and blood-sacrifice even, now and then, of human victims. Weird midnight orgies and mystic conjurations were invoked, the witch-woman and the voodoo-priest became the centre of Negro group life, and that vein of vague superstition which characterizes the unlettered Negro even to-day was deepened and strengthened.

In spite, however, of such success as that of the fierce Maroons, the Danish blacks, and others, the spirit of revolt gradually died away under the untiring energy and superior strength of the slave masters. By the middle of the eighteenth century the black slave had sunk, with hushed murmurs, to his place at the bottom of a new economic system, and was unconsciously ripe for a new philosophy of life. Nothing suited his condition then better than the doctrines of passive submission embodied in the newly learned Christianity. Slave masters early realized this, and cheerfully aided religious propaganda within certain bounds. The long system of repression and degradation of the Negro tended to emphasize the elements in his character which made him a valuable chattel: courtesy became humility, moral strength degenerated into submission, and the exquisite native appreciation of the beautiful became an infinite capacity for dumb suffering. The Negro, losing the joy of this world, eagerly seized upon the offered conceptions of the next; the avenging Spirit of the Lord enjoining patience in this world, under sorrow and tribulation until the Great Day when He should lead His dark children home,—this became his comforting dream. His preacher repeated the prophecy, and his bards sang,—

> "Children, we all shall be free
> When the Lord shall appear!"

This deep religious faralism, painted so beautifully in "Uncle Tom," came soon to breed, as all fatalistic faiths will, the sensualist side by side with the martyr. Under the lax moral life of the plantation, where marriage was a farce, laziness a virtue, and property a theft, a religion of resignation and submission degenerated easily, in less strenuous minds, into a philosophy of indulgence and crime. Many of the worst characteristics of the Negro masses of to-day had their seed in this period of the slave's ethical growth. Here it was that the Home was ruined under the very shadow of the Church, white and black; here habits of shiftlessness took root; and sullen hopelessness replaced hopeful strife.

With the beginning of the abolition movement and the gradual growth of a class of free Negroes came a change. We often neglect the influence of the freedman before the war, because of the paucity of his numbers and the small weight he had in the history of the nation. But we must not forget that his chief influence was internal,—was exerted on the black world; and that there he was the ethical and social leader. Huddled as he was in a few centres like Philadelphia, New York, and New Orleans, the masses of the freedmen sank into poverty and listlessness; but not all of them. The free Negro leader early arose and his chief characteristic was intense earnestness and deep feeling on the slavery question. Freedom became to him a real thing and not a dream. His religion became darker and more intense, and into his ethics crept a note of revenge, into his songs a day of reckoning close at hand. The "Coming of the Lord" swept this side of Death, and came to be a thing to be hoped for in this day. Through fugitive slaves and irrepressible discussion this desire for freedom seized the black millions still in bondage, and became their one ideal of life. The black bards caught new notes, and sometimes even dared to sing,—

> "O Freedom, O Freedom, O Freedom over me!
> Before I'll be a slave
> I'll be buried in my grave,
> And go home to my Lord
> And be free."

For fifty years Negro religion thus transformed itself and identified itself with the dream of Abolition, until that which was a radical fad in the white North and an anarchistic plot in the white South had become a religion to the black world. Thus, when Emancipation finally came, it seemed to the freedman a literal Coming of the Lord. His fervid imagination was stirred as never before, by the tramp of armies, the blood and dust of battle, and the wail and whirl of social upheaval. He stood dumb and motionless before the whirlwind: what had he to do with it? Was it not the Lord's doing, and marvellous in his eyes? Joyed and bewildered with what came, he stood awaiting new wonders till the inevitable Age of Reaction swept over the nation and brought the crisis of to-day.

It is difficult to explain clearly the present critical stage of Negro religion. First, we must remember that living as the blacks do in close contact with a great modern nation, and sharing, although imperfectly, the soul-life of that nation, they must necessarily be affected more or less directly by all the religious and ethical forces that are to-day moving the United States. These questions and movements are, however, overshadowed and dwarfed by the (to them) all-important question of their civil, political, and economic status. They must perpetually discuss the "Negro Problem,"—must live, move, and have their being in it, and interpret all else in its light or darkness.

With this come, too, peculiar problems of their inner life,—of the status of women, the maintenance of Home, the training of children, the accumulation of wealth, and the prevention of crime. All this must mean a time of intense ethical ferment, of religious heart-searching and intellectual unrest. From the double life every American Negro must live, as a Negro and as an American, as swept on by the current of the nineteenth while yet struggling in the eddies of the fifteenth century,—from this must arise a painful self-consciousness, an almost morbid sense of personality and a moral hesitancy which is fatal to self-confidence. The worlds within and without the Veil of Color are changing, and changing rapidly, but not at the same rate, not in the same way; and this must produce a peculiar wrenching of the soul, a peculiar sense of doubt and bewilderment. Such a double life, with double thoughts, double duties, and double social classes, must give rise to double words and double ideals, and tempt the mind to pretence or to revolt, to hypocrisy or to radicalism.

In some such doubtful words and phrases can one perhaps most clearly picture the peculiar ethical paradox that faces the Negro of to-day and is tingeing and changing his religious life. Feeling that his rights and his dearest ideals are being trampled upon, that the public conscience is ever more deaf to his righteous appeal, and that all the reactionary forces of prejudice, greed, and revenge are daily gaining new strength and fresh allies, the Negro faces no enviable dilemma. Conscious of his impotence, and pessimistic, he often becomes bitter and vindictive; and his religion, instead of a worship, is a complaint and a curse, a wail rather than a hope, a sneer rather than a faith. On the other hand, another type of mind, shrewder and keener and more tortuous too, sees in the very strength of the anti-Negro movement its patent weaknesses, and with Jesuitic casuistry is deterred by no ethical considerations in the endeavor to turn this weakness to the black man's strength. Thus we have two great and hardly reconcilable streams of thought and ethical strivings; the danger of the one lies in anarchy, that of the other in hypocrisy. The one type of Negro stands almost ready to curse God and die, and the other is too often found a traitor to right and a coward before force; the one is wedded to ideals remote, whimsical, perhaps impossible of realization; the other forgets that life is more than meat and the body more than raiment. But, after all, is not this simply the writhing of the age translated into black,—the triumph of the Lie which to-day, with its false culture, faces the hideousness of the anarchist assassin?

To-day the two groups of Negroes, the one in the North, the other in the South, represent these divergent ethical tendencies, the first tending toward radicalism, the other toward hypocritical compromise. It is no idle regret with which the white South mourns the loss of the old-time Negro,—the frank, honest, simple old servant who stood for the earlier religious age of submission and humility. With all his laziness and lack of many elements of true manhood, he was at least open-hearted, faithful, and sincere. To-day he is gone, but who is to blame for his going? Is it not those very persons who mourn for him? Is it not the tendency, born of Reconstruction and Reaction, to found a society on lawlessness and deception, to tamper with the moral fibre of a naturally honest and straightforward people until the whites threaten to become ungovernable tyrants and the blacks criminals and hypocrites? Deception is the natural defence of the weak against the strong, and the South used it for many years against its conquerors; to-day it must be prepared to see its black proletariat turn that same two-edged weapon against itself. And how natural this is! The death of Denmark Vesey and Nat Turner proved long since to the Negro the present hopelessness of physical defence. Political defence is becoming less and less available, and economic defence is still only partially effective. But there is a patent defence at hand,—the defence of deception and flattery, of cajoling and lying. It is the same defence which the Jews of the Middle Age used and which left its stamp on their character for centuries. To-day the young Negro of the South who would succeed cannot be frank and outspoken, honest and self-assertive, but rather he is daily tempted to be silent and wary, politic and sly; he must flatter and be pleasant, endure petty insults with a smile, shut his eyes to wrong; in too many cases he sees positive personal advantage in deception and lying. His real thoughts, his real aspirations, must be guarded in whispers; he must not criticise, he must not complain. Patience, humility, and adroitness must, in these growing black youth, replace impulse, manliness, and courage. With this sacrifice there is an economic opening, and perhaps peace and some prosperity. Without this there is riot, migration, or crime. Nor is this situation peculiar to the Southern United States,—is it not rather the only method by which undeveloped races have gained the right to share modern culture? The price of culture is a Lie.

On the other hand, in the North the tendency is to emphasize the radicalism of the Negro. Driven from his birthright in the South by a situation at which every fibre of his more outspoken and assertive nature revolts, he finds himself in a land where he can scarcely earn a decent living amid the harsh competition and the color discrimination. At the same time, through schools and periodicals, discussions and lectures, he is intellectually quickened and awakened. The soul, long pent up and dwarfed, suddenly expands in new-found freedom. What wonder that every tendency is to excess,—radical complaint, radical remedies, bitter denunciation or angry silence. Some sink, some rise. The criminal and the sensualist leave the church for the gambling-hell and the brothel, and fill the slums of Chicago and Baltimore; the better classes segregate themselves from the group-life of both white and black, and form an aristocracy, cultured but pessimistic, whose bitter criticism stings while it points out no way of escape. They despise the submission and subserviency of the Southern Negroes, but offer no other means by which a poor and oppressed minority can exist side by side with its masters. Feeling deeply and keenly the tendencies and opportunities of the age in which they live, their souls are bitter at the fate which drops the Veil between; and the very fact that this bitterness is natural and justifiable only serves to intensify it and make it more maddening.

Between the two extreme types of ethical attitude which I have thus sought to make clear wavers the mass of the millions of Negroes, North and South; and their religious life and activity partake of this social conflict within their ranks. Their churches are differentiating,—now into groups of cold, fashionable devotees, in no way distinguishable from similar white groups save in color of skin; now into large social and business institutions catering to the desire for information and amusement of their members, warily avoiding unpleasant questions both within and without the black world, and preaching in effect if not in word: *Dum vivimus, vivamus.*

But back of this still broods silently the deep religious feeling of the real Negro heart, the stirring, unguided might of powerful human souls who have lost the guiding star of the past and are seeking in the great night a new religious ideal. Some day the Awakening will come, when the pent-up vigor of ten million souls shall sweep irresistibly toward the Goal, out of the Valley of the Shadow of Death, where all that makes life worth living—Liberty, Justice, and Right—is marked "For White People Only."

The Sorrow Songs

W.E.B. DuBois

I walk through the churchyard
    To lay this body down;
I know moon-rise, I know star-rise;
I walk in the moonlight, I walk in the starlight;
I'll lie in the grave and stretch out my arms,
I'll go to judgment in the evening of the day,
And my soul and thy soul shall meet that day,
    When I lay this body down.

NEGRO SONG.

THEY that walked in darkness sang songs in the olden days—Sorrow Songs—for they were weary at heart. And so before each thought that I have written in this book I have set a phrase, a haunting echo of these weird old songs in which the soul of the black slave spoke to men. Ever since I was a child these songs have stirred me strangely. They came out of the South unknown to me, one by one, and yet at once I knew them as of me and of mine. Then in after years when I came to Nashville I saw the great temple builded of these songs towering over the pale city. To me Jubilee Hall seemed ever made of the songs themselves, and its bricks were red with the blood and dust of toil. Out of them rose for me morning, noon, and night, bursts of wonderful melody, full of the voices of my brothers and sisters, full of the voices of the past.

Little of beauty has America given the world save the rude grandeur God himself stamped on her bosom; the human spirit in this new world has expressed itself in vigor and ingenuity rather than in beauty. And so by fateful chance the Negro folk-song—the rhythmic cry of the slave—stands today not simply as the sole American music, but as the most beautiful expression of human experience born this side the seas. It has been neglected, it has been, and is, half despised, and above all it has been persistently mistaken and misunderstood; but notwithstanding, it still remains as the singular spiritual heritage of the nation and the greatest gift of the Negro people.

Away back in the thirties the melody of these slave songs stirred the nation, but the songs were soon half forgotten. Some, like "Near the lake where drooped the willow," passed into current airs and their source was forgotten; others were caricatured on the "minstrel" stage and their memory died away. Then in war-time came the singular Port Royal experiment after the capture of Hilton Head, and perhaps for the first time the North met the Southern slave face to face and heart to heart with no third witness. The Sea Islands of the Carolinas, where they met, were filled with a black folk of primitive type, touched and moulded less by the world about them than any others outside the Black Belt. Their appearance was uncouth, their language funny, but their hearts were human and their singing stirred men with a mighty power. Thomas Wentworth Higginson hastened to tell of these songs, and Miss McKim and others urged upon the world their rare beauty. But the world listened only half credulously until the Fisk Jubilee Singers sang the slave songs so deeply into the world's heart that it can never wholly forget them again.

There was once a blacksmith's son born at Cadiz, New York, who in the changes of time taught school in Ohio and helped defend Cincinnati from Kirby Smith. Then he fought at Chancellorsville and Gettysburg and finally served in the Freedman's Bureau at Nashville. Here he formed a Sunday-school class of black children in 1866, and sang with them and taught them to sing. And then they taught him to sing, and when once the glory of the Jubilee songs passed into the soul of George L. White, he knew his life-work was to let those Negroes sing to the world as they had sung to him. So in 1871 the pilgrimage of the Fisk Jubilee Singers began. North to Cincinnati they rode,—four half-clothed black boys and five girl-women,—led by a man with a cause and a purpose. They stopped at Wilberforce, the oldest of Negro schools, where a black bishop blessed them. Then they went, fighting cold and starvation, shut out of hotels, and cheerfully sneered at, ever northward; and ever the magic of their song kept thrilling hearts, until a burst of applause in the Congregational Council at Oberlin revealed them to the world. They came to New York and Henry Ward Beecher dared to welcome them, even though the metropolitan dailies sneered at his "Nigger Minstrels." So their songs conquered till they sang across the land and across the sea, before Queen and Kaiser, in Scotland and Ireland, Holland and Switzerland. Seven years they sang, and brought back a hundred and fifty thousand dollars to found Fisk University.

Since their day they have been imitated—sometimes well, by the singers of Hampton and Atlanta, sometimes ill, by straggling quartettes. Caricature has sought again to spoil the quaint beauty of the music, and has filled the air with many debased melodies which vulgar ears scarce know from the real. But the true Negro folk-song still lives in the hearts of those who have heard them truly sung and in the hearts of the Negro people.

What are these songs, and what do they mean? I know little of music and can say nothing in technical phrase, but I know something of men, and knowing them, I know that these songs are the articulate message of the slave to the world. They tell us in these eager days that life was joyous to the black slave, careless and happy. I can easily believe this of some, of many. But not all the past South, though it rose from the dead, can gainsay the heart-touching witness of these songs. They are the music of an unhappy people, of the children of disappointment; they tell of death and suffering and unvoiced longing toward a truer world, of misty wanderings and hidden ways.

The songs are indeed the siftings of centuries; the music is far more ancient than the words, and in it we can trace here and there signs of development. My grandfather's grandmother was seized by an evil Dutch trader two centuries ago; and coming to the valleys of the Hudson and Housatonic, black, little, and lithe, she shivered and shrank in the harsh north winds, looked longingly at the hills, and often crooned a heathen melody to the child between her knees, thus:

The child sang it to his children and they to their children's children, and so two hundred years it has travelled down to us and we sing it to our children, knowing as little as our fathers what its words may mean, but knowing well the meaning of its music.

This was primitive African music; it may be seen in larger form in the strange chant which heralds "The Coming of John":

"You may bury me in the East,
You may bury me in the West,
But I'll hear the trumpet sound in that morning,"

—the voice of exile.

Ten master songs, more or less, one may pluck from this forest of melody—songs of undoubted Negro origin and wide popular currency, and songs peculiarly characteristic of the slave. One of these I have just mentioned. Another whose strains begin this book is "Nobody knows the trouble I've seen." When, struck with a sudden poverty, the United States refused to fulfil its promises of land to the freedmen, a brigadier-general went down to the Sea Islands to carry the news. An old woman on the outskirts of the throng began singing this song; all the mass joined with her, swaying. And the soldier wept.

The third song is the cradle-song of death which all men know,—"Swing low, sweet chariot,"—whose bars begin the life story of "Alexander Crummell." Then there is the song of many waters, "Roll, Jordan, roll," a mighty chorus with minor cadences. There were many songs of the fugitive like that which opens "The Wings of Atlanta," and the more familiar "Been a-listening." The seventh is the song of the End and the Beginning—"My Lord, what a mourning! when the stars begin to fall"; a strain of this is placed before "The Dawn of Freedom." The song of groping—"My way's cloudy"—begins "The Meaning of Progress"; the ninth is the song of this chapter—"Wrestlin' Jacob, the day is a breaking,"—a paean of hopeful strife. The last master song is the song of songs—"Steal away,"—sprung from "The Faith of the Fathers."

There are many others of the Negro folk-songs as striking and characteristic as these, as, for instance, the three strains in the third, eighth, and ninth chapters; and others I am sure could easily make a selection on more scientific principles. There are, too, songs that seem to me a step removed from the more primitive types: there is the maze-like medley, "Bright sparkles," one phrase of which heads "The Black Belt"; the Easter carol, "Dust, dust and ashes"; the dirge, "My mother's took her flight and gone home"; and that burst of melody hovering over "The Passing of the First-Born" — "I hope my mother will be there in that beautiful world on high."

These represent a third step in the development of the slave song, of which "You may bury me in the East" is the first, and songs like "March on" (chapter six) and

"Steal away" are the second. The first is African music, the second Afro-American, while the third is a blending of Negro music with the music heard in the foster land. The result is still distinctively Negro and the method of blending original, but the elements are both Negro and Caucasian. One might go further and find a fourth step in this development, where the songs of white America have been distinctively influenced by the slave songs or have incorporated whole phrases of Negro melody, as "Swanee River" and "Old Black Joe." Side by side, too, with the growth has gone the debasements and imitations—the Negro "minstrel" songs, many of the "gospel" hymns, and some of the contemporary "coon" songs,—a mass of music in which the novice may easily lose himself and never find the real Negro melodies.

In these songs. I have said, the slave spoke to the world. Such a message is naturally veiled and half articulate. Words and music have lost each other and new and cant phrases of a dimly understood theology have displaced the older sentiment. Once in a while we catch a strange word of an unknown tongue, as the "Mighty Myo," which figures as a river of death; more often slight words or mere doggerel are joined to music of singular sweetness. Purely secular songs are few in number, partly because many of them were turned into hymns by a change of words, partly because the frolics were seldom heard by the stranger, and the music less often caught. Of nearly all the songs, however, the music is distinctly sorrowful. The ten master songs I have mentioned tell in word and music of trouble and exile, of strife and hiding; they grope toward some unseen power and sigh for rest in the End.

The words that are left to us are not without interest, and, deared of evident dross, they conceal much of real poetry and meaning beneath conventional theology and unmeaning thapsody. Like all primitive folk, the slave stood near to Nature's heart. Life was a "rough and rolling sea" like the brown Atlantic of the Sea Islands; the "Wilderness" was the home of God, and the "lonesome valley" led to the way of life. "Winter'll soon be over," was the picture of life and death to a tropical imagination. The sudden wild thunderstorms of the South awed and impressed the Negroes,—at times the rumbling seemed to them "mournful," at times imperious:

> "My Lord calls me,
> He calls me by the thunder,
> The trumpet sounds it in my soul."

The monotonous toil and exposure is painted in many words. One sees the ploughmen in the hot, moist furrow, singing:

> "Dere's no rain to wet you,
> Dere's no sun to burn you,
> Oh, push along, believer,
> I want to go home."

The bowed and bent old man cries, with thrice-repeated wail:

> "O Lord, keep me from sinking down,"

and he rebukes the devil of doubt who can whisper:

> "Jesus is dead and God's gone away."

Yet the soul-hunger is there, the restlessness of the savage, the wail of the wanderer, and the plaint is put in one little phrase:

Over the inner thoughts of the slaves and their relations one with another the shadow of fear ever hung, so that we get but glimpses here and there, and also with them, eloquent omissions and silences. Mother and child are sung, but seldom father; fugitive and weary wanderer call for pity and affection, but there is little of wooing and wedding; the rocks and the mountains are well known, but home is unknown. Strange blending of love and helplessness sings through the refrain:

> "Yonder's my ole mudder,
> Been waggin' at de hill so long;
> 'Bout time she cross over,
> Git home bime-by."

Elsewhere comes the cry of the "motherless" and the "Farewell, farewell, my only child."

Love-songs are scarce and fall into two categories—the frivolous and light, and the sad. Of deep successful love there is ominous silence, and in one of the oldest of these songs there is a depth of history and meaning:

A black woman said of the song, "It can't be sung without a full heart and a troubled sperrit." The same voice sings here that sings in the German folk-song:

> "Jetz Geh i' an's brunele, trink' aber net."

Of death the Negro showed little fear, but talked of it familiarly and even fondly as simply a crossing of the waters, perhaps—who knows?—back to his ancient forests again. Later days transfigured his fatalism, and amid the dust and dirt the toiler sang:

> "Dust, dust and ashes, fly over my grave,
> But the Lord shall bear my spirit home."

The things evidently borrowed from the surrounding world undergo characteristic change when they enter the mouth of the slave. Especially is this true of Bible phrases. "Weep, O captive daughter of Zion," is quaintly turned into "Zion, weep-a-low," and the wheels of Ezekiel are turned every way in the mystic dreaming of the slave, till he says:

> "There's a little wheel a-turnin' in-a-my heart."

As in olden time, the words of these hymns were improvised by some leading minstrel of the religious band. The circumstances of the gathering, however, the rhythm of the songs, and the limitations of allowable thought, confined the poetry for the most part to single or double lines, and they seldom were expanded to quatrains or longer tales, although there are some few examples of sustained efforts, chiefly paraphrases of the Bible. Three short series of verses have always attracted me,—the one that heads this chapter, of one line of which Thomas Wentworth Higginson has fittingly said, "Never, it seems to me, since man first lived and suffered was his infinite longing for peace uttered more plaintively." The second and third are descriptions of the Last Judgment,—the one a late improvisation, with some traces of outside influence:

> "Oh, the stars in the elements are falling,
> And the moon drips away into blood,
> And the ransomed of the Lord are returning unto God,
> Blessed be the name of the Lord."

And the other earlier and homelier picture from the low coast lands:

> "Michael, haul the boat ashore,
> Then you'll hear the horn they blow,
> Then you'll hear the trumpet sound,
> Trumpet sound the world around,
> Trumpet sound for rich and poor,
> Trumpet sound the Jubilee,
> Trumpet sound for you and me."

Through all the sorrow of the Sorrow Songs there breathes a hope—a faith in the ultimate justice of things. The minor cadences of despair change often to triumph and calm confidence. Sometimes it is faith in life, sometimes a faith in death, sometimes assurance of boundless justice in some fair world beyond. But whichever it is, the meaning is always clear: that sometime, somewhere, men will judge men by their souls and not by their skins. Is such a hope justified? Do the Sorrow Songs sing true?

The silently growing assumption of this age is that the probation of races is past, and that the backward races of to-day are of proven inefficiency and not worth the saving. Such an assumption is the arrogance of peoples irreverent toward Time and ignorant of the deeds of men. A thousand years ago such an assumption, easily possible, would have made it difficult for the Teuton to prove his right to life. Two thousand years ago such dogmatism, readily welcome, would have scouted the idea of blond races ever leading civilization. So wofully unorganized is sociological knowledge that the meaning of progress, the meaning of "swift" and "slow" in human doing, and the limits of human perfectability, are veiled, unanswered sphinxes on the shores of science. Why should Aeschylus have sung two thousand years before Shakespeare was born? Why has civilization flourished in Europe, and flickered, flamed, and died in Africa? So long as the world stands meekly dumb before such questions, shall this nation proclaim its ignorance and unhallowed prejudices by denying freedom of opportunity to those who brought the Sorrow Songs to the Seats of the Mighty?

Your country? How came it yours? Before the Pilgrims landed we were here. Here we have brought our three gifts and mingled them with yours: a gift of story and song—

soft, stirring melody in an ill-harmonized and unmelodious land; the gift of sweat and brawn to beat back the wilderness, conquer the soil, and lay the foundations of this vast economic empire two hundred years earlier than your weak hands could have done it; the third, a gift of the Spirit. Around us the history of the land has centred for thrice a hundred years; out of the nation's heart we have called all that was best to throttle and subdue all that was worst; fire and blood, prayer and sacrifice, have billowed over this people, and they have found peace only in the altars of the God of Right. Nor has our gift of the Spirit been merely passive. Actively we have woven ourselves with the very warp and woof of this nation,—we fought their battles, shared their sorrow, mingled our blood with theirs, and generation after generation have pleaded with a headstrong, careless people to despise not Justice, Mercy, and Truth, lest the nation be smitten with a curse. Our song, our toil, our cheer, and warning have been given to this nation in blood-brotherhood. Are not these gifts worth the giving? Is not this work and striving? Would America have been America without her Negro people?

Even so is the hope that sang in the songs of my fathers well sung. If somewhere in this whirl and chaos of things there dwells Eternal Good, pitiful yet masterful, then anon in His good time America shall rend the Veil and the prisoned shall go free. Free, free as the sunshine trickling down the morning into these high windows of mine, free as yonder fresh young voices welling up to me from the caverns of brick and mortar below—swelling with song, instinct with life, tremulous treble and darkening bass. My children, my little children, are singing to the sunshine, and thus they sing:

And the traveller girds himself, and sets his face toward the Morning, and goes his way.

THE AFTER-THOUGHT

Hear my cry, O God the Reader; vouchsafe that this my book fall not still-born into the world-wilderness. Let there spring, Gentle One, from out its leaves vigor of thought and thoughtful deed to reap the harvest wonderful. (Let the ears of a guilty people tingle with truth, and seventy millions sigh for the righteousness which exalteth nations, in this drear day when human brotherhood is mockery and a snare.) Thus in Thy good time may infinite reason turn the tangle straight, and these crooked marks on a fragile leaf be not indeed.

The Battle for Black Studies

Nathan Hare

In the beginning, white American education, particularly on the college level, was highly private, restricted to the few who were wealthy enough to afford it. Those persons, as social theorist Thorstein Veblen observed in his book, *The Theory of the Leisure Class*, were characterized by a peculiar mentality in which, owing to the necessity for displaying one's wealth, it was prestigious to be free from productive endeavor. Any work done could not be remunerative and preferably should be of no significant use to anybody, let alone oneself, to waste time, and to have the time to waste time were symbolic of prestige. Their educational enterprise, accordingly, was characterized by a "liberal arts" approach where students learned a little about a lot of things and a lot about nothing. The leisure-class syndrome and its snobbish motivations encouraged a preoccupation with lofty gobbledygook such as footnoting. Students might be compelled to labor in memorizing the idiomatic expressions and the verbal conjugations of dead languages; or, more currently, languages which invariably fade from the student's memory and, while remembered, are useless in post-graduate life.

As middle class aspirants began to emulate the leisure class, and education was largely socialized, the principle of exclusiveness was reinforced by the need to stem the flood of recruits to professional occupations. Hence a student might make A's and B's in all required courses only to fail the comprehensive exam or the language test, or pass all academic requirements only to fail the bar exam because of political beliefs or color of skin. Education lost much of its capacity for vitalizing the mind and, since the end-products became more important than the process, eventually amounted to a routine assimilation of approved bodies of knowledge, a process which fails particularly to inspire a black child of working class origin.

With the growing urbanization of the 1950's and 1960's, colleges emerged increasingly as the factories for producing the technicians needed to run an urbanized society—computer types, lawyers, and the like.

> The forces of production which eventually led to over-urbanization and industrialization have produced a concomitant specialization of learning, and a rise of gadgeteering, but the leisure-class legacy has nevertheless remained.

> Neither leisure class education or specialized education is sufficient to transform black consciousness—or white consciousness for that matter—into a revolutionary, creative instrument for dynamic change. Leisure class education creates dilettantes; specialized education creates pragmatists and moral zombies devoid of imagination or compassion in the exercise of their skills.[1]

Burdened by the duality of racial oppression, black American education likewise reflected white American education's dilemma, most strikingly exhibited in the educational philosophies for which Booker T. Washington and W.E.B. DuBois are known. With his job-training approach, Booker T. endeavored to create a race of skilled workers and a consolidated economic clout. DuBois' early talented-tenth theory was basically about creating a black vanguard of, essentially, radical black bourgeoisie who would become teachers/trainers and diffuse their skill and teach others through radicalized black colleges.

Booker T. provided for the masses and their economic plight in his thinking, but neglected the cultural-political theory, and the creation of a black inteligentsia. DuBois, or the other hand, directed attention to the intelligentsia, and cultural-political theoretics but, in his early and most famous approach, failed to provide sufficiently for the masses. Possibly as a consequence of historical circumstances—the location of most blacks of that day in the South and the intransigent mores of segregation—neither developed theoretics for invading white colleges.

This was left to more recent years, when the early advocates of "black studies" sought both the collective elevation of a people, with education of, from, and for the masses, and the training of a mass-minded black conscious middle class. Black studies was to provide a working model and theoretics for both black and white colleges, correcting the "Negro" college's fallacies and seizing equitable power and control at white colleges. Instead of searching merely for equality of education, its premise was 1) that there can be no equality of education in a racist society; 2) the type of education conceived and perpetrated by the white oppressor is essentially an education for oppression; and 3) black education must be education for liberation, or at least for change. In this respect, it was to prepare black students to become the catalysts for a black cultural revolution. All courses—whether history, literature, or mathematics—would be taught from a revolutionary ideology or perspective. Black education would become the instrument for change.

Its initial vehicle, black studies, was at best a mass movement and a mass struggle based on the notion that education belongs to the people and the idea is to give it back to them. Hence, most crucial to black studies, black education, aside from its ideology of liberation, would be the community component of its methodology. This was designed to wed black communities, heretofore excluded, and the educational process, to transform the black community, making it. more relevant to higher education, at the same time as education is made relevant to the black community. Such education would bring both the college to the community and the community to the college. The community and its problems would comprise a laboratory, and there-would be apprenticeships and field work components to every course.

Even a course such as history might have the requirement that students put on panel discussions on black history in church basement or wherever for younger children. A class project could be the formation of a black history club, over the years organizing the black community thereby and raising black consciousness, while helping to educate black youth through course-related tutorial programs. The black college student's mere presence in the community could provide an otherwise unavailable role model for young black children and, as the student tests out his theories learned in the classroom via the abovementioned activities and apprenticeships where applicable (say, in black politics, black economics, black journalism, black theater, etc.) he would gain an intensive knowledge of and commitment to the community he was being taught to serve after graduation.

Other than their opposition to incorporating an ideology of liberation (particularly in scientific and technical courses) to replace that of acquiescing to the status quo, administrators opposed the community component most. They soon succeeded in restricting black studies to culture and the humanities, to the study merely of blackness. But they did not do so without running into a battle with black students.

Let us now take up case studies of two of these struggles, one on a "Negro" campus, Howard University, the other on a white campus, San Francisco State College. I have chosen these not only because they were among the earliest and most intensive of their kind, but also because they are the ones I know best, having been a part of them firsthand.

"NEGRO" COLLEGES

Some years ago two Harvard University social scientists, David Riesman and Christopher Jencks, published a devastating article in the *Harvard Educational Review* on the failure of the American "Negro" college. It created a furor in Negro college circles. The anxious reaction of Negro college administrators and professors led to a number of lively, high-level faculty meetings and private threats—to my knowledge never carried out—to debate Riesman and Jencks in public print.

I do not think that the professors' hesitancy was simply a product of the fact that most of them had never published anything before. Rather, it is that they know, as I do, that Riesman and Jencks were as accurate as outsiders could manage to be. I know because I was graduated from a Negro college, taught for a total of seven years at two others, and lectured at many others across the country where I had occasion to observe the classroom behavior and engage students in casual conversation. I had gone to teach at Howard University in 1961 and hung on for six full years—against the advice of friends, relatives, and former professors—because of a keen interest, then unpopular, in helping to educate black students. It was my belief that they would become the leading black individuals of the future, if not black leaders, and that the entire race and the world would benefit from whatever they became.

This faith in the potential radicalization of the Negro college, before first radicalizing the white college as a model for them, soon appeared to be a bit naive. Part of the reason may be traced to the history of Negro colleges and the nature of their founding and motivation. A few grew out of abolitionist sentiment in the North but quickly became favorite places for guilt-ridden white slavemasters to send away their illegitimate offspring. Most early Negro colleges, however, were founded in the South by the missionary movement and religious preachers for missionary work in this country ("home missions") and Africa. They had the objective, writes Earl Conrad in *The Invention of the Negro*, "not only of teaching the freedmen how to read and write, but, by bringing the learning in the form of the Bible, to temper this teaching, perhaps to moderate the freed-man as well as free him."

Missionary-run colleges, for the most part, eventually folded, or were taken over or duplicated by state governments—but Negro colleges, to this day, have never escaped the missionary influence. Most are teachers' colleges with an occasional school of theology attached, though many, predictably, are called universities. Many students insist that they are more properly "puniversities," and complain that A&M (Agriculture and Mechanical) are Athletics and Music colleges A&I (Agriculture and Industrial), Athletics and Ignorance; and A&T (Agriculture and Technical), Athletics and Tomism.

As idealistic white teachers and administrators retreated, they were replaced by "colored" personnel who quickly instituted the mores of the plantation and sought to ape the academic trivia and adolescent fanfare of white colleges. These newcomers were mainly descendants of free blacks or "house nigger" slaves (those who worked in the house instead of the field and became domesticated emulators of upper-class Southern white manners). They longed to be accepted at all costs by white society and modeled their lives to approximate white thinking and behavior—even toward their own race—shunning association and identity with the lower class.[1]

> . . . instead of trying to promote a distinctive set of habits and values in their students, they were, by almost any standard, purveyors of super-American, ultra-bourgeois prejudices and aspirations. Fax from fighting to preserve a separate subculture, as other ethnic colleges did, the Negro colleges were militantly opposed to almost everything which made Negroes diffrent from whites, or the grounds that it was "lower-class."

By the mid-1960's, the Negro bourgeoisie administering Negro colleges had come so much to resent their multiplying lower class students they fell victim to an effort to "raise the quality" of Negro colleges by making them predominantly white. It was mainly the resistance of black students which halted this travesty, as we shall see. A case in point was Howard University.

As Howard became "the Capstone of 'Negro' education," it also became an epitome of its political docility and academic nothingness, groveling at the feet of outside (mainly government) expectations, real or imagined, and fawning upon white Congressional, appropriators. However, in an era of greater access to white colleges, just then emerging, and "rising Negro expectations," this footshuffling was proving inadequate, in the competition for top students and professors. Faced with this predicament, administrators merely intensified their Stepin' Fetchit tactics.

---

[1] **E. Franklin Frazier, *Black Bourgeoisie*, Clencoe, Illinois: Free Press, 1957.**

In early September 1966, then President James Narbit announced in the *Washington Post* a plan to make Howard "sixty per cent white" by 1970, a plan opposed by virtually every student on campus. To accomplish this goal, the University had devised an-ingenious program for excluding and/or removing black students while attracting white ones. Some professors were warned by the dean's office, through departmental chairmen instructed to "counsel" them, that their grade distributions for each class should include a minimum of six per cent failing marks.

At the same time, it was decided to "raise standards" by raising the required score on entrance tests standardized on children of urban middle-class white exposure. Many "culturally deprived" black students would not, of course, be expected to manage the new score. White students who flunked would not need to humiliate themselves enrolling in a pre-college sequence at Howard; hence, a proposed special division for students who fail the test would invariably be black. These "sub-normals" would have to spend a year preparing to enter the new white Howard. Having failed the test as individuals, their self-esteem would be further decimated, for they would be set apart as failures and subjected to an ego-mortifying curriculum.

Thus, according to Riesman and Jencks:
First, they were to receive a speech course (then already incorporated at Howard) frankly, calculated to force black students to "lose their in-group dialects," despite the fact that President Nabrit himself had been successful in Supreme Court presentations in a classical "Negro dialect." Such students also were to be given a course in reading skills and, simultaneously, one in masterpieces of world literature. It goes without saying that "masterpiece" authors would be invariably, if not exclusively, Caucasian. Still another course was history of *Western* civilization (not world civilization, as in the case of the masterpieces). This curriculum would say to black students, who already were failures as individuals, that they had no ennobling ancestral roots: thier kind had produced no civilization worthy of attention, no literary achievements, and indeed are guilty now of the wrong mode of speech.

Meanwhile, as integration at the college level increased (an overwhelming majority of all black college students now attend predominantly white colleges) the Negro bourgeoisie increasingly began to send their children to white colleges. The late sociologist E. Franklin Frazier complained to me, as we were walking across Howard University's campus one spring morning shortly before his death some years ago, that for forty years he for one had been unable to teach the Negro bourgeoisie or their children anything. Frazier once wrote prophetically in his book, *Black Bourgeoisie*: "As the children of the Negro masses have flooded the colleges, it was inevitable that the traditional standards of morals and manners would have to give way."

Thus, although the protest at Negro colleges in the 1960's sometimes took the form of black power cries (often exaggerated or concocted by administrators and public relations officials playing to public sentiment), the fight on Negro college campuses —in contrast to more nationalistic black tendencies on white campuses—more accurately reflected a desire to escape the doldrums of Negro bourgeois dalliance and administrative tyranny and mismanagement.

Even where black students at Negro colleges chanted "black power," it was mainly a rallying cry. Closer inspection of their demands revealed divergent provocations. Howard students, who launched the fad in 1968 of briefly taking over administration buildings finally wrangled some concessions out of their administrators. These concessions revolved around the following: the freedom to bring liquor into the dormitories, and the opportunity, in the case of girls, to take as many as three "unexplained" weekends. However, a cutback in the stiff prerequisites for the then existing course in "Negro history" was also being "considered." By contrast, black students at San Francisco State College already had sixteen courses in black studies! When students at Pennsylvania's Cheyney State College chased the existing administration out of its building, they demanded a state investigation of school policies. The students thrown out of Louisiana's Grambling College merely wanted less emphasis on athletics and more on academics.

Black students on Negro campuses were merely rejecting the paternalism (some say "maternalism") of their administrations and, like the black race generally, seeking a new-direction. They resented the fact that their colleges are fundamentally grotesque caricatures of white colleges, and that they are denied any place in helping to determine their own destinies.

Because administrators extend only puppet power even to official student government, most students disdained to take an active part in routine campus elections. Thus the students elected to office seldom represent genuine choices of the student bodies they purport to serve, and, except for occasional sham attempts to be relevant to student interests, serve largely antithetical goals. Students seeking self-determination accordingly feel impelled to take matters into their own hands and force the administration to serve them.

In all Negro colleges I have visited, I found students who wanted to know, as one of them put it recently, how to "break this administrative grip." At a college in South Carolina I was kept up all night long convincing students who had had enough to stay on in school so that someday, somehow, they might move into a better position to bring about more change.

A college registrar, before fleeing mid-year to a white university, once showed me figures indicating that his college, despite a high flunkout rate, lost more students each year who earn a "C" average and above than students with less than a "C" average. We could only speculate on the fact that most major leaders of black revolutionary groups such as SNCC (Student Nonviolent Coordinating Committee), RAM (Revolutionary Action Movement) and the Black Panthers, were above-average, frequently honor students, in predominantly black colleges or junior colleges, before dropping out in disgust. I have many times watched helplessly while my best students began to disdain most of their other classes and proceed to flunk out.

One student at a leading Negro college finally managed to graduate, after some hesitancy by his professors; then, after making *Who's Who in America* that self-same year, returned to his campus, where he was moved to remark that it should be burned down and cotton planted in its place, so that at least some economic benefit could accrue. Instead of teaching white colleges by example, the methods of a new and genuine freedom, Negro colleges merely compounded the most deplorable errors of white college ways.

Consequently, there is an ever-widening gulf between black students and Negro professors. The Negro professor's gleeful submission to a "melting pot" uniformity necessarily produces in a college involuntarily black an institutional schizophrenia. "Under such circumstances," wrote Riesman and Jencks in the *Harvard Educational Review*, "the Negro colleges could have maintained their self-respect only if they had viewed themselves as a pre-revolutionary holding operation, designed to salvage the victims of injustice." This they have never done. Part of the blame rests as much on the professors as on the administrators.

Negro professors are generally characterized by acquiescence to the administration and a resignation to academic nothingness. They disidentify with their work—for promotions are largely social or political in nature—and do enough to just get by. To compensate for this condition, professors ceremonialize the most minute achievements into regal grandiosity. More than half a dozen "academic processions" are pompously strutted through each term—Founders Day, Charters Day, Parents Day, May Day, baccalaureate ceremonies and commencement exercises—at which white and Negro dignitaries speak or receive "honorary" degrees.

There is a very high turnover of personnel, dampened by the addiction to the ownership of fine homes and the difficulty some of them experience in getting other jobs. "They are marginal," according to one former Howard professor, "and seldom publish anything," although some of them will pad their "bibliographies" with "letters to the editor" and the like. Those who dare to rebel are either dismissed on some pretext or labeled crazy or "confused."

Elaborate codes of conduct, vaguely defined, are set up to keep both faculty and students in lockstep and submission. I was criticized by superiors, for example, when Stokely Carmichael spoke one fall to two of my classes and, on another occasion I was asked to indicate a "Black Muslim" minister's qualification to speak on the mathematics of the black man's condition. It was known that the minister in question, Dr. Lonnie Shabazz, has a master's degree from the Massachusetts Institute of Technology and a Ph.D. from Cornell University in mathematics. He was for years the head of the mathematics department at Atlanta University before joining the Muslims. When a white Episcopalian priest was scheduled to speak, the storefront-sounding name of his church, "St. Philip the Evangelist," also broughtforth inquiries. I settled the problem by merely stating that he was white. On another occasion, the auditorium was closed down in an effort to prevent Muhammad Ali from speaking on the campus.

Many students increasingly came to realize the interdependence of faculty and student conditions. More and more of them are growing aware of the fact that freedom for them is freedom for the faculty which in turn will benefit them.

While such sentiments are on the rise in Negro colleges across the country, they are currently held by only a minority of students. However, the very apathy and inactivity of the student majority, bent mainly on hucklebucking through fraternity bazaars on the way to a bachelor's degree and a big-time job, will permit the militant minority to wield a disproportionate impact.

This was the case during our struggle at Howard in 1966–67. We wanted not only to prevent the proposed transformation of Howard into a white university but also contrarily to further "blacken" Howard, to "overthrow the Negro college with white innards and to raise in its place a black university relevant to the black community and its needs." That was not then a popular orientation of black students at Negro colleges. Thus, though we were able generally to excite mass protest on particular issues, the struggle mainly took the form of guerrilla propaganda and activity by a small vanguard whose goals frequently conflicted with moderate and liberal black student activists who then thought the vanguard too "extreme."

It was difficult to escalate to mass action, the most successful effort culminating in a boycott of merely one day. Part of this was due to the absence of provocation by visible (uniformed) police action on the campus, all violence being executed by the rebels. Containment took the form of police infiltration and student spies in the employ of the administration. At the same time, there was not a single arrest, even after a police infiltrator was quietly shot near the campus. This, like many other provocative events such as scattered fires and other terrorism, was totally kept out of the press, though the press, like the police, knew about the incidents. Also, there was almost no involvement by the faculty. What little there was included only white faculty members. This lessened the spread of support by students though many leaned toward change. In any case, the participation of a faculty member was a lonely one, leaving him subject to the most trivial forms of harassment.

One day while standing talking to my urban sociology class about the impact of urbanization on social norms, I got around to sexual norms. In order to assure the students of my adherence to society's regulations, I told of efforts the previous year to launch an association of virgins on the campus, but that one member grew sick and dropped out and the other flunked out. I also explained that the reason Howard's wall clocks always differed as to time of day was because every time a virgin at Howard passes a clock the clock stands still. Within thirty minutes after that class was over, the chairman of my department was calling me in excitedly to say that the dean had said that a student had said that I had said that I was the only virgin on Howard's campus.

School closed, and in the dead of early summer about twenty students and six professors (all but one of them white) received letters of dismissal for their "black power" activities. The courts readmitted the students, but, though pointing out that wo, were illegally dismissed (wihout a hearing) have not acted on our case to this day. Meanwhile, the student members of the Black Power Committee were imprisoned in another town in a summer "riot-prevention" roundup of black militants; in this case for allegedly "conspiring to incite a riot." No bail was set until October, leaving the student forces of the year before gravely decimated. The liberal-moderate students dillydallied but did little else. There also was no help, as promised the year before, from the community's black militants; including the Washington Committee for Black Power, an umbrella group of the activists in the area of which I was chairman. This also was to prove a problem at San Francisco State College, where community leaders sought to contain the strike by joining it; but, when they were not allowed to negotiate with the establishment in behalf of the students, simply tucked their tails and sneaked away. This is one of the most crucial failures in the black college student struggle, the lack of enduring community support.

At Howard, as in the case of the previous year's boycott, student militants exaggerated the united front approach to the point of fallacy. Excessive in their search for "wide participation," they turned the leadership over to establishment students. It was clear by then, at least to me, that the major reason for the Black Power Committee's relative strength in 1966–67 resulted from its exclusiveness, although this angered many students who regarded themselves as "black militants" and had reputations for constant espousals of the glories of blackness and revolutionary rhetoric. These students; years later, could still be found at that game, beating their chests and reading and parroting Frantz Fanon and Mao Tse-Tung; and it eventually became apparent that they could not be expected to do much else.

Then there were the grand organizers. One night I attended a unifying meeting of the representatives of nineteen different groups, each proposing to have the cure for Howard's ills. When I finally left the meeting at midnight they had not managed to get together on anything other than the prohibition of campus activity by any single member-group. Later, I learned that they agreed on a collective name whose acrostics formed an African word meaning "unity" but they never did do anything else. Which is what they agreed in the first place—remember?—that no member-group should do anything. There is a united front, apparently, and a united *front*.

The day before Christmas Eve of that year, 1967, I stopped by an asylum to visit a former Howard professor and friend incarcerated there. He had been one of the deans of black literature and black thought in the days when Howard was in its heyday, sought out for guidance by a generation of black students when Howard's faculty directory read like a Who's Who Among Black Scholars. In late November someone told me how he stood in a faculty meeting and angrily threatened, should Howard go through with a proposal to give all this year's honorary degrees to white individuals, he would write exposes to "make Nathan Hare's seem mild." Within two weeks they compelled him to retire ("leave of absence" beginning the second semester until the end of the academic year and then goodby) after over thirty years on the faculty. In a few days he was taken by force to St. Elizabeth's hospital. Coming down the corridor on the day of my visit, he looked well for his age and in good health. On approaching closer he recognized me and refused to see me, stating that he did not wish to see anybody from Howard again.

Not long after that, having been fired from Howard, my attention was turned to the black student on the white campus. My introduction took place at San Francisco State College, where I went to "coordinate" the nation's first black studies program. This soon dissolved into deception as I discovered that I had been brought there to appease black students. I refused the role of a troubleshooter and tumult was not long in breaking loose. I could not and did not try to stop the student protest. This too was instructive, but first a word on the situation of black students on white campuses in a general way.

WHITE COLLEGES

On white campuses, particularly those located in small college communities, black students live in social isolation (aggravated frequently by a skewed sex distribution) where their acceptance is superficial even when apparent. In less exclusive colleges located in large cities, the opportunities for social and romantic philandering are more prevalent, in both the greater number of their kind on campus and a relative access to the off-campus black community.

This quest for meaningful social relations, coupled with discriminatory housing and economic considerations, increases the black student's probability of becoming a campus commuter. Commuting each day between the black community and the white campus, black students experience a daily sense of discrepancy between two contrasting, even conflicting, worlds one world whose spirit has been largely broken in the quest for the social elevation, which the black student now holds dear; the other world characterized by a good deal of minutiae which the black student recognizes as profoundly "irrelevant" to himself, his fate, and his experience. And yet he knows so well that he must wade somehow through this "white" milieu in search of ratification for the "white rat race" (which is a chore for anybody). The chore is simply compounded by the fact that, psychologically and otherwise, it does not relate so well to what is crucial to the black student's life, inclining him in too many cases to give up. He eventually comes to see it as essentially "a bad set."

This sense of defeatism and despair is reinforced and magnified by the models of failure surrounding him in the black community. On top of that, exposure to harsh measures of discrimination, past or present, provoke a feeling of suspicion out of which can develop a negative definition of certain' phenomena which the white middle class employs for social acceptance, including not merely cultural symbols of status; it might become derogatory, for example, to be seen spending much time with books. Under the prevailing college system, structured so that an individual succeeds best by conforming most to middle class values, black students labor considerably less prepared (than white students of suburban training and experience) to cope. They grow naturally and indelibly alienated. It might become more "in" to be good at cards, for example, which only multiplies the probability of failure in the academic arena. The black student—covertly at first,—rightfully begins to question the nature of standards impassionately dangled above his head as obstacles to the acquisition of the stamp "qualified."

Early in his educational career, the black student encounters the subordinating slap of white supremacy. Modes of communication, for instance, compel him to lose his "in-group dialect" and imitate the snarls and twangs of the white race. "There" becomes "thear," "nine," "nigh-yun;" "law," "lower;" and so on. Verbal facility is frankly presented to the black student as the salient ingredient for admission to college, although I know young black men with more verbal facility than I will ever have who have either flunked out or dropped out of school.

Beyond this, the black student instinctively, if only faintly, is affronted by the fact that foreign languages required are exclusively of white European origin, though Oriental languages may be offered as electives. This, in spite of the fact that Chinese is spoken by more individuals than any other language in the world and Swahili, an African language, competes very favorably with German. This is just one of the examples of white snobbishness lurking behind the criteria of excellence which, by no means however, is entirely a product of racism alone. White students it is true, are victims of the same condition, but it is doubly alien to the experience of black students who, moreover, are burdened by many other unconscious assumptions of white supremacy.

Or, take the matter of cultural imperialism which white academic ethnocentrism produces. A white anthropology professor may think nothing of dividing African tribes into "primitive' and "westernized," then pointing out that primitive tribes are more characterized by the matrilineal system (tracing ancestry through the mother instead of the father) while neglecting to point out that this could be a more accurate procedure. The black student who first called my attention to this fact indicated that "you have to take the mother's word for it and sometimes she doesn't know herself." He swore that a boy in his Georgia bayou community came home from school one day and told his father happily that he was going to marry a girl—let us call her Pearlie Mae. His father said: "Son, I didn't know that you would go that far; you can't marry Pearlie Mae; that's my daughter; she's your sister; don't tell your mamma, now." The boy moped around, then broke down and told his mother what was wrong. "That's okay," his mother consoled, "you can marry Pearlie Mae. Don't tell your daddy but he ain't your father."

Sociology classes will discuss the merits of the Moynihan Report on the "Negro" family, for instance, incognizant of the implications of Moynihan's own figures showing, for example, that for every 100 nonwhite males between the ages of 25 and 40 in New York City there are 33 extra females. Somebody, of necessity, must carry a greater sexual burden than rightfully is his share, or a number of women will languish via induced celibacy. At the same time, the condition is being intensified by the disproportionate rates at which black males are `dying in Vietnam, depleting the supply of eligible black males. This cold demographic fact will lead to family disorganization and high rates of adultery, no matter how "moral" or "stable" (as social scientists say) black sexual codes may be.

Similarly, anthropology professors will subject black students to discussions on family disorganization among Africans in Kenya, for example, impervious to the fact that much family strife is a product of the Christian missionaries' importation of an alien monogamy which, replacing the existing polygamy evidently geared to the demography and socio-economic needs of the people, displaced surplus wives (in order to "save" them) and produced a good deal of the family disorganization which anthropologists get grants and trips abroad to "study."

Black students who wail about the absence of blackness in white college education accordingly are not trying to destroy American education so much as they are trying desperately to renovate it. Their compensatory response to black exclusion has taken a separatist flavor, for the most part, on the surface; but it may seem ironic to those who misunderstand them that, in the name of black nationalism, calling for the presence of more black students and professors, they actually are bringing about more desegregation of white colleges than ever there was before.

The name of the game is the elevation of a people by means of one important escalator —college education. Separatism and integrationism are possible approaches to that end; they lose their effectiveness when, swayed by dogmatic traces of absolutism, they become full ends in themselves. It'will be an irony of recorded history, I have written elsewhere, that "integration" was used in the second half of this century to hold the black race down just as segregation was so instituted in the first half. Black students increasingly seem to feel that integration; particularly in the token way in which it has been practiced up to now, and the neo-tokenist manner now emerging, elevates individual members of the group but, paradoxically, in plucking many of the strongest members from the group while failing to alter the lot of the group as a whole, weakens the collective thrust which the group might otherwise muster. Increasingly black students are turning their backs on the old tendency for black college graduates to escape from the black community instead of returning to help build it. This new mood is born of a greater awareness of the glories of their own past as a people, an image they now wish to convey also to others. Hence the clamor for more "black courses" and courses taught from a black perspective.

THE STRIKE AT SAN FRANCISCO STATE COLLEGE

Let us take up one such clamor, perhaps the most important single confrontation in campus history as of this writing, the San Francisco State College struggle, which included a five-month "strike" and was an experiment in the seizure of power over the educational destinies of black students.

It all began when black students, by then having exhausted all other avenues for redress, issued publicly a set of "demands" which, though "non-negotiable," were generally regarded as reasonable. They presented a comprehensive nationalist program for education, a blueprint in defining and directing their own lives as students. The only one not publicly understood was the one requesting that all black students wishing so be admitted in Fall, 1969.

Whites immediately envisioned hordes of black students flooding the campus by the thousands. However, experience had taught the black students the difficulty of finding even hundreds of blacks whose desires as persons customarily excluded from the educational process and whose socioeconomic circumstances would permit them to quit work or whatever and enroll at San Francisco State College. The student rebels were merely seeking to eradicate the existing racist and classist criteria for admission to the college. However, the demands spoke for themselves.

1. —That all Black Studies courses being taught through various other departments be immediately made part of the Black Studies Department, and that all the instructors in this department receive full-time pay.
2. —That Dr. Nathan Hare, Chairman of the Black Studies Department, receive a full professorship and a comparable salary according to his qualifications.
3. —That there be a Department of Black Studies which will grant a Bachelor's Degree in Black Studies; that the Black Studies Department, the Chairman, faculty and staff have the sole power to hire faculty and control and determine the destiny of its department.
4. —That all unused slots for black students from Fall 1968 under the Special Admissions Program be filled in Spring, 1969.
5. —That all black students wishing so be admitted in Fall, 1969.
6. —That twenty (20) full-time teaching positions be allocated to the Department of Black Studies.
7. —That Dr. Helen Bedesem be replaced from the position of Financial Aids Officer, and that a black person be hired to direct it, that Third World people have the power to determine how it will be administered.
8. —That no disciplinary action will be administered in any way to any students, workers, teachers, or administrators during and after the strike as a consequence of their participation in the strike.
9. —That the California State College Trustees not be allowed to dissolve the black programs on or off the San Francisco State College campus.
10. —That George Murray maintain his teaching position on campus for the 1968–69 academic year.

Having observed that most student rebels tend to engage in symbolic or expressive behavior, black leaders at San Francisco State College sought conversely to disdain confrontation as a major strategy (though it included confrontation) and instead to concentrate on an effort to "heighten the contradictions." For by heightening the contradictions, you prepare people for the confrontation which must come when they are fully sensitized, politicized, to the nature of their condition. Rushing into confrontations prematurely without having heightened contradictions weakens the force of the confrontation. The theory was that when contradictions in the system, contradictions in the status or behavior of the oppressor and the oppressed, are dramatized, the oppressed become correspondingly disaffected. For instance, when the Department of Health, Education and Welfare decreed that rebellious students would lose their grants-in-aid, that was a contradiction, a source of conflict, because it indicated or implied that only well-to-do students could afford to rebel.

In his speech before the Third World Liberation Front (nonwhite students) the day before the strike, Stokely Carmichael cautioned the students against focusing their planned struggle on the "specific" instead of the "general." To do so means that they would fight merely to re-hire a fired professor (a specific) instead of fighting for the right to significantly determine hiring and firing (the general which includes the specific). Thus, they would wind up fighting the same old battle over and over again; first, for George Murray, next for John Hatchett, or again, somebody else. We must fight for the general principle. But we must do more than that. We must distinguish between tactics, and strategy as well as between tactics and principles. A principle is a doctrine or assumption, a rule or code of conduct, and we discovered that once we had internalized our principles (an undying fight against racism and for the self-determination of oppressed peoples, combined with a policy of non-compromise), strategy was more clearly and more easily ascertained. Tactics, of course, are merely a variety of or instance of the use of strategy.

Naturally there developed conflicts over strategy and tactics, now and again within our own black ranks (stirred often by infiltrators); but also especially with our white allies. Mass confrontation, for instance, appeared to be favored by the white radicals who, as the majority of the studentry and faculty, constituted the majority of the strikers, though much of their prominence was due to widespread black student apathy. Mass behavior is the natural tendency of large collectivities and is more suited as well to America's myth of majority government which has been relatively more assimilated by the white middle class.

But, as in the case of most revolutionary action, the strike was launched initially by a minority of individuals who apparently articulated the latent needs, the powerlessness, the hopes, of the oppressed group at large. Revolution by definition is in discord with what most persons are accustomed to accept. Black revolutionaries too often wait for a majority vote before they move, and so they never do. Black students at San Francisco State College generally shunned the politics of ultra-democracy as a guiding principle, substituting "democratic centralism" instead. Their major strategy was the "war of the flea," scattered guerrilla action which in the strike as a whole, included some twenty bombings.

Some white professors, members of the American Federation of Teachers chapter on the campus, wanted to restore peace and harmony (the bourgeois liberal's phrase for "law and order" and all that it entails). They did not want, however, to risk their occupational security any more than they wanted to risk bodily harm earlier in the struggle from student terror and later from the clubs of the tactical squad police. Since they could not readily join the tactical squad they naturally joined the students, where the risk was smaller and they could execute the old "Tarzan-to-the-rescue-we-white-folks-can-solve-this-thing" white urges. They succeeded in jumping on a ready bandwagon—though this is not to say that there were not some genuinely dedicated—and when the going got rough, crawled off.

They sought to establish immediately the conventional definitions of the strike, which black students had early labeled their own struggle. This meant, for instance, that strikers were to ring the campus-with picket lines throughout active campus hours, marching single file, five feet apart, to the best of their ability. Nobody was ever to "cross the picket line" or enter the campus for any reason, even to so much as obtain their mail. Black students meanwhile preferred the strategy of the flea (an experimental variety of guerrilla tactics based on what a small flea can do to wear down a dog). The effect of the professors' picket line was to keep students on the periphery of the campus, which meant that "Allah's work could not be done" inside the campus grounds.

One night as I approached the campus with a famous black individual (who was one of several who from time to time sneaked out to try to negotiate), I almost fell into a fistfight with an AFT picketeer who angrily forbade me to enter the campus. I explained my purpose to no avail and at last remarked that I had been among those who helped start the skirmish, that he knew damn well that I was not "breaking the strike" by going onto campus after dark, then rolled my eyes at him and continued on my way.

The union-oriented AFT also set out to secure conventional reformist strike gains revolving around "stipulation of prerogatives" and better working conditions. But, though they were fighting ostensibly for occupational benefits, their reference group —the group to which they longed, even if unconsciously, to be a part of—remained the college's ruling class. Their unilateral clamor for "strike sanction" from the San Francisco Labor Council was testimony to that fact. A labor council sanction granted to a particular union is usually used as a reward whose aim is to procure conformity with the standards of behavior regarded as desirable by the sanctioning group—in this case the labor-establishment lackeys of the power structure.

The bourgeoisie, it has been recorded throughout history, has long tended to dampen revolutionary fervor via reform tactics whenever the status quo is shaken. These were some of the problems in trying to work with the white faculty's collaboration. They were gripped by what Robert Chrisman, then vice president and a black catalyst within the group, has referred to as the illusion of bourgeois privilege."

> Bourgeois privilege is the idea that the man of moderate means has full sanction under law, has full and unequivocal civil rights, has significance in the political fortune of his country, has the respect and esteem of his fellow-man because he is living a productive and morally righteous life, and that his voice is heard, will be heard and shall be obeyed, when it is collective, by all the power structures that obtain. Such is the illusion of bourgeois privilege—that the existence of man is ordered and reasonable and can be regulated through non-aggressive and articulate discussion, with full respect to follow.[2]

Thus, as intermediaries, they were able to lure the black student rebels into a three-day "convocation" (discussion and debate over issues) with the white administration. Until wiser heads finally broke up this farce, it is needless to say that the white administrators were getting the better of he confrontation, carried live each day over the local educational television station as college propaganda for the public.

---

[2] Robert Chrisman, "Observations on Race and Class at San Francisco State," *Black Power and Student Rebellion*, ed. by James McEvoy and Abraham Miller, Belmont, California: Wadsworth Publishing Company, 1969, p. 226.

Still, there is a challenge facing black students, as indeed all black revolutionaries, to work out their relationships with white collaborators, inasmuch as it is not possible to wish white people in America and the world away. We made some mistakes, but we learned a good deal in this regard via the San Francisco State College experiment. For instance, we pondered over the problem of white desires to take part directly and as one group in all of our actions. One day, when a group of white students came slobbering up to us, saying "what can we do to help?", we told them why not take the administration building. They trotted off to the task and ran into the big guns and clubs of the tactical squad which also sprayed mace into their faces. We learned, therefore, not to try that tactic ourselves.

Anyway, it is necessary to divide and weaken the enemy at least, if not to utilize the help of liberal factions without ourselves being co-opted. Hence it may be necessary to distinguish, as Maulana Ron Karenga has done, between an alliance (an association to further common interests) and a coalition (a temporary alliance of distinct parties for joint action).

HOWEVER, in the choice of any strategy, whether white radical are involved or not, it is necessary, we discovered at State, to consider both time and place. For example, colleges where revolutionary action of an intense nature has never taken place can utilize a bold form of confrontational tactics such as the Cornell students used in seizing the building with guns exhibited some years ago. Had black students at San Francisco State come on openly with weapons of any sort, let alone rifles and bullets around their shoulders, they would undoubtedly have been shot down on sight, as past activities would have suggested to police that the San Francisco State College students in those days had plans to use the guns for their proper purpose. Hence the limits of the confrontational tactic.

We discovered that not only was it more manageable by oppressive forces, it is more ephemeral. Confrontation is based on the notion of instant victory, that picketing for a day, taking over a building for a month, will achieve revolutionary change. This tactic is fruitful only in dramatizing one's discontent where there is no other way. Used exclusively, it becomes a new form of passive resistance even when it is accomplished by the exhibition of weapons never fired. This is in no way to detract from the efforts of black students who have used them, as their bravado at the least is admirable, just as it is not to give a pretext for apathy or virtual inaction by which we are currently gripped. Nor is it to say that the tactic is never useful; it is only to say that the seizure of power to control one's life and destiny will not be accomplished at one stroke, and hence the folly of instant strategems of any sort. The principle of the flea is based on the fact that a flea would never deign to jump into the mouth of a barking dog, to seize it, or even to bite it to death. The flea prefers to nibble along at his own pace, bit by bit, sometimes invisible to the dog, on his more remote and vulnerable parts, to worry him down.

At the time of the San Francisco State College strike, it had become a widespread fad to seize the symbols of power, to seize or "liberate," briefly, administration buildings and even hold the administrators themselves as hostages. Historically, however, successful revolutionaries have tended more to seize the instruments of power—weapons, land, wealth, tools, and the mind (which is what the fight for black studies is all about or should be). Administrators themselves seldom have the ultimate power. While the dean or the president is being held hostage, he is not able to go to the person who would give him the authority to implement the rebels demands. We must in general disdain the symbols of power and work toward seizing the instruments that are used to oppress us.

Many black students fall victim to tangential, expressive or symbolic behavior such as the once popular call for a "black university" at a time, when they could not even get a department or even a set of courses.

At San Francisco State College, students sought to supplant much symbolic behavior and the notions of instant victory with a concept of protracted struggle, cemented by the strategy of uncompromising non-negotiability. They might compromise, they said, on tactics, but never on principles. This added a do-or-die kind of spirit to their struggle, and, though it presented some problems of its own (hampering timing, in the analysis of Dr. Joe White, a black psychologist and then a San Francisco State dean), it nevertheless held students together in the strike longer than otherwise would have been the case. It was necessary time and again to gag would-be upstart negotiators who would have divided the ranks between those who wanted to negotiate at a given time and those who preferred to hang on a bit longer.

CONCLUSIONS

There were many other conclusions—both at San Francisco State and at Howard—which have implications for students everywhere, but they are difficult to draw. For one thing, the ancient Toms at Howard are being replaced now, at least in token degree, by a liberal black bourgeoisic. This new black bourgeoisic is not to be confused with the Negro bourgeoisic which E. Franklin Frazier described in his *Black Bourgeoisic.* The group of which we speak is a radicalized sector of the new black middle class, leaning neither toward the left-wing `Black Panthers nor the radical separatists such as the Republic of New Africa.

Its ideology revolves around black occupancy of crucial niches affecting black people. In the college situation, it is spurred more recently by a dream of converting the old Negro colleges into black colleges. They stress cultural atavism, while almost totally disdaining the politics of confrontation; few have ever participated in any form of activist struggle. Thus, despite their puffy tooting of "blackness," and the concomitant cover of black unity, they continue to receive strong criticism from their more revolutionary students. It is clear, then, that the Howard story has not yet ended. The developments there, in any case, are almost certain to be reflected more or less in other Negro colleges.

But what appears as at least a partial success (despite the firings of faculty participants) took place on the campus itself. By contrast, most of the consequences of the San Francisco Ctate College strike, hence most of its successes, occurred elsewhere and involved its impact on the campuses of the nation as a whole. In addition to the 1968–69 wave of campus rebellions in emulation of the San Francisco incident (some of them directly initiated by San Francisco State College students and faculty in an effort to combat the isolationism being perpetrated by authorities and the press), many college administrators turned a more attentive and receptive ear to black student needs in an effort to prevent holocausts on their own campuses similar to that of San Francisco State. In any case, the San Francisco State struggle, the longest and most intense in college history, though not the most publicized, did help radicalize colleges and students throughout the nation. According to the Urban Research Corporation,

> There were 292 major student protests on 232 college and university campuses in the first six months of 1969.
>
> Black students were involved in more than half of all protests.
>
> Black recognition was the issue raised more than any other.[3]

The result was that white college administrators agreed to assist in the creation of a new black middle class via college training—and administrators at Negro colleges soon began to ape them—but few of the mass-lumpen black students from whose ranks the major impetus of the 1969 struggle arose are admitted now and the administrators have achieved both direct and indirect control over the political/cultural content of the black studies courses. Hence the question arises: if there is going to be this new black middle class, what will be its values?

Much of this depends upon the kind of education they receive. Black students who would gain a relevant education must be prepared, as our case studies have shown, to deal with administrative cunning and deception. Typically, whenever black students call for relevant black education (using the black studies program as a model), a "coordinator of black studies" is brought in to spend up to a year planning the program and writing a proposal. Inasmuch as nobody chosen to submit a proposal by the scheduled date would need to spend that much time writing one, the coordinator is unofficially expected to do a lot of other things, not the least of which is to ride herd over student rebels, to be a troubleshooter whenever a crisis brews.

This and other subterfuge can only be subverted through a habit and commitment of prolonged struggle. It is necessary, black students must realize, to help make your own history, help shape your own destiny, or your history and your destiny will be shaped for you. Now is the time for all black intelligentsia, not the least of them black students, to rally around a prolonged struggle to rid the world of racism and achieve black self-determination. Black students must help to structure a new ideology, provide models of revolutionary zeal for others, and activate and energize the black intelligentsia toward giving greater and stronger direction to the people of the black captive nation in America. They must prepare themselves to become leaders, sharpen their tools and their understanding of the plight of the black race and the world. In so doing, black students will again seize the revolutionary initiative and begin the long march of a true vanguard in the making of a revolution.

---

[3] **"Student Strikes: 1968–69,"** ***The Black Scholar*****, (January-February, 1970), p. 66.**

PART 1 QUESTIONS

1. What makes a person an African American or Black?

2. How important are self-identification and self-designation to African Americans?

3. Can one identify an African American ethos and the culture that informs it?

4. How did the academic discipline of Black Studies or African American Studies or Africana Studies develop out of African American struggle for civil rights?

Part 2

Social Construction of Race and Social Reality

INTRODUCTION

Race as a biological term has been proven to be moot, while as a genetic reality or fact, it remains unsubstantiated, false, and nonexistent. Race is, however, a social reality and has been informing and influencing political, economic, social, and cultural thought, attitudes, activities, and interactions in America even before the birth of the nation. The African American experience has been impacted most significantly by the notion and practices of race imposed upon people of African descent for over four centuries with devastating consequences that they continually fight against and have been surmounting.

Howard Winant examines in "Race and Race Theory" the origins and underpinnings of the notion of race and race theory and their practice, especially in "biologistic racism" during the period of colonization on a global scale.[1] He points to race as a theme of study and discourse that sociology has been examining. Sociology of race has moved toward "a more critical, more egalitarian awareness of race," focusing on overcoming prejudice and discrimination.[2] He argues that global and domestic politics have entered a new period of crisis and uncertainty; therefore, deeper understanding of issues of race, race thought, and racism in contemporary society is required to tackle the pervasiveness of racism and racial politics.

In "Racism and Fascism," Toni Morrison goes to the heart of racism in its contemporary manifestations along with "its succubus twin fascism."[3] She maps out the contour and landscape of racial practices, racism, and fascism, identifying specific modus operandi, including, especially, "marketing for power."[4]

W.E.B. DuBois's intellectual attack of scientific racism on three issues of social Darwinism, the eugenics movement, and psychologists' measurement of intelligence epitomizes the African American intellectual challenge of racist thought and social and cultural impositions that racism engendered. In "W.E.B. DuBois's Challenge to Scientific Racism," Carol M. Taylor analyzes the DuBoisian challenge within the context of an undercurrent that swept through American intellectual circles among those who would defend racism and racial politics using the force of science and social sciences to uphold the notion of racial inferiority of Black people. DuBois challenged validity of scientific racism and exposed its unscientific and illogical methodology to reach the conclusion that "Blacks were not what American science said they were."[5]

---

[1] Howard Winant, "Race and Race Theory," *Annual Review of Sociology*, 26 (2000): 169.

[2] Ibid.

[3] Toni Morrison, "Racism and Fascism," *The Journal of Negro Education* 64, no. 3 (Summer, 1995): 384.

[4] Ibid., 385.

[5] Carol M. Taylor, "W.E.B. DuBois's Challenge to Scientific Racism," *Journal of Black Studies* 11, no. 4 (June, 1981): 459.

Robert K. Merton employs analysis of interpersonal interaction and response to racial stimuli in "Discrimination and the American Creed" to discern degrees of racial prejudice and animus on personal levels. The typologies he identifies—the fair-weather liberal, fair-weather illiberal, and all-weather illiberal—are relevant as markers of subtlety, fluidity, and ever-changing responses within the nuance of oppression that racism breeds. He surmises that any social policy dealing with prejudice, discrimination, and racism should take into account social and cultural milieu of the all-weather illiberal American.

Race and Race Theory

Howard Winant

ABSTRACT

Race has always been a significant sociological theme, from the founding of the field and the formulation of classical theoretical statements to the present. Since the nineteenth century, sociological perspectives on race have developed and changed, always reflecting shifts in large-scale political processes. In the classical period, colonialism and biologistic racism held sway. As the twentieth century dawned, sociology came to be dominated by US-based figures. DuBois and the Chicago School presented the first notable challenges to the field's racist assumptions. In the aftermath of World War II, with the destruction of European colonialism, the rise of the civil rights movement, and the surge in migration on a world scale, the sociology of race became a central topic. The field moved toward a more critical, more egalitarian awareness of race, focused particularly on the overcoming of prejudice and discrimination. Although the recognition of these problems increased and political reforms made some headway in combatting them, racial injustice and inequality were not surmounted. As the global and domestic politics of race entered a new period of crisis and uncertainty, so too has the field of sociology. To tackle the themes of race and racism once again in the new millennium, sociology must develop more effective racial theory. Racial formation approaches can offer a starting point here. The key tasks will be the formulation of a more adequate comparative historical sociology of race, the development of a deeper understanding of the micro-macro linkages that shape racial issues, and the recognition of the pervasiveness of racial politics in contemporary society. This is a challenging but also exciting agenda. The field must not shrink from addressing it.

INTRODUCTION

As the world lurches forward into the twenty-first century, widespread confusion and anxiety exist about the political significance and even the meaning, of race. This uncertain situation extends into the field of sociology, which has since its founding devoted great attention to racial themes.

The extent of the literature on the race concept alone, not to mention the mountains of empirical studies that focus on racial issues, presents difficulties for any attempt at theoretical overview and synthesis. A wide range of concepts from both the classical and modern traditions can readily be applied to racial matters.

Variations among national and cultural understandings of the meaning of race cry out for comparative appproaches. World history has, arguably, been racialized at least since the rise of the modem world system; racial hierarchy remains global even in the postcolonial present; and popular concepts of race, however variegated, remain in general everyday use almost everywhere. Thus, any effective sociological theory of race seems to require, at a minimum, comparative historical and political components, some sort of sociology of culture or knowledge, and an adequate microsociological account.

Over the past few decades, interest in racial matters, and the pace at which racial dynamics have been changing worldwide, have both increased dramatically. Controversy over the meaning and significance of race was greatly heightened after World War II. The war itself had significant racial dimensions and left a legacy of revulsion at racism and genocide. The social movements and revolutionary upsurges that succeeded the war and brought the colonial era to an end also raised the problematic of race to a new level of prominence. The civil rights movement in the United States and the anti-apartheid mobilization in South Africa are but the most prominent examples of this. As it gained its independence, the postcolonial world was quickly embroiled in the competition of the Cold War, a situation that placed not only the legacy of imperial rule but also the racial policies of the superpowers (especially those of the United States) under additional scrutiny. Another consequence of the war was enormous migratory flows from the world's rural South to its metropolitan North; in these demographic shifts the empire struck back, pluralizing the former mother countries (Centre for Contemporary Cultural Studies 1982). All these developments raised significant questions about the meaning of race.

SOCIOLOGY'S RACIAL ODYSSEY

In this article I survey the theoretical dimensions of race as the new century (and new millennium) commences. I begin with an account of the *origins of the race concept.* Here I consider how the theme of race, though prefigured in earlier ages, only took on its present range of meanings with the rise of modernity. The deep interconnection between the development of the modern world system—of capitalism, seaborne empire, and slavery—and the exfoliation of a worldwide process of racialization is not in doubt.

Next I examine how sociological theory has addressed the linkage between modernity and race. I argue that, not surprisingly, *the sociological study of race has been shaped by large-scale political processes.* The founding statements of sociological theory, the so-called classics, were above all concerned to explain the emergence of modernity in Europe. Whether they understood this to mean the dawn of capitalism, the advent of "disenchanted" forms of social organization, or the generation of complex dynamics of social integration and solidarity, they could hardly escape some reckoning with the problem of the Other, however s/he was defined: as plundered and exploited laborer, as "primitive" or "uncivilized," or as "traditional" or mechanically solidaristic.

After sociology's center of gravity migrated across the Atlantic, racial themes became more central. Dealing with social problems such as crime, poverty, and disease; addressing urbanization, stratification, and underdevelopment; and confronting social psychological issues as well, analysts again and again had recourse to racial themes.

Contemporary approaches to the race concept have by and large parted with the biologism of the past, although some vestigial viewpoints of this type can still be detected (such as those of *The Bell Curve* authors). The sociology of race was vastly stimulated by the political, cultural, and demographic shifts that took shape in the postwar decades.

But as we begin the twenty-first century, sociological theory is confronted with the obsolescence of the Big Political Processes, such as decolonization and civil rights, that drove the theoretical vehicle forward from the war's end. So now, racial theory finds itself in a new quandary. Empires have been ended and Jim Crow and *apartheid* abolished (at least officially). How then is continuing racial inequality and bias to be explained? Some would argue that since racial injustice is at least tendentially diminishing, the race concept is finally being obviated: In the globalized twenty-first century, world society and transnational culture will finally attain a state of colorblindness and racial (or better, ethnic) pluralism. Others note that this new situation—of multiculturalism or diversification—provides a much prettier fig leaf for policies of *laissez-faire* vis-a-vis continuing racial exclusion and inequality than any intransigent white supremacy could ever have offered. But whatever political disagreements underlie the ongoing difficulties of racial theory, there can be little doubt that these difficulties persist.

In the final section of this paper, I offer some *notes toward a new racial theory*, Any such account must take seriously the reformed present situation: postcolonial, postsegregationist (or at least post–official segregation), and racially heterogeneous (if not "integrated"). It must also note the continuing presence of racial signification and racial identity, as well as the ongoing social structural salience of race. Racial theory must now demonstrate comparative and historical capabilities, as well as addressing the formidable problem of the micro-macro linkage that inheres in racial dynamics. As this already suggests, such a theory would also incorporate elements (let us call them revisionist elements) of recent political sociology: process models of politics, new social movement theory, and constitution theories of society. Over the past two decades, racial formation theory has made the most serious attempt to fulfill this mission.

This is obviously no small assignment; only the contours of such a new theoretical approach to race can be outlined here. But I am confident that these notes, however elliptical, will facilitate access to a substantial body of work already underway, not only on race, but on the great multitude of issues, both substantive and conceptual, that it intersects. After all, the theme of race is situated where meaning meets social structure, where identity frames inequality.

ORIGINS OF THE RACE CONCEPT

Can any subject be more central or more controversial in sociological thought than that of race? The concept is essentially a modern one, although prefigured in various ways by ethnocentrism, and taking preliminary form in ancient concepts of civilization and barbarity (Snowden 1983), citizen (or *zoon politikon*) and outsider/slave (Hannaford 1996, Finley 1983). Yes, the Crusades and the Inquisition and the Mediterranean slave trade were important rehearsals for modem systems of racial differentiation, but in terms of scale and inexorability the race concept only began to attain its familiar meanings at the end of the middle ages.

At this point it would be useful to say what I mean by "race." At its most basic level, race can be defined as a *concept that signifies and symbolizes sociopolitical conflicts and interests in reference to different types of human bodies.* Although the concept of race appeals to biologically based human characteristics (phenotypes), selection of these particular human features for purposes of racial signification is always and necessarily a social and historical process. There is no biological basis for distinguishing human groups along the lines of race, and the sociohistorical categories employed to differentiate among these groups reveal themselves, upon serious examination, to be imprecise if not completely arbitrary (Omi & Winant 1994).

The idea of race began to take shape with the rise of a world political economy. The onset of global economic integration, the dawn of seaborne empire, the conquest of the Americas, and the rise of the Atlantic slave trade were all key elements in the genealogy of race. The concept emerged over time as a kind of world-historical *bricolage*, an accretive process that was in part theoretical,[1] but much more centrally practical. Though intimated throughout the world in innumerable ways, racial categorization of human beings was a European invention. It was an outcome of the same world-historical processes that created European nation-states and empires, built the dark satanic mills of Britain (and the even more dark and satanic sugar mills of the Brazilian Reconcavo and the Caribbean), and explained it all by means of Enlightenment rationality.

But this is not to say that the European attainment of imperial and world-encompassing power gave rise to race. Indeed it is just as easy to argue the opposite: that the modem concept of race gave rise to, or at least facilitated the creation of, an integrated

---

[1] Religious, philosophical, literary/artistic, political, and scientific discourses all were directed in a never ending flood of ink and image to the themes of "the Other"; variations in human nature; and the corporeal, mental, spiritual, sexual, and "natural historical" differences among "men." To the extent that this discussion addressed itself to the problem of patterns of human difference/identity and human variability, it may be fairly characterized as about race. To cite some valuable texts among a virtual infinity: Hannaford 1996, Gossett 1965, Todorov 1985, 1993, Kiernan 1969, Montagu 1997 [1942], Banton 1987.

sociopolitical world, a modern authoritarian state, the structures of an international economy, and the emergence over time of a global culture. We must recognize all these issues as deeply racialized matters.

THE SOCIOLOGICAL STUDY OF RACE HAS BEEN SHAPED BY LARGE-SCALE POLITICAL PROCESSES

The "Classics"

When we look at the treatment of racial matters in sociological theory, we find the concept present from the beginning, though often in an inchoate, undertheorized, or taken-for-granted form. Herbert Spencer, the usual example cited as the *ur*-sociologist, reads as a biological determinist today, preoccupied as he is with human evolution and the ranking of groups according to their "natural" characteristics.[2]

Marx's orientation to themes we would now consider racial was complex. His denunciation in *Capital* of the depredation, despoliation, and plunder of the non-European world in pursuit of primitive accumulation,[3] and his ferocious opposition to slavery, both commend him. But his insistence that the colonized pre-capitalist societies would ultimately benefit from their enmeshment in the brutal clutches of the European powers hints to present-day readers that he was not entirely immune to the hierarchization of the world that characterized the imperial Europe of his day.

Weber's treatment of the concept of *ethnie* under the rubric of "status" (a relational category based on "honor") presages a social constructionist approach to race; but in Weber's voluminous output there is no serious consideration of the modern imperial

---

[2] Early treatments of the race concept in Europe and the United States combined supposedly biologistic or natural history-based conceptions of race with a high degree of arbitrariness, if not outright incoherence, in their application. Numerous groups qualified as "races": national origin (the Irish) and religion (Jews) as well as the more familiar criteria of color were frequently invoked as signs of racial otherness. Although this fungibility has been somewhat reduced and regularized over recent decades, it still remains in effect and indeed can never be supplanted by "objective" criteria. See the discussion of racial formation below.

[3] "The discovery of gold and silver in America, the extirpation, enslavement, and entombment in mines of the aboriginal population, the beginning of the conquest and looting of the East Indies, the turning of Africa into a warren for the commercial hunting of blackskins, signalized the rosy dawn of the era of capitalist production. These idyllic proceedings are the chief momenta of primitive accumulation. On their heels treads the commercial war of the European nations with the globe for a theater. It begins with the revolt of the Netherlands from Spain, assumes giant dimensions in England's AntiJacobin War, and is still going on in the opium wars with China, etc." (Marx 1967:351).

phenomenon, there are numerous instances of European chauvinism,[4] and there is an occasional indulgence in—let us call it—racialist meditation.[5] Durkheim too ranks the world eurocentrically, distinguishing rather absolutely between "primitive" and "civilized" peoples based on the limited ethnology available to him; he also muses somewhat racialistically.[6]

It is not my purpose to chide these masters. Far from it: They acquit themselves well when compared to the rank-and-file pundits and even the *bien philosophes* who were their contemporaries. They can hardly be expected to have remained totally immune from the racial ideology of their times. But that is precisely the point: Sociological thought arose in an imperialist, eurocentric, and indeed racist era, both in Europe and in the United States. In its classical early statements, it was racially marked by the time and place of its birth.

Across the Atlantic

It was largely in the United States that the early sociology of race first forsook the library for the streets, partaking in the great empirical efflloresence that marked the field's establishment in that country. There was an inescapable association between the discipline's development in this period (the early twentieth century), and the rise of pragmatism in US philosophy and progressivism in US politics during the same epoch. Nor is it hard to understand why race was promoted to a more central sociological concern as the discipline acquired its foothold—indeed its headquarters—in the United States. This was, after all, a country where African slavery was still an artifact of living memory, where the frontier had only recently been declared closed, where immigration was a flood stage, and where debates over the propriety of imperial activity (in the Phillipines, for example) were still current.

At the beginning of the twentieth century, a nearly comprehensive view of the race concept still located it at the biological level. On this account, races were "natural": their characteristics were essential and given, immutable. Over the centuries such approaches had accomplished a wide range of explanatory work. Both the defense of slavery and its critique (abolitionism) had appealed to "natural" criteria in support of their views. In a similar vein the holocaust visited upon indigenous peoples, as well as the absorption of large numbers of former Mexican, Spanish, and Asian subjects through war and coercive immigration policies, had been justified as "natural," inevitable forms

---

[4] Especially during the World War I years, when Weber was seriously afflicted with German nationalism.

[5] In fairness, Weber also recognizes racism, notably anti-black racism in the United States. See his remarks on U.S. racial attitudes in Gerth & Mills 1958:405–6. Weber's sensitivity to U.S. racial matters may be attributed, at least in part, to the orientation provided him by DuBois. See Lewis 1993:225, 277.

[6] Racial categories are employed as "social types" in *Suicide*, for example. See Fenton 1980.

of human progress.[7] Even after emancipation and the "closing of the frontier" in the United States, scientific arguments still summoned "natural causes" to the defense of hierarchical concepts of race. In the late nineteenth and early twentieth centuries the impact of social Darwinism was enormous (not merely on Herbert Spencer), and the arguments of eugenics also acquired great support.

But the world racial system underwent significant shifts in the early twentieth century. As labor demands grew more complex and the agenda of democratization gradually assumed greater importance, biologistic racial theories became increasingly obsolete. The resurgence of anticolonial movements in Africa and Asia (a century after the success of such movements in the Americas), the spreading of democratic demands to countries considered "backward" and "uncivilized," and the increased mobility (both geographic and economic) of ex-slaves and former peasants during and after World War I, all motivated the gradual but inexorable development of a more sophisticated social scientific approach to race.

The two early twentieth century examples of pathbreaking racial theorizing that require mention here are the pioneering study by W.E.B. DuBois of black life in Philadelphia (DuBois 1998 [1899]), and the extensive body of work on racial matters that formed a crucial component of the Chicago School of sociology. Both these pioneers were oriented by the pragmatism that was the most original, and remains the most important, contribution of North American sociological theory.

DuBois's *The Philadelphia Negro*[8] sought both to make a significant advance over previous knowledge (overwhelmingly ignorant and stereotyped) about black life and

---

[7]The Chicago theorists, particularly Park, proposed a deterministic version of this argument in the form of a "race relations cycle" through which macrosocial encounters between "peoples" were argued to pass. The four stages of the "cycle" were held to succeed each other more or less inevitably: first contact, then conflict, succeeded by accommodation, and finally assimilation. Residues of the "natural history" logic of race can be detected here, to be sure, but there is also something of a social constructionism at work. For example, Park suggests that alternative power dynamics among racially defined groups are possible at each of the cycle's phases.

[8]One should cite much more of DuBois's contributions to the foundations of US sociology, and indeed to democratic theory and practice in respect to race: the Atlanta studies, the historical sociology (most notably *Black Reconstruction in America* (1977 [1935]), and an astounding wealth of other work (see Lewis 1995 for a good selection of materials). While DuBois was not entirely ignored by the "mainstream" of the field, he was hardly given his due recognition either. As noted, DuBois was associated with Weber, whom he had come to know in Berlin. The complex set of influences shaping DuBois's intellectual and political development has been much explored in recent scholarship: He combined a high German philosophical, historical, and social scientific training with solid roots in American pragmatism (notably his work with William James), and a deep engagement with the popular African-American traditions he first met as a college student in the South (see DuBois 1989 [1903]), DuBois 1991 [1940]), Lewis 1993, West 1989, Marable 1986).

US racial dynamics; and to build, upon a solid base of empirical data, a powerful and strategic argument for the democratization of race relations in turn-of-the-century America. Though slightly marred by concessions demanded of DuBois by his patrons (or perhaps imagined necessary by him) the work still stands, an entire century later, as a magisterial survey of the unique racial dementia of the United States: the country's foundational involvement with African enslavement and the permanent consequences of that involvement. In addition to his pathbreaking approach to racial theory, particularly evident in his concept of "the veil" and his understanding of racial dualism (DuBois 1989 [1903]), DuBois's early work is notable for its relentless empirical commitments and independent application of pragmatist philosophy (West 1989) to the sociological enterprise, both theoretical and practical. As Elijah Anderson points out in his introduction to the centennial reissue of *The Philadelphia Negro* (1996 [1899]), the tendency to attribute these innovations to more "mainstream" sociologists for many years banished DuBois from his rightful place in the disciplinary canon.

The large body of work on race produced by the researchers of the Chicago School also demonstrates the influence of pragmatism and progressivism. Oriented by a social problems approach and consciously viewing the city of Chicago as a sociological laboratory, the Chicago sociologists authored a group of studies focusing on crime, poverty, "slums," etc., all problems that were frequently seen racially. The approaches that developed in Chicago were notable for their attentiveness to their empirical subjects, and for their intrinsically democratic orientation. Moving from the preliminary work of Burgess, through the great creativity and comprehensiveness of Thomas & Znaniecki's massive study,[9] the Chicago engagement with the problematic of race culminated in the work of Robert E. Park on the macro-dimensions of race (Park 1950).[10] There was also an important micro-side of the Chicago tradition, which proceeded from Mead and deeply informed Blumer's work on the symbolic dimensions of race (Blumer 1958). Perhaps most important, the work of the Chicago sociologists broke definitively with the racial biologism that had characterized earlier treatments, asserting with increasing clarity the position that race was a socially constructed, not naturally given, phenomenon.[11] The influence of this view on crucial later treatments of race throughout the social sciences—for example, Myrdal's *An American Dilemma* (1944) or Drake & Cayton's magisterial work (Drake & Cayton 1993 [1945])—was enormous. The Myrdal study would not even have come into being, much less exercised the tremendous political influence it did (Southern 1987, Jackson 1990), without vast assistance from Chicago-trained scholars.

---

[9] *The Polish Peasant* prefigured the entire contemporary field of migration studies (Thomas & Znaniecki 1994 [1923]). Thomas & Znaniecki's book on what would now be considered a white ethnic group could easily be seen as a racial work at the time of its original appearance.

[10] For a good overview, see Bulmer 1984.

[11] In this developing analysis, Chicago sociology not only led the field, but established the beginning of an interdisciplinary social scientific consensus. In cultural anthropology, the early contributions of Franz Boas—whom DuBois invited to speak in Atlanta in 1911—were crucial here as well.

CONTEMPORARY APPROACHES TO THE RACE CONCEPT

The same dynamics that prompted the Americanization of sociology and sparked the shift from classical theorizing to empirical research were also at work in the development of contemporary approaches to race. Once again, pressing sociopolitical issues drove the theoretical vehicle forward.

Sociological argument could only properly challenge biologistic positions after the race concept had been fully reinterpreted sociohistorically. Given the onrushing European disaster of facism, the task of elaborating a democratic and inclusionist theory of race fell largely to US scholars from the 1930s onward.[12] Here the sociological work carried out by the Chicago scholars and their successors, and the continuously powerful voice of DuBois, combined with the insights and research of a growing number of progressive racial observers. To name but a few other important influences: the Boasian shift in anthropology, which refocused that discipline from physical to cultural preoccupations and had widespread effects in popular culture, was certainly significant. The association of fascism with eugenics—a movement that had developed strong bases both in Britain and the United States as well as in Germany—forced choices upon democratically and progressively inclined publics, both intellectual and political. The "retreat of scientific racism" was the result of these unsavory connections (Barkan 1992). Marxist accounts of race became more prominent in function of the upsurge of communism (a leading, though not unproblematic, antiracist influence, especially in the 1930s and 1940s). The growth of important black movements, both political and cultural,[13] also strongly affected the racial public sphere in the interwar period. And the liberal democratic ethos, strongly invoked in the United States by the wartime work of Myrdal, exercised tremendous influence (Myrdal 1944).

The Post-World War II Challenge

In the post–World War II period, the concept of race was more comprehensively challenged than ever before in modern history. Decolonization spread through the world's South, sometimes achieving its emancipatory aims by peaceful, or at least

[12] Not exclusively of course. Resistance to nazism also bred important works, as did anti-colonial struggle and cultural anthropology. A few examples: the Jewish and homosexual activist Magnus Hirschfeld first used (as far as I can tell) the term "racism" in a book he published with that title in 1935, whose topic was (logically) antisemitism. The pan-Africanist movement, which owed a lot to DuBois, was well underway by this time, generating important works by such scholar-activists (and marxists) as George Padmore, C.L.R. James, and others. Boas's students such as Gilberto Freyre and Ruth Benedict were producing important studies on race in Brazil, as was exiled anthropologist Claude Levi-Strauss.

[13] Notably the Garvey movement, the Harlem Renaissance, and the development of successful (though still effectively segregated) black media: music, film and theater, newspapers, etc.

largely political, means and sometimes requiring prolonged warfare to dislodge the occupying northern (aka "white") power. Migration and urbanization of previously impoverished ex-colonials and former peasants—largely people of color—landed millions of dark faces in the world's metropoles. These newly urbanized groups soon mobilized and pressed for their political and social rights, contesting entrenched customs and institutionalized patterns of white supremacy and racism in numerous countries. Especially in the United States, the hegemonic postwar nation, these racially based movements took the political center-stage.

These new demands for inclusion, in turn, induced serious crises in national political systems. As racial regimes steeped in discriminatory or exclusionist traditions were pressured to innovate and reform, sociological approaches to race were also transformed. A great (although quite belated) interest in patterns of discrimination and prejudice developed.[14] Interest in patterns of racial inequality grew at the international level. Not only the mainstream sociology, but also the radical sociology of race advanced, spurred on by the new movements as well as by dissatisfaction with the pace and scope of reform (Blauner 1972; Ladner, ed. 1973).

While an obvious advance over earlier views, postwar racial theory was subject to numerous limitations, in both its moderate and its radical versions. Most problematic was the tendency toward *reductionism:* The three main theoretical tendencies all subordinated the race concept to some supposedly more objective or "real" social structure. *Ethnicity*-based theories were generally the most mainstream or moderate. They saw race as a culturally grounded framework of collective identity. *Class*-based theories understood race in terms of group-based stratification and economic competition. *Nation*-based theories perceived race in the geopolitical terms largely given by the decolonization process so prominent in the postwar era. They focused attention on issues of peoplehood and race unity, rootedness, citizenship, and irredentism.[15]

As the twentieth century (whose "problem is the color-line," as DuBois had famously written) drew toward its end, these approaches to the race concept also neared their limits. They were informed by and oriented to the pressing sociopolitical problems of their time: notably racial prejudice and discrimination (especially state-sponsored discrimination). After these grievances had been forcefully raised in many countries by antiracist movements, they were generally at least ameliorated by democratic and inclusionist efforts at reform. Although hardly eliminated by shifts in state racial policy, racial injustice became less visible as a result of these reforms, and overt racism was generally stigmatized. In such a situation the racial theory that sought to explain such phenomena slowly became obsolete. Thus are we left at century's end with a range of unanticipated, or at least theoretically unresolved, racial dilemmas.

---

[14] A valuable survey of "mainstream" sociological approaches to race in the United States over the entire twentieth century is Pettigrew 1980. For a more critical perspective, see McKee 1993.

[15] For a more extensive critical review of the reductionism of 1960s racial theorizing in the United States, see Michael Omi & Howard Winant 1994).

The Limits of Contemporary Racial Theory

The inadequacy of the range of theoretical approaches to race available in sociology at the turn of the twenty-first century is quite striking. Consistent with the argument presented in this essay, this theoretical crisis can be seen as reflecting the continuing sociopolitical crisis of race. In particular, the *persistence of racially based distinctions*, distinctions that state-based racial reforms were supposed to overcome, poses major problems for racial theories inherited from the earlier post–World War II years.

Ethnicity-oriented theories of race had suggested that the suppression of prejudiced attitudes could be achieved through contact, integration, and assimilation; and that discrimination could be ended by laws and regulations that made jobs, education, housing, and so on equally accessible to all. But the endurance of obstacles to integration severely undermined ethnicity-based approaches to race,[16] while assimilation into white cultural norms was hardly desirable to most racially defined minorities. Faced with these impasses in the United States today, ethnicity theories of race have devolved into neoconservatism, which can do no better than reprove racially defined minorities for their continuing race-consciousness and supposed failure to take advantage of civil rights reforms (Thernstrom & Thernstrom 1997). In Western Europe, these theories take the form of differentialism, which repudiates the racist cultural hierarchies of the past, but affirms the exclusionist commitments of (French, German, British etc.) "national culture," thus upholding barriers to immigration and racial pluralism, not to mention integration (Taguieff 1988, Wieviorka 1995, Balibar & Wallerstein 1991).

Class-based theories of race had argued that racial conflict was the mode in which class conflict was lived out or expressed (Hall et al 1978). This suggested that racial stratification and intergroup competition were fairly well-defined in the post-war world (Bonacich 1972, 1976, Gordon et al 1982, Reich 1981). If the inequality among racially defined groups was to be overcome, then this would require not only interracial solidarity, but also race-conscious programs designed to remedy the *effects* of discrimination. Such programs, put into place in many countries and under various names, have come to be known under the rubric of "affirmative action." But two factors have undermined the plausibility of this account. First, a growing inequality *within* racially defined minority groups weakens group cohesion both politically and culturally; this undermines the case for affirmative action. Second, enduring white commitments to racial privilege—that is, persistent racism—largely trump interracial working-class solidarity, defeating whatever potential for economic redistribution such programs as affirmative action may have offered. Thus, class-based theories of

[16] At a deeper level, governments often enacted racial reforms that were more symbolic than substantive, and enforced those they had managed to enact indifferently if at all. See Lipsitz 1998, Massey & Denton 1993 for U.S. examples.

race have in practice been vitiated by the failure of the socialist (or social democratic, or New Deal) vision in the present epoch.[17]

Nation-oriented accounts of race have been called into question by the combined weight of international and intra-national heterogeneity. In a postcolonial era that has witnessed tremendous migration, that offers unprecedented ease of movement, and that boasts of communicative powers (mass media, particularly music and film, but also telephonic and computer-based resources) unimaginable even a few years ago, the nation-based dimensions of racial solidarity have atrophied. Trans- (or perhaps post-) national forms of racial correspondence persist, but now take the form of *diasporic* identities of various kinds (Kilson & Rotberg, eds., 1976, Appadurai 1996, Lemelle & Kelley, eds., 1994). At this point, however, transnational racial solidarity generally lacks the kind of political commitment and organization once displayed under the banners of pan-Africanism or the "non-aligned" movements. In this situation, nation-based theories of race have devolved into crude and retro forms of cultural nationalism, informed more by mysticism than by social analysis.[18]

NOTES TOWARD A NEW RACIAL THEORY

If the strength of earlier theoretical accounts has atrophied and a new approach is needed, what would be its outlines? As a new century begins, a convincing racial theory must address the persistence of racial classification and stratification in an era officially committed to racial equality and multiculturalism. The present moment is one of

[17] Perhaps the greatest effort to argue for a class-based contemporary racial theory in sociology has been that of William Julius Wilson. For more than two decades now Wilson has sought to present racial progress as dependent on generalized full-employment policies and politics. In recent work he has striven to revive well-used left arguments about the indispensability of interracial solidarity (Wilson 1996). But for all that is valuable in this approach, his dismissal of the continuing effects of racism, and of the experience of racial distinctions, is crippling. The sociocultural and organizational obstacles to interracial solidarity remain far more formidable than Wilson acknowledges.

[18] "Cultural nationalism" as politics and racial theory in the United States, Brazil, or South Africa may have entered a *cul-de-sac*, but it is essentially benign. The same cannot be said of the devolutionist nationalisms of the Balkans, Rwanda, or parts of South Asia, which have reintroduced the quasi-racist program of ethnic cleansing in forlorn and bloody attempts to achieve the utopian congruence of state and nation. Quite apart from the resemblance of such policies to genocides ancient and recent, they testify once again to the near-total hybridity of the human population and the impossibility of achieving any societal homogeneity, especially in the present. Such policies also reveal the flexibility of racialization, which has time and again been applied to exacerbate human distinctions not easily recognized (at least from "outside") as corporeal or phenotypic. Consider in this regard not only Hutu v. Tutsi or Bosnian Serb v. Bosnian Muslim, but also such cases of racialized conflict as: German "Aryan" v. German Jew, Palestinian Arab v. Israeli Jew, or British v. Irish.

increasing globalization and postcoloniality. It is a time when most national societies, and the world as a whole, are acknowledged to be racially multipolar, and when hybridity is frequently recognized as a key feature of racial identity. Today, in marked distinction to the situation that obtained before World War II, most states and members of state elites claim to oppose discrimination, deny their continuing adherence to racialized views of their populations, and may even claim to be colorblind or differentialist. How and why do racial distinctions endure in such changed circumstances?

Any minimally adequate theoretical response to this question must include recognition of the *comparative/historical dimension of race*. The mere fact that we are discussing race here and now (in a post-civil rights, post-cold war, post-colonial period) itself imposes significant theoretical constraints and opportunities. As I argued earlier, earlier racial theories too were products of their times and places. We remain in a similar situation today.

A second dimension in which any successful theory must operate is the ability to range over, and hopefully to link, *the micro- and macro-aspects of racial signification and racialized social structure*. Such a multileveled and interconnected account is a general obligation of social theory in the present.[19] It is an obligation incurred by any attempt to conceptualize the continuing significance of race. A notable and intriguing feature of race is its ubiquity, its presence in both the smallest and the largest features of social relationships, institutions, and identities.

A third theoretical dimension will involve recognition of the *newly pervasive forms of politics* in recent times. This may be alternatively regarded as a racially conscious conception of action or agency. In the United States, much of the impetus behind the reconceptualization of politics that has occurred in recent decades was derived from racially based and indeed anti-racist social movements. The democratizing challenge posed after World War II to normal systems of domination and power, accepted divisions of labor, and rational-legal means of legitimation, all had inescapable racial dimensions. Racially based movements, then, and the second wave feminism that followed and was inspired by them, problematized the public-private distinction basic to an older generation of political theory and political sociology.[20] This has been recognized in new approaches to political sociology, such as political process models (McAdam 1982, Morris & Mueller, eds., 1992), It also appears in the revival of interest in pragmatist sociology, in symbolic interactionism, in constitution theories of society (Joas 1996, Giddens 1984), and in the belated revival of interest in the work of W.E.B. DuBois (West 1989, Lewis 1993, Winant 1997).

---

[19] See Huber 1991, Giddens 1984, Collins 1987, Alexander et al, eds., 1987.

[20] In non-U.S. settings, the new social movement phenomenon has not always been so clearly recognized as racially structured. This is particularly notable in Europe where its study was prompted by the vicissitudes of the new left, the resurgence of feminism, the rise of green politics, and the upsurge of terrorism in the 1970s (Melucci 1989). But in the third world the rethinking of political theory and political sociology in terms of issues of subjectivity and of identity often took on a racial dimension. Consider the legacy of Fanon for example.

For the past few decades these themes have been developed in a body of theoretical work that goes under the general heading of *racial formation theory*. As one of the founders of this approach, I must stipulate from the beginning to the lack of consensus, as well as the overall incompleteness, of this theoretical current. Still, I submit that racial formation theory at least begins to meet the requirements for a sociological account of race, one capable of addressing the *fin-de-siecle* conditions adumbrated here.[21]

To summarize the racial formation approach: (*a*) It views the meaning of race and the content of racial identities as unstable and politically contested; (*b*) It understands racial formation as the intersection/conflict of racial "projects" that combine representational/discursive elements with structural/institutional ones; (*c*) It sees these intersections as iterative sequences of interpretations (articulations) of the meaning of race that are open to many types of agency, from the individual to the organizational, from the local to the global.

If we are to understand the changing significance of race at the beginning of the twenty-first century, we must develop a more effective theory of race. The racial formation perspective at least suggests some directions in which such a theory should be pursued. As in the past, racial theory today is shaped by the large-scale sociopolitical processes it is called upon to explain. Employing a racial formation perspective, it is possible to glimpse a pattern in present global racial dynamics.

That pattern looks something like the following: In the period during and after World War II an enormous challenge was posed to established systems of rule by racially defined social movements around the world. Although these movement challenges achieved some great gains and precipitated important reforms in state racial policy, neither the movements nor the reforms could be consolidated. At the end of the century the world as a whole, and various national societies as well, are far from overcoming the tenacious legacies of colonial rule, apartheid, and segregation. All still experience continuing confusion, anxiety, and contention about race. Yet the legacies of epochal struggles for freedom, democracy, and human rights persist as well.

Despite the enormous vicissitudes that demarcate and distinguish national conditions, historical developments, roles in the international market, political tendencies, and cultural norms, racial differences often operate as they did in centuries past: as a way of restricting the political influence, not just of racially subordinated groups, but of all those at the bottom end of the system of social stratification. In the contemporary era, racial beliefs and practices have become far more contradictory and complex. The old world racial order has not disappeared, but it has been seriously disrupted and changed. The legacy of democratic, racially oriented movements[22] and anticolonialist

---

[21] Numerous writers now employ racial formation perspectives, both within sociology and in other social scientific (as well as in cultural studies, legal studies, etc.). See for example Gilroy 1991, Crenshaw et al 1995, Davis and Lowe 1997, Almaguer 1994, Espiritu 1992).

[22] For example, the US civil rights movement, anti-apartheid struggles, *SOS-Racisme* in France, the *Movimento Negro Unificado* in Brazil.

initiatives throughout the world's South, remains a force to be reckoned with. But the incorporative (or if one prefers this term, hegemonic) effects of decades of reform-oriented state racial policies have had a profound effect as well: They have removed much of the motivation for sustained, anti-racist mobilization.

In this unresolved situation, it is unlikely that attempts to address worldwide dilemmas of race and racism by ignoring or transcending these themes, for example by adopting so-called colorblind or differentialist policies, will have much effect. In the past the centrality of race deeply determined the economic, political, and cultural configuration of the modern world. Although recent decades have seen a tremendous efflorescence of movements for racial equality and justice, the legacies of centuries of racial oppression have not been overcome. Nor is a vision of racial justice fully worked out. Certainly the idea that such justice has already been largely achieved—as seen in the "colorblind" paradigm in the United States, the "non-racialist" rhetoric of the South African Freedom Charter, the Brazilian rhetoric of "racial democracy," or the emerging "racial differentialism" of the European Union—remains problematic.

Will race ever be transcended? Will the world ever get beyond race? Probably not. But the entire world still has a chance of overcoming the stratification, the hierarchy, the taken-for-granted injustice and inhumanity that so often accompanies the race concept. Like religion or language, race can be accepted as part of the spectrum of the human condition, while it is simultaneously and categorically resisted as a means of stratifying national or global societies. Nothing is more essential in the effort to reinforce democratic commitments, not to mention global survival and prosperity, as we enter a new millennium.

LITERATURE CITED

Alexander J, et al, eds. 1987. *The Micro-Macro Link.* Berkeley: Univ. Calif. Press

Almaguer T. 1994. *Racial Faultlines: The Historical Origins of White Supremacy in California* Berkeley: Univ. Calif. Press

Appadurai A. 1996. *Modernity at Large: Cultural Dimensions of Globalization.* Minneapolis: Univ. Minn. Press

Balibar E, Wallerstein I. 1991. *Race, Nation, Class: Ambiguous Identities.* London: Verso

Banton M. 1977. *The Idea of Race.* London: Tavistock

Barkan E. 1992. *The Retreat Of Scientific Racism: Changing Concepts Of Race In Britain And The United States Between The World Wars.* New York: Cambridge Univ. Press

Bastide R, Fernandes F. 1971. *Brancos e Negros em São Paulo; Ensaio Sociológico Sôbre Aspectos da Formação, Manifestações Atuais e Efeitos do Preconceito de Côr na Sociedade Paulistana.* São Paulo, Brazil: Companhia Ed. Nacional. 3rd ed.

Blauner RA. 1972. *Racial Oppression in America.* New York: Harper

Blumer H. 1958. Race prejudice as a sense of group position. *Pac. Social. Rev.* 1(1) Spring:3–7

Bonacich E. 1972. A theory of ethnic antagonism: the split labor market. *Am. Sociol. Rev.* 37:547–59

Bonacich E. 1976. Advanced capitalism and black/white relations in the United States: a split labor market interpretation. *Am. Sociol. Rev.* 41:34–51

Bulmer M. 1984. *The Chicago School of Sociology: Institutionalization, Diversity, and the Rise of Sociological Research.* Chicago: Univ. Chicago Press

Centre for Contemporary Cultural Studies. 1982. *The Empire Strikes Back: Race and Racism in 70s Britain.* London: Hutchinson

Collins R. 1987. Iterated ritual chains, power and property: the micro-macro connection as an empirically based theoretical problem. In *The Micro-Macro Link*, ed. J Alexander, et al, pp. 193–206. Berkeley: Univ. Calif. Press

Cotler J. 1970. The mechanics of internal domination and social change in Peru. In *Masses in Latin America*, ed. IL Horowitz, pp. 407–44. New York: Oxford Univ. Press

Crenshaw K, et al, eds. 1995. *Critical Race Theory: The Key Writings That Formed the Movement.* New York: New Press

Davis A, Lowe L. Reflections on race, class, and gender in the U.S.A. In *The Politics of Culture in the Shadow of Capital*, ed. L Lowe, D Lloyd. Durham, NC: Duke Univ. Press

Drake St. C, Cayton H. 1993 [1945]. *Black Metropolis: A Study of Negro Life in a Northern City.* Chicago: Univ. Chicago Press

DuBois WEB. 1977 [1935]. *Black Reconstruction in America: An Essay Toward a History of the Part Which Black Folk Played in the Attempt to Reconstruct Democracy in America, 1860–1880.* New York: Atheneum

DuBois WEB. 1989 [1903]. *The Souls of Black Folk.* New York: Penguin

DuBois WEB. 1991 [1940]. *Dusk of Dawn: An Essay Toward an Autobiography of a Race Concept.* New Brunswick, NJ: Transaction

DuBois WEB. 1996 [1899]. *The Philadelphia Negro: A Social Study.* Philadelphia: Univ. Penn. Press

Espiritu YL. 1992. *Asian American Panethnicity: Bridging Institutions and Identities.* Philadelphia, PA: Temple Univ. Press

Fenton S. 1980. Race, class, and politics in the work of Emile Durkheim. In *Sociological Theories: Race and Colonialism.* Paris: UNESCO

Finley MI. 1983. *Politics in the Ancient World.* New York: Cambridge Univ. Press

Gerth H, Mills CW, eds. 1958. *From Max Weber: Essays in Sociology.* New York: Oxford Univ. Press

Giddens A. 1984. *The Constitution of Society.* Berkeley: Univ. Calif. Press

Gilroy P. 1991. *There Ain't No Black in the Union Jack: The Cultural Politics of Race and Nation.* Chicago: Univ. Chicago Press

Gordon D, Reich M, Edwards R. 1982. *Segmented Work, Divided Workers: The Historical Transformations of Labor in the United States.* New York: Cambridge Univ. Press

Gossett TF. 1965. *Race: The History of an Idea in America.* New York: Schocken

Hall S, et al. 1978. *Policing the Crisis: Mugging, the State, and Law and Order.* London: Macmillan

Hannaford I. 1996. *Race: The History of an Idea in the West.* Washington, DC: Woodrow Wilson Center Press; Baltimore: Johns Hopkins Univ. Press

Hechter M. 1975. *Internal Colonialism: The Celtic Fringe in British National Development.* Berkeley: Univ. Calif. Press

Huber J, ed. 1991. *Macro-Micro Linkages in Sociology.* Newbury Park, CA: Sage

Jackson W. 1990. *Gunnar Myrdal and America 's Conscience.* Chapel Hill: Univ. North Carolina Press

Joas H. 1996. *The Creativity of Action.* (Transl. J Gaines, P Keast). Chicago: Univ. Chicago Press

Kiernan VG. 1969. *The Lords of Human Kind: European Attitudes to the Outside World in the Imperial Age.* London: Weidenfeld & Nicolson

Kilson MA, Rotberg RI, eds. 1976, *The African Diaspora: Interpretive Essays.* Cambridge, MA: Harvard Univ. Press

Ladner JA, ed. 1973. *The Death of White Sociology.* New York: Random House

Lemelle SJ, Kelley RDG. 1994, *Imagining Home: Class, Culture, and Nationalism in the African Diaspora.* New York: Verso

Lewis DL. 1993. *W.E.B. DuBois: Biography of A Race.* New York: Henry Holt

Lewis DL, ed. 1995. *W.E.B. DuBois: A Reader.* New York: Henry Holt

Lipsitz G. 1998. *The Possessive Investment in Whiteness: How White People Profit from Identity Politics.* Philadelphia: Temple Univ. Press

Marable M. 1986. *W.E.B. DuBois: Black Radical Democrat.* Boston: GK Hall/Twayne

Marx K. 1967. *Capital,* Vol. 1. New York: Int. Publ.

Massey DS, Denton NA. 1993. *American Apartheid.* Cambridge, MA: Harvard Univ. Press

McAdam D. 1982. *Political Process and the Development of Black Insurgency, 1930–1970.* Chicago: Univ. Chicago Press

McKee JB. 1993. *Sociology and the Race Problem: The Failure of a Perspective.* Urbana: Univ. Ill. Press

Montagu A. 1997 [1942]. *Man's Most Dangerous Myth: The Fallacy of Race,* Walnut Creek, CA. 6th ed.

Morris A, Mueller CM, eds. 1992. *Frontiers in Social Movement Theory.* New Haven: Yale Univ. Press

Myrdal G. 1944. *An American Dilemma: The Negro Problem and Modern Democracy.* New York: Harper

Omi M, Winant H. 1994. *Racial Formation in the United States: from the 1960s to the 1990s.* New York: Routledge. Rev. ed.

Park RE. 1950. *Race and Culture.* Glencoe, IL: Free Press

Pettigrew TF, ed. 1980. *The Sociology of Race Relations: Reflection and Reform.* New York: Free Press

Reich M. 1981. *Racial Inequality.* Princeton, NJ: Princeton Univ. Press

Snowden FM. 1983. *Before Color Prejudice: The Ancient View of Blacks.* Cambridge, MA: Harvard Univ. Press

Southern DW. 1987. *Gunnar Myrdal and Black-White Relations: The Use and Abuse of An American Dilemma.* Baton Rouge: Louisiana State Univ. Press

Taguieff P-A. 2000. *The Force of Prejudice: On Racism and Its Doubles.* (Transl. Hassan Melehy) Minneapolis: Univ. Minn. Press. Forthcoming

Tarrow SG. 1998. *Power in Movement: Social Movements and Contentious Politics.* New York: Cambridge Univ. Press. 2nd ed.

Thernstrom S, Thernstrom A, 1997. *America in Black And White: One Nation, Indivisible; Race in Modern America.* New York: Simon & Schuster

Thomas WI, Znaniecki F. 1994 [1923]. *The Polish Peasant in Europe and America.* Ed. and abridged by E Zaretsky. Urbana: Univ. Ill. Press

Todorov T. 1985. *The Conquest of America: The Question of the Other.* [Transl. R. Howard] New York: Harper & Row

Todorov T. 1993. *On Human Diversity: Nationalism, Racism, and Exoticism in French Thought.* (Transl. C Porter) Cambridge, MA: Harvard Univ. Press

UNESCO. 1966. *Research on Racial Relations.* Paris: UNESCO

UNESCO. 1980. *Sociological Theories: Race and Colonialism.* Paris: UNESCO

West C. 1989. *The American Evasion of Philosophy: A Genealogy of Pragmatism.* Madison: Univ. Wisc. Press

Wieviorka M. 1995. *The Arena of Racism.* (Transl. C Turner) Thousand Oaks, CA: Sage

Wilson WJ. 1996. *When Work Disappears: The World of the New Urban Poor.* New York: Knopf

Winant H. 1967. Racial dualism at century's end. In *The House That Race Built: Black Americans, U.S. Terrain,* ed. W Lubiano, pp. 87–115. New York: Pantheon

Wolpe H. 1975. The theory of internal colonialism: the South African case. In *Beyond The Sociology of Development,* ed. I Oxall, pp. 229–52. London: Routledge & Kegan Paul

Racism and Fascism

Toni Morrison

In this address, given at Howard University during its 1995 Charter Day celebrations, Morrison spoke eloquently about the origins and social significance of Howard and other historically Black institutions of higher learning, about the education and miseducation of African Americans, and about the aberrant societal tensions wrought by racism and fascism. In this excerpt, she describes the persistent fallacies that emerge when racial and gender issues connect and intersect, and discusses the tendency of some to focus on a narrow sector rather than the full range of human abilities to differentiate, and most often disparage, members of minority and underrepresented groups.

. . . Let us be reminded that before there is a final solution, there must be a first solution, a second one, even a third. The move toward a final solution is not a jump. It takes one step, then another, then another. Something, perhaps, like this:

(1) Construct an internal enemy, as both focus and diversion.
(2) Isolate and demonize that enemy by unleashing and protecting the utterance of overt and coded name-calling and verbal abuse. Employ *ad hominem* attacks as legitimate charges against that enemy.
(3) Enlist and create sources and distributors of information who are willing to reinforce the demonizing process because it is profitable, because it grants power and because it works.
(4) Palisade all art forms; monitor, discredit or expel those that challenge or destabilize processes of demonization and deification.
(5) Subvert and malign all representatives of and sympathizers with this constructed enemy.
(6) Solicit, from among the enemy, collaborators who agree with and can sanitize the dispossession process.
(7) Pathologize the enemy in scholarly and popular mediums; recycle, for example, scientific racism and the myths of racial superiority in order to naturalize the pathology.
(8) Criminalize the enemy. Then prepare, budget for and rationalize the building of holding arenas for the enemy—especially its males and absolutely its children.

Morrison, Toni (1995). Racism and Fascism. *The Journal of Negro Education*, 64, 384-385.

(9) Reward mindlessness and apathy with monumentalized entertainments and with little pleasures, tiny seductions, a few minutes on television, a few lines in the press, a little pseudo-success, the illusion of power and influence, a little fun, a little style, a little consequence.
(10) Maintain, at all costs, silence.

In 1995 racism may wear a new dress, buy a new pair of boots, but neither it nor its succubus twin fascism is new or can make anything new. It can only reproduce the environment that supports its own health: fear, denial and an atmosphere in which its victims have lost the will to fight.

The forces interested in fascist solutions to national problems are not to be found in one political party or another, or in one or another wing of any single political party. Democrats have no unsullied history of egalitarianism. Nor are liberals free of domination agendas. Republicans may have housed abolitionists and white supremacists. Conservative, moderate, liberal; right, left, hard left, far right; religious, secular, socialist—we must not be blindsided by these Pepsi-Cola, Coca-Cola labels because the genius of fascism is that any political structure can become a suitable home. Fascism talks ideology, but it is really just marketing—marketing for power.

It is recognizable by its need to purge, by the strategies it uses to purge and by its terror of truly democratic agendas. It is recognizable by its determination to convert all public services to private entrepreneurship; all nonprofit organizations to profit-making ones—so that the narrow but protective chasm between governance and business disappears. It changes citizens into taxpayers—so individuals become angry at even the notion of the public good. It changes neighbors into consumers—so the measure of our value as humans is not our humanity or our compassion or our generosity but what we own. It changes parenting into panicking—so that we vote against the interests of our own children; against their health care, their education, their safety from weapons. And in effecting these changes it produces the perfect capitalist, one who is willing to kill a human being for a product—a pair of sneakers, a jacket, a car—or kill generations for control of products—oil, drugs, fruit, gold.

When our fears have all been serialized, our creativity censured, our ideas "market-placed," or rights sold, our intelligence sloganized, our strength downsized, our privacy auctioned; when the theatricality, the entertainment value, the marketing of life is complete, we will find ourselves living not in a nation but in a consortium of industries, and wholly unintelligible to ourselves except for what we see as through a screen darkly.

W.E.B. DuBois's Challenge to Scientific Racism

Carol M. Taylor

In 1929 several hundred people gathered in Chicago's North Hall to witness a debate on the question, "Should the Negro Be Encouraged to Cultural Equality?" The affirmative position was argued by W.E.B. DuBois. His opponent was Theodore Lothrop Stoddard, Harvard Ph.D. and author of dozens of popular articles and twenty-two books. During the course of the debate, Stoddard (1929: 1) summarized the conclusions to which "modern science" had led him: "To-day, as never before, we possess a clear appreciation of racial realities. . . . We know that *our* America is a *White* America. . . . And the overwhelming weight of both historical and scientific evidence shows that only so long as the American people remain white will its institutions, ideals and culture continue to fit the temperament of its inhabitants—and hence continue to endure."

Stoddard had excellent reason to celebrate the clarity of his perceptions and the self-evidence of his conclusions. Quite literally, he had it on the best authority. His concept of race as a determining factor in human affairs was supported with virtual unanimity by the leading figures in American social science. Utilizing both professional and popular channels, biologists, psychologists, and sociologists proclaimed with one voice the inherent and immutable inferiority of the black race.

During the late nineteenth and early twentieth centuries, scientific racism formed a vital link in the oppression of American blacks. If established social science defined blacks as inferior beings who could naturally be expected to occupy the position in society which they in fact held, then occasional social reformers could be dismissed as romantic dreamers who had neither knowledge nor appreciation of hard scientific fact. The thesis of this article is that a direct and authoritative challenge to the scientific racism of this period was urgently necessary, and that issuing such a challenge was one of the leading rhetorical contributions of W.E.B. DuBois. Specifically, I will examine the clash between social scientists and DuBois on three issues: social Darwinism, the eugenics movement, and psychologists' measurement of intelligence.

In both ability and opportunity, DuBois was admirably equipped to confront the scientific community. After earning a Ph.D. from Harvard in 1895, DuBois amassed an impressive

Republished from *Journal of Black Studies, Vol. 11, No. 4 (June 1981)* by Carol M. Taylor.

list of scholarly and popular publications. Between 1897 and 1910 he chaired the Department of Sociology at Atlanta University, where he inaugurated studies of American blacks, establishing him as "the father of Negro sociology" (Broderick, 1969). A respected social scientist himself, DuBois was well qualified to join battle with his white counterparts.

Although DuBois engaged the enemy on a wide variety of battlegrounds, he reached his largest audience through the editorial pages of *The Crisis*. As editor of the NAACP's official organ from its inception in 1910 until his resignation in 1934, DuBois saw a peak circulation of more than 100,000. Approximately 80% of those readers were black (Kellogg, 1967). Armed with impeccable credentials and access to a massive audience, DuBois attacked the scientific underpinnings of racial discrimination.

I.

In the late nineteenth and early twentieth centuries, American science enjoyed enormous prestige. The rapid advancement of scientific knowledge lent scientists a "halo." Since they had produced palpable achievements in their own fields, they seemed worthy of imitation, and their doctrines were reapplied to other areas. Those arguments which could claim scientific sanction were not open to further attack. The scientific and the true were indistinguishable (Platt, 1967).

In no area were scientists of this period more unified, and thus more influential, than in the area of race theory. Their primary unifying agent was the Darwinian theory of evolution. Under the leadership of Herbert Spencer, Darwin's principle of natural selection was reapplied to society. If biological organisms evolved gradually by eliminating those individuals least fitted for survival, it was thought, then social organisms must evolve at the same geologic rate and by the same process of elimination. The analogy had several corollaries. No society or segment of society could be improved substantially beyond the level to which evolution had brought it. "It is at any rate a tough old world," admonished sociologist William Graham Sumner (1924: 245). "It has taken its trend and curvature and all its twists and tangles from a long course of formation. All its wry and crooked gnarls and knobs are therefore stiff and stubborn." Reformist schemes were futile and dangerous attempts to tamper with the natural and inexorable progress of evolution. A second corollary was that social conflict, such as the conflict between races, was natural and desirable. Lester Frank Ward, who has been described as the "St. Augustine of the American cult of science" (Gabriel, 1940: 204), believed that organized society had originated in the conquest of one race by another, and that subsequent racial conflict represented the continual striving of society to improve itself through competition (Hofstadter, 1955).

If evolution eliminated the unfit, then the loser in racial conflict must be, by definition, inferior. One argument frequently used in support of black inferiority was that the race was dying out. Nathaniel Shaler, dean of the Lawrence Scientific School at Harvard, suggested in 1884 that blacks were becoming extinct. Frederick L. Hoffman's *Race Traits and Tendencies of the American Negro* (1896) warned that the high incidence of tuberculosis and venereal disease among blacks arose from their inherent immorality, and would eventually destroy them.

Social scientists discerned further evidence of black inferiority in the actions of Southern lynch mobs. The prevalence of lynching, Ward (1914) explained, was a by-product of evolution. Whites lynched the black man because he insisted upon raping white women. The black man raped white women in response to the "unheard but imperious voice of nature commanding him at the risk of 'lynch law' to raise his race to a little higher level." Whites reacted violently because of an equally instinctive determination to protect their race from inferior strains (1914: 359–360). Although Ward demurred from the next logical step, the obvious conclusion was that a high incidence of lynching (not to mention raping) was inevitable and attempts to reduce it unnatural. Perhaps more clearly than any other issue, the rape argument illustrates the circular nature of evolutionary thought in the area of race theory. How do we know that the black man has rapist tendencies? Because he is inferior. How do we know that he is inferior? Because he has rapist tendencies.

The biological determinism suggested by the social Darwinists was further supported by the eugenicists. In 1869 the English scientist Francis Galton published *Hereditary Genius,* in which he argued that individual characteristics were determined solely by heredity. Heredity dictated that "the average intellectual standard of the negro race is some two grades below our own," for, as Galton (1962: 394) pointed out, "It is seldom that we hear of a white traveller meeting a black chief whom he feels to be the better man."

Under the stimulus of Galton's work, the eugenics movement flourished in the United States from the 1880s to the mid-1920s. The movement's central tenet was that such traits as genius, feeblemindedness, criminal tendencies, and pauperism were part of the human germ plasm, and that the unfit must be limited in numbers through social application of scientific knowledge (Pickens, 1968).

For the eugenicists, the issues of heredity and race were intertwined. Madison Grant, an officer in the American Eugenics Society, announced in 1916 that "races vary intellectually and morally just as they do physically," and he scolded idealists who refused to confront biological reality:

> There exists to-day a widespread and fatuous belief in the power of environment . . . to alter heredity. . . . Such beliefs have done much damage in the past and if allowed to go uncontradicted, may do even more serious damage in the future. Thus the view that the Negro slave was an unfortunate cousin of the white man, deeply tanned by the tropic sun and denied the blessings of Christianity and civilization, played no small part with the sentimentalists of the Civil War period and it has taken us fifty years to learn that speaking English, wearing good clothes and going to school and church does not transform a Negro into a white man [1918: 226].

In place of such fuzzy thinking, Grant advocated "a rigid system of selection" through sterilization of the unfit, beginning with the criminal and the insane and extending ultimately to "worthless race types" (1918: 16, 51).

In the early 1900s scientific racism gained an additional impetus from the psychologists. In 1916 Lewis Terman and his associates "perfected" the Stanford Binet intelligence tests. The I.Q. tests demonstrated that the children of college professors, bank presidents, and the like displayed superior mental ability. The results were considered conclusive proof of the value of good heredity (Boring, 1950). They provided a powerful weapon for the racists. Ability was inherited; the greatest ability was to be found in the upper classes; the upper classes included few blacks.

The response to exceptional blacks illustrated the closed nature of scientific thought. A highly intelligent black was not an argument against the race's incurable inferiority. Science had decreed that blacks were not intelligent. Therefore, any intelligent person had some amount of white blood, regardless of how black he or she appeared to be (Fanon, 1967). To believe otherwise was logically impossible. As long as scientific sanction for racism remained a closed system, a persuasive argument for significant progress of American blacks was impossible to construct.

The mid-1920s marked the high point of racism's scientific respectability. By the early 1930s, scientific pronouncements on race were under fire from members of the scientific community. Cultural anthropologist Franz Boas denounced racist doctrines as clearly lacking in scientific proof. Moreover, the work of the anthropologists pointed up the intimate relationship between ideas and culture, and thus began to focus attention on environment rather than heredity (Gossett, 1965). In a speech before the Third International Eugenics Congress in 1932, Herbert J. Muller, pioneer geneticist, launched a fiery attack upon the eugenics movement as a mere reflection of upper-class bias (Pickens, 1968). Psychologists began to stress the importance of learning in the development of intellectual ability (Boring, 1950).

Yet race theory had become deeply embedded in the national consciousness. If the scientific definition of blacks was correct, then the justice of their position in American society was unassailable. In order to challenge the validity of social and political discrimination, it was necessary to argue that blacks were not what American science said they were.

II.

In his editorials in *The Crisis*, DuBois developed an extensive rationale for challenging whites' definitions of blacks. As DuBois saw it, no one, including blacks themselves, was denying the current assumptions:

> For now nearly twenty years we have made of ourselves mudsills for the feet of this Western world, We have echoed and applauded every shameful accusation made against 10,000,000 victims of slavery. Did they call us inferior half-beasts? We nodded our simple heads and whispered: "We is." Did they call our women prostitutes and our children bastards? We smiled and cast a stone

> at the bruised breasts of our wives and daughters. Did they accuse of laziness 4,000,000 sweating, struggling laborers, half paid and cheated out of much of that? We shrieked; "Ain't it so?" We laughed with them at our color, we joked at our sad past, and we told chicken stories to get alms [May, 1914: 24].

"This is the lie which *The Crisis* is here to refute," he announced. "It is a lie, a miserable and shameful lie, which some black men have helped... to spread and been well paid for their pains" 1912: 153). Whites' assumptions about the Negro demanded refutation; W.E.B. DuBois would supply it. As DuBois saw it, scientific racism was a closed system which reached untenable conclusions by weak methodology in the hands of biased researchers.

DuBois set out to refute the social Darwinist assumption that racial conflict was a means of evolutionary progress. There were, DuBois contended, three arguments for racial antagonism, and all of them were false. First, social Darwinists hypothesized that racial antagonism represented an instinctive repulsion from something harmful and was, therefore, a condition of ultimate survival. Nonsense, DuBois snorted; white and black children played together willingly. Race hatred was learned. Second, social Darwinists argued that racial antagonism was an avoidance of poor racial traits, such as poor health and low ability. There was no evidence, DuBois replied, that whites were innately more healthy than blacks. As for low ability, the prejudice against Jews was hardly a function of their intellectual inferiority. Third, social Darwinists considered racial antagonism a method of race development. But, DuBois observed, it is hardly necessary to suppress one race in order to develop another (September, 1914: 232–233).

Acceptance of racial antagonism presumed the inferiority of one race, and Dubois attacked the presumption. A popular scientific argument for blacks' inferiority was the belief that they were dying out. By 1918 DuBois was sufficiently certain of his facts to deny the assertion outright: "It is unfortunate that many calamity howlers follow the example of Dr. Shirley Wynne of the New York Department of Health and seek to prove, in the face of all reliable statistics, that the Negro is 'deteriorating.' This is flatly false. He is rapidly improving in health" (May, 1918: 11). Three years later DuBois noted that, according to the census of 1920, "our increase in time of war and stress has been healthy and encouraging" (August, 1921: 150). The disappearance of blacks might fit the theoretic framework of social Darwinism, but it did not fit the facts.

Equally at variance with the facts was the social Darwinist pronouncement that black men were lynched because they were instinctive rapists driven by an overpowering desire for white women. Fundamentally racist, the accusation provoked DuBois's full wrath:

> For a generation we black folks have been the sexual scapegoats for white American filth in literature and lynching. Every time a black man commits a crime, the story is garnished and embellished by unbelievable sadism in order to make a beast out of the criminal. It is not enough that a black man robs or kills or fights. No! In addition to that, the world must be made to believe him a wild beast of such inconceivable and abnormal appetites that he turns from red force and white anger to filthy lust. No proof is asked for such incredible lies [October, 1930: 353].

Actually, DuBois pointed out, a careful study by the NAACP in 1922 demonstrated that only 19% of blacks lynched had been accused of rape, much less convicted (February, 1922: 166). Sexual relations, DuBois scoffed, were "about the last of the social problems" which disturbed blacks. On the other hand, whites "for the most part profess to see but one problem: 'Do you want your sister to marry a nigger?'" (February, 1913: 180).

It was much more likely, DuBois retorted, that his sister would be raped by a white man. Mulattoes had resulted from the white man's lust, not the black man's: "We have not asked amalgamation; we have resisted it. It has been forced on us by brute strength, ignorance, poverty, degradation, and fraud. It is the white race, roaming the world, that has left its trail of bastards and outraged women and then raised holy hands to heaven and deplored 'race mixture'" (December, 1921: 56). The black man did not desire white women; he much preferred that black women be left alone. Again, social Darwinists had defined the black man incorrectly.

The eugenecists were similarly unreliable in their delineation of the hereditary characteristics of the black race. DuBois was exasperated by the theory of innate characteristics, which allowed commentators to ignore observable behavior which contradicted theory: "There is always a whisper for your private ear—confidential information relating to certain innate characteristics, by which this man, though personally clean, sprang from dirty seed and to dirty seed must inevitably return; by which this man, though a gentleman of ability, must be treated like a dog on account of a temporarily hidden (but absolutely certain) dog nature" (May, 1911: 21). In short, the closed nature of race theory dictated that, when theory and facts conflicted, the facts were insignificant.

Appalled by the eugenecists' total disregard of the influence of environment, DuBois attacked the notion that blacks betrayed a genetic predisposition toward criminality. "Crime," DuBois lectured, "is a social disease; it is a complex result of poverty, ignorance and other sorts of degradation. As the peculiar victim of these things the Negro in the United States suffers more from arrest and punishment . . . than any other element" (May, 1926: 9).

If scientific assumptions about race were logically untenable and contrary to fact, they were also based on weak methodology, In 1913 DuBois commended the "deep insight and superb brain power" of Dr. Ulrich B. Phillips of the University of Michigan, who knew "all about the Negro." Phillips compared cotton production among Mississippi blacks before and after emancipation and concluded that it had declined. By contrast, he noted that during the same period cotton production among whites in Oklahoma and Texas had increased. DuBois was scathing:

> We are delighted to learn all this, for in the dark days of our college economics we were taught that it was labor *and* land, together, that made a crop. . . . It seems that we were grievously in error. This is apparently true only of *white* labor. If you wish to judge *white* labor, judge it by the results on rich Texas and Oklahoma prairies, with fertilizers and modern methods; if, on the other hand, you would judge *Negro* labor, slink into the slavery-cursed Mississippi bottoms

> where soil has been raped for a century. . . . Then, rolling you eyes and lifting protesting hands, point out that, whereas the slave drivers of 1860 wrung 1200 pounds of cotton from the protesting earth, the lazy blacks are able . . . to get only 700 pounds for their present white masters.

DuBois concluded that he fully expected to see the "astute" Dr. Phillips at the head of the Department of Agriculture, not because the job required intelligence, but because it did call for "adroitness in bolstering up bad cases" (March, 1913: 239–240). Scientific methodologies were often questionable.

The scientists themselves, DuBois charged, would not bear scrutiny. Specifically, they were biased. In 1925 DuBois took a delighted swipe at the psychologists:

> Have you noticed, brethren, that since the afflatus of postwar "science" and the great *ex-cathedra* utterances of those mighty scientists [psychologist William] McDougall of Harvard and what-you-may-call-him [probably psychologist Carl C. Brigham] of Princeton—that since all this flareup and proof of Negro "inferiority" by "intelligence" tests, there has dropped a significant silence? . . . Well, here is one of the reasons: In Louisville, Kentucky, they have been testing school children . . . white and black. And then? Well and then, silence; Silence! [After two inquiries from DuBois, the superintendent replied that the results would not be published.] What is wrong? Why all this heavy secrecy? . . . If the truth must be known, those damned tests went and came out wrong! In other words, instead of proving white children superior, they actually proved—but no: We cannot write it; it's too awful [October, 1925; 270–271].

DuBois was, of course, guessing. He had no evidence of the motive for withholding the results. However, the message was clear, Scientists were not objective seekers of truth, but biased whites who suppressed evidence which did not support their prejudices.

DuBois found similar evidence of bias in scientific pronouncements on blacks' insanity. In former years, DuBois noted, census reports had indicated a low incidence of insanity and suicide among blacks. Scientists had found it easy to explain the statistics: "'Naturally,' said American science, 'for Negroes have not enough brains to go insane with and are too good-natured to kill themselves.'" In more recent years, the rates had risen sharply. "But American science" DuBois reported, "is unperturbed." The mounting suicide rates simply indicated that the black man's inferior mind was unequal to the strain of civilization. "And there you are," DuBois concluded. "How can we possibly satisfy our friends?" (July, 1926: 111). DuBois's answer was, of course, that scientists could not be satisfied, and that the "scientific facts," whatever they happened to be, would be manipulated by biased investigators to demonstrate their preconceived and unshakable convictions. As scientists, DuBois suggested, Americans made good racists.

By 1929 DuBois was relieved to note that the respectability of scientific racism was declining. "It is becoming more and more difficult," he exulted, "for them [whites] to state frankly the case against the Negro. The reason for this is that the main facts upon which they have been relying are no longer plausible and the thesis [that blacks should not seek cultural equality] without them in barbarous, unscientific and unchristian" (May, 1929: 167). In other words, if the Negro was not as American science defined him, then American society's treatment of him was unconscionable. And, DuBois argued, scientific definitions were illogical and unsupported assumptions of a closed system, derived from a laughable methodology, and interpreted by biased investigators. Blacks were not what American science said they were.

According to social psychologist Kenneth B. Clark (1966: 600), W.E.B. DuBois "may well have been the most important figure in the American civil rights movement in the twentieth century." The fact that, more than any other spokesman, DuBois issued a direct and authoritative challenge to scientific racism may not determine whether he merits election as the most important figure in black protest in the twentieth century. It may suggest, however, appropriate grounds for his nomination.

REFERENCES

BORING, E. G. (1950) "The influence of evolutionary theory upon American psychological thought," in S. Persons (ed.) Evolutionary Thought in America. New Haven, CT: Yale University Press.

BRODERICK, F. L. (1969) W.E.B. DuBois: Negro Leader in a Time of Crisis. Stanford, CA: Stanford University Press.

CLARK, K. B. (1966) "The civil rights movement: momentum and organization," in T. Parsons and K. B. Clark (eds.) The Negro American Boston: Beacon.

DuBOIS, W.E.B. (1910–1934) Editorials in The Crisis.

FANON, F. (1967) Black Skin, White Masks (C. L. Markmann, trans.). New York: Grove Press.

GABRIEL, R. H. (1940) The Course of American Democratic Thought. New York; Ronald Press.

GALTON, F. (1962) Hereditary Genius. Cleveland: Meridian. (Originally published 1869.)

GOSSETT, T. F. (1965) Race: The History of an Idea in America. New York: Schocken.

GRANT, M. (1918) The Passing of the Great Race. New York: Scribner.

HOFFMAN, F. (1896) Race Traits and Tendencies of the American Negro. New York: Macmillan.

HOFSTADTER, R. (1955) Social Darwinism in American Thought. Boston: Beacon.

KELLOGG, C. F. (1967) NAACP. Baltimore: Johns Hopkins University Press.

PICKENS, D. (1968) Eugenics and the Progressives. Nashville, TN: Vanderbilt University Press.

PLATT, O. (1967) "Invention and advancement," in H. N. Smith (ed.) Popular Culture and Industrialism, 1865–1890. Garden City, NY: Anchor.

SHALER, N. (1884) "The Negro problem." Atlantic Monthly 54 (November): 696–709.

STODDARD, T. L. (1929) "Should the Negro be encouraged to cultural equality?" Typed manuscript, DuBois papers, Fisk University, Nashville, Tennessee.

SUMNER, W. G. (1924) "The absurd effort to make the world over," in A. Keller and M. Davi (eds.) Selected Essays of William Graham Sumner. New Haven, CT: Yale University Press.

WARD, L. F. (1914) Pure Sociology. New York: Macmillan.

Discrimination and the American Creed

Robert K. Merton

QUESTIONS TO CONSIDER

Have you ever been in a situation in which social, economic, or peer pressure forced you to treat someone from a different racial group in an inappropriate way? Robert Merton suggests that individuals who are not *prejudiced often act in bigoted and discriminatory ways. How and why does this happen? Is it possible to live our lives in the category Merton calls the "unprejudiced non-discriminator"?*

The primary function of the sociologist is to search out the determinants and consequences of diverse forms of social behavior. To the extent that he succeeds in fulfilling this role, he clarifies the alternatives of organized social action in a given situation and of the probable outcome of each. To this extent, there is no sharp distinction between pure research and applied research. Rather, the difference is one between research with direct implications for particular problems of social action and research which is remote from these problems. Not infrequently, basic research which has succeeded only in clearing up previously confused concepts may have an immediate bearing upon the problems of men in society to a degree not approximated by applied research oriented exclusively to these problems. At least, this is the assumption underlying the present paper: clarification of apparently unclear and confused concepts in the sphere of race and ethnic relations is a step necessarily prior to the devising of effective programs for reducing intergroup conflict and for promoting equitable access to economic and social opportunities. . . .

THE AMERICAN CREED: AS CULTURAL IDEAL, PERSONAL BELIEF AND PRACTICE

The American creed as set forth in the Declaration of Independence, the preamble of the Constitution and the Bill of Rights has often been misstated. This part of the cultural heritage does *not* include the patently false assertion that all men are created equal in capacity or endowment. It does *not* imply that an Einstein and a moron are equal in intellectual capacity or that Joe Louis and a small, frail Columbia professor (or a Mississippian Congressman) are equally endowed with brawny arms harboring muscles as strong as iron bands. It does *not* proclaim universal equality of innate intellectual or physical endowment.

Instead, the creed asserts the indefeasible principle of the human right to full equity—the right of equitable access to justice, freedom and opportunity, irrespective of race or religion or ethnic origin. It proclaims further the universalist doctrine of the dignity of the individual, irrespective of the groups of which he is a part. It is a creed announcing full moral equities for all, not an absurd myth affirming the equality of intellectual and physical capacity of all men everywhere. And it goes on to say that though men differ in innate endowment, they do so as individuals, not by virtue of their group memberships.

Viewed sociologically, the creed is a set of values and precepts embedded in American culture, to which Americans are expected to conform. It is a complex of affirmations, rooted in the historical past and ceremonially celebrated in the present, partly enacted in the laws of the land and partly not. Like all creeds, it is a profession of faith, a part of cultural tradition sanctified by the larger traditions of which it is a part.

It would be a mistaken sociological assertion, however, to suggest that the creed is a fixed and static cultural constant, unmodified in the course of time, just as it would be an error to imply that as an integral part of culture, it evenly blankets all subcultures of the national society. It is indeed dynamic, subject to change and in turn promoting change in other spheres of culture and society. It is, moreover, unevenly distributed throughout the society, being institutionalized as an integral part of local culture in some regions of the society and rejected in others.

. . . Learned men and men in high public positions have repeatedly observed and deplored the disparity between ethos and behavior in the sphere of race and ethnic relations. In his magisterial volumes on the American Negro, for example, Gunnar Myrdal called this gulf between creed and conduct "an American dilemma," and centered his attention on the prospect of narrowing or closing the gap. The President's Committee on Civil Rights, in their report to the nation, and . . . President [Truman] himself, in a message to Congress, have called public attention to this "serious gap between our ideals and some of our practices."

But as valid as these observations may be, they tend so to simplify the relations between creed and conduct as to be seriously misleading both for social policy and for social science. All these high authorities notwithstanding, the problems of racial and ethnic inequities are not expressible as a discrepancy between high cultural principles and low social conduct. It is a relation not between two variables, official creed and private practice, but between three: first, the cultural creed honored in cultural tradition and partly enacted into law; second, the beliefs and attitudes of individuals regarding the principles of the creed; and third, the actual practices of individuals with reference to it.

Once we substitute these three variables of cultural ideal, belief and actual practice for the customary distinction between the two variables of cultural ideals and actual practices, the entire formulation of the problem becomes changed. We escape from the virtuous but ineffectual impasse of deploring the alleged hypocrisy of many Americans into the more difficult but potentially effectual realm of analyzing the problem in hand.

To describe the problem and to proceed to its analysis, it is necessary to consider the official creed, individuals' beliefs and attitudes concerning the creed, and their actual behavior. Once stated, the distinctions are readily applicable. Individuals may *recognize* the creed as part of a cultural tradition, *without having any private conviction of its moral validity or its binding quality.* Thus, so far as the beliefs of individuals are concerned, we can identify two types: those who genuinely believe in the creed and those who do not (although some of these may, on public or ceremonial occasions, profess adherence to its principles). Similarly, with respect to actual practices: conduct may or may not conform to the creed. But, and this is the salient consideration: *conduct may or may not conform with individuals' own beliefs concerning the moral claims of all men to equal opportunity.*

Stated in formal sociological terms, this asserts that attitudes and overt behavior vary independently. *Prejudicial attitudes need not coincide with discriminatory behavior.* The implications of this statement can be drawn out in terms of a logical syntax whereby the variables are diversely combined, as can be seen in the following typology.

By exploring the interrelations between prejudice and discrimination, we can identify four major types in terms of their attitudes toward the creed and their behavior with respect to it. Each type is found in every region and social class, though in varying numbers. By examining each type, we shall be better prepared to understand their interdependence and the appropriate types of action for curbing ethnic discrimination. The folklabels for each type are intended to aid in their prompt recognition.

Type I: The Unprejudiced Non-Discriminator or All-Weather Liberal

These are the racial and ethnic liberals who adhere to the creed in both belief and practice. They are neither prejudiced nor given to discrimination. Their orientation toward the creed is fixed and stable. Whatever the environing situation, they are likely to abide by their beliefs: hence, the *all-weather* liberal:

This is, of course, the strategic group which *can* act as the spearhead for the progressive extension of the creed into effective practice. They represent the solid foundation both for the measure of ethnic equities which now exist and for the future enlargement of these equities. Integrated with the creed in both belief and practice, they would seem most motivated to influence others toward the same democratic outlook. They represent a reservoir of culturally legitimatized goodwill which can be channeled into an active program for extending belief in the creed and conformity with it in practice.

Most important, as we shall see presently, the all-weather liberals comprise the group which can so reward others for conforming with the creed, as to transform deviants into conformists. They alone can provide the positive social environment for the other types who will no longer find it expedient or rewarding to retain their prejudices or discriminatory practices.

But though the ethnic liberal is a *potential* force for the successive extension of the American creed, he does not fully realize this potentiality in actual fact, for a variety of reasons. Among the limitations on effective action are several fallacies to which the ethnic liberal seems peculiarly subject. First among these is the *fallacy of group soliloquies.* Ethnic liberals are busily engaged in talking to themselves. Repeatedly, the same groups of like-minded liberals seek each other out, hold periodic meetings in which they engage in mutual exhortation and thus lend social and psychological support to one another. But however much these unwittingly self-selected audiences may reinforce the creed among themselves, they do not thus appreciably diffuse the creed in belief or practice to groups which depart from it in one respect or the other.

More, these group soliloquies in which there is typically wholehearted agreement among fellow-liberals tend to promote another fallacy 'limiting effective action. This is the *fallacy of unanimity.* Continued association with like-minded individuals tends to produce the illusion that a large measure of consensus has been achieved in the community at large. The unanimity regarding essential cultural axioms which obtains in these small groups provokes an overestimation of the strength of the movement and of its effective inroads upon the larger population which does not necessarily share these creedal axioms. Many also mistake participation in the groups of like-minded individuals for effective action. Discussion accordingly takes the place of action. The reinforcement of the creed for oneself is mistaken for the extension of the creed among those outside the limited circle of ethnic liberals.

Arising from adherence to the creed is a third limitation upon effective action, the *fallacy of privatized solutions* to the problem. The ethnic liberal, precisely because he is at one with the American creed, may rest content with his own individual behavior and thus see no need to do anything about the problem at large. Since his own spiritual house is in order, he is not motivated by guilt or shame to work on a collective problem. The very freedom of the liberal from guilt thus prompts him to secede from any *collective* effort to set the national house in order. He essays a *private* solution to a *social* problem. He assumes that numerous individual adjustments will serve in place of a collective adjustment. His outlook, compounded of good moral philosophy but poor sociology, holds that each individual must put his own house in order and fails to recognize that privatized solutions cannot be effected for problems which are essentially social in nature. For clearly, if each person *were* motivated to abide by the American creed, the problem would not be likely to exist in the first place. It is only when a social environment is established by conformists to the creed that deviants can in due course be brought to modify their behavior in the direction of conformity. But this "environment" can be constituted only through collective effort and not through private adherence to a public creed. Thus we have the paradox that the clear conscience of many ethnic liberals may promote the very social situation which permits deviations from the creed to continue unchecked. Privatized liberalism invites social inaction. Accordingly, there appears the phenomenon of the inactive or passive liberal, himself at spiritual ease, neither prejudiced nor discriminatory, but in a measure tending to contribute to the persistence of prejudice and discrimination through his very inaction.

The fallacies of group soliloquy, unanimity and privatized solutions thus operate to make the potential strength of the ethnic liberals unrealized in practice.

It is only by first recognizing these limitations that the liberal can hope to overcome them. With some hesitancy, one may suggest initial policies for curbing the scope of the three fallacies. The fallacy of group soliloquies can be removed only by having ethnic liberals enter into organized groups not comprised merely by fellow-liberals. This exacts a heavy price on the liberal. It means that he faces initial opposition and resistance rather than prompt consensus. It entails giving up the gratifications of consistent group support.

The fallacy of unanimity can in turn be reduced by coming to see that American society often provides large rewards for those who express their ethnic prejudice in discrimination. Only if the balance of rewards, material and psychological, is modified will behavior be modified. Sheer exhortation and propaganda are not enough. Exhortation verges on a belief in magic if it is not supported by appropriate changes in the social environment to make conformity with the exhortation rewarding.

Finally, the fallacy of privatized solutions requires the militant liberal to motivate the passive liberal to collective effort, possibly by inducing in him a sense of guilt for his unwitting contribution to the problems of ethnic inequities through his own systematic inaction.

One may suggest a unifying theme for the ethnic liberal: goodwill is not enough to modify social reality. It is only when this goodwill is harnessed to social-psychological realism that it can be used to reach cultural objectives.

Type II: The Unprejudiced Discriminator or Fair-Weather Liberal

The fair-weather liberal is the man of expediency who, despite his own freedom from prejudice, supports discriminatory practices when it is the easier or more profitable course. His expediency may take the form of holding his silence and thus implicitly acquiescing in expresions of ethnic prejudice by others or in the practice of discrimination by others. This is the expediency of the timid: the liberal who hesitates to speak up against discrimination for fear he might lose status or be otherwise penalized by his prejudiced associates. Or his expediency may take the form of grasping at advantages in social and economic competition deriving solely from the ethnic status of competitors. This is the expediency of the self-assertive: the employer, himself not an anti-Semite or Negrophobe, who refuses to hire Jewish or Negro workers because "it might hurt business"; the trade union leader who expediently advocates racial discrimination in order not to lose the support of powerful Negrophobes in his union.

In varying degrees, the fair-weather liberal suffers from guilt and shame for departing from his own effective beliefs in the American creed. Each deviation through which he derives a limited reward from passively acquiescing in or actively supporting discrimination contributes cumulatively to this fund of guilt. He is, therefore, peculiarly vulnerable to the efforts of the all-weather liberal who would help him bring his conduct into accord with his beliefs, thus removing this source of guilt. He is the most amenable to cure, because basically he wants to be cured. His is a split conscience which motivates him to cooperate actively with those who will help remove the source of internal conflict. He thus represents the strategic group promising the largest returns for the least effort. Persistent re-affirmation of the creed will only intensify his conflict; but a long regimen in a favorable social climate can be expected to transform the fair-weather liberal into an all-weather liberal.

Type III: The Prejudiced Non-Discriminator or Fair-Weather Illiberal

The fair-weather illiberal is the reluctant conformist to the creed, the man of prejudice who does not believe in the creed but conforms to it in practice through fear of sanctions which might otherwise be visited upon him. You know him well: the prejudiced employer who discriminates against racial or ethnic groups until a Fair Employment Practice Commission, able and willing to enforce the law, puts the fear of punishment into him; the trade union leader, himself deeply prejudiced, who does away with Jim Crow in his union because the rank-and-file demands that it be done away with; the businessman who forgoes his own prejudices when he finds a profitable market among the very people he hates, fears or despises; the timid bigot who will not express his prejudices when he is in the presence of powerful men who vigorously and effectively affirm their belief in the American creed.

It should be clear that the fair-weather illiberal is the precise counterpart of the fair-weather liberal. Both are men of expediency, to be sure, but expediency dictates different courses of behavior in the two cases. The timid bigot conforms to the creed only when there is danger or loss in deviations, just as the timid liberal deviates from the creed when there is danger or loss in conforming. *Superficial similarity in behavior of the two in the same situation should not be permitted to cloak a basic difference in the meaning of this outwardly similar behavior*, a difference which is as important for social policy as it is for social science. Whereas the timid bigot is under strain when he conforms to the creed, the timid liberal is under strain when he deviates. For ethnic prejudice has deep roots in the character structure of the fair-weather bigot, and this will find overt expression unless there are powerful countervailing forces, institutional, legal and interpersonal. He does not accept the moral legitimacy of the creed; he conforms because he must, and will cease to conform when the pressure is removed. The fair-weather liberal, on the other hand, is effectively committed to the creed and does not require strong institutional pressure to conform; continuing interpersonal relations with all-weather liberals may be sufficient.

This is the one critical point at which the traditional formulation of the problem of ethnic discrimination as a departure from the creed can lead to serious errors of theory and practice. Overt behavioral deviation (or conformity) may signify importantly different situations, depending upon the underlying motivations. Knowing simply that ethnic discrimination is rife in a community does not, therefore, point to appropriate lines of social policy. It is necessary to know also the distribution of ethnic prejudices and basic motivations for these prejudices as well. Communities with the same amount of overt discrimination may represent vastly different types of problems, dependent on whether the population is comprised by a large nucleus of fair-weather liberals ready to abandon their discriminatory practices under slight interpersonal pressure or a large nucleus of fair-weather illiberals who will abandon discrimination only if major changes in the local institutional setting can be effected. Any statement of the problem as a gulf between creedal ideals and prevailing practice is thus seen to be overly-simplified in the precise sense of masking this decisive difference between the type of discrimination exhibited by the fair-weather liberal and by the fair-weather illiberal. That the gulf-between-ideal-and-practice does not adequately describe the nature of the ethnic problem will become more apparent as we turn to the fourth type in our inventory of prejudice and discrimination

Type IV: The Prejudiced Discriminator or the All-Weather Illiberal

This type, too, is not unknown to you. He is the confirmed illiberal, the bigot pure and unashamed, the man of prejudice consistent in his departure from the American creed. In some measure, he is found everywhere in the land, though in varying numbers. He derives large social and psychological gains from his conviction that "any white man (including the village idiot) is 'better' than any nigger (including George Washington Carver)." He considers differential treatment of Negro and white not as "discrimination," in the sense of unfair treatment, but as "discriminating," in the sense of showing acute discernment. For him, it is as clear that one "ought" to accord a Negro and a white different treatment in a wide diversity of situations, as it is clear to the population at large that one "ought" to accord a child and an adult different treatment in many situations.

This illustrates anew my reason for questioning the applicability of the unusual formula of the American dilemma as a gap between lofty creed and low conduct. For the confirmed illiberal, ethnic discrimination does *not* represent a discrepancy between *his* ideals and *his* behavior. His ideals proclaim the right, even the duty, of discrimination. Accordingly, his behavior does not entail a sense of social deviation, with the resultant strains which this would involve. The ethnic illiberal is as much a conformist as the ethnic liberal. He is merely conforming to a different cultural and institutional pattern which is centered, not about the creed, but about a doctrine of essential inequality of status ascribed to those of diverse ethnic and racial origins. To overlook this is to overlook the well-known *fact* that our national culture is divided into a number of local subcultures which are not consistent among themselves in all respects. And again, to fail to take this fact of different subcultures into account is to open the door for all manner of errors of social policy in attempting to control the problems of racial and ethnic discrimination.

This view of the all-weather illiberal has one immediate implication with wide bearing upon social policies and sociological theory oriented toward the problem of discrimination. The extreme importance of the social surroundings of the confirmed illiberal at once becomes apparent. For as these surroundings vary, so, in some measure, does the problem of the consistent illiberal. The illiberal, living in those cultural regions where the American creed is widely repudiated and is no effective part of the subculture, has his private ethnic attitudes and practices supported by the local mores, the local institutions and the local power-structure. The illiberal in cultural areas dominated by a large measure of adherence to the American creed is in a social environment where he is isolated and receives small social support for his beliefs and practices. In both instances, the *individual* is an illiberal, to be sure, but he represents two significantly different *sociological types.* In the first instance, he is a *social conformist*, with strong moral and institutional reinforcement, whereas in the second, he is a *social deviant*, lacking strong social corroboration. In the one case, his discrimination involves him in further integration with his network of social relations; in the other, it threatens to cut him off from sustaining interpersonal ties. In the first cultural context, personal change in his ethnic behavior involves alienating himself from people significant to him; in the second context, this change of personal outlook may mean fuller incorporation in groups meaningful to him. In the first situation, modification of his ethnic views requires him to take the path of greatest resistance whereas in the second, it may mean the path of least resistance. From all this, we may surmise that any social policy aimed at changing the behavior and perhaps the attitudes of the all-weather illiberal will have to take into account the cultural and social structure of the area in which he lives. . . .

IMPLICATIONS OF THE TYPOLOGY FOR SOCIAL POLICY

... In approaching problems of policy, two things are plain. First, these should be considered from the standpoint of the militant ethnic liberal, for he alone is sufficiently motivated to engage in positive action for the reduction of ethnic discrimination. And second, the fair-weather liberal, the fair-weather illiberal and the all-weather illiberal represent types differing sufficiently to require diverse kinds of treatment.

Treatment of the Fair-Weather Liberal

The fair-weather liberal, it will be remembered, discriminates only when it appears expedient to do so, and experiences some measure of guilt for deviating from his own belief in the American creed. He suffers from this conflict between conscience and conduct. Accordingly, he is a relatively easy target for the all-weather liberal. He represents the strategic group promising the largest immediate returns for the least effort. Recognition of this type defines the first task for the militant liberal who would enter into a collective effort to make the creed a viable and effective set of social norms rather than a ceremonial myth. . . .

Since the fair-weather liberal discriminates only when it seems rewarding to do so, the crucial need is so to change social situations that there are few occasions in which discrimination proves rewarding and many in which it does not. This would suggest that ethnic liberals self-consciously and deliberately seek to draw into the social groups where they constitute a comfortable majority a number of the "expedient discriminators." This would serve to counteract the dangers of self-selection through which liberals come to associate primarily with like-minded individuals. It would, further, provide an interpersonal and social environment for the fair-weather liberal in which he would find substantial social and psychological gains from abiding by his own beliefs, gains which would more than offset the rewards attendant upon occasional discrimination. It appears that men do not long persist in behavior which lacks social corroboration.

We have much to learn about the role of numbers and proportions in determining the behavior of members of a group. But it seems that individuals generally act differently when they are numbered among a minority rather than the majority. This is not to say that minorities abdicate their practices in the face of a contrary-acting majority, but only that the same people are subjected to different strains and pressures according to whether they are included in the majority or the minority. And the fair-weather liberal who finds himself associated with militant ethnic liberals may be expected to forgo his occasional deviations into discrimination; he may move from category II into category I. . . .

Treatment of the Fair-Weather Illiberal

Because his *beliefs* correspond to those of the full-fledged liberal, the fair-weather liberal can rather readily be drawn into an interpersonal environment constituted by those of a comparable turn of mind. This would be more difficult for the fair-weather illiberal, whose beliefs are so fully at odds with those of ethnic liberals that he may, at first, only be alienated by association with them. If the initial tactic for the fair-weather liberal, therefore, is a change in interpersonal environment, the seemingly most appropriate tactic for the fair-weather illiberal is a change in the institutional and legal environment. It is, indeed, probably this type which liberals implicitly have in mind when they expect significant changes in behavior to result from the introduction of controls on ethnic discrimination into the legal machinery of our society.

For this type—and it is a major limitation for planning policies of control that we do not know his numbers or his distribution in the country—it would seem that the most effective tactic is the institution of legal controls administered with strict efficiency. This would presumably reduce the amount of *discrimination* practiced by the fair-weather illiberal, though it might *initially* enhance rather than reduce his *prejudices*. . . .

A second prevalent tactic for modifying the prejudice of the fair-weather illiberal is that of seeking to draw him into interethnic groups explicitly formed for the promotion of tolerance. This, too, seems largely ineffectual, since the deeply prejudiced individual will not enter into such groups of his own volition. As a consequence of this process of self-selection, these tolerance groups soon come to be comprised by the very ethnic liberals who initiated the enterprise.

This barrier of self-selection can be partially hurdled only if the ethnic illiberals are brought into continued association with militant liberals in groups devoted to significant common values, quite remote from objectives of ethnic equity as such. Thus, as our Columbia-Lavanburg researches have found, many fair-weather illiberals *will* live in interracial housing projects in order to enjoy the rewards of superior housing at a given rental. And some of the illiberals thus brought into personal contact with various ethnic groups under the auspices of prestigeful militant liberals come to modify their prejudices. It is, apparently, only through interethnic collaboration, initially enforced by pressures of the situation, for immediate and significant objectives (other than tolerance) that the self-insulation of the fair-weather illiberal from rewarding interethnic contacts can be removed.

But however difficult it may presently be to affect the *prejudicial sentiments* of the fair-weather illiberal, his *discriminatory practices* can be lessened by the uniform, prompt and prestigeful use of legal and institutional sanctions. The critical problem is to ascertain the proportions of fair-weather and all-weather illiberals in a given local population in order to have some clue to the probable effectiveness or ineffectiveness of anti-discrimination legislation.

Treatment of the All-Weather Illiberal

It is, of course, the hitherto confirmed illiberal, persistently translating his prejudices into active discrimination, who represents the most difficult problem. But though he requires longer and more careful treatment, it is possible that he is not beyond change. In every instance, his social surroundings must be assiduously taken into account. It makes a peculiarly large difference whether he is in a cultural region of bigotry or in a predominantly "liberal" area, given over to verbal adherence to the American creed, at the very least. As this cultural climate varies, so must the prescription for his cure and the prognosis for a relatively quick or long delayed recovery.

In an unfavorable cultural climate—and this does not necessarily exclude the benign regions of the Far South—the immediate resort will probably have to be that of working through legal and administrative federal controls over extreme discrimination, with full recognition that, in all probability, these regulations will be systematically evaded for some time to come. In such cultural regions, we may expect nullification of the law as the common practice, perhaps as common as was the case in the nation at large with respect to the Eighteenth Amendment, often with the connivance of local officers of the law. The large gap between the new law and local mores will not *at once* produce significant change of prevailing practices; token punishments of violations will probably be more common than effective control. At best, one may assume that significant change will be fitful, and excruciatingly slow. But secular changes in the economy may in due course lend support to the new legal framework of control over discrimination. As the economic shoe pinches because the illiberals do not fully mobilize the resources of industrial manpower nor extend their local markets through equitable wage-payments, they may slowly abandon some discriminatory practices as they come to find that these do not always pay—even the discriminator. So far as discrimination is concerned, organized counteraction is possible and some small results may be expected. But it would seem that wishes father thoughts, when one expects basic changes in the immediate future in these regions of institutionalized discrimination.

The situation is somewhat different with regard to the scattered, rather than aggregated, ethnic illiberals found here and there throughout the country. Here the mores and a social organization oriented toward the American creed still have some measure of prestige and the resources of a majority of liberals can be mobilized to isolate the illiberal. In these surroundings, it is possible to move the all-weather illiberal toward Type III—he can be brought to conform with institutional regulations, even though he does not surrender his prejudices. And once he has entered upon this role of the dissident but conforming individual, the remedial program designed for the fair-weather illiberal would be in order.

PART 2 QUESTIONS

1. Can one scientifically prove the existence of race?

2. How is race a social construction?

3. What causes racism?

4. Why would an unprejudiced person discriminate based on race?

Part 3

Sexualization, Gender and Culture

INTRODUCTION

During the period of American slavery, nuance of oppression manifested itself in sexual impositions that turned some slave women into mistresses of their owners, forced others into prostitution, and made some mistresses of white men, while children born out of such forced unions were caught in the hypocritical web of race, slavery, and dehumanization of Black people. Sexual objectification of Black women during slavery set the tone through the centuries into the present, during which time the real targets and embodiment of racial oppression and animus have been, first, Black women and, second, their children. However, the most visible and maligned people have been Black men. Internalization of racism and sexism, emasculation and stereotypes of Black male sexuality within a phallocentric context, and pressure on African American families—a centuries-old siege—have to be contended with in contemporary society because popular culture, to a great extent, feeds on residual stereotypical expressions of Black sexuality.

In "Sex and Racism" Mary Frances Berry and John W. Blassingame trace and examine the intertwined character of sex and racism in the American experience of Black people over the centuries. They analyze the depth of sexual exploitation of Black women and the victimization of Black men arriving at an underlying psychosexual relationship across racial lines and within racial boundaries that is hinged on myths, stereotypes, prejudice and racism, and internalized racism and sexism. They bring interracial relationships and marriages to the fore and argue that despite progress, "sexual myths and fear and oppression continue to be barriers to a democratic society in America."[1]

Bernice Johnson Reagon argues in "African Diaspora Women: The Making of Cultural Workers" that Black culture taught and sensitized her to communicating and bringing people together in that she has spent her life in "gatherings, seeing people who were masters of gathering" people to do cultural work. She affirms that women traditionally in Africa and in the African Diaspora have been central to continuance of these practices and, therefore, are heads of their communities, "keepers of the tradition". She points to cultural work being done in Sao Paulo in Brazil, New York and South Carolina in the United States, and in Jamaica as examples that are indicative of non-sexist leadership roles of women in African-derived communities in which "mothering/nurturing is a vital force and process in establishing relationships". She concludes that by linking intellectual, academic and cultural work and seeing them as one and the same, a choice could be made to mother and nurture, thus, transform space and opportunity to do cultural work.

---

[1] Mary Frances Berry and John Blassingame, "Sex and Racism," in *Long Memory: The Black Experience in America* (Oxford: Oxford University Press, 1982). 140.

In "The Hip Hop Generation: African American Male–Female Relationships in a Nightclub Setting," Janis Faye Hutchinson studies the subculture of the hip-hop generation to discern the nature of male-female relationships in the space where African Americans who participate in hip-hop culture conglomerate and socialize. She focuses on perceptions of female–male relationships from the viewpoint of African American women. Given stereotypical ideas projected on young-adult African American women in low-income urban environments and sexist and misogynistic trends exhibited in "gansta-rap" and performance, Hutchinson's analysis of male-female relationships gives an insight into the reality of young poor Black women.[2]

[2] **Janis Faye Hutchinson, "The Hip Hop Generation: African American Male–Female Relationships in a Nightclub Setting," *Journal of Black Studies* 30, No. 1 (September, 1999): 84.**

Sex and Racism

Mary Frances Berry
John W. Blassingame

Throughout American history, one important indicator of the unequal status of blacks was the taboo against interracial sexual contact and the legal prohibition of interracial marriage. The sexual fear and curiosity about blacks that white males exhibited reflected their desire to subordinate and exploit blacks and was in itself a significant barrier to black progress in America. Some white men seemed to fear that if a black earned a living wage, received a better education, or moved into a white neighborhood, he would then succeed in obtaining a white wife. The white man's fear was as persistent as it was unfounded, for it was fueled by myths instead of by reality.

One expression of sexual fears, the penis envy of whites, for example, is revealed clearly in the treatment of blacks in pornographic literature. When two psychologists, Eberhard and Phyllis Kornhauser, studied this literature, they found in scenes describing sexual relations between black males and white females that the males always had a massive penis and were lovers *par excellence*. The books they examined illustrated the popular belief of whites that blacks "are extraordinarily virile, sensuous, and given to all kinds of perversions." Believing that black males had more physical prowess, fewer inhibitions, inexhaustible sexual appetites, and uncontrollable passions, many white males naturally were afraid to compete with them for sexual favors. In life and literature, it might be said without much exaggeration that the black male was America's phallic symbol.

SEXUAL ATTITUDES TOWARD WOMEN

Until the last decades of the twentieth century white men, often suffering from puritanical and psychological inhibitions and taught that sex was somehow sinful and unnatural, put up many barriers to interracial sexual contacts. Yet, blacks fascinated them. Many of the white man's sexual fantasies, dreams, and desires that he considered sinful were projected onto blacks. The fantasies appeared most clearly in the myths about black women. The image of the black woman was that she was the most sensuous, exotic, mysterious, and voluptuous female in the world—the embodiment of passion. In the traditional sexual and racial mythology of the United States, the white woman was just the opposite. By creating a mythological black Venus and a white Virgin Mary, the white man dehumanized both. In myth, considered frail, cold, and concerned only with the ennobling aspects of life, the white woman was not expected to show passion or erotic interests. In effect, as the sociologist John Dollard observed in *Caste and Class in a Southern Town* in 1949, "the idealization of the white woman . . . especially in the South . . . made her sexually untouchable." But not the black woman. Obviously, if the black Venus was as passionate as the white man's image of her suggested, then she had to be exploited for the sexual pleasure of the white man. Similarly, if the black male was the Apollo white men said that he was, white women might be seduced by him. To prevent this from happening the middle- and upper-class white man cloistered his women, sheltering them from contact with black men. Contrary to the evidence and his own fears, he argued that the white woman was too angelic, too concerned with preserving the purity of the superior race, to have sexual relations with black men. And just to be on the safe side, he passed laws banning interracial marriage.

Tragically, blacks were victimized in many ways by the white man's centuries-old mythology. Given the belief in the ungovernable passion of blacks, the rape of a black woman by a white man was a legal *non sequitur*. She stood defenseless before the bar of justice because it was always assumed that she had been the seducer. The South Carolina demagogue Senator Cole Blease once declared that there was a "serious doubt as to whether the crime of rape can be committed upon a negro." That such beliefs were still prevalent in the United States in the 1970s was indicated by the case of Joanne Little. When Ms. Little killed a white policeman who was allegedly raping her in 1975, the state of North Carolina tried her for murder—in spite of the fact that the man was naked, had obviously used a weapon to force her to submit, and had dried semen on his leg. Reflecting on similar cases in *Crisis* magazine in 1913, W. E. B. Du Bois pointed to the operation of myths and laws that left black women "absolutely helpless before the lust of white men." The legal system had created a population of black women "the ownership of whose bodies no one is bound to respect."

INTERRACIAL MARRIAGE BANS

Although leaving all avenues open to his exploitation of black women, the white man consistently tried to ban interracial marriage. Because prohibitions against interracial sex were so important to whites, they generally represented an almost impassable barrier to the equal treatment of blacks. The Swedish scholar Gunnar Myrdal pointed out in his classic, *The American Dilemma* (1944), that American whites were most fearful of sexual contacts with blacks and felt that desire for interracial sex was what lay behind all black demands for equality. Blacks, on the other hand, had the least desire for interracial sexual contacts. White males were rarely able to separate sexual from other kinds of equality. For them, forbidding contacts between black men and white women while making black women freely available to them was another expression of the unequal condition of blacks in the society. It was still possible in the last quarter of the twentieth century to stop practically any discussion of black rights with the query, "Would you want your daughter to marry one?" The relationship between this and other forms of oppression was stated succinctly by race-baiting William Pickett in 1909: "Forbidden matrimonial equality . . . [the Negro] cannot obtain social privileges. Denied social equality, his political status becomes that of an inferior. Refused political equality, his progress in business is hampered, his education retarded, and his industrial subordination assured." The 1910 Oklahoma law banning interracial marriage was consciously designed to promote the kind of subordination that Pickett supported. Oklahoma whites, desiring to obtain Indian lands, banned not only black-white marriages but black-Indian unions as well. In this regard, one of the primary reasons for twentieth-century opposition to integrated schools was the white man's fears of fostering interracial sex contact. In Louisiana, for example, there were proposals in 1969 to segregate the schools by sex if they were racially integrated.

PRE-CIVIL WAR INTERRACIAL SEXUAL CONTACTS

Despite the existence of legal bans, there was a great deal of interracial sex contact. Miscegenation was, during the antebellum period, part of the "southern way of life." Although there was considerable sexual exploitation of black women by white males in the South, it is impossible to determine precisely how extensive it was. Statistics on the question are unbelievably treacherous. Many categories of literary sources, on the other hand, are very suggestive. Southerners, black and white, commented on the pervasiveness of miscegenation.

When asked whether the planters in South Carolina had sexual intercourse with their slave women, ex-slave Harry McMillan declared in 1863: "There was a good deal of it. They often kept one girl steady and sometimes two on different places; men who had wives did it too sometimes, if they could get it on their own place it was easier but they would go wherever they could get it." Frederick Douglass echoed McMillan's claim and asserted that the planter, "in cases not a few, sustains to his slaves the double relation of master and father." After living thirty-two years in North Carolina, Hiram. White wrote, "Amalgamation was common. There was scarce a family of slaves that had females of mature age where there were not some mulatto children."

The sexual exploitation of black women began in African slave castles when the European soldiers and slave traders raped captured African women. European and American sailors and traders continued the practice during the Middle Passage. Zephaniah Kingsley, a wealthy Florida planter and slave trader, is a good example of the transfer of racial mixing from Africa to America. When Kingsley came to Florida in 1803 he brought his wife Anna Jai, the daughter of an African prince, with him. One of the South's most famous polygamous miscegenators, Kingsley chose other mistresses from among his slaves during the next twenty years and had several children by them.

The scarcity of white women in most of the early European colonies in the New World guaranteed miscegenation a prominent role in the new societies. Eleven years after the first blacks landed at Jamestown, one Hugh Davis was accused of "defiling his body in lying with a negro," and in 1640 Robert Sweet had to do penance "for getting a negro woman with child."

The slave woman was at the mercy of her master, his sons, the overseer, and most other white men John Thompson, a slave, reported that his master "was the father of about one-fourth of the slaves on his plantation" and that none of the black women "could escape" the planter's "licentious passion." Another bondsman, William Anderson, claimed that the sexual exploitation of slave women "was carried on to an alarming extent in the far South." An overwhelming majority of these women submitted to white males because of their fear of punishment for refusing. Others did so for material rewards, in hopes of being freed at a later date, or because they loved the white men. Occasionally, slave women became the concubines of white planters and maintained a liaison with them extending over several years. In *The Peculiar Institution* (1956), Kenneth Stampp, quoting from court cases, noted several such relationships: A South Carolinian "lived for many years in a state of illicit intercourse" with a slave woman "who assumed the position of a wife"; another permitted a female slave "to act as the mistress of his house" and control his domestic affairs. A Kentuckian owned a woman who was his concubine and "possessed considerable influence over him." And a Virginian, his colored mistress, and their mulatto children lived "as a family upon terms of equality, and not as a master with his slaves." Most slave women were caught on the horns of a dilemma. If they rejected the advances of the planter, they would be flogged until they submitted. If they submitted and the planter's wife discovered the relationship, the mistress would flog or sometimes try to kill them or their mulatto children.

In southern cities, miscegenation was institutionalized in brothels where black women consorted with white men and in quasi- or common-law marriages in which they were concubines of middle- and upper-class white males. There was so much interracial mixing in New Orleans that weekly dances were held at which white men met the nearly white quadroons. Even that staunch defender of slavery, Gov. James H. Hammond of South Carolina, felt that interracial mixing was "perpetrated for the most part in cities." A northern white visiting Mobile in 1850 found "few southern boys who would not sleep with Negresses." Writing from New Orleans, a Virginia white drew a similar conclusion: "The fair skin and the Quadroon here intermingle promiscuously." Sometimes the white man deserted his black concubine when he married a white woman; on other occasions he maintained two families. Practically all classes of white males made such alliances. One result of this practice was that almost 50 percent of the antebellum nonwhite population in such cities as New Orleans, Baltimore, and St. Louis consisted of mulattoes. Even if some of the mulattoes were children of mulatto parents, interracial contacts were a part of their lineage. Another consequence was the humiliation of white women, who knew they had been rejected as sexual partners by white males. This was certainly the case of the white women in New Orleans, who often complained that their husbands "deposited" them at white socials and then rushed to attend quadroon balls.

WHITE WOMEN AND BLACK MEN

White women bitterly resented the white man's philandering and some of them chose black lovers. A Virginia white woman symbolized their defiance in 1815 when she admitted that she had given birth to a mulatto and asserted that "she had not been the first nor would she be the last guilty of such conduct, and that she saw no more harm in a white woman's having been the mother of a black child than in a white man's having one, though the latter was more frequent." Although the white woman's role in miscegenation has been repeatedly denied by southern romantics, the number of mixed couples listed in the manuscript census returns, public records of white women giving birth to mulatto children, court cases, and the research of such scholars as Letitia Brown, Richard Wade, and James Hugo Johnston refute such denials. And, however extravagant some of his claims, Joel A. Rogers unearthed an impressive amount of evidence on the white woman's role in miscegenation.

Though not as numerous as their black counterparts, white concubines of black men were not unknown in the South. One Louisiana free black, described by a white contemporary as a handsome man with "a body of Hercules and with eyes as black as the moonless nights of Africa," had two white concubines simultaneously in Lafayette Parish. He had nineteen children by them. The daughters of planters were sometimes the lovers of the black men they had associated with since childhood. For instance, a Kentucky minister, John Rankin, wrote in 1837 that he knew of several cases of slaves "actually seducing the daughters of their masters. Such seductions sometimes happened in the most respectable families." Several white men divorced their wives when they had mulatto children, ran off with, or publicly consorted with black men. Many indiscretions of white women went undetected until they became pregnant. But in innumerable cases (and especially when the father was a mulatto), the children of black men and white women were light-skinned enough to be accepted as white.

Sexual contacts between black men and white women were most visible in southern cities. For example, between October 15 and November 13, 1859, the police in Mobile, Alabama, arrested five white women on charge's of "amalgamation." In one of the cases a policeman discovered two black males and two white females in a bedroom with "only one garment on apiece." The police caught another white woman "laying on the same bed with a well known negro driver of a baggage wagon." Journals reported similar incidents in Richmond, Memphis, Charleston, Nashville, and New Orleans. Morris Helpler found in his investigation of crime in New Orleans that "each year during the 1850s police arrested several white women for taking up with slave men."

In addition to the casual sexual contacts between black men and white women, there were many long-term unions. David Dodge, a white native of North Carolina, recalled in 1866 that in his state "hardly a neighborhood was free from low white women who married or cohabited with free negroes." The U.S. census for Nansemond County, Virginia, in 1830 included eight white women listed as the "wives" of free blacks.

Few blacks lived in the antebellum North; consequently, there was less miscegenation there than in the South. However, considerable sexual contact between the races in northern cities did take place. In Philadelphia, Thomas Branagan wrote in 1805, "I solemnly declare, I have seen more white women married to, and deluded through the arts of seduction by negroes in one year in Philadelphia than for the eight years I was visiting [in the West Indies and in the South]. . . . There are perhaps hundreds of white women thus fascinated by black men in this city, and there are thousands of black children by them at present."

In 1821 a group of whites from Greene County, Pennsylvania, agreed with Branagan, for they declared that many of the blacks settling in the state had "been able to seduce into marriage the minor children of white inhabitants." Similarly, in 1857 a committee of the New York State legislature found, upon visiting one tenement house in New York City, that "in answer to inquiries, and in fact by ocular demonstration, it was ascertained that nearly all the inhabitants were practical amalgamationists—black husbands and white (generally Irish) wives making up the heads of constantly increasing families." The same patterns prevailed in New England. Rhode Island's colonial historian, William Weeden, asserted that "illicit intercourse between white men and colored women in Rhode Island marked a numerous progeny." The high percentage of mulattoes in the black population of northern cities confirmed the impressionistic data. Prostitution houses which had both an integrated staff and clientele, the exploitation of black women by slaveholders, the intermingling of indentured servants and slaves, and the keeping of black mistresses by upper-class white males accounted for a large number of these mulattoes.

MISCEGENATION AFTER THE CIVIL WAR

Many historians contend that miscegenation decreased in the South after the Civil War. All indications are that it simply changed in character. First, many white men who had had black concubines before the war married them in those states that abolished bans against intermarriage. Second, because of the breakdown of customary antebellum societal restraints and the dislocation attendant to war, the number of white women who had sexual intercourse with black men increased. Slave patrols disappeared with the end of the war, and when blacks joined southern law enforcement agencies the police were less effective in preventing miscegenation. As a result of the civil rights acts of 1866 and 1875, the poverty of white women, the refusal of many Reconstruction governments to ban interracial marriage, and the loss of many white males in the war, white southerners saw an increase in "promiscuous mixing." Black soldiers, as the members of victorious armies have always done, found love and sexual gratification in the arms of the women of the vanquished. For instance, the Freedmen's Bureau noted in 1866 that there were six white women married to black soldiers in Jacksonville, Florida.

Whatever the reasons, miscegenation continued in the South after 1865. Even after Reconstruction ended and many states and municipalities enacted antimiscegenation laws, interracial sexual intimacy was still prevalent in the South. For example, historian Howard Rabinowitz, in *Race Relations in the Urban South*, 1865–1890 (1978), observed, "In Nashville during the 1880s the annual number of arrests for interracial cohabitation never dropped below thirteen couples. One year it reached a total of fifty-seven individuals, some charged with more than one offense. . . . Couples brought to trial ranged from those who were married or in love to those who had a single sexual liaison." Contemporary observers often noted the continuation of interracial sexual contact after the Civil War. In 1887 the editor of the Montgomery *Herald* asked, "Why is it that white women attract Negro men now more than in former days? There was a time when such a thing was unheard of. There is a secret to this thing, and we greatly suspect it is the growing appreciation of white Juliets for colored Romeos." The editor was run out of town, but he had touched an essential truth. Speaking on January 31, 1887, a black minister in Baltimore, P. H. A. Braxton, observed, "In sight of the capitol at Richmond, white men, and not a few, cohabit with colored women daily; they build fine houses for them, and stay with them, and get children by them. It is said that there are hundreds of colored women in Richmond, saying nothing of the other part of the state, who are kept and supported by white men for their lascivious purposes. . . . Go where you may in this country, and especially in the South, and you will find that two-thirds of the so-called Negroes are Negroes only in name; many of them are as white as the children of their father by his white wife."

Frederick Hoffman, a prominent statistician, declared in 1896, "It is my firm conviction that unlawful intercourse between the sexes is excessively prevalent at the present time in the large cities as well as in the rural sections of the country." In 1910 John James Holm, an Alabama anthropologist, asserted that 25 percent of the white males of the South had sexual intercourse with black women. There were numerous interracial couples in Florida, Louisiana, and most southern cities during this period. All of the statistical indices support the observations of Holm and Hoffman. There was, for instance, a phenomenal increase in the number of mulattoes in the South after the Civil War. While the number of blacks increased by 129 percent between 1850 and 1920, the number of mulattoes increased by 498 percent.

THE ATTACK ON RACE MIXING

Reflecting on the evil of the "promiscuous mixing" that occurred during Reconstruction, the white South developed a monolithic assault on miscegenation. It began as part of the campaign to wrest control of the political structure from blacks, but the ideology did not emerge in its final form until the 1880s. First, the whites convinced themselves that interracial sex was unnatural, that whites had an "instinctive repugnance" to mating with blacks. Writing in *Century Magazine* in 1885, T. U. Dudley, Protestant Episcopal bishop of Kentucky, said, "Instinct and reason, history and philosophy, science and revelation, all alike cry out against the degradation of the race by the free commingling of the tribe which is highest with that which is lowest in the scale of development." Drawing on the concepts of Social Darwinism, whites expressed great fear that miscegenation would lead to an irrevocable degradation of the superior white race. There were those who disagreed, of course, but generally most whites believed that blacks were so far down on the scale of humanity that the descendants of white-black unions would be low in intelligence, capacity for self-government, self-control, and morality—as well as weak, short-lived, and sterile. In short, miscegenation threatened to destroy civilization.

This destruction, they contended, had begun during Reconstruction, when all of the "false" rhetoric about equality had undermined the instinctive aversion of whites to blacks and the laws permitting interracial marriage had encouraged black men to rape white women. The trend could be reversed only by rigid separation of the races and the prevention, by any means, of the pollution of white women, in whom rested all hope of preserving racial purity. As one Texas editor screamed in 1897, "If the South is ever to rid herself of the Negro rape-fiend, she must take a day off and kill every member of the accursed race that declines to leave the country." The antimiscegenation rhetoric of white politicians and editors so inflamed the popular imagination that the anti-intermarriage laws and subsequent constitutional bans were not considered sufficient to prevent race mixing and especially rape.

The southern white man's sense of manhood and chivalry, so battered by his defeat in the Civil War and by his subjection to "black rule" during Reconstruction, demanded that he avenge the "honor" of white women by resorting to the rope and faggot. One of the major reasons for the lynching campaign was the postwar increase in voluntary sexual contact between black men and white women (who often claimed that they had been raped when the liaisons were discovered). The number of lynchings was also closely correlated with the disfranchisement of blacks, greater segregation, and the enlarged role of the poor white in southern politics.

The heyday of these trends, the 1890s, also represented the high point in the yearly average of lynchings for rape-related "crimes." Between 1882 and 1936, allegations of rape accounted for the lynching of 1,093 blacks and 97 whites. Of the 3,383 blacks lynched during this period, 32.3 percent were accused of raping white women.

By the 1890s, copulation between a black man and a white woman had become synonymous with rape in the white mind. But the antimiscegenation proponents were frustrated time and time again when white women who had mulatto children refused to identify their "rapist." The frustration was revealed clearly in a story appearing in the Memphis *Ledger* on June 8, 1892:

> If Lillie Bailey, a rather pretty white girl seventeen years of age who is now at the City Hospital would be somewhat less reserved about her disgrace there would be some very nauseating details in the story of her life. She is the mother of a little coon. The truth might reveal fearful depravity or it might reveal the evidence of a rank outrage. She will not divulge the name of the man who has left such black evidence of her disgrace, and, in fact, says it is a matter in which there can be no interest to the outside world. . . . She is a country girl. She came to Memphis from her father's farm, a short distance from Hernando, Miss. . . . When the child was born an attempt was made to get the girl to reveal the name of the Negro who had disgraced her, she obstinately refused and it was impossible to elicit any information from her on the subject.

The fact that most interracial sexual contact was voluntary and not a proper subject for control through the lynching bee eventually became evident to thoughtful observers. In examining the southern rape complex in 1941, Wilbur J. Cash concluded the obvious when he asserted in *The Mind of the South* that the chance of a white woman being raped by a black man was "much less, for instance, than the chance that she would be struck by lightning." Realizing this, noting the frequent occasions on which white men raped black women with impunity, and angered by the continuation of clandestine sexual relations between white men and black women, southern white women rebelled. Between 1900 and 1932 southern women denied that there was any need to resort to lynching to protect them and publicly deplored the practice. The declaration of the Georgia Women's

Interracial Commission was typical: "We believe no falser appeal can be made to Southern manhood than that mob violence is necessary for the protection of womanhood, or that the brutal practice of lynching and burning of human beings is an expression of chivalry."

In spite of the appeal of white women, white males insisted on preserving their racial purity through violent means. Two twentieth-century cases illustrated so obviously the barbaric insanity of such violence prevalent in white America that they made news throughout the world. In 1951 a black sharecropper in Yanceyville, North Carolina, was convicted and sentenced to prison for the "rape by leer" of a white girl. Although he was seventy-five feet away from the woman, Matt Ingram was convicted of assault because of the way he allegedly looked at her. He obtained his freedom only after two and a half years of court maneuvers. Emmett Till, a fourteen-year-old boy, was kidnapped and killed in Money, Mississippi, in 1955 because he allegedly whistled at a white woman.

The American rape complex was productive of much injustice. Because of the social taboos associated with interracial sex, even the habitual white prostitute could assure a black man of death or imprisonment by shouting that vile four-letter word. The fact that two promiscuous Alabama white girls who consented to have sexual relations with nine black boys in Scottsboro, Alabama, in 1931 could cause a long incarceration for them was simply one famous case that proved the point.

In his reaction to reports of interracial sex contacts, the white man sometimes transformed himself into a primitive savage. When a black man was accused of raping a white woman in the second half of the nineteenth century and early part of the twentieth, southern whites usually castrated him, lynched him, riddled his body with bullets, and then burned it. In fact, any crime involving interracial sex seemed to plunge the white man into the very depths of antediluvian barbarism. The 1934 case of Claude Neal, a black man arrested in Marianna, Florida, for the murder of his white mistress, is an example. After an enraged mob kidnapped him from an Alabama jail (whore he had been placed for his "safety"), they traveled toward the Florida state line as fifteen southern newspapers announced the date of the coming lynching and the route and progress of the mob. The white men tortured Neal for twelve hours. They hung him until he was almost dead, forced him to eat his own penis, burned him with red-hot irons, slashed his side and stomach, and cut off his fingers and toes before they murdered him and hung his body in the Marianna courthouse square.

The number of such lynchings decreased dramatically after 1940 as American whites depended more and more on the police to harass, beat and imprison black men caught dating or having sexual relations with white women. Closely related to this was another development: judicial lynching for alleged rape. A black lawyer, Haywood Burn, described this process perfectly in 1970:

> White America still reserves special penalties for blacks convicted of sex crimes—especially interracial sex crimes. National Prison Statistics show that of the 19 jurisdictions that have executed men for rape since 1930, almost one-third of them—six states—have executed *only* blacks. There have been some years in which everyone who was executed for rape in this country was

> black. Detailed state-by-state analysis has shown that the discrepancy in death sentences for rape is related to the race of the victim. . . . For example, in Florida between 1960 and 1964, of the 125 white males who raped white females, six—or about 5 percent—received death sentences. Of the 68 black males in the same period who were convicted in Florida of raping black females, three—or about 4 percent—received death sentences; and this when in two cases the victims were children. However, of the 84 blacks convicted of raping white women, 45—or 54 percent—received the death sentence. *None* of the eight white men who raped black women were sentenced to death.

The injustice revealed in the statistics is compounded by studies of criminologists suggesting that in more than 80 percent of all allegations of rape, the woman lies. Yet until the 1970s scores of black men were executed every year for allegedly raping white women. Obviously, as the imposition of the death penalty shows, rape was, for all practical purposes, a "Negro crime." Of the 455 men executed for rape between 1930 and 1969 in the United States, 405 or 89 percent were black.

DEFINING THE RACES

Throughout American history the great problem faced by the foes of miscegenation was to define who was black and who was white. By the first decades of the nineteenth century it had become virtually impossible in many instances to designate southerners by race. Fugitive slaves, for example, were frequently described as having "straight hair and complexion so nearly while that a stranger would suppose there was no negro blood in him," or as having "light sandy hair, blue eyes, ruddy complexion; he is so nearly white as to easily pass for a white man." So many mulattoes succeeded in concealing their black ancestors and intermarrying with "pure whites" that many southerners found themselves in the position of the Virginia woman who declared in 1831 that she "did not know whether she was entirely white or not."

Southern racial patterns were so complicated that they sometimes defied description. The racial admixture that designated a person "Negro" varied from place to place. Often a combination of wealth and light skin color was enough for a mulatto to be defined legally as "white." As a South Carolina jurist ruled in 1835, "The condition [of mixed ancestry] . . . is not to be determined solely by . . . visible mixture . . . but by reputation . . . and it may be . . . proper, that a man of worth . . . should have the rank of a white man, while a vagabond of the same degree of blood should be confined to the inferior caste." Such judicial and social attitudes enabled many descendants of blacks to be absorbed by whites. One of the clearest cases of this occurred in Sumter County, South Carolina. In 1790, a group of mulattoes successfully petitioned the legislature to be relieved from acts discriminating against blacks. By the 1860s they were accepted as whites, and many of them fought as "white men" in the rebel army.

The legal definitions of race that evolved in the United States were nothing short of bizarre; for foreigners they were incomprehensible. But if law is to ban interracial marriage, then it has to define race. In 1967, a person was considered black in Alabama, Arkansas, Georgia, Oklahoma, and Texas if he had in his "veins any negro blood whatever" or any black ancestors. One-third "negro-blood" made one black in Maryland, North Carolina, and Tennessee; one-fourth in Florida; one-eighth in Mississippi and Missouri. Georgia and South Carolina complicated matters further. In the nineteenth century they defined anyone with "one-eighth negro blood" as black; in the twentieth century they changed the definition to "any ascertainable trace" of black ancestors. Between 1919 and 1930, the Virginia legislature annually considered, passed, amended, and repealed several acts defining a black person. In applying for school admission in some states "one drop of Negro blood" made one a black, while in applying for a marriage license seven-eighths "white blood" made one "white."

In the final analysis, visibility and reputation appeared to be the most important factors in determining racial identity. Both methods were fallible. Some blacks were not only legally white in several southern states, they appeared so to any observer. This was certainly the case with the families of Walter White, the Hunts, Westmorelands, and Millers. Poppy Cannon, a rather dark brunette white woman from South Africa, indicated how bewildering the whole phenomenon was when she and her black husband, Walter White, went to India in 1949:

> We were guests of the Calcutta Association for the United Nations, a meeting hurriedly arranged. The president of the Association turned to me. "I have read in the journals," he said, "that you are white." He pointed to his snow-white cuff. "And your husband," pointing now to his coat sleeve, "is black."
>
> Both of us looked across the table at Walter. "Obviously," I answered. And the whole table, up to the moment formal and solemn, broke into a roar of laughter. "These mad Americans."

The southerner's preoccupation with racial definitions indicated his well-founded paranoia about "passing." The incredible geographical mobility of the American people defeated all attempts to prevent passing. In the 1890s, for example, W. E. B. DuBois found several "white" families in Philadelphia who were descendants of mulattoes: "Between 1820 and 1860 many natural children were sent from the South and in a few cases their parents followed and were legally married here. Descendants of such children in many cases forsook the mother's [black] race; one became principal of a city school, one a prominent sister in a Catholic church, one a bishop, and one or two officers in the Confederate Army." In Louisiana and other southern states, mulatto women and their white lovers often bribed officials to register their newborn children as white; baptismal records of mulattoes were regularly destroyed. They were mutilated so often in New Orleans that one observer thought the baptismal books looked as though a rat had eaten his way through them with a pair of shears. Even without the records in such places, Ohio State University sociologist Robert Struckert estimated in a 1958 article in the *Ohio Journal of Science* that one out of every five American whites had some Afro-American ancestors. It is no wonder, then, that twentieth-century America added a new genre to the world's literature, "the passing novel and autobiography." James Weldon Johnson began it in 1912 when he published the *Autobiography of an Ex-Coloured Man*, Sinclair Lewis explored a similar phenomenon in *Kingsblood Royal* (1947) and Reba Lee wrote *I Passed for White* in 1955.

OPPOSING INTERRACIAL MARRIAGE

Unable as they were to determine with any precision who was "white" and who was "black." American whites nevertheless consistently opposed racial intermarriage. Prohibition laws began appearing in the colonial period: Virginia and Maryland, 1662; Massachusetts, 1705; North Carolina, 1715; Delaware, 1721; and Pennsylvania, 1725. Most of these laws were reenacted after the American Revolution. During the nineteenth century thirty-eight states banned interracial marriage, though seven repealed such laws: Pennsylvania, 1780; Massachusetts, 1843; Rhode Island, 1881; Maine and Michigan, 1883, New Mexico, 1886, and Ohio, 1887. Most of the laws fined the minister performing the ceremony (sometimes as much as $10,000), imprisoned the black involved (for up to twenty years), and fined or imprisoned the white partner in the union. According to the colonial Pennsylvania law, a free black marrying a white person was to be sold into slavery for life. In several southern colonies the mulatto children of a white woman were taken away from her and indentured for between eighteen and thirty years, and the woman herself was bound to service for seven years.

Generally, antebellum whites expressed their opposition to mixed marriage by resorting to violence whenever such unions occurred. When whites found that a black man had married a white girl in Indianapolis in 1840, a mob gathered at the house where they were spending their wedding night, dragged them outside, rode the bride on a rail, and chased the groom out of town (the couple was eventually reunited in Cincinnati). A similar case occurred in New York in 1853 when William G. Allen, a black professor at the integrated New York Central College, proposed to one of his white students, Mary King. On January 30, the couple met at the house of friends in Mary's hometown, Phillipsville. Mary's white townsmen, on hearing about the intended match, decided then and there to prevent such a "foul connection." A mob gathered in front of the house, forced Mary to return to her home, and threatened to kill Allen if he did not leave the village. Mary was placed under virtual house arrest, and some of the townsmen and her enraged relatives pursued Allen to Syracuse. He soon found refuge with friends in Pennsylvania. In March, Allen wrote to Mary renewing his proposal and asking if she would go to England with him. Mary answered, "Yes; gladly and joyfully will I hasten with you to a land where unmolested, we can be happy in the consciousness of the love which we cherish for each other." Through subterfuge Mary escaped from her family and married William Allen in New York City on March 30, 1853. The Liberty Party of New York, Harriet Beecher Stowe, Gerrit Smith, Frederick Douglass, and Sarah D. Porter expressed their indignation over the mob attack and their approval of the marriage. On April 9, the Allen sailed to England, where they were received cordially by such abolitionists as Joseph Sturge and George Thompson.

ABOLITION SUPPORT FOR INTERRACIAL MARRIAGE

Although most abolitionists opposed intermarriage, a few of them spoke out against the marriage restriction. One of them, the editor of Indiana's *Free Labor Advocate*, wrote in 1842, "Such legislation is not only pitiably contemptible, but it is wicked and tyrannical; tending directly to increase that abominable prejudice which is crushing to earth the free people of color in the professedly free states." The most successful attack on a law banning intermarriage was led by William Lloyd Garrison in Massachusetts. Garrison contended in January, 1831, that a 1786 Massachusetts law banning interracial marriage was "an invasion of one of the inalienable rights of man, namely, 'the pursuit of happiness'—disgraceful to the state—inconsistent with every principle of justice—and utterly absurd and preposterous." The next month Garrison asked, "Does a man derive or lose his right to choose his wife from his color? Yes, say our sapient legislators. Why, then, let us have a law prohibiting tall people from marrying short ones. Here is a more palpable and unpardonable distinction than the other!" When the opponents charged the abolitionists with being consumed with a passionate desire to marry blacks and declared that repeal of the law would lead to a spate of interracial marriages, Garrison retorted, "The blacks are not so enamored of white skins as some of our editors imagine. The courtship, the wooing, the embrace, the inter-mixture—in nine cases out of ten—will be proposed on the part of the whites, and not of the opposite color."

Though the Massachusetts legislators refused to be prodded into action between 1831 and 1832, they did respond to an avalanche of abolitionists' petitions between 1839 and 1843. The campaign began when white women in Lynn, Rehoboth, and Dorchester petitioned for a repeal of all the state's laws discriminating against blacks. George Bradburn of Nantucket supported the petitions and contended that the 1786 law violated the first article of the Massachusetts Declaration of Human Rights and encouraged "vicious connections between the races," led to licentiousness, and "legalized prostitution of the marriage covenant." In March, 1839, the Massachusetts Anti-Slavery Society gave its support to the movement for repeal. Among the prominent abolitionists who supported the repeal campaign were Edmund Quincy, Caroline Chase, John Greenleaf Whittier, Lydia Maria Child, Maria Weston Chapman, Henry B. Stanton, Charles Francis Adams, Henry Wilson, John A. Collins, Wendell Phillips, James Birney, and William E. Channing. By the spring of 1840 the legislature had received ninety-two different petitions with 8,700 signatures for repeal of the law. Three years later an overwhelming majority of the legislators voted to repeal the anti-intermarriage law.

Some abolitionists were unequivocal in their support of interracial marriage. Theodore Tilton felt that "when a man and woman want to be married it is *their* business, not mine nor anybody else's. . . . So far from denouncing the marriage of blacks and whites, I would be glad if the banns of a hundred thousand such marriages could be published next Sunday." The Virginia-born abolitionist Moncurs D. Conway espoused one of the most extreme positions when he asserted in 1864, "I, for one, am firmly persuaded that the mixture of the blacks and whites is good; that the person so produced is, under ordinarily favourable circumstances, healthy, handsome, and intelligent. Under the best circumstances, I believe that such a combination would evolve a more complete character than the unmitigated Anglo-Saxon. . . . Every race has a genius in some sort, to be unfolded by proper culture; and so long as that of the African, or any other race, however lowly, is excluded, some function will be absent from every brain, some flaw will be in every heart."

Regardless of the well-publicized views of the abolitionists, whites continued to react hysterically whenever an interracial union took place. When Frederick Douglass took as his second wife a white clerk in his office in Washington, D.C., in 1884, there was a storm of protest, and Congress received several petitions to prohibit such marriages. Douglass, who said his father had been white, answered the protesters in characteristic fashion. He allegedly said that when he married his first wife he honored his mother's people, the blacks, and when he married his second wife, he honored his father's.

The black who caused more nightmares for white America than any other was bullet-headed, braggadocious heavyweight boxing champion Jack Johnson. Publicly consorting with white prostitutes, Johnson married five times; four of his wives were white. His first marriage to a white woman in 1911 caused such a sensation that anti-intermarriage bills were introduced in ten of the states which did not at that time have them. Georgia Congressman Seaborn A. Roddenberry proposed a constitutional amendment to ban such unions and said that Johnson's action was "more revolting than white slavery. . . . No brutality, no infamy, no degradation in all the years of southern slavery possessed such villainous character and such atrocious qualities as the provisions of laws . . . which allow the marriage of the negro Jack Johnson to a woman of the caucasian strain." Newspapers throughout the country were whipped into a mad frenzy by Johnson's marriage. Eventually, the U.S. government launched a vendetta against the world champion and convicted him in 1913 of violating the Mann Act, that is, of transporting a woman across state lines for purposes of prostitution. Primarily as a result of Johnson's sexual exploits, twenty-one anti-intermarriage bills were introduced in Congress between 1909 and 1921. Between 1925 and 1930, attempts were made to ban racial intermarriage in eleven states (Connecticut, Illinois, Iowa, Maine, Massachusetts, Michigan, New Jersey, Ohio, Pennsylvania, Rhode Island, and Wisconsin).

FEATURES OF INTERRACIAL MARRIAGES

Statistics on interracial marriages are so difficult to obtain and so frequently contradictory that we can only draw tentative conclusions about the nature and extent of such marriages. Because of legal prohibitions, most of our statistics are for a few places in the North. In Michigan, Rhode Island, and Connecticut, between 1874 and 1893 there were an average of 5.6 black-white marriages annually.

It is obvious that even in states permitting interracial marriage, these unions were rare. Only 27 of them occurred in Philadelphia between 1900 and 1904. The 6 consummated in 1900 represented less than 1 percent of the 633 marriages in the city that year. In Boston from 1914 to 1938 only 276, or 3.9 percent, of all marriages involving blacks were interracial. In Connecticut between 1953 and 1959, there were 285 black-white marriages. Only 11 out of every 1,000 marriages in New York State between 1924 and 1933 were interracial. As for the total number of interracial families in America by the 1960s, the best estimate we have was made by an N.A.A.C.P. lawyer in 1967: 550,000.

Some features of the interracial marriage emerge clearly from an examination of the statistics. First of all, these marriages occurred primarily in cities. For example, 90 percent of the black-white marriages that occurred in Rhode Island from 1881 to 1940 were in Providence. Second, in the North a black male was far more likely to marry a white woman than a black woman a white male. About 70 percent of the interracial marriages in Rhode Island between 1900 and 1916 were between black males and white females. In the 1890s W. E. B. DuBois found that 29 of the 33 blacks married to whites in one ward in Philadelphia were men, or 87 percent. The percentage was even higher in Boston; 210 of the 227 interracial marriages between 1900 and 1907, or 92 percent, were between black males and white females. In southern states that permitted interracial marriage in the nineteenth century, the pattern was just the reverse. For example, there were 255 black-white marriages in New Orleans between 1868 and 1880. In 176, or 78 percent, of these unions the husband was white.

Most whites insisted that only poor whites who were either debased or criminal married or engaged in sexual relations with blacks. As one southern historian, Philip A. Bruce, asserted in 1889, "The few white women who have given birth to mulattoes have always been regarded as monstrosities, and without exception they have belonged to the most impoverished and degraded caste of whites. . . ." Much of the evidence, however, suggests just the opposite.

Many of the white women in these unions were clearly upper class. In 1938, wealthy Mary B. Dawes, a descendant of the man who rode with Paul Revere on his famous ride, married a black. Similarly, in 1951 steel heiress Ann Mather, a descendant of the Puritan divine Cotton Mather, married a black. Studies of the occupations of interracial couples in Boston indicate that the black groom tended to be superior in status to the general black population. In other words, upper-class black males were more likely to choose white brides than were lower-class blacks. While in the nineteenth century the white bride in such marriages was generally lower on the occupational scale than the general white population, the reverse was true by the 1960s. The partners in an interracial marriage after 1960 were generally superior in education and economic status to the general population.

Numerically, black-white marriages were insignificant. In regard to race relations, however, they were very important. At first glance, for instance, the predominance of the black male-white female union between the 1870s and the 1930s seemed to substantiate the white man's fear that all black men were secretly lusting after white females. In actuality, this pattern developed because the number of black males exceeded the number of black females in northern cities in the first part of the twentieth century, while the number of white females often exceeded the number of white males.

THE NATURE OF INTERRACIAL MARRIAGES

Given the violent opposition to such unions, several questions emerge when interracial marriages are considered. Why did whites and blacks intermarry? What was the nature of the interracial family? What pressures did interracial couples face? And finally, what adjustment problems confronted the children of interracial couples, and how did the parents help them to overcome them? When one cuts through the mythology, the reasons for interracial marriages are not difficult to fathom. The myth that the partners in interracial marriages had deep psychological problems must be rejected. In spite of social taboos, love and passion are "color-blind." Some factors which seem to facilitate interracial marriages are mutual interests, shared values, geographical propinquity, physical attraction, curiosity, and desire for forbidden fruit.

Generally, interracial sex contacts occur where there is social and spatial proximity and similarities of culture between different races. Joel A. Rogers, the famous black student of miscegenation, for instance, concluded that "propinquity and personality are more than a match for prejudice." Integrated housing and the anonymity that city life afforded created many opportunities for interracial sexual contacts and the softening of racial antipathies. Another important factor in facilitating interracial marriages is a large foreign-born population. With far less antipathy to blacks than native-born whites, especially Anglo-Saxons, immigrants are much more willing to have sexual relations with and to marry them. This fact is reflected in the relatively high percentage of the foreign-born among white partners in interracial marriages in many cities.

Most scholars also believe that blacks seek out white partners as a way of raising their status and achieving equality. This was especially true, they argue, in the case of the black male. The Martinican psychiatrist Frantz Fanon asserted that the black male in these unions unconsciously says, "I wish to be acknowledged not as *black* but as *white*. Now . . . who but a white woman can do this for me? By loving me she proves that I am worthy of white love. I am loved like a white man. Her love takes me onto the noble road that leads to total realization. . . . I marry white culture, white beauty, white whiteness. When my restless hands caress those white breasts, they grasp white civilization and dignity and make them mine." While there may be an element of truth in Fanon's poetically expressed theory, sociologists and psychologists appear to have exaggerated the black male's desire to obtain status by marrying a white woman. Status seeking seemed to play a lesser role in interracial marriages than in conventional ones. On the other hand, it was a very strong factor in casual interracial sex contacts. In these liaisons, the black male frequently felt that he was enhancing his status by violating one of the strongest taboos of white America.

The most important factor in promoting interracial marriage was not the dream life of the black male. The opportunity for social contact and childhood experiences were the keys. Josephine, the white wife of journalist George Schuyler, gave the following among the reasons for her marriage:

> The fact that he was dark and I fair gave an added fillip to our association This was not surprising for I, as the daughter of a Midwest Texas cattleman and

> banker, had been pleasantly associated with Negroes all my life. As a child, the activities of the Negroes fascinated me. They were always doing something interesting. . . . Goodnaturedly, they let us white children follow them as they went about their work. Thus I had much pleasant association with Negroes from the very beginning. I also knew of such association, in the reverse, among the grown-ups. Early I had found out that the deacon of a local Baptist church, a most respectable man, had had a colored companion for twenty years with everyone aware of the intimacy. I knew, too, that an important family there had numerous colored "cousins" whom they privately acknowledged and visited. I knew, besides, that the same system existed in my own family, with my father drawing no color line in his love life, and that my eldest brother, publicly thought to be childless, had a colored daughter attending school outside the state. So interracial love was not unknown in my environment.

Although there are few statistics on the matter, there is little evidence to support the popular belief that interracial marriages were less stable than other marriages. In fact, when we consider that one in every three marriages in America ended in divorce in the 1970s, the interracial family seemed remarkably stable. The most revealing study of black-white marriages was conducted by Eugene Cash in Philadelphia in the 1950s. Based on questionnaires and intensive interviews of seventeen interracial couples, the study showed that a surprisingly high percentage of the white partners were attracted to their black spouses (76 percent of whom were males) because they had discovered that their parents had consistently lied to them about the character of black people. More than 90 percent of the marriages were stable, and the spouses were psychologically well-adjusted individuals. Their intelligence was far above the average of the general population, and they had completed an average of two years in college. The women had been attracted to the males, white or black, because they were aggressive, poised, forceful, and considerate. The general, psychological profile of the partners in these seventeen interracial marriages showed that they were unusually confident, independent, individualistic, emotionally mature persons who had broad intellectual and cultural interests. The courtship preceding most of the marriages was a long one, and the opposition raised by the relatives of the whites tended to cement the relationships. Often the relatives relented and accepted the marriages after their initial opposition.

These unions survived in spite of being subjected to every weapon in the arsenal of the oppressive American system. Parents frequently disowned the white partners, and so-called friends ostracized them. White divorcees who won custody of their children suddenly had them taken away by the courts when they married black men. People stared at interracial couples on the streets as if they were circus curiosities. The police harassed them, sometimes arresting the women as prostitutes. The F.B.I. occasionally investigated them. Sick people wrote the couples vulgar, obscene letters and sick employers fired them upon learning of their union. Banks refused to give them loans. When Walter White and his white wife, Poppy Cannon, tried to buy a house in 1951, for instance, no bank in New York City would finance it.

Mixed couples found it almost impossible to rent apartments. After 1950 they adopted a subterfuge in their efforts to obtain housing; the white partner applied to white realtors and the black partner to black ones. When the white partner in the union was male the couple usually resided in a white neighborhood. If the husband was white, the mixed couple suffered far less harassment from white neighbors than when the husband was black. The experience of Tamara and her black husband, Vincent Wright, was typical. When the Wrights moved into a predominantly white middle-class neighborhood in East Meadow, Long Island, in 1963 they were "plagued by anonymous 'hate' phone calls, obscene letters, and . . . a cross-burning on their front lawn and a firecracker blast through their living room windows." After the cross-burning, the Wrights received an avalanche of scurrilous letters. Generally, there was considerably more opposition to mixed couples than to black families moving into predominantly white neighborhoods.

White America's opposition to mixed marriages was sometimes maddening in its intensity and led to personal tragedy. Helen Lee Worthing, for example, the "Golden Girl" of the 1920s, was the star of the Ziegfeld Follies and considered one of the five most beautiful women in the world. She was frequently a cover girl on American magazines and became a co-star in movies with John Barrymore and Adolf Menjou. Then Helen met and fell in love with a wealthy black California doctor. She married him because, as she asserted, "I thought then that our love was strong enough to whip a thousand dragons." She had, unfortunately, underestimated white America. Her marriage ended her movie career, and she found she could not bear the stares of strangers and the snubs of her friends. After a few weeks of marriage, Helen wrote, "We continued to go out to night clubs and theaters as I thought that surely my friends would come at last to accept him as my husband. But it wasn't easy to bear the snubs, the surreptitious glances and the whispers. I began carrying a small flask or liquor in my bag and when I couldn't bear it any longes, I would go to the powder room and take a drink. It helped a lot and only thus was I able to face the cold scrutiny of the eyes that looked at me." Eventually she was committed to a sanitarium, her paranoia deepened, once she tried to kill her husband, and frequently she attempted suicide. After separating from her husband, she became a dope addict and an inhabitant of skid row. Helen Worthing died in Los Angeles in 1948.

Frequently inner-directed individuals who were deeply in love, the partners of an interracial marriage insisted that although society might oppress them, love would enable them to survive. Still, before the 1960s the oppression often led interracial couples into a strange way of life. Their activities sometimes took on a secretive air. Frequently they did not go out together. Generally the white woman in such unions was excluded from white society and had to find all of her friends among blacks. On occasion, interracial couples organized in an effort to fight oppression and lead meaningful social lives. One of the first clubs of interracial couples, the Manassah Society, was founded in Chicago in 1890, and one of the great social events in the early part of the twentieth century was its annual ball. At one point the club had 700 members. A similar organization, the Penguin Club, was organized in New York City in 1936 with 100 couples. There were nine of these clubs in Washington, D.C., Los Angeles, and Detroit in 1950. Among middle- and upper-income mixed couples, a different pattern of life prevailed after 1950 in the North. Growing toleration, the broad social and intellectual interests of the partners, and the steadfastness of former friends led to wide social contacts for the couples.

However mixed couples were able to make adjustments in their social lives, they often faced a crisis in rearing their children. Indeed, they were often urged not to have any. White relatives frequently recommended that the wives have abortions when they became pregnant. The birth of the child added to the long line of insults the couple received. The question of the racial identity of the children and the inevitable discrimination they would face perplexed many of the mixed couples, especially the white partner. Most of them, however, rejected the suggestions of white friends that the children "pass for white." The child-rearing credos of the mixed couples were remarkably similar: teach the children to have pride in being black, give them plenty of love, affection, and solid values, and instill self-confidence.

BLACK REACTIONS TO INTERRACIAL MARRIAGE

Crucial to the problems faced by an interracial couple was the reaction of blacks to the union. Unfortunately, most studies of sex and racism ignore the attitudes of blacks to interracial marriage. But these attitudes can be traced from the pre-Civil War era to the last decades of the twentieth century by a careful reading of primary sources. Fearing a violent backlash from whites, blacks rarely expressed a desire to abolish the restrictions on interracial marriage during the antebellum period. Samuel E. Cornish, David Ruggles, and Henry Highland Garnet argued the inevitability of miscegenation and found nothing inherently wrong with racial intermarriage. There were so many circumlocutions in their arguments, however, that they seemed to come down on both sides of the fence simultaneously. Even during the campaign to repeal the 1786 Massachusetts anti-intermarriage law, blacks were largely silent. The greatest public display occurred in 1843 when a group of Boston black males called for the abolition of all discriminatory laws and especially the 1786 act which "we rejoice to believe . . . will soon be wiped away." William Wells Brown, a novelist, playwright, and fugitive slave who had frequently written about Thomas Jefferson's mulatto children, was an uncompromising exponent of miscegenation. Writing in the *Anglo-African* newspaper in February, 1864, Brown contended that "the blending of races is requisite to peace, good feeling and the moral, mental, and physical development of mankind. It breaks down caste and teaches the brotherhood of man."

Spurred on by the optimism of Reconstruction, more confident of their own strength, and less fearful of reprisals, the stance black leaders took on racial intermarriage after the Civil War starkly contrasted to their silence before 1865. North and South, they demanded the removal of bans against intermarriage and fought against their adoption in states where they did not exist. Black newspapers in New Orleans led a campaign against such bans in the 1860s and 1870s. On March 7, 1872 the New Orleans *Louisianian* questioned whether it was "anybody's business whether a white man chooses to [marry] a colored woman, or vice versa? Is it not one of those transactions in which individuals should preeminently consult their own tastes?" Such attitudes continued to be expressed by black opinion leaders until the end of the nineteenth century. For instance, a state convention of Indiana blacks petitioned the legislature to remove the "invidious distinctions" in the marriage laws in 1875.

One of the foremost black champions of unrestricted marriage laws in the nineteenth century was T. Thomas Fortune, editor of the New York *Globe*. Fortune argued against the anti-intermarriage laws because they encouraged immorality, left the black woman defenseless, and represented the white man's belief in the inferiority of blacks. The Indianapolis *Journal*, Cleveland *Gazette*, New York *Freeman*, the black historian and Ohio legislator George Washington Williams, Ida Wells Barnett, and South Carolina Congressman Robert Smalls expressed similar views between 1880 and 1900. There was near unanimity among black leaders regarding bans on intermarriage after 1900. The editorial position of New York's *Messenger Magazine* was typical:

> We favor the intermarriage between any sane, grown persons who desire to marry—whatever their race or color. . . . We therefore demand the repeal of all laws against intermarriage as being inimical to the interests of both races. We further call attention to the fact that there is no desire to check the association of white men with colored women, colored women with white men, nor to serve any interests of Negro men. And inasmuch as no law requires any woman under any circumstances to marry a man whom she does not will or want to marry, these laws narrow themselves down to the prevention of *white women marrying colored men* whom they desire to marry.

Traditionally, the major opposition to intermarriage in the black community was expressed by black women. A group of twenty black women in Boston set the tone for the debate in 1843 when they appealed to the Massachusetts legislature to retain the 1786 ban on interracial marriage. Repeal of the law would, the women felt:

> exert a most pernicious influence on the condition of colored women. If the proposed change of the laws takes place, we shall be deserted by our natural protectors . . . and thrown upon the world friendless and despised, and forced to get our bread by any vile means that may be proposed to us by others, or that despair may teach us to invent. . . . If this request be granted . . . Colored husbands will regret that they married before the change of the law, and will wish their wives out of the way. The least evil that we can expect . . . is the utter destruction of domestic happiness. The petition of the colored men show that we are despised. . . . we . . . beg that you will not, by a legislative act, plunge us into an abyss of wretchedness, temptation and ruin. . . .

Middle-class black women led the campaigns against intermarriage because of the propensity of middle- and upper-class black males to marry white women. One black woman argued in 1947 that every black man "who has changing clothes is looking for a near-white or white woman for his mate." Since traditionally more black women obtained college degrees than black males and the American economy did not permit many black males to rise to middle-class status, there were generally not enough men to go around in this class. Obviously, when these men began to marry white women the supply of eligible bachelors declined further. Writing to *Ebony* magazine in 1970, a black woman asserted, "I am not a racist but white women are a threat to black women. In the near future there aren't going to be enough black men around for us to marry."

The psychological burden of rejection was heightened by the constant emphasis in the press on the famous black males who married white women. Many of the black women propounded the same views as whites regarding mixed marriages. Some of them felt that only degenerate poor whites married blacks. One black minister, Nannie Burroughs, argued in 1904 that such unions indicated that the black man had no self-respect or racial pride. Besides, she claimed, interracial marriages violated God's divine plan: "The Negro has native charm, spirit and endurance. Amending a race by the infusion of fresh blood from another race tends to modify to some degree the divinely-bestowed characteristics of that race. It also tends to pass on into offspring weaknesses of each and little of the strength, if there, by such commingling of blood. The white man has sent oceans of blood into the Negro race by the back door and the race is no better off by his gratuitous contribution."

Historically, however, and in spite of such feelings, many Afro-Americans viewed mixed marriages as signs of racial progress, as indications of the acceptance of blacks on equal terms by whites. At the same time, more cautious blacks frowned on such unions because they might increase the white man's fears and make progress in other areas of life more difficult. As blacks became increasingly more revolutionary in the 1960s, their attitudes toward mixed marriages became increasingly complex. Their emphasis on black being beautiful and on black manhood made blacks more desirable as sex objects and as marriage partners for whites. Greater desirability, coupled with the decline in legal barriers to interracial contacts, led to a rise in mixed marriages. Conversely, the growing emphasis on racial pride and repudiation of integration as an end in itself led to an absolute rejection of mixed marriages by many blacks.

By the 1970s, even though the nexus between racial oppression and sex was still painfully obvious, there was less concern with prohibiting free association among individuals. Public opinion polls showed a sharp decline in white opposition to interracial marriages after 1950, and after 1967 the U.S. Supreme Court systematically and consistently ruled that anti-intermarriage laws were unconstitutional. Progress in this area was revealed in the fact that by 1967 only seventeen states prohibited interracial marriage. One state, Maryland, repealed its anti-intermarriage law in 1969, and there were no violent outbursts over the 566 black-white marriages that took place in the first nineteen months after the law was stricken from the books.

Despite this progress, however, sexual myths and fears and the oppression they reflected and perpetuated still represented one of the greatest barriers to a democratic society in America. These barriers will be broken down only when most Americans agree with the declaration made by William Lloyd Garrison in the May 7, 1831, edition of the *Liberator*:

> The pursuit of happiness is among the inalienable rights of man: it is inseparable from his existence, and no legislative body has a right to deprive him of it. . . . A union of the sexes is a matter of choice, as well as duty. To limit this choice to a particular family, neighborhood or people, is to impoverish and circumscribe human happiness, and to create an odious aristocracy. These propositions we conceive to be reasonable, plan undeniable, self-evident. . . . The standard of matrimony is erected by affection and purity, and does not depend upon the height, or bulk, or color, or wealth, or poverty, of individuals. Water will seek its level; nature will have free course; and heart will answer to heart. To attempt to force or obstruct the flow of the affections, is ridiculous and cruel.

African Diaspora Women: The Making of Cultural Workers

Bernice Johnson Reagon

I mark my beginnings as a cultural worker with my involvement in the civil rights movement. This was my first experience with distancing myself from the culture in which I was living and selecting things from that culture, organizing them, and using them to bring back information, positions, and political stances to the community that had created the material in the first place. All of my work—in the civil rights movement; as a student of William Lawrence James at Spelman College; as a graduate student at Howard University; as a vocal director of the D.C. Black Repertory Company, a theater workshop executed by Robert Hooks and Vantile Whitfield in Washington, D.C; and my work with the Smithsonian Institution and with Sweet Honey in the Rock—would fall into this category. It was after some ten years in this kind of activity that I began to think that maybe the culture offered more than data content; that maybe the culture also offered a process, the way things were to be done, the way material was to be collected, assembled, presented; that maybe the culture offered a methodology for these activities, a theory for use, and an analysis of the conditions of Black people in the larger world.

As I began to think on this matter, I discovered that, to some extent, I was already operating on the premise that the culture you are studying also has its methodology for study and archiving and analysis, presentation, and practice. When I became the program coordinator of the Albany Georgia Movement, which things informed my execution of my responsibilities? I knew already how a mass meeting was done. It was to be done the way all gatherings of Black people were done. There was always a song without a word. Always first a song. Then a statement of definition about why we had come together. Then another song followed by a prayer that, in some way, acknowledged the presence in the gathered group of the totality of the history of the people.

In the civil rights movement, our base was Christian and we prayed to God, announcing our understanding of our commonness with all life in the universe, calling on that force to be with us. Then came another song and then announcements. Then came the sermon or speech or the testimonies and another song, with singing all the way through the collection to support the movement. (Some progressives put the offering before the sermon in order to say that people should give money in a very conscious moment and not be manipulated by the higher, spiritual state that is more likely to occur after the

From *Feminist Studies, Vol. 12, No. 1 (Spring 1986)* by Bernice Johnson Reagon. Reprinted by permission, Feminist Studies.

sermon.) An even newer position, opposed to the use of song as background for other activity, advocates collecting money during talk—the sermon or speech—as well as song, believing that song should not be used to cull money out of people. Once the sermon and the money collection were over, you would close, unless the police were present and you deemed it best to continue. In that case you could just start again and go on forever. Continuance or expansion of the structure was always done through singing.

My culture had already educated me to be a program coordinator. I had spent my life in gatherings, seeing people who were the masters of gathering us together to do this work. When I began to understand that I already operated out of a Black American cultural context, I began to look to that source for patterns of analysis and theory that I could use in my investigative research. I had the opportunity, while developing the African Diaspora program at the Smithsonian Institution, to witness the role of women in the development of New World African Diaspora societies. In this program, which brought together African and African Diaspora cultural expressions, especially those traditions that had illuminating value when viewing the Black American experience, we found that women were central to the continuance of many of the traditional practices.

In the following examples, the women I would like you to meet were the heads of their communities, the keepers of the tradition. The lives of these women were defined by their culture, the needs of their communities, and the people they served. They and their work are available to us today because they accepted the responsibility when the opportunity was offered—when they were chosen. There is the element of transformation in all of their work. Building communities within societies that had enslaved Africans, they and their people had to evolve in at least dual realities. These women are best seen as a central part of the community structure and process. Their role was to resolve areas of conflict and to maintain, sometimes create, an identity that was independent of a society organized for the exploitation of natural resources, people, and land.

Olga Da Alaketu, translated as Olga of the Ketu Nation or, as she is called, Dona Olga Regis Alaketu, is queen of the Ketu nation, which according to her oral tradition existed in West Africa in what is now Benin.[1] She is also known as the mother of saints, Ialorixa. Olga lives in Bahia, Brazil. She is the highest priestess of Candomblé in Bahia and is recognized throughout Brazil and West Africa, especially Yoruba West Africa, for her rituals and ceremonies. Descendant of a long line of queens and priests, she was trained in the priest-craft by her great-aunt.

I was introduced to Olga Alaketu when she came to Washington, D.C., to participate in the Smithsonian's African Diaspora program, as the head of a cultural delegation from Brazil.[2] The African Diaspora program had as its goal the investigation of Black American culture as part of a larger family of culture rooted in Africa, extending through African-derived communities in the Caribbean and Latin American countries. Olga represented Brazil as a nation but, as her name demonstrates, she represented another nation as well. Brazil was the country to which Africans were brought by the Portuguese as slaves. The story of Olga Alaketu and the culture she represents is the story of an evolving or rebirthing in Brazil of a people and culture which was at the same time of and beyond Brazil.

Candomblé is the culture and religion evolved by slaves in Brazil, and a way of continuance and transformation, required in order to survive as a people in a new place. Survival here does not simply address the questions of staying alive but in fact addresses the need to survive beyond the narrow definitions afforded by the slave and post-slave structure. To function as slaves within the society would be much too narrow to ensure that a people would prosper. There was a need to establish a structure and system with its own content that would allow an improved situation for survival beyond the confines of carrying out the required functions as slaves.

For many years, the development of Candomblé took place as a subcultural activity, for slave owners had no need for slaves to maintain or evolve an identity beyond their slave status. The lacing or intermingling of the identities of Candomblé deities with the saints of Roman Catholicism was one dimension of insuring the survival of African-based culture. Today, Candomblé is widely practiced in Bahia, its devotees extending beyond racial and class boundaries. In structuring presentations for sacred rituals, we encouraged our guest groups to become hosts and to reorder the presentation space according to their ceremonial and ritual needs. When Olga began her presentation, people who entered the space were separated: men were asked to sit on one side and women on the other. When Olga entered, the audience was asked to stand because she was a high priest. When the American audience stood, it taught us on a physical participatory level who she was among her people, because in our society you stand in courtrooms when judges come in, in deference to the position of the office. During the ceremony people were asked not to cross their legs and hands because to do so would block the spirits. This reminds me of old Black women sitting wide-legged with their skirts looped between their legs, never crossing their legs, whether on the porch or in the church or in the streets. However, within the Black American community, as class enters the picture as a behavioral force, we are taught that this is improper for women. The correct position is to be seated with your legs closed very tightly or crossed at the ankles. Occasionally, with the full skirts, you can cross at the knee, but that indicates a bit of daring flash.

I always have trouble with sexual delineations because of the oppressive and exploitative power of sexism in my life as a Black American woman. In the physical act of separating men from women, there seemed to be acknowledgment that we were not the same, and that our functions within society were different. In Dona Olga's services, it did not convey inequality in any sense, especially since everyone stood when Olga entered and everyone sat with their legs open to the spirits. Olga herself held the highest position in the house and, as a woman, took rank over the men in her group who were drummers. The fact also that Olga learned her craft from a great-aunt indicates that within African and Brazilian religious practices there was a tradition of powerful women in leadership roles.

Olga traveled with six of her children. Her four sons were drummers and her two daughters were dancers. There were dancing and drumming ceremonies to Obu, the hunting god; to Obawehey, the god of skin disease; to the deities of the sun and wind; to Shango and Isla who is his wife; to Osia, the god of leaves and medicine; to Osun, goddess of the river; to Eshu, the messenger between man and God; to Shuman, the rainbow God; and to Yemanjah, the mother of all gods. When they did the dances to Shango and Isla, they were dressed in their colors: red, gold, and white. On Friday, the day of Oshawa, the dancers were in white and Olga was in blue. Oshawa is the supreme deity within Candomblé.

Olga's responsibility as a participant in the program of Candomblé culture was to share what she could with us, maintaining her own sense of cultural and sacred integrity. At the same time she was present, there were also Santeria worshipers from New York City and a group from Oyotunji, the reconstructed Yoruba village in South Carolina. The Yoruba village group was always in her audience. At one point, she called on the high priest, Oba Enfuntola, to join in the dance to Shango. Near the end of that ceremony, she gave roots to each member of the Yoruba village.

What we were able to gather from our experiences with Olga Alaketu was that there had evolved in Brazil a powerful culture that was based in African tradition with infusions of European culture. Today, as Candomblé is no longer submerged or oppressed by the Brazilian government, there is the active participation of Olga in more modern areas of the society. In addition to her responsibilities as head of the oldest Candomblé house in Bahia, Olga has been a consultant at the psychiatry department of the university of São Paulo, especially in diagnostic determinations when the problem of a patient is religious or spiritual and not mental. If the problem is of the first category, Olga is trained to identify the problem and, through initiation, resolve it. This acknowledgment of the spiritual life of the human unit is very important in Africa and African-derived communities and is many times blurred or ignored in Western disciplines which deal with the nonphysical aspect of human life and behavior.

The presence of Olga Alaketu working as part of the training process for psychiatrists at the university indicates, in some way, how far the nurturing and mothering process has to extend in order to take care of the needs of the people. Candomblé was initially submerged as a part of the subculture in slave and postslave society. As Brazilian culture evolved and those barriers lifted, it became important for Candomblé to be an overt, valid part of the national culture, as well as the culture of the descendants of the Ketu nation. In some way, Brazil and the Ketu nation must acknowledge each other as compatible if future generations are to be nurtured.

Another cultural worker to participate in the African Diaspora Festival was Imogene Kennedy, queen of the Kuminas from Jamaica.[3] Her people call her Queenie and say that she is an African queen. The Kumina, a Jamaican cult group, blend Christian concepts with those of West Africa. Their ceremonies open with Baila songs, phrases from Christian hymns and prayers, including some Ashanti words. These songs, used for mourning and healing, (1) call the spirits to the earth and (2) address them with the needs of the group when they arrive. The Kumina members state that the Ashanti words were taught to them by the spirits, referring to the role of possession in the ceremony and the belief that everything that happens in that state comes from the spirits.

During the festival, each Sunday was devoted to ceremonies. The first Sunday, Imogene Kennedy chose to do a selection of songs rather than a full ceremony. She began all songs sung by the full group in union and antiphony. The melodies were modal, with the voices spanning three octaves: low-medium to Queenie's high piercing lead soprano, characteristic of the African soprano. This very clear, piercing tone, without vibrato, is made by sounding the note forward in the head. Drumming, which signaled the beginning of the ceremony, was from the kbandu and cast or playing drums, the kbandu establishing the snap rhythm and the cast drum establishing the overlay rhythm.

The troupe was with the festival for two weeks. At the beginning of the second week, Queenie came to us and stated that she wanted to do a table ceremony. We had not heard of a table ceremony. It seemed that initially the Kumina group had viewed the African Diaspora program as a part of the dominant society and had, as way of protecting the integrity of their culture, presented a series of selections. It was not until they had lived for several days with other participants from the United States and Africa and had gotten a sense of the structure of the program and of the energy that was from the Black community of the festival that they decided they were an integral part of this community and that this was a community with which they could celebrate.

Preparations for the table ceremony were elaborate. Queenie was taken shopping to select the necessary ingredients. James Early, staff member in charge of programming, remarked that when Queenie picked up what was to him a bottle of soda pop, he knew she was picking up something that to her was part of a ritual. It was a lesson for him in the ways in which a thing that means something in one context can be redefined when the context is changed. In this case, a bottle of grape soda became a drink of ritual and celebration.

On the day of the ceremony, a long table was spread, laden with bread, soda, watermelon, bananas, other fruit, and a large number of candles. To begin the ceremony, Queenie selected four bananas and threw one to each of the four corners of the room. This fruit was an offering to the four sources of the universe. It was to fly freely. As she threw the fruit, American members of the audience, who thought all was for them, tried to catch it. It took a while before it was understood that the fruit was supposed to be offered to the gods and not the audience. Queenie began the ceremony with phrases from conventional Christian hymns and the Lord's Prayer and then moved into more African lyrics. While the hymns were sung, the drums beat African rhythms. Members of the audience came up, gave a contribution, and received a blessing and a symbolic candle lit by Queenie or one of her assistants. The structure of the Kumina table ceremony was very similar to the Baptist communion. However, in the Kumina ceremony, food preparation was more elaborate, in contrast to the bland fare of bread and wine in Christian communion, and offerings seemed to be made to the deities from the participants as well as from the deities.

The decision by Queenie to do this ceremony at a festival, which had so much that was not from the Kumina culture, signaled a redefinition of the Diaspora area. It became for that period of time a Kumina community where Queenie held the highest status as a spiritual leader. It was in her position as leader of her community and keeper of the tradition that Queenie was able to come into a new situation and, after some observation, determine that she could practice more fully the rituals and ceremonies that were sacred. The experience of the Kumina at the African Diaspora program within the larger Smithsonian Institution Festival of American Folklife might be analogous to how our people move or are moved into new situations. There is the need to, first, carry out the basic requirements for our continued existence and then slowly work out the ways in which we can really continue to be who we are. The Kumina tradition in Jamaica, like so many of the African traditions—such as Candomblé in Brazil—survives in spite of a period of oppression when it was outlawed and had to go underground. It was always left to those like Queenie who assumed the responsibility of protecting and nurturing the community to work out ways to keep the traditions strong for the people, whether banned or in the open.

Bessie Jones was another cultural worker during the festival. She was born in 1902 in Smithville, Georgia, and grew up in nearby Dawson, about twenty miles from Albany, Georgia, where I was born.[4] I met Bessie Jones for the first time at the Newport Folk Festival in 1963. I was there as a singer with the SNCC Freedom Singers. We were traveling all over the country to develop support for the movement and to raise funds for specific activities in the South. Bessie Jones was singing with the Georgia Sea Island Singers, led by John Davis. When I listened to the group, I was so excited and deeply moved to hear songs and the style of singing with which I had grown up. There were also songs I had never heard, seemingly of the same family, but slightly different. The group did a dance called "The Buzzard Lope" and another where John Davis beat a broomstick in a cross-rhythm to the song, like beating a drum. The songs were introduced by Alan Lomax, who recorded this group during the 1930s when he was taken to Sea Islands by Zora Neale Hurston. In his introduction, Lomax said that the Georgia Sea Island Singers spoke with such a deep Gullah dialect that it would be difficult for the Newport audience to understand them.

What I remember most strongly about Bessie that first time, when we ran up to the stage after the group came off and surrounded them, was Bessie saying, "I usually speak for the group, you know, but Mr. Lomax has been so nice in bringing us here that we let him introduce us." She wanted to make it clear to this group of young Black singers that the Georgia Sea Island Singers were more than singers, that they were able to represent their songs and their stories to any audience. When I heard her many times since, talking about the songs and games, Bessie Jones has remained consistent in her role to make very clear that a song was more than a song, and a game was more than a game, and that some games that people call games were plays and, as such, carried in their content and structure a foundation piece of Black American culture, or a basic unit for the building of a Black American community. She seemed to want us to know that during slavery and afterwards we as a people had to take care of ourselves and, sometimes, in ways that went far beyond European or Euro-American culture or knowing.

There was a song she taught us called "Gimme the Gourd to Drink Water." This song would not be clear without the story, she said. The call is, "Regular, rollin under/ Gimme the gourd to drink the water." One verse: "Never heard the likes since I been born, bull cow kicking on the milk cow's horn." Bessie said the song was about the glass and tin dippers that white people drank out of and did not want the Blacks, who worked in their houses or fields, to drink out of. Black people drank out of a gourd because water from a gourd was cooler than water from a glass or tin dipper. The bull cow verse: the bull is dependent on the milk cow in similar ways that men were dependent on women or slave owners on slaves. So why kick something that you need to survive. The insanity of abusing something that supports your life is clearly expressed in these lyrics.

Bessie Jones learned her field songs, work chants, and game songs from her grandfather, a former slave named Jed Samson whom she describes as "a natural born African who wore a braid all the way down his back." Samson, who lived to be 105 and worked as a brickmaker, also taught his granddaughter about herbs and how to make teas to deal with certain ailments. With this knowledge, she was for many years a midwife and "worked on" people. She curtailed these activities when they began to license midwives and therefore what she was doing became, by state law, illegal. Bessie Jones also grew up surrounded by music in her home, her church, and in school. Her mother was a fine singer and dancer and her father played several musical instruments.

When Bessie Jones was 31, she moved to her husband's home on St. Simon's Island, off the Georgia coast. The relative isolation of these islands provided an atmosphere in which the African and Afro-American cultural traditions of the predominantly Black population flourished. There Bessie Jones gained a reputation as a powerful singer and was asked by John Davis to join the Coastal Georgia Singers. This group sang indigenous island songs at the A.W. Jones plantation's hotel for the tourists, who had begun to "discover" the coastal island. "The singers," recalled Bessie Jones, "were paid a little but not much" and were required to wear "a big white apron and a head-rag." The group also sang in their own community, adding to their repertoire dances and games such as "Sandy Rose," "The Horses and the Buggy," and "Step, Uncle Jesse," which Bessie Jones had brought from the mainland.

Jones states that many times she felt members of her community wanted to forget the traditions and mores of slavery along with the oppression. "People wouldn't listen to the music and what it meant. Some people acted like they were embarrassed by what they were." Bessie Jones believes that being the grandchild of a slave is nothing to be ashamed of. What we were doing was important. "It's like with Jesus. If nobody preached about him, how would other folks know? If we didn't teach what we're teaching, some would never learn how far we've come and how hard it was."

For me as a Black American woman and singer and cultural scholar, she had been a mother, giving me content-songs, stories, and traditions that I needed in order to develop, and also showing me how to witness and be in a sort of apprenticeship to her. Jones showed me how traditions, content, and structure are transmitted within the boundaries of Black American culture. Being able to walk in her shadow was very much like a womb experience. The relationship was a strong, nurturing one.

Many times when we think of nurturing life, we think of a healthy mother who comes with the food that is best for her baby. That, in fact, is an ideal. The reality allows one to investigate what shape the mother is in, what she is taking into her system on a day-to-day basis, thus what she can possibly feed to her children. Utilizing the mothering mode as a way of analyzing data for the quality of a relationship is good because it affords the researcher the potential of examining the phenomenon from the range of the ideal, where each generation is really brought into a situation that is very healthy and affirming for them. It can also handle the situations of exploitation, where the experience in which a group might find themselves is like a baby taking milk from the mother's breast that might really be poisonous; or worse, that the mother might be in such poor shape that the next generation does not come. It might seem that in using the mothering process as a method of analyzing data, I will be eliminating the role of the father or the sisters and brothers. However, it is in the mothering process that all of these can be included. My primary examples are female. However, one can use the concept of a mothering generation, meaning the entire community and the way it organizes itself to nurture, during a womb stage and newborn stage, the community and future communities that have to follow it if the people are to continue.

When I began to look at relationships between people in the community as a major way of developing models to investigate and evaluate data, I look to the same relationships in the larger, natural world, beyond and before, sometimes, the human family. Among all living things in the universe, there is a nurturing process. It is the holding of life before birth, the care and feeding of the young until the young can care for itself. This process is called mothering. When applied to the examination and analysis of cultural data, it can reveal much within the historical picture of how culture evolves and how and why changes occur in order to maintain the existence of a people. It is important, as you review the data, to look for the nurturing space or ground. Look for where and how feeding takes place. Look for what is passed from the mothering generation to the younger generation.

Within the African Diaspora story, there is the opportunity to see a process of continuance and transformation at work among women cultural workers. There is the struggle to contend with a new space where their people and children are defined in new ways. That definition disrupted and threw into severe trauma cultural practices that had been nursed in African societies. Mothering therefore required a kind of nurturing that would both provide food and stamina for survival within a cruel slave society and the passing on of nurturing that would allow for the development of a community that was not of but beyond the slave society. These women had to take what they were given from their mothers and fathers and make up a few things. Nurturing was not only reconciling what was passed to them with the day-to-day reality, but also sifting and transforming this experience to feed this child, unborn, this new Black community, in preparation for what it would face.

Mothering/nurturing is a vital force and process establishing relationships throughout the universe. Exploring and analyzing the nature of all components involved in a nurturing activity puts one in touch with life extending itself. This is the feminine presence. The earth is a woman. Africa is a woman. The earth holds and feeds it there. The fathering energy in the universe is the seed. It will drop from the tree but if there is a wind, there's no telling where it may fall. Sometimes, if it falls to the earth, there is new life. When you use the earth as mother, it is important to also grapple with the capacity for violence, as in earthquakes, so that you don't overdue that overworn concept of mothering being an unending process. Mothers are not forever. Mothering within human communities requires conscious choice. One has to come to terms with herself, her life, her sanity, and her health, and also of the health of life around her.

Mothering here does not refer to biologically having babies out of your body. These women—Olga Da Alaketu, Imogene Kennedy, Bessie Jones—are nurturers and holders, womblike, of a people, of a birthing community in a strange land. They, through their lives, challenge those of us who have already begun to go through the process of knowing the system of the larger society, as academic scholars, to find what it is that we nurture. What are the unions we hold in our wombs? What do we have to transform? Their lives stand as invitations to do what? To apply the same principles in our work. Black women from the Diaspora, with our Ph.D.'s, who used the struggle and history of our people as data to get our Ph.D.'s, who offer our people's stories up for the highest salary, for assistant, associate, and full professorships, for tenure. We can choose to be mothers, nurturing and transforming.

We have the opportunity to nurture a union between the knowledge we gather which is of the Black community and that of the larger society we live in. There is the need to create a new space larger than the space that Olga or Queenie or Bessie created, larger than the space we now occupy, large enough for our people to continue as a people, sharing a commonness of humanity with other people and a unity with all that is living. We are today looking at a reality that the space we have is no longer sufficient. Most of us cannot talk to the teenagers of today. We are afraid of them. When we get on the bus or the subways, we hope they won't knife us or steal something from us. If they wear dreadlocks, at any age, we know they have already signed off from the inadequate non-employment space that society offers them.

We can choose to do this other job, mothering for our people, even as we hold our positions as the heads of Black studies. It is in fact the blood and struggle of our people which created the space that we hold. Too many of us spend time dissociating ourselves from the protestors and the radicals. When we get our budgets cut and our tenure rejected, we don't even know how to organize a response. We can choose to know that even though we look like Ph.D.'s—a few of us even sound like Ph.D.'s—we can choose to be mothers, nurturing and transforming a new space for a new people in a new time.

NOTES

1. Information on Olga Da Alaketu was documented during her presentations at the 1976 Smithsonian Institution Festival of American Folklife, and the reports of Smithsonian field researcher James Early, and Luisa Marquez, scholar for the Brazilian delegation; Program in Black American Culture, Smithsonian National Museum of American History, African Diaspora Files, Washington, D.C.

2. The Smithsonian African Diaspora Program developed out of a series of meetings organized in 1972 by Dr. Gerald Davis, then the associate director of the Smithsonian Institution's Festival of American Folklife. It was then that I began to work in the areas of Black Diaspora culture. In large part, through the effort of this gathering of scholars, the African Diaspora concept began to be recognized as a legitimate and valuable term to conduct comparative cross-continental studies in African-based communities around the world. This is a term that was in full use during the mid- and late-1960s. The concept existed within the Black political community. Many of us who were involved in political activism during the 1960s had consciously chosen to train ourselves within the Black American culture and within Western formal educational institutions. We were scholars and cultural workers. We were theoreticans and poets and singers.

   When Davis pulled together a nationally based panel of scholars in Black American culture to discuss the scope and definitions of a Black presentation program, many of the Blacks in the room came with degrees in various disciplines—folklore, cultural history, anthropology, art history—and with years of radical political organizing. When the overall concept of the Bicentennial Festival was explained—Old Ways in the New World as a way of celebrating the diversity and plurality of American culture—we insisted that the proper nomenclature for a Black presentation was African Diaspora. Some of our white colleagues who worked in the fields of African, Afro-Caribbean, or Afro-American culture questioned the terminology as one unrecognized by the field. My response then—and it is a view I continue to hold—will serve as the centering point of my discussion.

   The role of native scholars is very much the process of collecting and analyzing, from the perspective of the cultures they study as well as from the perspective of the disciplines and methodologies in which they were trained. A big part of this is bringing into or onto the mainstream and formalized stage of sharing and increasing knowledge of the evolution and analysis and change that occurs within the communities from which they come.
3. Information on Imogene Kennedy was documented during her presentations at the 1975 Festival of American Folklife, the reports of Smithsonian field researcher Leonard Goines, and Olive Lewin, scholar for the Jamaican delegation, AD Files.
4. Information on Bessie Jones comes from, *Oh What A Time*, (Nashville: Southern Folk Cultural Revival Project, 1982) and "Bessie Jones and Bess Hawes," Introduction, *Step It Down* (New York: Harper & Row, 1972).

The Hip Hop Generation
African American Male-Female Relationships in a Nightclub Setting

Janis Faye Hutchinson

In examining Black male-female relationships, Bell, Bouie, and Baldwin (1990) noted that most of the research is pathology-centered. This research focuses on a worldview or cultural orientation whose center is Euro-American. It is assumed that Black heterosexual relationships are based on the same values, lifestyles, and beliefs as those of Euro-American heterosexual relationships. To support this belief, the research emphasizes Black-White comparisons that are not cross-culturally sensitive to variation (Allen, 1978). Any deviation from the Euro-American pattern is considered abnormal.

Asante (1980) proposed that African American cultural orientation is distinct from that of Euro-Americans. African American cultural orientation and worldview are situated in the cultural, historical, and philosophical tradition of African people. This world-view is defined by two principles: "oneness with nature" and "survival of the group." In this holistic perspective, each partner provides for the other's intellectual, emotional, physical, and social stimulation. Neither partner exploits the relationship (Bell et al., 1990).

Other social scientists, such as Page (1997), Hutchinson (1997), and Michaels (1995), discussed the heterogeneity and variation within African American communities. For example, Michaels used a historical examination of writers such as Paul Lawrence Dunbar, Zora Neal Hurston, and W.E.B. DuBois to discuss variation among African Americans. Page also suggested that promoters of the traveling photographic exhibit *Songs of My People* showed only the positive attributes of African American life from a Eurocentric perspective. She believed the exhibit did not present the heterogeneous nature of African American communities. Hutchinson provided an examination of negative portrayals of African Americans and their varied responses to these portrayals. In doing so, she described African Americans as socially and economically varied and continually changing within and among their communities.

This study should be interpreted within the context of a socially heterogeneous population of young adult African American women in a low-income urban environment. The aim of the ethnography was to identify perceptions of female-male relationships from the viewpoint of African American women and to provide a context for understanding these perceptions by examination of theory.

METHODS

The ethnography took place at a local gangsta rap nightclub (Club X, fictitious name) in Houston, Texas, from May 1993 to the summer of 1995. This nightclub is not unique among Blacks or the general population of Houston. It is similar to other Black clubs in terms of age and gender composition and percentage of non-Whites (small numbers of Whites and Hispanics). Only a few clubs in Houston play gangsta rap music. It is the controversial type mentioned in the local news. These rappers espouse themes of killing, use of guns, extremely derogatory statements about women, and explicit sexual statements. The music also portrays realistic views of life in the African American community and what it is like to be Black in a White-dominated American society. This music appeals to diverse groups of younger African Americans. Club X was chosen because it has the previously discussed characteristics and because many young African Americans frequent this club. A former student who frequented the club introduced me to the club. She was infected with HIV by one of the "regulars" at the club. Through discussions with her, I learned about sexual transactions in her network and that this club was a focal point for their interactions.

Participant Observations

Ethnographers describe cultures or certain aspects of a culture and attempt to understand the culture from the perspective of the people living within it. The ethnography involved participant observation on Thursday, Friday, and Monday nights. Observations focused on female-male interactions and the general atmosphere of the club. Public interactions between men and women were observed. Participant observation at the nightclub was concerned with issues such as: What do they do at the club? How do men approach women and how do women respond? I observed interactions, listened to peoples' conversations, and talked to women about men (this usually took place in the restroom).

Intensive Interviews

Five African American women between the ages of 25 and 32 years old were intensively interviewed. Interviews lasted between 1 and 4 hours and were conducted at their homes, my biocultural laboratory at the University of Houston, at a park, and at a McDonald's restaurant. Intensive interviews dealt with determining who to date, categorization of men, sexism, dancing, personal appearance, economics, female-male relationships, use of the word "bitch," rap music, and condom use and nonuse. The interviewed women were very diverse in terms of their backgrounds. Two respondents were students with no children (Latasha, 22 years old, and Yvonne, 25 years old), LaQuita (28 years old) was unemployed and on welfare with three children, Shontele was a 25-year-old woman with one child who lives with her parents, and the eldest was Anna, a 32-year-old professional working woman with no children (all names are fictitious).

RESULTS

Categorization of Men and Women

Categorization of men by women was based on a number of criteria. For instance, a student informant stated that different areas of the club are allocated to certain drug dealers, and men form a hierarchy. Drug dealers are at the top and are ranked by the amount of money they spend at the club. Rappers who have recorded an album are next in the ranking, and men who work for the drug dealers are beneath the rappers in rank, followed finally by the regulars—men who do not fall into the other categories (they have a regular job)—who are at the bottom of the hierarchy. Certain women are associated with different groupings of men and also form a hierarchy based on the men's rank. There is a desire among some women to date men in the upper echelon of the club. This means dating the top drug dealers and their friends or rappers.

Shontele said:

> You're in it but you're looking out. Yeah, I know I'm hanging out with these people. That's not me. I'm in the front of all of them. I'm not in the back of them or in the middle. So I have a better chance of getting out. Some women still get respect because of boyfriends they used to have.

Unfortunately, "to get in front of them," you have to date the high-level drug dealers. This is an attempt at social elevation and an economic categorization that symbolizes the attempt at upward mobility.

Another way women categorize men is through their personal appearance. This includes physical attractiveness and clothing. Clothes add to a man's physical attractiveness and also provide a clue about economic status (although women reported that this sometimes can be misleading). Finally, women group men based on their potential as a husband or sexual partner. A potential short-term sexual partner is one who is a good dancer, spends money, and may have money (as shown by a Lexus or Tommy Hilfiger clothes). Potential husbands are men with an education, those who spend money and appear to have money, and who do not appear to have a lot of women. As a mate, women want someone they can talk to (compatible with) and someone they feel will "treat me right."

Manning (1973) stated that these symbols represent sensory and ideological poles of meaning. The sensory pole contains clusters of meaning related to the physiological, for instance, physical attractiveness and dancing. At the other end of the spectrum is the ideological (education, employment status, and perceived sex experience). Whereas education and employment status attest to a man's positive motivation and show maturity and responsibility, perceived sex experience is not viewed as a negative attribute for men. Men can have a number of sexual liaisons as long as they are not perceived as a "player," someone with a number of sexual partners at the same time.

Concerning reputations, Yvonne said "I don't like one-night stands. But plenty of it goes on." Women who frequent the club weekly may get a bad reputation.

> Some men they'll say like I slept with her. My homeboy slept with her. They do get reputations being in there all the time. Some women don't care about their reputation. They're having a good time and trying to see what they can get out of someone. Or saying, "Hey I met this guy in a Suburban and I met a guy in a Lexus and he took me to breakfast and we went to the hotel" and things like that. Some people like that. It's a status thing. It raises their status. Then you have some people with real low self-esteem. So when they go out and have guys approaching them, and say "Well, I'll do this and that for you and I have this and that," it makes them feel I am something. I am somebody. At one time I had low self-esteem. Now I'm at the point where I can dress the way that I want to dress and it doesn't bother me if anyone talks to me or if not. Women feel that if no one talks to them then maybe I'm not cute enough maybe this or that is not right with me. They feel like something is wrong with them. So next time I come I'll wear something different and I'll do this or that. (Latasha)

> My roommate sleeps with a lot of men. I said to my roommate "Don't you worry about your reputation?" She said, "Girl I don't care. I do what I want to. This is my body." Things like that. (Latasha)

Some women have bad reputations, because, as Anderson (1990) noted, not only must young men have sexual conquests, but also they must prove it. Therefore, they must talk about sex and girls with other young men (Anderson, 1990). Others have reputations because of their sexual orientation. Anna said,

> It's a girl, I don't know her name but she's a lesbian, right. I see her all the time and I never knew she was one. I see her talking to males and females. This guy told me like, see her, she's a lesbian. She comes in here all the time and she talks to this person and that person.

The standards for marriage and nonmarital relationships are different. Marriage at Club X is with the "good girl." For nonmarital relationships, the ideal woman may be identified at the club by frequency of attendance, skimpy clothing, and sexual dancing, Women believe that men perceive these women as "hard up" and desperate for a man.

Sexual Dancing

The dancing is very sexual at Club X and, to some degree, mimics the physical act of sex. "Sexual dancing" takes place on the dance floor and while standing around watching people dance. Off the dance floor, some women dance in front of their boyfriends. For example, one night a woman was dancing with her back to her boyfriend. She put her "butt" in his crotch and proceeded to move in a circular motion against his genital area. He was not dancing, just standing. She took his beer out of his hand and took a few swallows and then handed it back to him. Then she continued dancing, which was really a grinding of his crotch area. Later, she turned around and danced face-to-face with him.

LaQuita said,

> It's just something they just like to do. I just dance regular. I hear guys say she can roll her body good. I bet she's good in bed. I might see a guy dancing and say "Ooh, he's something else" and I might say a little something. Dancing is an indication of something else. Guys say, "Oh, she can get down. I'm going to try to get with her." I've seen it where a guy is laying on the floor and a girl is on top of him. Just dancing and stuff. I wouldn't do that, it's degrading.
>
> Guys look at the way you dance. The guys check it out. Guys watch the way you dance. Guys watch the way you move when you dance. They figure if you can move like that on the dance floor you can do that in bed. It is important in terms of finding someone. If you can dance and move like that they are going to try to talk to you, even if you're ugly.

Dancing is part of the public performance in attracting a partner. The dance floor is a place to display and to pique the interests of potential suitors. Manning (1973) studied recreational clubs in Bermuda and described similar sexual dancing at clubs where men and women dance in sexually suggestive manners.

Date Selection

In terms of selecting a date, attractiveness must be considered. Factors involved in attractiveness include not only biological appearance, but economic status and personality. Anna said,

> I look at the way they're dressed, casual, decent, not too much jewelry. Then if he tries to talk to me I check out his attitude. See if he has that "ladies' man attitude." Does he think he's got it going on. Have I seen him with this girl and that girl every time I come. I watch the guys, what they do, how they talk, and how they act. I ask if they're talking to somebody else. If he says he doesn't have a girlfriend we can talk. I would have to get to know him before I go to bed with him. I'll tell him we need to be friends right now.

In describing the clothes men wear, Latasha said that,

> Guys wear the Tommy Hilfiger. It's a little emblem on the shirt. You buy them at places like Palais Royal. The shirt runs from $65 on up. They are nice shirts, similar to the polo shirt, but it's Tommy Hill. They like to wear the Guess jeans and the Tommy Hill jeans. Then you have a tew who like to put on some slacks and a nice shirt. Then you have ones that like to throw on jeans and a T-shirt. Sometimes people try to tell how much money they have from what they wear.

> But you know what I've come to realize, like I might look at a guy and I'll be like he's dressed real sharp. He probably has a little money and what have you. But then once you get to know them, they really don't have anything.

As for the women,

> I've noticed some of the women like me like to put on a nice casual type outfit. Some of them like to wear the short short, daisy dukes you'd call them, I guess, with a little halter top to show off their breast, figure, what have you. You have some of them that don't wear anything. . . . When I dress casual with bell bottoms, guys will be attracted to me. They'll be like, "Hi, how are you doing." But I noticed when I put on my daisy dukes, the men are "Ooh baby you look so cute" and I have men coming from everywhere. All out the woodwork with the daisy dukes on. I get a lot of stares for my physical appearance. But I don't want them to like me for that. I want them to like me for what I am on the inside. (Anna)

Dress varies at the club. To some degree, this determines the likelihood that a man will approach a woman and also if the woman will be responsive. Manning (1973) noted that women in clubs used clothing as a symbol of sexuality:

> Women's fashions, in addition to projecting the mod and Afro images, are designed to enhance sex appeal. Flesh-clinging dresses with plunging necklines, miniskirts that suggestively expose the thighs, two-piece ensembles that daringly bare the midriff, hot pants outfits that accentuate the pubes, hips, and buttocks, and tight-fitting pants suits that gloriously contour the cantilevered dimensions of their wearers, are popular attire. (p. 157)

This raises the issue of how men think about women who wear little in the way of clothing. Latasha said some men look at them as "Ooh, they're cheap."

> Some men look at them like that and some don't. Most of the men, I come to realize now, they're into sex. You know what I'm saying. That's all they think about is sex. So when they see a woman dressed like that they're like "Wow, she'll probably give it up easy." So they go after her and try to pursue her and see what she's all about and if they feel they can take her home they will. That's when I noticed a lot of them will pull out their money. "Well here, I'll buy you and your friends a drink." That's supposed to make you go "Wow. He has money so I might talk to him and go home with him." Men love it. Most guys go "She's a whore. She can give it up." They look at another person, "She's decent. She's nice." (Latasha)

So, depending on how you are dressed, men and women classify women as "decent" and "whore." A decent person is someone with whom you have a relationship and a whore is someone you can go to bed with anytime.

> Women know they're getting a reputation but they figure they can get anybody they want. Some women wear the shorts real short. We call them "whore shorts." Women like the attention. All eyes are on them. They catch all the

> men. They like the attention. When guys say that looks fine on you. They love the attention. (Anna)

For women, attention seems to be their focus. They dress in "skimpy clothes although they may create a negative image. Then again, who determines that it is a negative image? To them, it is positive. They get the attention they desire.

Brooks (1995) discussed the "centerfold syndrome" and its impact on sexual relationships. The basic thesis of the syndrome is the belief among men (and women) that physically attractive women's bodies are magnificent and men are destined to desire them. The centerfold syndrome has five components: voyeurism, objectification, the need for validation, trophyism, and the fear of true intimacy. In terms of voyeurism, the unique features of a woman's or man's physical appearance—the outline of a man's biceps or contour of a woman's breast in a dress—can be strong sexual stimuli. The harm in this is that glorification of the body leads to unreal images of women, creates an obsession with visual stimulation, and minimizes other aspects of a healthy psychosexual relationship (Brooks, 1995).

Objectification is related to voyeurism. In the centerfold syndrome, men observe women and therefore women are the object and men are the objectifiers. In American society, men have the right to look at women and women are expected to accept the role of visual stimulators for men. When men see women as objects, imperfect women (those with varicose veins, cellulite legs, etc.) are less appealing. Also, one fantasy woman is not enough, because images that were exciting can soon cease to be so (Brooks, 1995). Outward physical features, clothes, jewelry, hairstyle and hair texture, and biological features are used to objectify both genders at Club X.

Men crave validation of their masculinity and view women's bodies as an avenue for that validation. A woman has tokens to manhood (sex) that she can dispense whenever she likes. Although women may have little power in other spheres, women do have power in the sexual arena; this sets the background for misunderstandings and antagonisms between women and men (Brooks, 1995).

When women are viewed as objects, they also become trophies, testaments to a man's power and skillful sexual performance. The trophy hunting man must realize that his prize eventually will lose her irresistible allure. Also, he can never be sure that the trophy will remain his (Brooks, 1995).

According to Brooks (1995), the centerfold syndrome "prevents real intimacy, mature discourse, and honest interpersonal connection, it creates barriers to understanding and becomes a significant obstacle to healthy relationships" (p. 12).

Economic Interactions

Part of the social interaction involves economic power plays. In *Sexual Games in Black Male/Female Relations*, Burgest (1990) discusses a variety of games played between Black men and women. Burgest calls one game "if you dance to the music, you got to pay the piper." The aim of the performance is to create indebtedness in Black women to Black men. This is accomplished through economic and financial dependency. In return for economic favors provided by Black men, the woman is to provide sexual favors (Burgest, 1990). This may be observed in the simple offer to buy a woman a drink (and maybe buy her friends a drink). "Some men think if you buy them a drink they have to be with them all night." Yvonne said she tells them that "'If you buy me a drink it doesn't mean that I'm going to be with you all night.' A guy told me that if I buy you this drink, well I think you need to be with me. I told him, 'Well, that's okay. I'll get my own drink.'"

Latasha had the following experience:

> At [Club X], I had an experience with this guy that I had been knowing. He was kind of drunk. He bought me a drink and I was walking around, you know, looking for my friends and he saw me. He grabbed the drink out of my hand and poured it out. He just poured it out. He said, "Well, I wanted you to be with me," and I didn't want to be with him. [She laughed]

He thought that she should be attentive to him because he bought her a drink.

> Others don't mind, they just want to buy you a drink. Some women at [Club X] might go to bed with someone because they bought them some drinks. It's the dollar bill. One of my roommates probably feels obligated to go to bed with him if he buys her drinks and clothes. (Latasha)

This is popular among Black men who value property and economic resources. They use these resources as a means to manipulate and control women (Burgest, 1990).

Another game, played mainly by women, is "I won't . . . if you don't or you can't . . . if you don't." Black women negotiate with their bodies for favors in the relationship. Black men and women view sex as a commodity (Burgest, 1990). Women at Club X discussed money and clothes in exchange for sex. They look at the clothes men wear and the cars they drive to determine their economic potential.

> Other guys may feel that you owe them if they buy you clothes or give you money. Others are girls who come out strictly to meet someone to go home with. I see them and they are always talking to the guys in the flashy cars. Every time you see them. It's certain ones. I see them. One week she may be talking to somebody in a Lexus. Next time I see her she's talking to somebody in a BMW. My roommate will say something like, "Girl, we're going to go out tonight and I'm going to meet me a man in a Lexus." She doesn't necessarily go to bed with them, but that is what she is looking for. Some women do do that. We call them "car hoppers." They're not necessarily considered whores, but maybe. If someone acts, you know what I'm saying, if she likes flaunting herself, dressed like a slut. They are whores. (Anna)

> I see girls that are like real wild. I don't know what they do. But just from hearing the conversation as I pass by, a guy might say, "Well, I want to take

you home tonight," and he looks like a big spender. So the female might go home with him. Then you have some people like me who just like to go out and have fun. I' m a people person and I just like to go out, dance, socialize. (Yvonne)

There is a continual bartering system in Black female-male relationships.

Male-Female Relationships

I asked questions about the importance of a relationship and whether it is a status symbol.

> It's security. I just got out of a relationship. I like to be in a relationship because of sexwise I don't like to have a lot of partners. I like to have one main partner and he's with me and no one else. Then again he could be with someone else. I always use protection. Security. Sometimes I wouldn't have money for rent and he'd say okay I'll pay your rent for you this month. I don't fool with a lot of females. So when I come home from work I'll talk to my boyfriend. This happened today. He knows that I'm talkative so if I come home and I'm quiet he's like, "What's wrong?" It's fun to do things, go to the movies, double date. (Anna)

So there are a variety of reasons for being in a relationship: security, companionship, and sex. It is also a status symbol. When asked this question, they all said, "Yes, pretty much so."

> A prestigious guy might marry a woman because she has a degree and if we get together and get married we'll have *X* amount of dollars. It's a prestige thing. Then I see it leads to a unhappy marriage if they get married for the financial thing. (Yvonne)

> Women don't want to be alone. They want someone to hold them and tell them it's going to be all right. You have to have a man. Everyone looks down on you if you're not in a relationship. They ask why you're not married yet. "Are you going to get married?" What do they say in the Bible, fornication is a sin. I would love to get married. Most people just go from one person to the next. It's a cycle. It's all about money. The younger generation are about he's going to do this for me. Give me this, buy me this. If he's not going to buy it, then the next person will. (Anna)

Also, if you're not in a relationship, women feel that men think you're a whore.

> When guys see that some women don't want to be in a relationship or want to be single, guys think that they're whore hopping. They want to be with that man and that man. If you're not in a relationship, you may be whore hopping. In terms of power in the relationship, men have the power. (Yvonne)

LaQuita said it is hard to say no to a man when you love him.

> Hard to say "No, you can't come over here." I do want to see him. It's hard to say no when you're in love. It's hard to say no you can't kiss me. That's how it is when you're in love. That's how weak you get when you're in love. If he's in my face it's hard for me to say no. If we're on the phone, no. Face to face is hard.

> Most men have the upper hand. I figure if you know how to do it you can work it. If a man can satisfy you they have the upper hand because they know you want it. If a man is good in bed then he has control. Men have control because they have more money. For women if you don't have that car and job they don't want you. Men are the same way. Whoever has those things can be in control. If the man is good in bed it's hard to say who has control. They may be controlling each other.

I noticed that it is difficult for women to say no during my interviews, as I noted in the journal I kept during the study:

> One woman agreed to do the interview and then didn't show up. I paged her and she never returned my call. I'm not going to page her again. If she didn't want to take part she could have said so, but she didn't. I wonder how they can negotiate condom use and sex when they can't tell someone they don't even know that they don't want to be interviewed.

One woman felt that it is extremely important for a woman to be with a man.

> There is no woman who wants to be alone without a man. Someone to hug, someone to care for them. Someone to be there for them. (Yvonne)

> The man feels that he has power but I look at it as the woman has power. I've had several men say, "I don't want to use a condom." Well, if you don't want to use a condom, then you don't want to have sex. But you do have some individuals who feel, "Well, I don't want to lose this guy so I'll just go along with what he says so I won't use a condom this time." (Yvonne)

This attitude goes along with the game, "if you love me, you will." It is played by Black men and is usually introduced by young lovers who attempt to coerce a partner into a sexual encounter. The outcome of this game is for Black men to gain satisfaction against the explicit wishes of the woman (Burgest, 1990).

Women feel that men are going to have more than one woman and there is nothing they can do about it. "Some men are never satisfied with one woman."

> My roommate has been with this guy for 3 years. The second year into the relationship he told her he had been dating someone else. He made that particular person his girlfriend, but he's still messing with her. I feel like this, if you let it happen it will happen. I don't like to play second fiddle. I like to

> be number one. But my momma told me, you may be number one but you're not the only one. I believe it because a man is going to do what he wants to do. Some of them you can talk to them, mold them in a sense, but some of them: "I'm going to do this." I've come to realize it's a big ego thing too. "I had this girl this week and I can get her." They like to see what they can do and how far they can go. It boosts their ego. (Latasha)

"This guy told me that sometimes I have to have more than one woman. It takes more than one woman to satisfy me." LaQuita said she believes it.

> Sometimes you lose the attraction. You don't lose the feelings for the person you're with, but there's something different. I caught my boyfriend with another girl. He told me that the feeling wasn't there any more. He said he loves me, but the feelings aren't there any more. He said I still love and care for you, but the feelings aren't there. It's something different. He said he wanted to be single. We were going to break up and I agreed to it. He told me he loved me and didn't want me to be with anyone else. When I caught him with the girl he said the girl doesn't mean anything to him. They're just friends. Now he said he wants to be with her. I said, "Last week you said something different. Why did you lie?" He said I didn't lie. He can cut me off. He still calls me and comes by. He said it's just something different. He came over yesterday. . . . I would take him back because I'm in love with him. For four and a half years it was me and him. I can't be with him while he's with another woman. I can't accept that. He said he was happy with this girl. I said, "Didn't I make you happy?" He said, "You did, but the feeling isn't there anymore." I would still take him back because I miss him. I miss the time we spent together. Him taking me places. It's hard for me to start over. I think it was because he didn't have a decent job and wasn't dressed. Now he has a new car and he's dressing nice. He's getting a lot of attention now. (LaQuita)

> All men are going to have someone else. My dad is like that. He's married. He's been married for 17 years, but he's out there. He has another woman. Stepmom might know and it's security. She came up with hardly anything. My dad's a chemical engineer. He brings home a lot of money. He has her living in a nice two-story house. She's driving a Jag. He has a BMW. It's security. As long as he's bringing home the money he can do whatever. Then again, she might be naive and don't know. My dad's always going out of town. "Well, I'm flying to Dallas." He doesn't take her. Sometimes he does but a lot of times he doesn't take her. When I was little I don't know if he knew I wouldn't tell or what, but I remember meeting a number of his girlfriends. One of them claimed that she was pregnant and he had a blood test and it wasn't his. (Shontele)

Although they are young, one participant sees herself as "spoiled" and that she must get a mate before no one wants her, Shontele said,

> Men are more interested in what's untouched, in what's pure. They're not interested in a woman with a baby. Some men are more interested in women

> who are untouched, more pure and clean. Most men like women with the perfect measurements, no children, no sex or they only had a little sex, but you don't know a lot about sex. You don't have to have a mind or brain, you can be dumb, but you have the looks, the body. If I knew then what I know now my children would come a whole lot later and I wouldn't have had as much sex as I did. I'm old to him now. I'm going to be really old as far as a spouse or partner is concerned in a few years. I'm worried about that. I worry about it all the time.

Women strive to show that they have had little in the way of sexual experience. In the recreational clubs studied by Manning (1973), there was no stigma from extramarital affairs. This is not true for women at Club X. Although some women admitted having past relationships with married men, such affairs are not considered acceptable behavior. The married man can provide short-term and long-term economic support, but they cannot provide the status symbol of "Mrs."

Women at Club X may see the individual only for the night or have a longer-term relationship. However, a longer-term relationship with one individual does not necessarily exclude sexual contact with others.

Baby's Mother

"Baby's mother" is a special category. Two of the interviewees in this study were baby's mother. Anna explained it the following way:

> They are not called girlfriends. Your girlfriend is someone else, a completely different person. Everybody's got one. Everybody has a baby's mother. They have no plans to marry these people but they will do everything they can to be nice to them so they won't file child support.

Many poor Black women have a prolife philosophy, and abortion is often not an option. Children are wanted regardless of the circumstances, and the child is genuinely valued. A baby brings a woman praise, a welfare check, and some independence (Anderson, 1990). Adult status is placed on women who become mothers (Collins, 1990).

Baby's mother is a good position to be in for financial reasons and also because the woman has an ongoing relationship with the father. Baby's mother is a socially prestigious position, and she may or may not date other men. Shontele said,

> You're sort of like property then. The father can always go back and sleep with the baby's mother. It's like a given. He'll say I'll give you money. She'll say if you give me money I won't file child support. It's sort of like an intricate bartering system.

Anderson (1990) argued that because such men are unemployed or underemployed, they could not form economically self-reliant families, the usual marker of the transition to manhood. As a consequence, young men's peer groups stress sexual activity to prove manhood, and a baby is proof of sexual activity. Young girls are lured to have sex by the hopes of love and marriage and may become pregnant and abandoned. Some view this as an opportunity to be eligible for welfare that allows them to establish their own households and to attract other men who need money. Anderson views it as a cultural manifestation of persistent urban poverty. Although the sexual codes of the youth in this ethnography probably do not differ from those of other young people, the consequences vary by social class. Exploitative sexual relationships are prevalent in all social classes, but middle-class youths have stronger interest in their future and realize that a pregnancy can derail that future (Anderson, 1990).

> The girls have a dream, the boys a desire. The girls dream of being carried off by a Prince Charming who will love them, provide for them, and give them a family. The boys often desire sex without commitment or babies without responsibility for them. It becomes extremely difficult for the boys to see themselves taking on the responsibilities of conventional fathers and husbands in view of their employment prospects. Yet the boy knows what the girl wants and plays that role to get sex. In accepting his advances, she may think she is maneuvering him toward a commitment or that her getting pregnant is the nudge he needs to marry her and give her the life she wants. What she does not see is that the boy, despite his claims, is often incapable of giving her that life. For in reality he has little money, few prospects for earning much, and no wish to be tied to a woman who will have a say in what he does. (Anderson, 1990, pp. 113–114)

This scenario outlines the dilemma faced by both genders in trying to form a sexual relationship. The bartering system has short-term gains but long-term disadvantages. Consequences of the bartering system for women are unplanned pregnancies, increased prevalence of sexually transmitted diseases (STDs), continued poverty, and lowered quality of life, especially unhappiness.

DISCUSSION

Families in the United States have undergone significant demographic changes. These important changes include an overall decline in marriage rates, older ages at first marriage, a higher prevalence of births to unmarried women, increases in female-headed households, more children in female-headed households, and a larger percentage of children living in poverty. Although these trends affect both Blacks and Whites, Black families are disproportionately affected. In 1993, more than half of Black men (58%) and women (61%) in the United States were not married, compared with 41% of White women and 38% of White men. A large proportion of this decline in marriage occurred because of an increase in the percentage of those who were never married (Taylor, Tucker, Chatters, & Jayakody, 1997). Relative to other groups, Blacks will spend a greater percentage of their lives as singles (Tucker & Taylor, 1997). The declines in marriage have been offset by increases in cohabitation (Taylor et al, 1997). McLanahan and Casper (1995) suggested that because marriage differentials between White and Black women is equally high for mothers as for nonmothers, the cause of the decline in marriage is similar for all women, not just mothers.

A number of theories have been put forth to explain the relatively high prevalence of "unmarriedness" among African Americans. These same theories may help elucidate observed patterns of male-female interpersonal relationships.

Sex Ratio Imbalance

There is a gender imbalance among Whites and Blacks, but not Hispanics. For example, the gender ratio in 1991 was 100 to 100 among Hispanics, 95 to 100 among Whites, and 88 to 100 for African Americans. This scarcity of men is more marked among young, sexually active age groups. The gender ratio imbalance for those below the poverty line is more striking than the overall figures. For instance, the gender ratio for those below the poverty level is 73 to 100, whereas the ratio drops to 69 to 100 among African Americans living in poverty (Aral, 1996).

Guttentag and Secord (1983) advanced the argument that societies with gender ratio imbalance have different patterns of marital values and social organization; shortage of men is related to more divorce, singlehood, adultery, out-of-wedlock births, transient relationships, less commitment among men to relationships, lower societal value on family and marriage, and a rise in feminism. They also argued that a shortage of men among African Americans is associated with an increase in extramarital childbearing and marital decline. Secord and Ghee (1986) also argued that this gender ratio imbalance destabilizes existing relationships because viable alternative mates are always available to the gender in short supply.

The gender ratio hypothesis considers how gender ratio imbalances interact with gender inequality to influence marriage patterns. Members of the scarcer gender have a bargaining advantage because they have more potential mates (Guttentag & Secord, 1983). But how members of the scarcer gender use their advantage depends on their structural power and control of economic and political resources. It is assumed that women depend on marriage for financial support and therefore use their bargaining power when potential mates are abundant to marry, and they marry men with higher status than they otherwise could attract. Men are more likely to marry when the gender ratio is near 100. When women are scarce (i.e., when the ratio is less than 100), men are less likely to marry, and when men are in short supply (less than 100), they are also less likely to marry because they do not need commitment to gain sexual relationships (Guttentag & Secord, 1983).

Low gender ratios are also believed to weaken husbands' commitment to marriage because men do not place great value on marriage. Therefore, husbands provide fewer benefits to wives, which results in lower marital satisfaction for women than for men. A consequence of this scenario for married couples is higher risk of separation and divorce (Guttentag & Secord, 1983).

The African American gender ratio has declined since the 1920s. This disparity between the number of women and men is partly due to higher male mortality and increased female longevity (Taylor et al., 1997). However, researchers such as Epenshade (1985) noted that although Black gender ratios declined since the 1920s, marital decline did not begin until the 1960s.

Economic Factors

The declining economic condition of Black men also has been cited as a causative factor in the decline in marriage and bonding. The decline in the industrial sector, which provided employment for Black men without higher education, resulted in Black men being less attractive as potential husbands and also made them less confident that they could financially support a family (Darity & Myers, 1987; Wilson, 1987). Another economic explanation of marital decline is the growing disparity between Black female and male income levels and increased economic independence of women. Research indicates that the most economically independent Black women, those most highly educated, are more likely to marry than less educated women (Taylor et al., 1997). The effects of the gender ratio and employment on marital status are more evident under conditions of poverty (Taylor et al., 1997).

Feminist Theory

Those who espouse the view that Black men experience more severe oppression than Black women and that therefore Black women must support Black male sexism do not consider the overarching gender ideology that constrains both Blacks and Whites (Collins, 1990).

Objectification of subordinate groups is part of domination and is central to female oppression.

> The foundations of complex social hierarchy become grounded in the interwoven concepts of either/or dichotomous thinking. . . . [D]omination based on difference . . . impl[ies] relationships of superiority and inferiority, hierarchical bonds that mesh with political economies of race, gender, and class oppression. African American women occupy a position whereby the inferior half of a series of these dichotomies converge, and this placement has been central to our subordination. (Collins, 1990, p. 70)

Eurocentric gender ideology objectifies both genders. Some African American men believe that they can only be men by dominating Black women (Collins, 1990). Sexism and internalized sexism play major roles in the dynamics of Black male-female relationships.

CONCLUSIONS

Attributes of women's beliefs and behaviors described in this article can be found in any club and among any ethnic group. These young people are not afraid to say how they feel. They want to have fun. They are "the hip hop generation," a generation that is concerned about pleasure and enjoyment, and they are not afraid to say so. During the hippie movement, people talked about free love. However, they discussed it in political and liberation tones. Today, young people are living a free love devoid of the political rhetoric, sometimes pretentious, of the 1960s.

Karenga (1978) discussed Black female-male relationships. He said the dynamics of Black love fall within one of the following categories: dependency connection, flesh connection, and the cash connection. According to Karenga, the root of social problems in Black male-female relationships rests on these stereotypical connections. However, these connections are probably more widespread and real than simply stereotypical. These connections form the base for many female-male relationships. In a society where women, especially Black women, have little social and economic status and power, these connections are survival strategies in a Eurocentric-structured world.

This study indicates the importance of social status, economic security, and male-female companionship among young adult African American women. The bartering of material resources, companionship, and social status in exchange for sex within a sexist context are driving forces in Black sexual interpersonal interactions. Although all men are viewed as unfaithful, women have unprotected sex because the relationship is more important than the perceived risk of STDs, including HIV. Having a baby is another way, like sex, to gain attention, social status, companionship, and economic security. It may be that African Americans are still in transition in terms of redefining female-male relationships in the New World Eurocentric environment. Poor Black women often use male-female bonding to attain companionship, social status, and economic security.

REFERENCES

Allen, W. (1978). The search for applicable theories of Black family life. *Journal of Marriage and the Family, 35*, 117–128.

Anderson, E. (1990). *Streetwise: Race, class and change in an urban community.* Chicago: University of Chicago Press.

Aral, S. O. (1996). The social context of syphilis persistence in the southeastern United States. *Sexually Transmitted Diseases, 23*(1), 9–15.

Asant, M. K. (1980). *Afrocentricity: A theory of social change*. Buffalo, NY: Amulefi.

Bell, Y. R., Bouie, C. L., & Baldwin, J. A. (1990). Afrocentric cultural consciousness and African-American male-female relationships. *Journal of Black Studies, 21*, 162–189.

Brooks, G. R. (1995). *The centerfold syndrome: How men can overcome objectification and achieve intimacy with women.* San Francisco: Jossey-Bass.

Burgest, D. R. (1990). Sexual games in Black male/female relations. *Journal of Black Studies, 21*, 103–116.

Collins, P. H. (1990). *Black feminist thought.* New York: Routledge.

Darity, W., & Myers, S. (1987). Public policy trends and the fate of the Black family. *Humboldt Journal of Social Relations, 14*, 134–164.

Epenshade, T. J. (1985). Marriage trends in America: Estimates, implications, and underlying causes. *Population and Development Review, 11*, 193–245.

Guttentag, M., & Secord, P. F. (1983). *Too many women: The sex ratio question.* Beverly Hills, CA: Sage.

Hutchinson, J. F. (1997). Creating a racial identity. In J. F. Hutchinson (Ed.), *Cultural portrayals of African Americans: Creating an ethnic/racial identity* (pp. 139–137). West-port, CT: Bergin & Garvey.

Karenga, M. R. (1978). *Beyond connections: Liberation in love and struggle.* New Orleans, LA: Ahidiana.

Manning, F. E. (1973). *Black clubs in Bermuda.* Ithaca, NY: Cornell University Press.

McLanahan, S. S., & Casper, L. (1995). Growing diversity and inequality in the American family. In R. Farley (Ed.), *State of the union: America in the 1990s* (Vol. 2, pp. 1–45). New York: Russell Sage.

Michaels, W. B. (1995). *Our America: Nativism, modernism, and pluralism.* Durham, NC: Duke University Press.

Page, H. (1997). Visual images of the postcolonial blues on the corner of Toulouse and Royal: Discord and identity in songs of my people. In J. F. Hutchinson (Ed.), *Cultural portrayals of African Americans: Creating an ethnic/racial identity* (pp. 75–111). West-port, CT: Bergin & Garvey.

Secord, P., & Ghee, K. (1986). Implications of the Black marriage market for marital conflict. *Journal of Family Issues,* 7, 21–30.

Stack, C. (1974). *All our kin.* New York: Harper & Row.

Taylor, R. J., Tucker, M. B., Chatters, L. M., & Jayakody, R. (1997). Recent demographic trends in African American family structure. In R. J. Taylor, J. S. Jackson, & L. M. Chatters (Eds.), *Family life in Black America* (pp. 14–62). Thousand Oaks, CA: Sage.

Tucker, M. B., & Taylor, R. J, (1997). Gender, age, and marital status as related to romantic involvement among African American singles. In R. J. Taylor, J. S. Jackson, & L. M. Chatters (Eds.), *Family life in Black America* (pp. 79–94). Thousand Oaks, CA: Sage.

Wilson, W. J. (1987). *The truly disadvantaged: The inner city, the underclass, and public policy.* Chicago: University of Chicago Press.

Janis Faye Hutchinson, Ph.D., M.P.H., is a medical anthropologist in the Department of Anthropology at the University of Houston. Her research interests include condom use, HIV/AIDS, racism and health, and unplanned pregnancies. Her publications focus on these topics and African American identity, as shown in her book Cultural Portrayals of African Americans: Creating an Ethnic/Racial Identity *(1997). She currently is examining the long-term health consequences of domestic violence among women of various ethnicities.*

PART 3 QUESTIONS

1. How do racism and sexism affect African American women?

2. How are color complex, sexism and racism interwoven in lives of African Americans?

3. Do psycho-sexual relations exist within and across racial and ethnic groups?

4. What factors color relationships between African American women and men?

Part 4

Facing the Present

INTRODUCTION

The end of the first decade of the twenty-first century was marked by the election of Barack Obama to the U.S. presidency, the first African American to be so elected. The American experience has proven that constitutional rights are attainable despite centuries of oppression and impediments placed in the path of African Americans in their odyssey toward freedom and equality. Present realities, however, indicate that like some of their compatriots, African Americans face economic problems. Unlike them, however, because of a history of unequal treatment, their condition is harsher and persistent. In addition, despite the demise of *de jure* racism and the amelioration of overt racism, prejudice, stigmatization, and discrimination continue via covert racism that is more difficult to expose, so that *de facto* racism and socioeconomic and political ramifications still hamper full realization of the pursuit of happiness and the American ideal.

Robert Joseph Taylor, Linda M. Chatters, and James S. Jackson[LLC4], in "A Profile of Familial Relations among Three-Generation Black Families," examine the African American family—the extended family—using statistical data and make comparative analysis with other American ethnic groups. They find that intergenerational relationships are significant in Black families and that grandparents assume surrogate parenting roles, thus providing supplemental support in times of crisis, easing pressure on the extended families. On obligational and reciprocal levels, children in African American intergenerational families help their parents with respect to personal trauma in the later years of life.

"The Streets: An Alternative Black Male Socialization Institution" by William Oliver examines the network of public and semipublic social settings and space in which primarily lower- and working-class Black males tend to congregate and socialize. He posits that "the streets" is an institution that exists primarily to meet the psychological and social needs of socially and economically marginalized Black males."[1] He makes a link between "the streets," hip-hop culture, and the contemporary social construction of gender identity among poor and non-poor African American males. Oliver also discusses problematic consequences associated with the pursuit of valued manhood identities in the streets and points to vulnerability and exposure to influences that undermine African American families and communities.

Rebecca M. Blank brings a wealth of data to bear on the social and economic conditions of Americans in "An Overview of Trends in the Social and Economic Well-Being, by Race." She examines seven indicators of well-being: population/demographic change, education, labor markets, economic status, health status, crime and criminal justice,

[1] **William Oliver, "The Streets: An Alternative Black Male Socialization Institution," *Journal of Black Studies* 36, no. 6 (July 2006): 922.**

and housing and neighborhood. She concludes that the indicators "underscore the ongoing importance of disparities by race and Hispanic origin in U.S. society."[2]

In "Demand-Side Changes and the Relative Economic Progress of Black Men: 1940–90," [LLC5]Elaine Reardon examines data spanning fifty years to ascertain if there was stagnation or progress in the economic life of African American men. She looks at shifts in the demand for labor, industrial and technological change, and increased competition from other workers. Reardon sees some evidence suggesting that worsening job prospects for middle-skilled white men has heightened competition for jobs that African American men tend to hold. She arrives at the conclusion that policy makers should concern themselves with the fortunes of African American men and of less-skilled men of both races as well as middle-skilled workers.

[2] **Rebecca M. Blank, "An Overview of Trends in the Social and Economic Well-Being, by Race." 67.**

A Profile of Familial Relations among Three-Generation Black Families*

*Robert Joseph Taylor, Linda M. Chatters, James S. Jackson***

This profile of demographic structure and family relationships among a national sample of three-generation black American families revealed important variation across generations in several key demographic (e.g., age, gender, marital status, socioeconomic status, and region) and family (e.g., affection and support) factors. The findings are discussed in relation to current demographic trends affecting the generational age structure of American families and the implications of these changes for practice with multigeneration families.

In the last 30 years, the demographic structure of American families has undergone rapid change (Bengtson, Rosenthal, & Burton, 1990). The increased longevity of Americans has resulted in an overall increase in the number of living generations in families. Presently, it is not uncommon for American families to consist of four or five generations. Also, reduction in the number of children born per couple since 1960 has meant a decrease in the number of aunts, uncles, and cousins within families. Instead of large numbers of people in each generation, as was often the case in the 1950s, the contemporary American family has fewer people in each generation, but more generations. In addition, older black adults in the 1980s were more likely than previous generations to be the oldest members of a kin network in which recent generations are composed of single parents (Burton & Dilworth-Anderson, 1991). Some of the consequences of these changes are that adults now spend more years of their lives as grandparents and there is more interaction across generations (Bengtson et al., 1990). Although changes in mortality, fertility, single parenthood, and intergenerational structure do not determine the interpersonal framework of family relations, they do create the general parameters within which family relationships occur (Burton & Dilworth-Anderson, 1991; Gee, 1987). As such, intergenerational family relationships and the changing generational structure of American families profoundly affect the work of family practitioners in at least two important ways.

First, changes in the generational structure of families will influence the range of life circumstances that clients and their families experience, as well as increase diversity in family forms and functioning. Higher rates of divorce, single-parent families, and adolescent parenthood have generally resulted in a more active family role for grandparents. Similarly, it is not unusual for individuals in their 60s and 70s who are grandparents to also be the major caregivers for their own elderly parents. With these added responsibilities comes a tremendous amount of stress associated with both the physical and emotional demands of caregiving and role incongruities (e.g., individuals in their 50s who are the primary caregivers of preschool children). Practitioners and therapists who have clients with intergenerational role demands will need to assist them in coping with their added responsibilities and stresses.

Second, changes in the generational age structure of American families mean that family generations have more years of contact with one another (Bengtson et al., 1990). For most families, the increase in generational contact will constitute an important resource for the family as a whole and its individual members. However, for those families that experience problems in functioning, added years of contact may constitute a continuing source of stress and conflict. Many of the major family problems, such as domestic violence and substance abuse, have a recognized intergenerational component. Family practitioner interventions that are aimed at breaking the intergenerational transmission of these problems will have to accommodate both the lengthened opportunities for contact between generations and the existence of several generations that may manifest dysfunction. Consequently, it is crucial that family practitioners have an appreciation for the generational age structure of American families and the nature of intergenerational family relationships.

INTERGENERATIONAL FAMILY RELATIONSHIPS AMONG ANGLOS AND MEXICAN AMERICANS

The pioneering research of Hill (1965) and Hill, Foote, Aldous, Carlson, and MacDonald (1970) helped to establish an interest in the empirical investigation of intergenerational family relations (Adams, 1968; Bengtson, 1975; Sussman, 1965). Although the majority of these studies focus on two generations, concentrating on the relationships between adult children and their elderly parents, several investigations (Bengtson, 1975; Hill et al., 1970; Managen, Bengtson, & Landry, 1988; Markides, Boldt, & Ray, 1986; Rossi & Rossi, 1990) have examined intergenerational relations within three-generation families. A variety of interest areas has been explored using this perspective, including interaction and activity patterns, value consensus, affectional ties, and support transactions. One aspect of this research documents intergenerational similarities and differences in attitudes and values and the factors associated with generational transmission, while a separate area of interest involves the investigation of intergenerational support transactions and exchanges.

Several investigations of familial relations and support transactions within multigenerational families are found in the literature. Hill et al.'s (1970) investigation of 120 three-generation families (i.e., married child, parent, and grandparents) demonstrated that respondents were extensively involved in intergenerational relations. In particular, they were frequent participants in shared kinship activities (e.g., weddings and holidays), reported almost weekly contact with family and relatives, and were involved in a vast network of mutual assistance. Respondents participated in within-generation support transfers, but most instances of reciprocal assistance involved members of different generations. With regard to generational differences in support, members of the middle generation tended to give more assistance than they received and interacted more frequently with members of other generations. The grandparent generation both gave and received the least amount of assistance. Grandparents required substantial assistance with illness problems, household management, and emotional gratification, while married children received substantial support in the areas of child care and economic assistance. Based on these and other results, Hill et al. (1970) concluded that the modified extended family effectively links the three generations into one functioning network. The efforts of the middle generation were particularly critical in assisting the development of the child generation and in providing care for the grandparent generation.

Bengtson and Cutler's (1976) examination of generational differences in interaction and assistance identified two dimensions of intergenerational interaction: (a) informal activities (e.g., recreation, conversation, and discussions of important matters) and (b) ceremonial or family ritual activities (e.g., family gatherings, reunions, funerals, birthdays, and weddings). Their findings revealed no significant generational differences between middle-aged adults and elderly parents; both groups reported high levels of each type of activity. Troll and Smith's (1976) examination of a three-generation sample of women found that regardless of age or generation, strength of family bonds was unaffected by distance or physical separation. Brody, Johnsons, Fulcomer, and Lang's (1983) examination of attitudes toward family support among three generations of women found that the majority of women in each generation believed that adult children should help their parents with everyday activities, household tasks, and financial assistance; no generational differences were found in women's expressed attitudes toward reciprocal support. Markides' study (Markides et al., 1986) of a three-generation sample of Mexican Americans in the San Antonio area revealed the presence of strong familial ties, with a considerable amount of reciprocal assistance exchanged between the grandparent and parent generation. There were, however, minimal levels of interaction and intergenerational helping occurring between grandparents and grandchildren. The Mangen et al. (1988) analysis of three-generation families described a typology of intergenerational relationships that included level of affect, interaction, proximity, and reciprocal exchanges between grandparents (G1) and adult children (G2). Over half of the sample, who were termed *moderates*, were described as having average levels of intergenerational proximity, affect, interaction, and exchange. Persons identified as *exchangers* (12.6%) were well above average in the amount of assistance they provided. The *geographically distant* (15.7%) resided at a considerable distance from each other and had low levels of interaction and providing assistance. Lastly, the *socially distant* (18.5%) were characterized by average geographical proximity, but low levels of affect, interaction, and reciprocal assistance.

One of the more recent three-generation studies was conducted by Rossi and Rossi (1990) using a Boston-based sample. Their analysis revealed a fairly high degree of familial proximity, interaction, and kinship exchange among the three-generation families. The predominant characteristic of the middle generation respondents (G2) was the widespread access they had to both their parents (G3) and adult children (G1). Sixty percent of these middle generation respondents lived less than 35 miles from their parents, and 70% lived less than 35 miles from their adult children. This degree of proximity was consistent with the high levels of intergenerational contact, with over a third of the middle generation respondents reporting face-to-face contact and almost half reporting telephone contact with their parents on a weekly basis. The majority of middle generation respondents were satisfied with their level of contact with parents, but among those who were dissatisfied, there was a strong preference for greater contact. Analysis of the type of assistance exchanged between the G1 (grandparents) and G2 (adult children) indicated extensive exchanges of aid in both directions. For many types of assistance, the incidence of help given to a child and help given to a parent were equally high. However, children were more likely to receive instrumental assistance, whereas parents were more likely to receive personal assistance (e.g., care during an illness).

INTERGENERATIONAL RELATIONSHIPS IN BLACK FAMILIES

Historical (Genovese, 1974; Gutman, 1976) and anthropological research on black families (Aschenbrenner, 1973, 1975; Ladner, 1971; Stack, 1972, 1974) document the existence of strong three-generation family systems that contribute to child rearing and the maintenance of family stability. The presence of extensive family and friend networks among blacks (Jackson, 1980; McAdoo, 1981; Shimkin, Shimkin, & Frate, 1978; Stanford, 1978; Wilson, 1986, 1989) provides the basis for the frequent exchange of goods, services, and socioemotional support. Elderly black adults occupy a significant place in the family (Martin & Martin, 1978), particularly in relation to their participation in intergenerational relations and interactions with children and grandchildren (Cantor, 1979; Dowd & Bengtson, 1978; Hirsch, Kent, & Silverman, 1972; Shanas, 1982).

Research on household living arrangements documents that blacks are more likely than whites to reside in three-generation and other types of extended family households (Angel & Tienda, 1982; Beck & Beck, 1989; Farley & Allen, 1987; Freedman, 1991; Hofferth, 1984; Tienda & Angel, 1982), even when controlling for socioeconomic status. Older black adults are more likely than older whites to reside with children and grandchildren (Freedman, 1991; Lopata, 1979; Mitchell & Register, 1984; Shanas, 1982) and to take children and grandchildren into their households (Mitchell & Register, 1984). A longitudinal analysis of the incidence of extended family households among middle-aged black women (Beck & Beck, 1989) revealed that approximately one half of all black women lived in a three-generation household at some point during the period from 1969 to 1984.

A collection of findings on four subpopulations—adolescent mothers, single mothers, grandparents, and elderly adults—indicates that intergenerational relationships are significant for black American families. Mothers of adolescent parents play an important role in the lives of their children and grandchildren, and the support they provide their daughters has a positive impact on the daughter's subsequent educational achievement and parenting skills. Adolescent mothers who remained in their mother's home were more likely to comptlet high school and were less likely to continue to receive public assistance, compared to adolescent mothers who established independent households (Brooks-Gunn & Furstenberg, 1986; Furstenberg & Crawford, 1978). Further, those adolescent mothers who remained at home were more likely to consult their mothers for help with childrearing problems and were able to develop responsive parenting styles (Stevens, 1984, 1988). Wilson (1989) argues that, in single-parent families, the involvement of family members of different generations facilitates the mother's participation in self-improvement activities, increases the quality of child care, and enhances the parenting skills of single mothers. Research on child care and grandparenthood suggests that, in comparison to whites, black grandparents take a more active role in the parenting of grandchildren and are more likely to participate in the administration of discipline (Cherlin & Furstenberg, 1986). In addition, black single mothers are more likely than white single mothers to utilize grandmothers for child care (Hogan, Hao, & Parish, 1990).

A number of comparative analyses indicate that blacks are less likely than whites to provide and receive assistance. Eggebeen and Hogan (1990) found that blacks are less likely than whites to be involved in exchanges with parents as either recipients or providers. The disparity is particularly pronounced with regard to financial assistance (Cooney & Uhlenberg, 1992; Hoffcrth, 1984; Parish, Hao, & Hogan, 1991), and reflects both a decreased likelihood of providing aid of this type and of giving smaller amounts on average (Rosenzweig & Wolpin, 1990). Recent work (Jayakody, 1993) suggests that the race disparity for exchanges of financial assistance is diminished when accurate assessments of financial resources (i.e., wealth and assets) for both recipient and provider are taken into account. Racial discrepancies in wealth are much larger than racial differences in income. Specifically, the median net worth of white households is 10 times greater than the median net worth of black households (Jaynes & Williams, 1989; Oliver & Shapiro, 1989). Comparisons of median wealth for black and white households reveal that whites have nearly three times greater wealth than blacks, despite equivalent annual incomes. Consequently, a thorough understanding of financial resources available for intrafamily transfers should include measures of wealth and assets (Jayakody, 1993).

Recent work (Taylor & Chatters, 1991) suggests that adult children are particularly important in facilitating the integration of older adults in family networks. Older black adults with children expressed more positive appraisals of family life and resided in closer proximity to their relatives than childless elderly persons (Taylor & Chatters, 1991). Adult children were critical in determining the form and function of the informal support networks of elderly black adults, such that those who had an adult child tended to have larger informal helper networks (Chatters, Taylor, & Jackson, 1985; Chatters, Taylor, & Neighbors, 1989) that were comprised exclusively of immediate family members (Chatters, Taylor, & Jackson, 1986). The presence of an adult child was also related to a greater likelihood of receiving assistance from both extended family members (Taylor, 1985, 1986) and church members (Taylor, 1986).

The present study provides a profile of familial relations within a national sample of three-generation black American families (Jackson & Hatchctt, 1986). First, a demographic description of these families is presented, followed by an examination of generational differences in factors that characterize the nature of familial relations. Percentage differences in these traits across family generations are examined for: (a) levels of family interaction, (b) family closeness, (c) satisfaction with family life, and (d) frequency and type of support received from extended family members.

METHOD

Sample

The Three-Generation Family Study was conducted in conjunction with the National Survey of Black Americans (NSBA). Both surveys were conducted by the Program for Research on Black Americans at the Institute for Social Research, University of Michigan (Jackson, 1991). The NSBA sample is the first nationally representative cross-section of the adult (18 years old and older) black population living in the continental United States (Jackson, Tucker, & Gurin, 1987). There are 2,107 respondents in the NSBA data set, which represents a response rate of nearly 70 percent. A more detailed description of the NSBA sample is provided by Hess (1985); a comparison of the sample with 1980 Census data is provided by Taylor (1986).

The Three-Generation Family Study sample was based on the original NSBA sample. Respondents in the NSBA study were asked a series of questions to determine whether they were members of eligible three-generation families. The basic requirements for eligibility included the presence of three contiguous generations of the same family lineage, with the youngest generation member being at least 14 years of age. If a respondent was a member of an eligible three-generation family, then, depending upon the nature of the three-generation configuration, the appropriate family members (i.e., parent/child, grandparent/parent, or child/grandchild) were interviewed. In addition, the original NSBA respondent was reinterviewed on a separate instrument. In sum, a member of each family generation was interviewed. Coresidence was not a selection requirement, so family members might live in separate households. The original respondent received the Reinterview Questionnaire, while the respondent's two family members (parent/child, grandparent/parent or child/grandchild) were given the Three-Generation Questionnaire. The Three-Generation Family Study yielded a total of 2,241 interviews, which included 866 Reinterviews and 1,375 three-generation interviews. Of this total, there were 510 three-generation triads. A detailed analysis of the three-generation sampling techniques and sample is presented in Jackson and Hatchett (1986).

There are several additional advantages in using the National Survey of Black Americans and the Three Generation Family Study data sets. In particular: (a) the quality of the sampling permits generalization of the findings to the entire black population; (b) the findings can be used as baseline estimates against which to compare the results of smaller, regional studies of the family relations of blacks; (c) closer attention can be paid to the heterogeneity of families and family life that exist within the black communities; and (d) the size of the sample permits greater power of testing than had previously been possible (Jackson & Hatchett, 1986).

Family Network Variables

Research on the family lives of older adults (Troll, Miller, & Atchley, 1979) has described four dimensions of kinship structure: (a) family interaction, (b) residential propinquity, (c) qualitative aspects of family relationships, and (d) informal support. Reflecting these dimensions, several variables that relate to various aspects of family networks were used in this analysis. They include: (a) family contact; (b) subjective family closeness; (c) subjective closeness to children, parents, and grandparents; (d) satisfaction with family life; (e) receipt of informal support; and (f) type of informal support received.

Frequency of family contact was measured by the question, "How often do you see, write or talk on the telephone with family or relatives who do not live with you? Would you say nearly every day, at least once a week, a few times a month, at least once a month, a few times a year, or hardly ever?" Family closeness was measured by the question, "Would you say your family members are very close in their feelings to each other, fairly close, not too close, or not close at all?" A separate set of items assessed affective closeness to children, parents, and grandparents. Respondents were asked, "How close do you feel to the following people in your ideas and feelings about things? How close do you feel to your parents (grandparents, children)? Do you feel very close, fairly close, not too close, or not close at all to them in your ideas and feelings about things?"

Satisfaction with family life was measured by the question, "How satisfied are you with your family life, that is, the time you spend and the things you do with members of your family? Would you say that you are very satisfied, somewhat satisfied, somewhat dissatisfied, or very dissatisfied?" Frequency of informal social support from family members was measured by the question, "How often do people in your family help you out? Would you say very often, fairly often, not too often, or never?" An additional response category was created for respondents who volunteered that they never needed help from family. Finally, respondents who indicated that they received help from their family members were asked the follow-up question to indicate the type of support, "In what ways are they most helpful to you?"

RESULTS

Descriptive findings for the demographic and family factors (Tables 1 and 2) are presented as aggregate information for grandparent (G1), parent (G2), and child (G3) generations.

Demographic Composition by Generation

Table 1 presents a demographic profile of the Three-Generation Family sample by generational status. The child generation (G3) has a slightly higher percentage of males than is found in either the parent (G2) or grandparent (G1) generations. Age differences in generational composition are as anticipated; 72.9% of the grandparent

TABLE 1 Demographic Distribution of Three Generations of Black Families by Generational Membership

Variable	Grandparents %	Grandparents *n*	Parents %	Parents *n*	Children %	Children *n*
Gender						
Male	27.9	(163)	30.9	(247)	45.7	(331)
Female	72.1	(422)	69.1	(553)	54.3	(394)
TOTAL	100.0	(585)	100.0	(800)	100.0	(725)
Age						
14–34	0.0	(0)	6.0	(48)	96.1	(696)
35–54	3.4	(20)	77.2	(617)	3.9	(28)
55–64	23.6	(138)	14.4	(115)	0.0	(0)
65–99	72.9	(426)	2.4	(19)	0.0	(0)
TOTAL	100.0	(584)	100.0	(799)	100.0	(724)
Marital Status						
Married and common law	36.4	(213)	53.9	(431)	23.8	(172)
Divorced	5.6	(33)	16.3	(130)	5.0	(36)
Separated	7.0	(41)	13.5	(108)	4.1	(30)
Widowed	49.7	(291)	11.4	(91)	0.4	(3)
Never Married	1.2	(7)	4.9	(39)	66.7	(482)
TOTAL	100.0	(585)	100.0	(799)	100.0	(723)
Education						
0 to 11 years	87.8	(510)	52.8	(421)	37.1	(263)
High school graduate	8.1	(47)	29.3	(234)	33.7	(239)
Some college	2.4	(14)	10.8	(86)	20.3	(144)
College graduate	1.7	(10)	7.1	(57)	8.9	(63)
TOTAL	100.0	(581)	100.0	(798)	100.0	(709)
Annual Personal Income						
$0 to $4,999	71.0	(347)	37.1	(271)	59.5	(399)
$5,000 to $9,999	19.1	(93)	28.0	(203)	18.8	(126)
$10,000 to $19,999	6.8	(33)	24.9	(182)	17.2	(115)
$20,000 and above	3.1	(15)	10.0	(74)	4.5	(30)
TOTAL	100.0	(488)	100.0	(730)	100.0	(670)
Annual Family Income						
0 to $4,999	51.0	(232)	18.2	(131)	16.3	(96)
$5,000 to $9,999	27.0	(123)	23.4	(168)	22.3	(131)
$10,000 to $19,999	13.4	(61)	30.5	(219)	29.6	(174)
$20,000 and above	8.6	(39)	27.9	(201)	31.8	(187)
TOTAL	100.0	(455)	100.0	(719)	100.0	(588)
Region						
Northeast	11.5	(67)	17.8	(142)	16.7	(121)
North Central	15.0	(88)	21.8	(174)	21.4	(155)
South	69.9	(409)	54.3	(435)	55.6	(403)
West	3.6	(21)	6.1	(49)	6.3	(46)
TOTAL	100.0	(585)	100.0	(800)	100.0	(725)

Note. Due to rounding error percentages may not equal 100%.

generation are 65 years of age or older, 77.3% of the parent generation are between the ages of 35 and 54 years, and 96.1% of the child generation are 35 years of age or younger. Marital status profiles across generations indicate that the grandparent generation is most likely to be widowed (49.7%), a majority of the parent generation is married (53.9%), and two out of three members of the child generation (66.7%) never married. Respondents in the grandparent generation have both lower personal and family incomes and formal education levels than persons in the parent and child generations, Regional differences indicate that the grandparent generation is the most likely of the three groups to reside in the South.

Family Factors

Table 2 presents the univariate distributions for the family interaction, affection, and support variables by generational membership. Respondents in the grandparent and parent generations interact more frequently with family members than do persons in the child generation. Overall, nine out of 10 respondents in each of the three generations indicate that they are either "very" or "fairly close" to their family members. Generational differences indicate that respondents in the grandparent generation are most likely to state that they feel "very close" to their family members, followed by respondents in the parent generation and those in the child generation. With respect to statements of feeling "fairly close," the gradient is reversed, with the child generation endorsing this view most strongly, followed by the parent and grandparent generations.

Percentage distributions for degree of family satisfaction are similar to those for family closeness. Overall, roughly 90% of respondents report satisfaction with family life. Grandparents again report the highest level of family satisfaction ("very satisfied"), followed by parents and children, while perceptions of being "somewhat satisfied" are highest among the child generation, followed by the parent and grandparent generations. Univariate distributions for degree of affective closeness to specified target groups (i.e., children, parents, and grandparents) reveal that, regardless of generational membership, the majority of respondents report feeling close to these groups. The grandparent generation reports the highest percentages for feeling "very close" to all three groups, followed by the parent and child generations, respectively.

Turning to reports of support from family (see Table 3), respondents in the child generation indicate receiving assistance from family more frequently (73.2% report "very often" or "fairly often") than persons in either the parent (44.0% report "very often" or "fairly often") or grandparent (43.0% report "very often" or "fairly often") generations. A profile of the most important type of support provided by family indicates that the grandparent generation is most likely to receive companionship, goods and services, transportation, help when sick, and total support. Persons in the child generation are the most likely to receive advice and problem-solving, encouragement, and financial assistance. In addition, parent and child generations are more likely to report that they receive assistance with child care. Finally at least 20% of respondents in each generation indicate that financial assistance is the most important type of support they receive.

TABLE 2 Univariate Distribution of Selected Indicators of Familial Relations by Generational Membership

Variable	Grandparents %	Grandparents *n*	Parents %	Parents *n*	Children %	Children *n*
Family Interaction						
Nearly every day	41.3	(190)	40.6	(271)	33.3	(209)
At least once a week	24.8	(114)	30.4	(203)	30.0	(188)
A few times a month	16.1	(74)	13.0	(85)	16.0	(100)
At least once a month	9.1	(42)	7.5	(50)	6.9	(43)
A few times a year	3.3	(18)	4.6	(32)	7.3	(46)
Hardly ever	3.9	(18)	3.6	(24)	5.9	(37)
Never	1.5	(7)	0.4	(3)	0.6	(4)
TOTAL	100.0	(460)	100.0	(667)	100.0	(627)
Family Closeness						
Very close	75.4	(439)	63.2	(502)	58.8	(424)
Fairly close	17.8	(104)	29.5	(234)	34.0	(245)
Not too close	5.8	(34)	5.4	(43)	5.5	(40)
Not close at all	1.0	(6)	1.9	(15)	1.7	(12)
TOTAL	100.0	(583)	100.0	(794)	100.0	(721)
Closeness to Children						
Very close	94.8	(427)	88.1	(542)	86.5	(211)
Fairly close	3.6	(16)	10.4	(64)	11.1	(27)
Not too close	0.9	(4)	1.3	(8)	2.0	(5)
Not close at all	0.7	(3)	0.2	(1)	0.4	(1)
TOTAL	100.0	(450)	100.0	(615)	100.0	(244)
Closeness to Parents						
Very close	89.3	(159)	75.1	(455)	66.6	(378)
Fairly close	5.6	(10)	17.2	(104)	26.0	(148)
Not too close	1.7	(3)	5.9	(36)	5.8	(33)
Not close at all	3.4	(6)	1.8	(11)	1.6	(9)
TOTAL	100.0	(178)	100,0	(606)	100.0	(568)
Closeness to Grandparents						
Very close	73.4	(69)	67.4	(137)	58.5	(330)
Fairly close	9.6	(9)	15.3	(31)	28.0	(158)
Not too close	2.1	(2)	8.4	(17)	10.3	(58)
Not close at all	14.9	(14)	8.9	(18)	3.2	(18)
TOTAL	100.0	(94)	100.0	(203)	100.0	(564)
Family Satisfaction						
Very satisfied	78.8	(457)	55.3	(440)	45.9	(329)
Somewhat satisfied	17.9	(104)	34.3	(273)	42.0	(301)
Somewhat dissatisfied	2.2	(13)	9.5	(76)	10.0	(72)
Very dissatisfied	1.0	(6)	0.9	(7)	2.1	(15)
TOTAL	100.0	(580)	100.0	(796)	100.0	(717)

Note. Due to rounding error percentages may not equal 100%.

TABLE 3 Univariate Distribution of Selected Indicators of Familial Support by Generational Membership

Variable	Grandparents		Parents		Children	
	%	*n*	%	*n*	%	*n*
Family Support						
Very often	27.9	(162)	24.6	(196)	41.2	(297)
Fairly often	15.1	(88)	19.4	(155)	32.0	(231)
Not too often	27.9	(162)	29.8	(238)	19.4	(140)
Never	20.3	(118)	17.9	(143)	4.7	(34)
Never need	8.8	(51)	8.3	(66)	2.6	(19)
TOTAL	100.0	(581)	100.0	(798)	100.0	(721)
Type of Family Support						
Advice/problem solving	0.7	(3)	4.3	(25)	15.2	(100)
Companionship	18.3	(76)	9.9	(58)	6.1	(40)
Encouragement	3.6	(15)	12.9	(76)	16.4	(108)
Anything/everything	7.7	(32)	5.6	(33)	6.2	(41)
Goods/services	25.7	(107)	18.1	(106)	6.1	(391
Financial assistance	20.2	(84)	21.8	(128)	26.6	(175)
Child care-related	1.0	(4)	10.5	(62)	9.4	(62)
Transportation	10.4	(43)	4.1	(24)	2.1	(14)
Help when sick	6.0	(25)	3.4	(20)	1.7	(11)
Other assistance	5.4	(23)	8.7	(54)	9.4	(62)
TOTAL	100.0	(412)	100.0	(586)	100.0	(652)

Note. Due to rounding error percentages may not equal 100%.

DISCUSSION

These data provide important descriptive information on the demographic and family characteristics of individuals who comprise three-generation black families. The findings suggest that family generations differ from one another with respect to gender and age composition, as well as income and educational levels, marital status, and regional distribution. Turning first to overall demographic characteristics, one of the more unique features of this three-generation sample is the high proportion of women. This is due to several factors, including the higher incidence of male mortality which affects the gender and marital status composition of the black population. For example, the Sweet and Bumpass (1987, p. 203, Table 5.14) analysis of 1980 Census data revealed that for women between the ages of 40 and 69, black women had a much higher incidence of widowhood than did white women. As a result, widowhood is a much more normative event among blacks than whites; this has profound consequences for the gender composition of three-generation families.

Jackson and Hatchett's (1986) earlier analysis of the Three-Generation Family sample provided several explanations for the prevalence of women in three-generation black families that are related to the manner in which the sample was generated. For this discussion, it is important to remember that eligible family triads must reflect generations that are both contiguous and blood-related, as opposed to marriage-related lineages. The types of eligible family triads were: (a) parent-child triads comprised of the respondent (G2) and his or her eligible parent (G1) and child (G3); (b) grandparent-parent triads consisting of the respondent (G3) and his or her eligible parent (G2) and grandparent (G1); and (c) child-grandchild triads consisting of the respondent (G1) and his or her eligible child (G2) and grandchild (G3).

Gender and Age Composition

The higher mortality rate for men relative to women has differential impacts on the availability of female versus male family members across particular generational triads (Jackson & Hatchett, 1986). For example, more than two thirds of eligible NSBA respondents who were part of a parent-child triad had only one living parent, and of these parents, the majority (over three fourths) were mothers. In contrast, sons and daughters were available for selection in roughly the same proportions. The gender composition of parent-grandparent triads in the sample was similarly affected by the higher mortality rates for males. As mothers were more likely to be living than fathers, maternal grandparents were more likely to be eligible for selection than were paternal grandparents (this fulfills the requirements of contiguous and blood-related lineages). Consistent with the mortality data for blacks, when only one grandparent was alive (whether they were maternal or paternal grandparents), more than three fourths of them were female. Finally, with regard to the child-grandchild triad, NSBA respondents were more likely to have daughters with eligible children than sons with eligible children.

With regard to the age structure of three-generation families, because the sample is based on family lineage, the age ranges for family generations overlapped to some extent. The overlap in age ranges emphasizes the heterogenous composition of three-generation black families. For example, persons in the grandparent generation who are between 35 and 54 years of age (3.4% of this generational group) comprise a group of relatively young grandparents. By definition, the youngest generation in the family triad must be at least 14 years of age, so that at the uppermost limit, grandparenthood would have been attained by the age of 40. These grandparents are members of three-generation families in which both they and their children became parents at a young age. Similarly, respondents in the parent generation who are in the age category of 34 years or younger (6.5%), had (at the uppermost limit) become parents by the time they had reached the age of 20.

The overlap in age ranges for the three generations is consistent with Burton's (Burton & Bengtson, 1985; Hagestad & Burton, 1986) work on the timing of grandparenthood and its relationship to role behaviors and expectations. Burton distinguishes between women who experience, in a normative sense, early versus on-time entry into the role of grandmother. Early grandmothers had a median age of 32 years as compared to on-time grandmothers, whose median age was 46 years. The pattern of early grandmotherhood tended to result from two generations of teenage pregnancy: their own and that of their daughters. The present data document the existence of heterogenous age patterns in the generational configurations of black families. Although there are instances of successive generations of early parenthood, this configuration is not representative of all three-generation black families. Finally, although the focus of this profile was three-generation families, a number of respondents were members of families with four and five generations (Table 2). The existence of five generations was indicated by grandparents who reported that they themselves had grandparents (n = 94), while families with four generations were represented by child generation members who themselves had children (n = 244), grandparent generation respondents who had parents (n = 179), and parent generation members who had grandparents (n = 203).

Education, Income, Marital Status, and Regional Distributions

Education, income, marital status, and regional distributions by family generation were largely consistent with information on how age status is correlated with these factors. Research on the correlates of socioeconomic status indicates that elderly adults as a group have lower incomes and fewer years of educational attainment; elderly black adults, in particular, have exceedingly low socioeconomic status. The present data indicate that of the three groups, respondents in the grandparent generation (who were also on average the oldest) had the lowest levels of educational attainment and personal and family incomes. Generational differences in personal income were curvilinear, reflecting the fact that the middle-aged, parent generation had higher personal incomes than members of the child and grandparent generations. The contribution of other family members' incomes in deriving overall family income was evident among the child generation who, despite lower personal incomes, had family incomes comparable to those of the parent generation. With regard to marital status, the younger, child generation (G3) respondents were more likely to be never married; the middle-aged, parent generation respondents (G2) were more likely to be married, divorced, or separated; and the older grandparent generation (G1) respondents were more likely to be widowed. Finally, the regional distribution of this sample is consistent with Census data which indicate that a little over half of the overall black population are Southern residents (Taylor, 1986; U.S. Health and Human Services [US HHS], 1980) and roughly six out of 10 blacks over the age of 65 are Southerners (US HHS, 1980).

Family Network Factors

Turning to the family network factors, we found that regardless of generational membership, respondents interacted with family members on a frequent basis, displayed a high degree of family affection, and were fairly frequent recipients of informal help from extended kin. These findings are consistent with other research indicating the critical importance of family ties among black Americans (Aschenbrenner, 1973, 1975; McAdoo, 1981; Stack, 1972, 1974). Two thirds of respondents reported interacting with family members at least once a week or nearly every day. Similar to other work indicating that the middle generation interacts most often with other generational members (Hill et al., 1970), the parent generation had the highest reported level of interaction with family, followed by the grandparent and child generations, respectively.

Findings for family support indicated that the majority of respondents reported receiving informal assistance from extended family members. Respondents in the child generation were most likely to indicate that they received support and that they received assistance either "very" or "fairly often." This finding is consistent with other research on the National Survey of Black Americans data which indicates that, generally, age is negatively associated with the probability of receiving assistance from family members (Taylor, 1986). Generational differences in reports of the most important type of support received tend to correspond to the needs and challenges facing specific generations. Rossi and Rossi (1990) found that parents assisted children in their transition to adulthood by providing money and advice or information helpful to securing or advancing in a job, whereas children helped their parents with respect to personal traumas (i.e., illness and loss events) that are prevalent in the later years of life.

In the present analysis, respondents in the child generation indicated that advice/help with problem solving and encouragement were important types of assistance that they received from family. Comparable percentages of respondents in the child and parent generations rated child care as the most important type of assistance received from family members. The salient needs of older blacks were reflected in the type of help they considered the most important; a large percentage of respondents in the grandparent generation stated that goods and services (e.g., cooking, housekeeping, grocery shopping, and making small repairs), companionship, and transportation were the most important types of help they received. In addition, help during an illness was mentioned most often by respondents in the grandparent generation, followed by respondents in the parent and child generations, respectively. Consistent with low income levels for large segments of the black population, a substantial number of respondents in each generation indicated that financial assistance was the most important type of support received.

The majority of intergenerational research has focused on interaction patterns and informal helping, while qualitative aspects of intergenerational relationships generally have been neglected (Aizenberg & Treas, 1985). Bengtson's work on the *developmental stake* (Bengtson, Burton, & Mangen, 1985; Bengtson & Cutler, 1976; Bengtson & Kuypers, 1971) addresses generational differences in affective perceptions of family relationships. This work suggests that family generations hold contrasting representations of their common relationship. Generational members' investment in and perception of their relationship vary according to how the relationship relates to the attainment of their personal goals. Younger family members, whose developmental stake involves the establishment of their independence and individual identity, tend to maximize family and generational differences. Older family members, conscious of their own mortality and concerned with the continuation of the family lineage, tend to perceive greater subjective closeness and similarity between generation members. Consistent with this interpretation, the present analyses indicated that blacks expressed a high degree of affection for family members in general, and for intergenerational members (i.e., grandparents, parents, and children) in particular. Across all five measures assessing family closeness and satisfaction, at least 80% of respondents expressed positive sentiments toward their families. Differences by generation indicated that the grandparent generation consistently reported the highest levels of family closeness and satisfaction, followed by the parent generation, and lastly, the child generation.

PRACTICE IMPLICATIONS

Findings from this study serve to underscore the inherent diversity in three-generation black families and further suggest ways that these differences potentially affect family practice. Normative expectations as to the age structure and functions of intergenerational family roles and relationships are pervasive. Shaped in part by the popular media and other sources, these idealized images of family structure and the nature of family relationships often do not reflect contemporary demographic realities. This is particularly true during periods of rapid change in families (e.g., increases in divorce rates and single-parent households). Family practitioners, as members of U.S. society, often share these normative expectations of family roles. As the present data indicated, three-generation black families vary considerably with respect to their age structure, and these differences have an important influence on the content and process of practice with families.

Effective practitioner-client relations can be jeopardized when societal expectations of intergenerational family structure and their manifest demographic characteristics are incompatible. For example, common expectations regarding the normative age for grandparenthood is late midlife and older. An actual incident in a major metropolitan city illustrates what happens when expectations are at odds with reality. A young single mother was incarcerated by the authorities, and her children were placed with child protective services. When a 34-year-old woman who identified herself as their grandmother attempted to pick them up, she was refused custody. The practitioner in this case refused to release the children to the woman, believing that she was an impostor because she was considered too young to be a grandmother. Although this mistake was rectified a few hours later, this negative interaction did irreparable damage to the relationship between the family and the agency. As this example demonstrates, accurate information that describes the diversity of family structure is crucial for effective family practice and program development.

Opportunities for Intergenerational Support

The truncation of the generational age structure in families caused by increased longevity and earlier childbearing means that there will be more generations within a family. Further, findings from this study indicated the presence of four- and five-generation families. Under these conditions, there are increased opportunities for intergenerational support that can be mobilized in response to events such as shifts in the local labor market, unemployment, physical or mental incapacity, homelessness, adolescent parenting, and substance abuse. These circumstances may result in grandparents playing a more active and central role in the lives of their grandchildren, sometimes functioning as surrogate parents and assuming formal custody (Apfel & Seitz, 1991; Burton, 1992; Minkler et al., 1992). This intensification in role expectations and obligations (i.e., surrogate parenting) represents a distinct difference in the nature of the traditional grandparent role in which individuals have more restricted involvement and provide only supplemental care. The preponderance of women within three-generation families, and particularly the grandparent generation, observed in these data indicates that grandmothers will be assuming these surrogate parenting roles.

There are a number of ways that social service agencies and family practitioners can assist grandparents and great-grandparents in their parenting roles. Group work is a very effective therapeutic modality. Therapy, self-help, and psychoeducational groups are all accepted intervention approaches for older adults (Smyer, Zarit, & Qualis, 1990). The distinctions between these three types of groups are not rigid, and they share several important features. Self-help groups such as Grandparents As Parents (GAP) have developed in response to the needs of surrogate parents. The positive outcomes of these groups include: (a) giving advice, suggestions, and guidance about problems; (b) providing interaction that leads to a normalization of experiences; (c) linking group members to a new social network; (d) facilitating reciprocal support among group members; (e) developing new coping skills; (f) helping to mitigate anger and depression; and (g) enhancing self-efficacy and esteem. Individual and family counseling may be needed for anxiety, depression, difficulties arising from competing role demands (other caregiving responsibilities), and coping with drug-dependent family members.

Respite Care and Education Needs

In a discussion of other types of services that would benefit black grandparents and great-grandparents who are surrogate parents, Burton (1992) found that respite care from parenting responsibilities was a frequently mentioned need. Surrogate mothers indicated a desire for time for themselves and modest leisure activities. Many reported that they could not afford the costs of highquality child care or baby sitting. Concerned that child protective services would remove the grandchild if there were any question about the quality of child care, these women chose to forego the opportunity to have a break from caregiving (Burton, 1992). Surrogate parents may require educational interventions focusing on parenting skills, as well as information on the mental, physical, and emotional development of children; appropriate medical care; and childhood diseases and immunizations. Burton's grandparents (1992) expressed a need for parenting education and child rearing strategies, along with techniques for coping with the stresses associated with parenting and other social roles. Disadvantaged socioeconomic status among members of the grandparent generation may present financial and educational barriers to effectively accessing various health and social service agencies. Legal counseling that addresses issues of guardianship and foster care, financial guidance and assistance, and access to appropriate resources and care for their own health concerns are among the additional services that are required by surrogate parents (Burton, 1992).

The example of surrogate parenting by grandparents and great-grandparents has been used to illustrate how changes in the generational structure of families might influence intergenerational relationships and modify interventions with families. However, as these data on three-generation families demonstrated, persons in their mid-30s, as well as those who are late midlife and older, may be involved as surrogate parents. Further, the existence of four and five generations of family members may mean that the grandmother who functions as a surrogate parent to her grandchild may also be caring for her own mother and grandmother. These different profiles of grandparenthood demonstrate the diversity that exists among this group and suggest the importance of developing programs and services that uniquely suit individual needs and circumstances.

Individual Assistance

Up to this point, we have discussed practice implications that concern specific members of multigeneration families, that is, persons in the grandparent and great-grandparent generations who are involved in surrogate parenting. However, other models of practice application are concerned with the preliminary task of assessing features of an individual's social network and using this information to design and implement interventions. Israel and Rounds (1987) discuss the employment of network assessment and intervention strategies to enhance an individual's existing support resources. Their work suggests that the selection and effectiveness of any intervention strategy will depend upon a number of general factors that describe the nature of the problem, the network, and the broader context within which they occur. Findings from the present study suggest that an understanding of how differences in the age structure of families affect family functioning provide additional information that is relevant in designing interventions.

Information about the sociodemographic and family characteristics of three-generation families would be useful in constructing profiles that could be matched with appropriate intervention strategies. One network intervention (Israel & Rounds, 1987) attempts to strengthen already existing network ties by identifying persons with particular needs and utilizing significant members of their present network in meeting those needs. Information about the three-generation family could identify whether a person has viable ties with the family network, participates in reciprocal exchanges, and is not presently overburdened, in addition to whether the network, itself, is capable of providing support. Conversely, information about the three-generation family structure can be used to identify those networks that are characterized by relationships that are limited, detrimental, overburdened, or unable to provide support. This might be the case when a grandmother is involved as primary caregiver to grandchildren under adverse social circumstances, such as drug or alcohol addiction (Burton, 1992). An appropriate intervention in this situation might involve the development of new network ties that unite those who require assistance with another person(s) who is outside of the three-generation family network.

Family and individual norms may mitigate against the use of professional helpers to resolve problems. This may be a particular difficulty for older family members who, due to previous life experiences and limited resources, may not be inclined to seek professional help. In these instances, interventions can be designed to strengthen an already existing network by involving individuals known as *natural helpers*, who currently exist in the community. This process identifies lay helpers who are customarily relied upon by others for informal assistance and involves them in training activities to extend the provision of social support. Successful employment of this strategy requires careful selection of natural helpers and development of the collaborative relationship. Finally, there are network interventions that bring together overlapping networks or communities to meet identified needs (Israel & Rounds, 1987).

An advantage of this network assessment strategy is that it recognizes that family networks and their individual members possess different resources and liabilities that can be employed in the development of effective interventions. In addition, information as to the affective dimensions of family networks and the extent to which families conceive of themselves and operate as a cohesive unit (i.e., possess a multigeneration family identity) are vital. The strategy is versatile, in that it can be adapted for use among various types of social networks. However, the effective application of this assessment and intervention strategy with black multigeneration families requires detailed information with respect to family network characteristics (e.g., generational structure, coresidence, and interaction patterns), as well as affective and supportive dimensions.

CONCLUSION

The present investigation focused attention on a variety of methodological and substantive concerns and issues that are pertinent to the conduct of intergenerational research. The methodological innovations employed in this study permitted an in-depth exploration of generational differences (Jackson & Hatchett, 1986). The use of family lineage as opposed to age status as the basis for determining generational position revealed substantial age overlap in generation categories. The unit of analysis employed in this study was the individual respondent, and the descriptive information represented aggregate data on persons who were categorized as members of one of three generations in a family. Although the observed age variability within generations indicated the presence of substantial heterogeneity in generational structure, precise information on respondent age at the time of actual generational transition was not available. The examination of issues related to the timing of, and transition into, different generational statuses (i.e., age at first parenthood and grandparenthood) requires more detailed data and prospective observation of families.

The generational structure observed in these data bear upon a number of important substantive issues with respect to the functioning of black families. One example is the possible effects of truncated family generations of the type reported by Burton and her associates (Burton & Bengtson, 1985; Hagestad & Burton, 1986) on the functioning of families. It has been suggested that the truncation of generational structure within a family has negative consequences in terms of socioeconomic status attainment and economic mobility patterns within families and the socialization of adolescents to the adult roles of spouse and parent (i.e., learning of appropriate role behaviors and expectations). The investigation of these questions requires the linkage of data from separate generations in a family (Jackson & Hatchett, 1986). Similarly, questions related to generational similarities and differences in tangible and affective exchanges within a family are appropriately addressed when data are organized with the family as the unit of analysis. This approach permits, for example, an examination of whether family generations are similar with regard to demographic characteristics and if certain types of families are characterized by high levels of support. A number of significant methodological and analytic concerns remain in the study of multi-generation families. This descriptive profile provided background for the investigation of multigeneration families, as well as information regarding diversity in generational structure among black families and their implications for practice.

REFERENCES

Adams, B. N. (1968). *Kinship in an urban setting*. Chicago: Markham.

Aizenberg, R., & Treas, J. (1985). The family in later life: Psychosocial and demographic considerations. In J. Birren K. W. Schaie (Eds.), *Handbook of the psychology of aging* (2nd ed.) (pp. 169–189). New York: Van Nostrand Reinhold.

Angel, R., & Tienda, M. (1982). Determinants of extended household structure: Cultural pattern or economic model? *American Journal of Sociology*, 87, 1360–1383

Apfel, N. H. & Seitz, V. (1991). Four models of adolescent mother-grandmother relationships in black inner-city families. *Family Relations*, 40, 421–429.

Aschenbrenner, J. (1973). Extended families among black Americans. *Journal of Comparative Family Studies*, 4, 257–268.

Aschenbrenner, J. (1975). *Lifelines: Black families in Chicago*. New York: Holt, Rinehart and Winston.

Beck, R. W., & Beck, S. H. (1989). The incidence of extended households among middle-aged black and white women: Estimates from a 5-year panel study. *Journal of Family Issues*, 10, 147–168.

Bengtson, V. L. (1975). Generation and family effects in value socialization. *American Sociological Review*, 40, 358–371.

Bengtson, V. L., Burton, L., & Mangen, D.J. (1985). Generations, cohorts and relations between age groups. In R. H. Binstock & E. Shanas (Eds.), *Handbook of aging and the social sciences* (2nd ed) (pp. 304–338). New York: Van Nostrand Reinhold.

Bengtson, V. L., & Cutler, N. (1976). Generations and intergenerational relations: Perspective on age groups and social change. In R. H. Binstock & E. Shanas (Eds.), *Handbook of aging and the social sciences* (pp. 130–159). New York: Van Nostrand Reinhold.

Bengtson, V. L., & Kuypers, J. A. (1971). Generational differences and the developmental stake. *Aging and Human Development*, 2, 249–260.

Bengtson, V. L., Rosenthal, C., & Burton, L. M. (1990). Families and aging: Diversity and heterogeneity. In R. H. Binstock & L. George (Eds.), *Handbook of aging and the social sciences* (3rd ed.)(pp. 263–287). New York: Van Nostrand Reinhold.

Brody, E. M., Johnsons, P. T., Fulcomer, M. C., & Lang, M. A. (1983). Women's changing roles and help to elderly parents: Attitudes of three generations of women. *Journal of Gerontology*, 38, 597–607.

Brooks-Gunn, J., & Furstenberg, F. F., Jr. (1986). The children of adolescent mothers: Physical, academic, and psychological outcomes. *Developmental Review*, 6, 224–251.

Burton, L. M. (1992). Black grandparents rearing children of drug-addicted parents: Stressors, outcomes, and social service needs. *The Gerontologist*, 32, 744–751.

Burton, L. M., & Bengtson, V. L. (1985). Black grandmothers: Issues of timing and continuity of roles. In V. L. Bengtson & J. F. Robertson (Eds.), *Grandparenthood* (pp. 61–77). Beverly Hills, CA: Sage.

Burton, L. M., & Dilworth-Anderson, P. (1991). The intergenerational family roles of aged black Americans. *Marriage and Family Review*, 16, 311–330.

Cantor, M. H. (1979). The informal support system of New York's inner city elderly: Is ethnicity a factor? In D. E. Gelfand & A. J. Kutzik (Eds.), *Ethnicity and aging: Theory, research, and policy* (pp. 153–174). New York: Springer.

Chatters, L. M., Taylor, R. J., & Jackson, J. S. (1985). Size and composition of the informal helper networks of elderly blacks. *Journal of Gerontology*, 40, 605–614.

Chatters, L. M., Taylor, R. J., & Jackson, J. S. (1986). Aged blacks' choices for an informal helper network. *Journal of Gerontology*, 41, 94–100.

Chatters, L. M., Taylor, R. J., & Neighbors, H. W. (1989). Size of informal helper network mobilized during a serious personal problem among black Americans. *Journal of Marriage and the Family*, 51, 667–676.

Cherlin, A.J., & Furstenberg, F. F., Jr. (1986). *The new American grandparent: A place in the family, a life apart*. New York: Basic Books.

Cooney, T. M., & Uhlenberg, P. (1992). Support from parents over the life course: The adult child's perspective. *Social Forces*, 71, 63–84.

Dowd, J. J., & Bengtson, V. (1978). Aging in minority populations: An examination of the double jeopardy hypothesis. *Journal of Gerontology*, 33, 427–436.

Eggeheen, D. J., & Hogan, D. P. (1990). Giving between the generations in American families. *Human Nature*, 1, 211–232.

Farley, R., & Allen, W. R. (1987). *The color line and the quality of life in America*. New York: Russell Sage Foundation.

Freedman, V. A. (1991). Intergenerational transfers: A question of perspectives. *The Gerontologist*, 31, 640–647.

Furstenberg, F., & Crawford, G. (1978). Family support: Helping teenagers to cope. *Family Planning Perspectives*, 10, 322–333.

Gee, E. M. (1987). Historical change in the family life course. In V. Marshall (Ed.), *Aging in Canada* (2nd ed.)(pp. 120–132). Ontario: Fitzhenry and Whiteside.

Genovese, E. (1974). *Roll, Jordan roll*. New York: Pantheon Press.

Gutman, H. G. (1976). *The Black family in slavery and freedom* 1750–1925. New York: Random House.

Hagestad, G. O., & Burton, L. M. (1986). Grandparenthood, life context, and family development. *American Behavioral Scientist*, 29, 471–484.

Hess, I. (1985). Sampling for social research surveys: 1947–1980. Ann Arbor, Ml:

Institute for Social Research, University of Michigan.

Hill, R. (1965). Decision making and the family life cycle. In E. Shanas & G. F. Streib (Eds.), *Social structure and the family: Generational analysis* (pp. 113–139). Englewood Cliffs, NJ: Prentice-Hall.

Hill, R., Foote, N., Aldous, J., Carlson, R., & MacDonald, R. (1970). *Family development in three generations*. Cambridge, MA: Schenckman.

Hirsch, C., Kent, D. P., & Silverman, S. L. (1972). Homogeneity and heterogeneity among low-income negro and white aged. In D. P. Kent, R. Kastenbaum & S. Sherwood (Eds.), *Research planning and action for the elderly: The power and potential of social science* (pp. 400–500). New York: Behavioral Publications.

Hofferth, S. L. (1984). Kin networks, race, and family structure. *Journal of Marriage and the Family*, 46, 791–806.

Hogan, D. P., Hao, L.-X., & Parish, W. L. (1990). Race, kin networks, and assistance to mother-headed families. *Social Forces*, 68, 797–812.

Israel, B., & Rounds, K. (1987). Social networks and social support. *Advances in Health Education and Promotion*, 2, 311–351.

Jackson, J. J. (1980). *Minorities and aging. Belmont*, CA: Wadsworth.

Jackson, J. S. (Ed.) (1991). *Life in black-America*. Newbury Park, CA: Sage.

Jackson, J. S., & Hatchett, S. J. (1986). Intergenerational research: Methodological considerations. In N. Datan, A. L. Greene, & H. W. Reese (Eds.), *Intergenerational relations* (pp. 51–75). Hillsdale, NJ: Erlbaum.

Jackson, J. S., Tucker, M. B. & Gurin, G. (1987). *National survey of black Americans*, 1979–1980 [machine-readable data file]. 1st ICPSR ed. Ann Arbor: Uiversity of Michigan, Program for Research on Black Americans (Producer). Inter-university Consortium for Political and Social Research (Distributor).

Jayakody, R. (1993). *Race, family structure and socio-economic differences in intergenerational financial assistance*. Unpublished manuscript.

Jaynes, G. D., & Williams, R. M., Jr. (1989). *A common destiny: Blacks and American society*. Washington, DC: National Academy Press.

Ladner, J. (1971). *Tommorow's tommorow: The black woman*. Garden City, NY: Doubleday.

Lopata, H. Z. (1979). *Women as widows*. New York: Elsevier.

Mangen, D. J., Bengtson, V. L., & Landry, P. H. (1988). *Measurement of intergenerational relations*. Beverly Hills, CA: Sage.

Markides, K. S., Boldt, J. S., & Ray, L. A. (1986). Sources of helping and intergenerational solidarity: A three generational study of Mexican-Americans. *Journal of Gerontology*, 41, 506–511.

Martin, E. P., & Martin, J. M. (1978). *The black extended family*. Chicago: University of Chicago Press.

McAdoo, J. L. (1981). Black father and child interactions. In L. E. Gary (Ed.), *Black men* (pp. 115–130). Beverly Hills, CA: Sage.

Minkler, M., Roe, K. M., & Price, M. (1992). The physical and emotional health of grandmothers raising grandchildren in the crack cocaine epidemic. *The Gerontologist*, 32, 752–761.

Mitchell, J. S., & Register, J. S. (1984). An exploration of family interaction with the elderly by race, socioeconomic status and residence. *The Gerontologist*, 24, 48–54.

Oliver, M. L., & Shapiro, T. M. (1989). Race and wealth. *The Review of Black Political Economy*, 17(4), 5–25.

Parish, W. L., Hao, L.-X., & Hogan, D. P. (1991). Family support networks, welfare, and work among young mothers. *Journal of Marriage and the Family*, 53, 203–215.

Rosenzweig, M. K., & Wolpin, K. I. (1990). *Intergenerational support and the life-cycle income of children: Coresidence and interhousehold financial transfers*. Unpublished manuscript, University of Minnesota, Minneapolis.

Rossi, A. S., & Rossi, P. H. (1990). *Of human bonding: Parent-child relations across the life course*. New York: Aldine de Gruyter.

Shanas, E. (1982). *National Survey of the Aged* (DHHS Publication No. 83–20425). Washington, DC: Department of Health and Human Services.

Shimkin, D., Shimkin, E., & Frate, D. (1978). *The extended family in black societies*. Chicago: Aldine.

Smyer, M. A., Zarit, S. H., & Qualis, S. H. (1990). Psychological intervention with the aging individual. In J. E. Birren & K. W. Schale (Eds.), *Handbook of the psychology of aging* (3rd ed.) (pp. 375–403). San Diego, CA: Academic Press.

Stack, C. (1972). Black kindreds: Parenthood and personal kindreds among urban blacks. *Journal of Comparative Family Studies*, 3, 194–206.

Stack, C. (1974). *All our kin: Strategies for survival in a black community*. New York: Harper and Row.

Stanford, E. P. (1978). *The elder black*. San Diego, CA: Campanile.

Stevens, J. H., Jr. (1984). Black grandmothers' and black adolescent mothers' knowledge about parenting. Developmental Psychology, 20, 1017–1025.

Stevens, J. H. (1988). Social support, locus of control, and parenting in three low-income groups of mothers: Black teenagers, black adults, and white adults. *Child Development*, 59, 635–642.

Sussman, M. B. (1965). Relationships of adult children with their parents in the United States. In E. Shanas & G. F. Streib (Eds.), *Social structure and the family: Generational relations* (pp. 62–92). Englewood Cliffs, NJ: Prentice Hall.

Sweet, J. A., & Bumpass, L. L. (1987). *American families and households*. New York: Russel Sage Foundation.

Taylor, R. J. (1985). The extended family as a source of support to elderly blacks. *The Gerontologist*, 25, 488–495.

Taylor, R. J. (1986). Receipt of support from family among black Americans: Demographic and familial differences. *Journal of Marriage and the Family*, 48, 67–77.

Taylor, R. J., & Chatters, L. M. (1991). Extended family networks of older black adults. *The Journal of Gerontology*, 46, S210–S217.

Tienda, M., & Angel, R. (1982). Headship and household composition among blacks, Hispanics, and other whites. *Social Forces*, 61, 508–531.

Troll, L., Miller, S., & Atchley, R. (1979). *Families in later life*. Belmont, CA: Wadsworth.

Troll, L. E., & Smith, J. (1976). Attachment through the life span: Some questions about dyadic bond among adults. *Human Development*, 19, 156–170.

U.S. Department of Health and Human Services. (1980). *Characteristics of the black elderly*. Washington, DC: U.S. Government Printing Office.

Wilson, M. (1986). The black extended family: An analytical consideration. *Developmental Psychology*, 22, 246–259.

Wilson, M. N. (1989). Child development in the context of the black extended family. American Psychologist, 44, 380–385.

REFERENCES

Bailey, W. C., Hendrick, C., & Hendrick, S. S. (1987). Relation of sex and gender rate to love, sexual attitudes, and self-esteem, *Sex Roles*, 16, 637–648.

Baxter, L. A., & Bullis, C. (1986). Turning points in developing romantic relationships. *Human Communication Research*, 12, 469–493.

Bell, R. R., & Chaskes, J. B. (1970). Premarital sexual experience among coeds, 1958 and 1968. *Journal of Marriage and the Family*, 32, 81–84.

Carroll, J. L., Volk, K. D., & Hyde, J. S. (1985). Differences between males and females in motives for engaging in sexual intercourse. *Archives of Sexual Behavior*, 14, 131–139.

Christopher, F. S., & Cate, R. M. (1984), Factors involved in premarital sexual decision-making. *The Journal of Sex Research*, 20, 363–376.

Christopher, P. S., & Cate, R. M. (1985). Premarital sexual pathways and relationship development. *Journal of Social and Personal Relationships*, 2, 271–288.

Christopher, F. S., & Frandsen, M. M. (1988, October). *Strategies of influence in sex and dating; Trying to change a partner's behavior*. Paper presented at the national meeting of the National Council on Family Relations, Philadelphia, PA.

Christopher, F. S., & Frandsen, M. M. (1990). Strategies of influence in sex and dating. *Journal of Social and Personal Relationships*, 7, 89–105.

Christopher, F. S., & Roosa, M. W., (1991). Factors affecting sexual decisions in the premarital relationships of adolescents and young adults. In K. McKinney & S., Sprecher (Eds.), *Sexuality in close relationships* (pp. 111–133). Hillsdale, NJ: Lawrence Erlbaum.

Clayton, R. R. (1972). Premarital sexual Intercourse: A substantive test of the contingent consistency model. *Journal of Marriage and the Family*, 35, 273–281.

D'Augelli, J. R., & Cross, H. J., (1975). Relationship of sex guilt and moral reasoning to premarital sex in college women. *Journal of Consulting and Clinical Psychology*, 43, 40–47.

Gunderson, M. P., & McCary, J. L. (1979). Sexual guilt and religion. *The Family Coordinator*, 28, 353–357.

Harvey, J. H., Flanary, R" & Morgan, M. 0986). Vivid memories of vivid loves gone by. *Journal of Social and Personal Relationships*, 3, 359–373.

Howard, M., & McCabe, J. B. (1990). Helping teenagers postpone sexual involvement. *Family Planning Perspectives*. 22, 21–26.

Hudson, W. W. Murphy, G. J., & Nurius, P. S., (1983). A short-form scale to measure liberal vs. conservative orientations toward human sexual expression. *The Journal of Sex Research*, 19, 258–272.

Huston, T. L., McHale, S. M., & Crouter, A. C. (1986). When the honeymoon's over: Changes in the marriage relationship over the first year. In S. Duck & R. Gilmour (Eds.), The emerging field of personal relationships (pp. 109–132). Hillsdale, NJ: Lawrence Erlbaum.

Huston, T. L., & Robins, E. (1982). Conceptual and methodological issues in studying close relationships. *Journal of Marriage and the Family*, 44, 901–925.

Kelley, H. H., Berscheid, E" Christensen, A., Harvey, J. H., Huston, T. L., Levinger, G., McClintock, E., Peplau, L. A., & Peterson, D. R. (Eds.). (1983). *Close relationships*. New York: W. H. Freeman.

Kelly, C., Huston, T. L., & Cate, R. M. (1985). Premarital relationship correlates of the erosion of satisfaction In marriage. *Journal of Social and Personal Relationships*, 2, 179–194.

Kirby, D., Barth, R. P., Leland, N., & Fetro, J. V. (1991). Reducing the risk: Impact of a new curriculum on sexual risk'taking. *Family Planning Perspectives*, 23, 253–263.

Lane, K. E., & Gwartney-Gibbs, P. A. (1985). Violence in the context of dating and sex. *Journal of Family Issues*, 6, 45–59.

Lang, A. R., Scarles, J., Laucrman, R., & Adesso, V. (1980). Expectancy, alcohol, and sex guilt as determinants of interest in the reaction to sexual stimuli. *Journal of Abnormal Psychology*, 89, 644–653.

LaPlante, M. N., McCormick, N., & Brannigan, G. G. 0980). Living the sexual script: College students' views of influence in sexual encounters. *The Journal of Sex Research*, 16, 338–355.

Leigh, B. C. (1989). Reasons for having and avoiding sex: Gender, sexual orientation, and relationship to sexual behavior. *The Journal of Sex Research*, 26, 199–209.

Lewis, R. J., Gibbons, F. X., & Gerrard, M. C. (1986). Sexual experience and recall of sexual vs. nonsexual information. *Journal of Personality*, 54, 676–693.

Markman, H. J. (1979). The application of a behavioral model of marriage in predicting relationship satisfaction of couples planning marriage. *Journal of Consulting and Clinical Psychology*, 47, 743–749.

Markman, H. J. (1981). Prediction of marital distress; A five-year follow-up. *Journal of Consulting and Clinical Psychology*, 49, 760–762.

Markman, H. J. (1984). The longitudinal study of couples' interactions: Implications for understanding ant predicting the development of marital distress. In K. Hahlweg & N. Jacobson (Eds.), *Marital interaction: Analysis and modification* (pp. 253–281). New York: The Guilford Press.

Markman, H. J., Floyd, F., Stanley, S. M., & Storaasli, R. (1988). The prevention of marital distress: A longitudinal investigation. *Journal of Consulting and Clinical Psychology*, 56, 210–217.

Mctts, S., & Cupach, W. R. (1989). The role of communication in human sexuality. In K. McKinney & S. Sprecher (Eds.), *Human sexuality: The societal and Interpersonal context* (pp. 139–161). Norwood, NJ: Ablex.

Mosher, D. L. (1961). *The development and validation of a sentence completion measure of guilt*. Unpublished dissertation, Ohio State University, Columbus.

Mosher, D. L., & Anderson, R. D. (1986). Macho personality, sexual aggression, and reactions to guided imagery of realistic rape. *Journal of Research in Personality*, 20, 77–94.

Muehlenhard, C., & Cook, S. W. (1988). Men's self-reports of unwanted sexual activity. *The Journal of Sex Research*, 24, 58–72.

Olson, D. H. (1976), Bridging research, theory, and application: The triple threat in science. In D. Olson (Ed.), *Treating relationships* (pp. 565–579). Lake Mills, 1A: Graphic Press.

Peplau, L. A., Rubin, Z., & Hill, C. T., (1977). Sexual intimacy in dating relationships. *Journal of Social Issues*, 33, 86–109.

Pinney, E. M., Gerrard, N., & Denney, N. W., (1987). The Pinney sexual satisfaction inventory. *The Journal of Sex Research*, 23, 233–251.

Renick, M. J., Blumberg, S. L., & Markman, H. J. (1992). The Prevention and Relationship Enhancement Program (PREP): An empirically based preventive intervention program for couples. *Family Relations*, 41, 141–147.

Robinson, I., Ziss, K., Ganza, B., & Rati, S. (1991). Twenty years of the sexual revolution, 1965–1985: An update. *Journal of Marriage and the Family*, 53, 216–220.

Schwartz, R. C., & Breunlin, D. (1983). Research: Why clinicians should bother with it. *Family Therapy Networker*, 7, 23–27, 57–59.

Sherwin, R., & Corbett, S. (1985). Campus sexual norms and dating relationships: A trend analysis. *The Journal of Sex Research*, 21, 258–274.

Spanier, G. B. (1976). Measuring dyadic adjustment: New scales for assessing the quality of marriage and similar dyads. *Journal of Marriage and the Family*, 38, 15–28.

Williams, L. M. (1991). A blueprint for increasing the relevance of family therapy research. *Journal of Marital and Family Therapy*, 17, 355–362.

Wynne, L. C. (1983). Family research and family therapy: A reunion? *Journal of Marital and Family Therapy*, 9, 113–117.

"The Streets"
An Alternative Black Male Socialization Institution

William Oliver

The primary purpose of this article is to describe the social significance of "the streets" as an alternative to the family, church, and other community-based institutions that facilitate Black male socialization. A major assumption of this discussion is that for many marginal Black males, "the streets" is a socialization institution that has a major influence on their psychosocial development and life-course trajectories and transitions. In addition, the article addresses some of the problematic consequences associated with the pursuit of manhood and social recognition in "the streets."

The primary purpose of this article is to describe the social significance of "the streets" as an alternative site of Black male socialization. Socialization is a formal and informal interactive process in which the adults in a society, through the use of the institutions that they control, deliberately seek to inculcate in young people the beliefs, values, and norms that will allow them to functionally adapt as members of society (Coser, Rhea, Steffan, & Nock, 1983). In most discussions of the socialization process, the emphasis is on the role and function of conventional socialization institutions (e.g., the family, church, educational system, community-based organizations, and mass media) in shaping identity and behavior. In contrast, there is a lack of research on the role and function that unconventional social institutions play in facilitating the socialization of adolescents and young adults.

The phrase "the streets" is used here to refer to the network of public and semipublic social settings (e.g., street corners, vacant lots, bars, clubs, after-hours joints, convenience stores, drug houses, pool rooms, parks and public recreational places, etc.) in which primarily lower and working-class Black males tend to congregate. Hence, a major assumption guiding this discussion is that for many marginalized Black males, "the streets" is a socialization institution that is as important as the family, the church, and the educational system in terms of its influence on their psychosocial development and life course trajectories and transitions. Furthermore, the view developed here expands on a finding reported nearly 30 years ago by Useni Perkins

(1975) in his seminal work, *Home is a Dirty Street*, in which he concluded that "the streets... constitute an institution in the same way that the church, school, and family are conceived as institutions" (p. 26).

AMERICAN SOCIAL STRUCTURE AND THE STREET INSTITUTION

The streets as a ghetto institution is the creation of the American social structure (Clark, 1965; W. J. Wilson, 1996) as well as functional and dysfunctional individual and cultural adaptations to intergenerational structural challenges confronting African American males (Feagan & Vera, 1995; Perkins, 1975; Welsing, 1974; W. J. Wilson, 1996). For example, high rates of unemployment, underemployment, poverty, substance abuse, incarceration, and inadequate family and fatherhood role functioning are major characteristics of Black males who center their lives in "the streets" (Anderson, 1999; W. J. Wilson, 1996).

The idleness of many underclass Black males, resulting in part from chronic unemployment, is a major factor contributing to their being available to participate in street-related activities. For example, Black male unemployment on average is 2 times greater than the unemployment rate among White males. In addition, Black males earn 62 cents for every dollar earned by White males. Also, as a result of the decline of low-skill, high-wage heavy industrial jobs and the expansion of low-wage service jobs and high-wage, high-skill information and technology jobs, Black males have born the brunt of the loss of low-skill, high-wage manufacturing jobs resulting from the geographical shift in the concentration of jobs from the inner cities to the suburbs and Third World countries (Kasarda, 1990; W. J. Wilson, 1996). Indeed, although all Americans must adapt to shifts and transformations in the national economy, among Black males the adverse effects of the restructuring of the economy are enhanced as a result of their intergenerational exposure to historical and contemporary patterns of racial discrimination, particularly blocked access to educational and employment opportunities (Freeman, 1996; Liebow, 1967; W. J. Wilson, 1996).

INDIVIDUAL AND COLLECTIVE ADAPTATION TO THE STREETS

Most lower and working-class Black males do not center their lives in "the streets" and street-related activities (Anderson, 1990, 1999; Hannerz, 1969). Indeed, the majority of lower and working-class Black men are resilient and conform to a decency orientation in response to adverse structural conditions that tend to limit their capacity to successfully compete with White men in the arenas of politics, education, economics, and the maintenance of a stable family life (Anderson, 1999; Hannerz, 1969; Hunter & Davis, 1994; White & Cones, 1999). However, there is a substantial number of Black males who lack the resiliency and personal and social resources that are necessary to cope effectively with the adverse structural conditions directed against them (Madhubuti, 1990; Taylor-Gibbs, 1988). Consequently, it is this population of marginalized lower and working-class Black males who are most prone to seek respect and social recognition by constructing their identities as men in the social world of "the streets" (Anderson, 1999; Hannerz, 1969; Perkins, 1975; Staples, 1982). Among such men, it is during adolescence that they learn that an important step toward social recognition and respect as a man, given the social realities of marginalized Black men, involves developing the ability to successfully navigate life in the streets (Anderson, 1999; Perkins, 1975).

The importance of "the streets" as an alternative Black male socialization institution is related to the manner that macro-level, life-sustaining institutions (e.g., the political system, the economic system, the educational system, the criminal justice system, and mass media) have historically been managed by the White majority, and particularly White men, to prevent African American males from achieving political, economic, and social equality (Feagin & Vera, 1995; Madhubuti, 1990; Welsing, 1974). According to White and Cones (1999),

> White males have constructed a society in which they have empowered themselves in positions of wealth, decision making, and prestige. They exercise controlling vetoes over aspirations and choices in most of the political, economic, and legal areas of American life. In empowering themselves, they have reduced the opportunities and choices of Black males. (p. 142)

Hence, the cumulative effects of intergenerational exposure to historical and contemporary patterns of racial and gender oppression directed against Black males has served as a catalyst leading many marginalized Black males to socially construct masculine identities that place emphasis on toughness, sexual conquest, and street hustling (Anderson, 1999; Hannerz, 1969; White & Cones, 1999; Whitehead, Peterson, & Kaljee, 1994) as a means of coping with and transcending what some researchers have characterized as "frustrated masculinity" (Hare, 1964) or "fragmented gender identity" (Whitehead et al., 1994). Indeed, individual and collective perceptions of systematic exclusion from the conventional means of achieving identity and status as a man within the legitimate opportunity structure, along with individual-level variation in access to supportive family and community support, has had the effect of enhancing the attraction and institutionalization of the streets as an alternative setting to pursue personal and social significance (Anderson, 1999; Hannerz, 1969; W. J. Wilson, 1996). Consequently, for many lower and working-class Black males, a significant stage in their rite of passage into manhood involves learning how to successfully manage the challenges of street life by constructing masculine identities that are respected and feared by other men in and outside the social world of "the streets" (Anderson, 1999). As a result of this social process, "the streets" is an institution that exists primarily to meet the psychological and social needs of socially and economically marginalized Black males (Anderson, 1999; Perkins, 1975; White & Cones, 1999).

Although there are a number of gathering places (e.g., basketball courts, churches, Masonic lodges, social clubs, community centers, parks, liquor and convenience stores, bars and clubs, skating rinks, bowling alleys) in which Black males congregate and use to bond and enact what A. J. Franklin (1999) described as "brotherhood rites of passage and activities," none is more significant in constructing Black male gender identities that are associated with problematic behavior than the network of settings that are colloquially referred to by Black men as "the streets."

The emergence and intergenerational existence of "the streets" as an important ghetto institution is also the product of exposure to inadequate family and community support, community tolerance of various patterns of dysfunctional behavior routinely engaged in by marginalized Black males, and the lack of organized and sustained community resistance directed toward Black males who embrace street-related values, norms, and roles (Madhubuti, 1990; Perkins, 1975; W. J. Wilson, 1996). The psychologist A. N. Wilson (1992) has characterized marginalized Black males who are most at risk for becoming involved in street-related violence as men

> whose training for positive manhood is nonexistent or inadequate; whose avoidance of masculine responsibility or confusion about what it means to be a man under oppression, have moved them to accept an incomplete, distorted, self-defeating and, sometimes self-destructive definition and expression of masculinity. (p. 340)

Consequently, street-related values, norms, and roles are culturally transmitted across succeeding generations of Black males, particularly among those males whose daily lives are entrenched in the social realities and experiences of the urban underclass (Anderson, 1999; W. J. Wilson, 1987, 1996). It is for this reason that the various street-corner settings where many marginalized Black males spend an inordinate amount of time socializing and "hanging out" have importance based on their routine use as social stages that allow and tolerate the ritualized enactment of street-oriented masculine identities (Perkins, 1975; White & Cones, 1999). Furthermore, it is in "the streets" that many marginalized Black males proactively assume masculine identities that are adopted for the purpose of transcending what Franklin (1999) has described as an "invisibility syndrome," that is, "an inner struggle with the feeling that one's talents, abilities, personality, and worth are not valued or even recognized because of prejudice and racism" (p. 761). Thus, from the perspective of marginalized Black men, the achievement of success and status in "the streets" is a means to become highly visible in the social world of the urban underclass.

HIP HOP AND STREET CULTURE SOCIALIZATION

Hip hop culture, particularly gangsta rap music and videos, has had a major influence on the evolution and transmission of contemporary street culture socialization and the social construction of gender identity among poor and nonpoor African American males (Kitwana, 2002). For example, prior to the emergence of hip hop, exposure to and socialization into street culture involved investing time and energy in being physically present in the various street-corner social settings that provide familiarity with street life and opportunities to develop various street-related skills (Hannerz, 1969; Horton, 1972; Majors & Mancini-Billson, 1992). According to Horton (1972), for example, "the more or less organized center of street life is the 'set'–meaning both the peer group and the places where it hangs out. It is the stage and central marketplace for activity, where to find out what's happening." Thus, prior to the emergence of hip hop, to learn "the game" as it is played on "the streets," one had to be physically present in various street settings. In contrast, hip hop music, music videos, gangsta films, hip hop magazines, and television programs featuring hip hop artists have provided Black youth as well as youth and young adults of other races and class levels opportunities to be exposed to street-related values, norms, roles, and activities without being physically present in street-corner settings (Kitwana, 2002). Hence, technological advances in the dissemination of Black popular culture have functioned to glorify and reinforce urban street culture, particularly among those Black males who are most vulnerable to pursuing social recognition in "the streets."

The thematic concerns and images presented in hip hop music and videos often depict members of the hip hop generation in street-corner settings (e.g., street hangouts, nightclubs, parties, and various social situations, etc.) engaging in patterns of behavior ritually expressed in a manner associated with urban street culture (Best & Kellner, 1999). In addition, the worldview and expressive style of so-called old-school pimps, players, hustlers, and street women are prominent in rap and hip hop videos and in the public personas that many rap and hip hop artists present for public consumption (Dyson, 2003; Kitwana, 2002, p. 136; Pough, 2004; Powell, 2003). For example, in his song "One More Chance," the rapper Biggie Smalls raps about his player skills and his ability to steal another man's girl because he is president of the players club. However, unlike previous generations of lower and working-class Black males who learned the content of street-corner socialization by being physically present on "the streets" observing and emulating the attitudes and behavior of more seasoned players and hustlers (Allen, 1978; Hannerz, 1969), the contemporary generations of young street-corner males are exposed to various media products that constitute an urban street-corner soundtrack. That is, values, norms, roles, and behavior associated with the streets are often depicted in hip hop music videos and gangsta films and reinforced by lyrics and video images that tend to glorify life in "the streets." According to Best and Kellner (1999),

> The images and lyrics show and tell us that it is a time of intense poverty and differences between the haves and the have-nots, that it is a time of urban crime and violence, a time of gangs and drugs, a time of STDs, HIV, and AIDS, a time of buck wilding and extreme sexuality, a time when the urban underclass is striking out and striking back, and thus is a tense and frightening time for the culture at large. (p. 8)

Furthermore, rap artists present "a highly articulated awareness and sense of place" (Best & Kellner, 1999, p. 7). Thus, the significance of rap music is that it is a music that expresses views about the conditions, experiences, and aspirations of Blacks living in urban ghettos (Dyson, 1996; Kitwana, 2002). Indeed, gangsta rap is about existing on the margins of American society (Dyson, 1996; Kitwana, 2002). For example, in the early years of its origin as a Black youth cultural art form, hip hop's lyrical content reflected the challenges, concerns, and aspirations of marginalized Black men and women whose lives were not centered in street culture but who were very aware of the types of social pressures that compel individuals to seek social recognition in "the streets" (Dyson, 1996). This type of thematic concern is most evident in Grandmaster

Flash & the Furious Five's (1983) classic hit "The Message," in which they describe life in the ghetto as a jungle in which residents are on the edge of loosing their minds due to poverty and hatred toward the larger society. In addition, the group raps about their admiration for the street hustlers who as big money makers used their wits to transcend ghetto poverty and achieve a measure of material success unattainable to most ghetto residents. The popularity and social significance of "The Message" was that its incisive social commentary describing the challenges confronting lower and working-class Blacks resonated with a broad segment of the Black community.

In contrast, over the past decade and a half, hip hop soul and rap, as a musical genre, have tended to glamorize America's obsession with achieving status through material acquisition and the manner through which material and social success is sometimes alternatively pursued and ritualized by underclass Black males who maintain a street culture orientation (Dyson, 1996; Kitwana, 2002). In this sense, not only does rap music describe the rage and anger that exists in the ghetto, but it also describes the extreme means that a distinct segment of the Black male population are willing to use to transcend poverty and hopelessness.

In addition, contemporary rap music increasingly reflects the larger society's misogynistic attitudes and behaviors toward women (Dyson, 1996; Kitwana, 2002; Pough, 2004). In recent years, so-called gangsta rap has fell out of vogue to be replaced by what Neal (2002) referred to as "playa/pimp/balla/high-roller" (p. 189) rap. Thus, the promotion of street-oriented manhood roles, in which men achieve significance as players and ballas, is a prominent feature of contemporary rap and hip hop music and videos (Kitwana, 2002). Consequently, in response to the potential wealth and status associated with achieving success in the hip hop industry as an artist or entrepreneur, an alternative to drug dealing as a means of achieving the American dream for many marginalized Black males has emerged. That is, the economic opportunities associated with hip hop culture are now perceived by many young Black men as the new "street game" and a viable and legitimate alternative to selling drugs or committing burglaries or robberies and other forms of street hustling as a means of acquiring money, various material goods, and status in and outside the ghetto (Kitwana, 2002). It is because of this that rap and hip hop artists, record producers, record executives, and various hip hop merchandisers have emerged as role models for a generation of young Black men and women who are obsessed with achieving success and status through acquiring wealth and material consumption (Kitwana, 2002).

Rap and hip hop video images in which young Black men are portrayed as gangstas, ballas, and players is problematic because these images of masculinity serve to promote and glorify masculine behavior that condones exploiting others to achieve material success, resorting to violence as a means of resolving disputes and to indiscriminate pursuit of sexual relationships with women (Kitwana, 2002). Equally problematic is the portrayal of young Black women as hypersexed, promiscuous, devious, violent, and willing to do anything to gain access to a man's money and other material resources (Morgan, 1999; Pough, 2004). Consequently, portrayals of Black women by male artists in hip hop culture serve to perpetuate existing stereotypes (e.g., Jezebel and Sapphire) or reformulate new stereotypes (e.g., "skeezers," "bitches," "hoes" and "ride-and-die chicks") that render Black women vulnerable to aggression and violence perpetrated by Black males who have internalized misogynistic messages that provide justifications for engaging in acts of violence against Black women (Wyatt, 1997).

The Content of Street Socialization

The essence of the streets as an important ghetto institution is not its physical location as a place of excitement and danger but its social function as a ghetto-based institutional site in which the worldview (i.e., ideology, values, and norms) and manhood roles that dominate Black male street culture are ritually expressed and continuously reformulated and embraced by successive generations of marginalized Black males (Anderson, 1999; Liebow, 1967; Kitwana, 2002). Equally important is the social function of the streets as an institutional site in which various street-corner settings are available for use as social stages on which valued masculine identities can be enacted in the presence of significant others, who serve to validate one's manhood (Hannerz, 1969; Oliver, 1998). Among Black males who center their lives in street culture, an individual's efforts to achieve manhood are not regarded as valid unless they can be successfully enacted in the presence of a social audience who possesses the credibility to validate competent enactment (Oliver, 1998). For example, Horton (1972) reported,

> Here [in "the streets"] peer socialization and reinforcement also take place. The younger dude feels a sense of pride when he can be on the set and throw a rap to an older dude. He is learning how to handle himself, show respect, take care of business, and establish his own rep. (p. 25)

Thus, "the streets" is a social stage in which marginalized Black males become exposed to street-related values, norms, and roles and subsequently engage in behavior that reflects an effort to achieve respectability (Anderson, 1999; Majors & Mancini-Billson, 1992).

Anderson (1999) has characterized the worldview of "the streets" as the "code of the streets," that is, a set of informal rules governing interpersonal public behavior in underclass communities. According to Anderson, the heart of the code is the emphasis on respect, which is described as the desire to be treated right or granted deference in all interpersonal relations. Routine adherence to the code of the streets is generally expressed through the enactment of masculine identities that are valued among males who center their lives in street culture. Hence, the code of "the streets" is a normative standard that marginalized and nonmarginalized Black males who adhere to street culture rely on to assess the extent to which their peers and others adhere to values and norms that place emphasis on toughness, sexual conquest, and hustling. Consequently, in the course of social interaction, such assessments influence how street-corner men behave toward others and how street-oriented men are responded to by those who are ghetto insiders and outsiders (Anderson, 1999; Oliver, 1998; W. J. Wilson, 1996).

There are three masculine roles that constitute the core of the hierarchy of manhood roles that are valued by Black males who seek social recognition in "the streets." These roles include the tough guy/gangsta, the player, and the hustler/balla. These roles are not mutually exclusive in that individuals may adopt elements of all three in their construction of masculine identity and presentation of self. However, in the encounters of everyday life, the concerns, normative expectations, and behavior associated with a particular masculine role orientation may predominate over others based on the circumstances, the participants, and what is at stake in a given situation.

The Tough Guy/Gangsta

For males, successful participation in street settings on a regular basis is dependent on an individual's ability to convey to other males through symbolic (e.g., demeanor and cool poses) and overt displays (e.g., tough talk, threats, actual acts of violence) of toughness that he is willing to resort to violence as a means of resolving disputes (Majors & Mancini-Billson, 1992; Oliver, 1998). Although conventional conceptualizations of manhood emphasize toughness, what is unique about adherence to the toughness norm in the streets is that street-oriented men are more likely to become involved in interpersonal encounters in which their commitment to toughness will be challenged in ways that threaten both their reputation and physical safety (Oliver, 1998). Thus, males who are unable to convey a credible commitment to toughness are at risk of being harassed, exploited, and physically assaulted (Oliver, 1998). Hence, marginalized Black males who frequent various street settings are hypersensitive to conducting themselves in a manner in which they can avoid attempts by others to violate their desire to be free from external interference. Thus, in street lore and in the social world of "the streets," respect and deference are attributed to those males who are able to present credible portrayals of themselves as being "bad niggas," "thugs," and "hard" (Roberts, 1990).

The Player of Women

Overt emphasis on sexual conquest and sexual promiscuity is not unique to lower and working-class Black men (Pleck & Pleck, 1980). However, what is unique is the manner in which Black men ritualize the sexual conquest orientation as a feature of masculine identity and social practice in the social world of the underclass community (Majors & Mancini-Billson, 1992). Limited access to the legitimate means necessary to support establishing manhood in terms of being an independent self-sufficient adult and/or providing for one's family has served as a catalyst for some Black men to define and claim manhood in terms of sexual conquest and exploitation of women (Anderson, 1999; Hannerz, 1969; Staples, 1982; W. J. Wilson, 1996). Among Black males generally, and particularly those who organize daily life around their involvement in street life, there is substantial support and respect for those males who successfully demonstrate their proficiency in enacting the player of women role (Anderson, 1999; Hannerz, 1969). In his ethnographic study of urban Black males, Anderson (1990) found that "casual sex with as many women as possible, impregnating one or more, and getting them to have your baby brings a boy the ultimate esteem from his peers and makes him feel like a man." Indeed, a major theme in contemporary hip hop is the sexual objectification and exploitation of Black women (Kitwana, 2002; Morgan, 1999; Pough, 2004).

The Hustler/Balla

The hustler/balla role is a role orientation in which manhood is defined in terms of using one's wits to aggressively pursue access to legitimate economic opportunities and the illicit resources of the ghetto to improve one's economic and material condition. In his ethnography of urban street life, Horton (1972) concluded, "Hustling is the central street activity. It is the economic foundation for everyday life. Hustling and the fruit of hustling set the rhythm for social activities" (p. 23) in the social world of the streets. The social significance of the hustler/balla role among marginalized Black men is that it represents an alternative to more legitimate means of acquiring material goods, constructing a valued manhood identity, and achieving status in an environment in which many men believe that they lack the skills and resources to achieve success through legitimate means (Whitehead, Peterson, & Kaljee, 1994). Hence, street hustling may involve selling drugs, operating an afterhours joint, selling stolen merchandise or merchandise purchased wholesale and presented to the buying public as stolen, gambling, pimping, and so forth (Horton, 1972). Furthermore, the emergence and popularity of hip hop as the most salient expression of contemporary Black popular culture has provided many marginalized Black males with an ever-widening range of illegitimate and legitimate alternatives to traditional forms of street hustling. Thus, the ideology and principles of street hustling, also referred to as "the game," are now being incorporated in marginalized Black males' efforts to pursue money, material goods, and status by engaging in entrepreneurial activities, ranging from hip hop artists, record producers, concert promoters, sellers of bootleg CDs, sellers of hip hop clothing at the retail and street-corner level, and detailers of automobiles to those providing a host of goods and services that are essential to those who identify with hip hop culture.

THE CONSEQUENCES OF STREET SOCIALIZATION

"The streets" is an important setting in the lives of many marginal Black males because it provides an alternative to the traditional opportunity structure as a means of achieving status and respect. However, there are a number of problematic consequences associated with the pursuit of valued manhood identities in the streets.

Disconnection from Employment Opportunities

Centering a major portion of one's life in street-related activities (hanging out, drinking, pursuing indiscriminate sexual relations, using drugs, selling drugs, robbing, and stealing) increases already weak labor force attachments emanating from the lack of marketable skills, the transformation of the economy, and the loss of low-skill, high-wage manufacturing jobs. That is, commitment to dysfunctional manhood roles and involvement in routine activities associated with such roles weaken marginalized Black males' attachment to the conventional labor force (Van Haitsma, 1989; W. J. Wilson, 1996). Furthermore, routine enactment of social roles and participation in activities associated with street life reduces the likelihood that underclass Black males will have access to social networks, information, training, and employment opportunities that are likely to lead to a strong attachment to a changing economic market place (W. J. Wilson, 1987, 1996). Thus, the transformation of the national economy is a major source of structural pressure confronting marginalized Black men and is compounded as a result of their assumption of manhood roles that reinforce economic marginality and social isolation.

Disruption of Family Life and Abdication of Fatherhood Responsibilities

Routine participation in street-related activities renders street-oriented Black men less desirable as husbands and long-term intimate partners and also contributes to high rates of family and relationship disruption (e.g., high divorce rates, female-headed families, out-of-wedlock births, less commitment of men to relationships, and negative perceptions of Black men on the part of Black women) (Hare & Hare, 1989; Tucker & Mitchell-Kernan, 1995). In addition, participation in street culture contributes to the scarcity and shortage of marriageable Black males. For example, research suggests that among Black men, participation in street-related activities is linked to increased rates of substance abuse and drug trafficking (Whitehead, Peterson, & Kaljee, 1994), violent crime offending (Oliver, 1998; Wright & Decker, 1997), incarceration (Mauer, 1999), unemployment (W. J. Wilson, 1996), poverty (W. J. Wilson, 1996), firearm injuries resulting in paralysis, other forms of disability, and premature death due to homicide (Oliver, 2000; Zawitz, 1994).

Furthermore, participation in street-related activities diminishes a man's capacity to function as a responsible father. For example, among the conventional norms associated with fatherhood is an expectation that fathers will mentor and provide financial support for their children. However, commitment to and involvement in street life decreases street-oriented males' attachment to family life and their capacity to fulfill the responsibilities associated with fatherhood (W. J. Wilson, 1987, 1996).

Interpersonal Conflict and Violence

The pursuit of money, status, and respect in the streets is a major source of interpersonal conflict leading to violent confrontations involving marginalized Black men as perpetrators and victims (Oliver, 1998; Wright & Decker, 1997). Although the streets are regarded as exciting, they are also perceived by those who spend an inordinate amount of time in these settings as dangerous places where reputations, freedom, and even lives may be lost (Anderson, 1999; Oliver, 1998). For example, in his focused interviews with violent Black men, Oliver (1998) found that violent confrontations among Black men are generally precipitated by one or both combatants' adherence to values, norms, and routine activities associated with enactment of manhood roles that are valued in Black male street culture.

Furthermore, Black women who are romantically involved with male partners who are actively engaged in street-related activities (e.g., drug use, drug dealing, hustling, gangs, and street violence) may be at increased risk of experiencing intimate partner violence. For example, men who construct their identities in terms of manhood role orientations that are valued in the streets (the tough guy, the gangsta, the player, etc.)

are likely to import pro-violence values, norms, and expectations into their intimate relationships (Dunlap, Johnson, & Rath, 1996; Richie, 1996).

High Rates of Incarceration

Black males' involvement in street life is directly related to their high rates of incarceration (Whitehead, 2000). For example, at year end 2002, the incarceration rate of Black males (4,810/100,000) was 8 times higher than the incarceration rate of White males (649/100,000) (Harrison & Karberg, 2003). Moreover, in 1991, the Bureau of Justice Statistics reported that African American males had a 29% lifetime risk of serving at least 1 year in prison, which is 6 times higher than the risk for White males (Bonczar & Beck, 1997). Currently, an estimated 10% of Black males ages 25 to 29 were incarcerated at year end 2002, compared to 2.4% of Hispanic males and about 1.2% of White males in the same age group (Harrison & Beck, 2003).

Consequently, the prevalence of incarceration among Black males has come to be recognized as an expected reality and a significant aspect of the rite of passage into manhood among Black males who reside in underclass neighborhoods (Whitehead, 2000). The anticipation of experiencing imprisonment is enhanced by their exposure to Black youth popular culture that has promoted prison-style clothing and glamorized images of prison life (Clayton & Moore, 2003). Furthermore, following a period of imprisonment, it is not uncommon that the challenges associated with finding a job, housing, or reuniting with family leads many Black males back to the streets and their pre-prison associations and activities (Clayton & Moore, 2003).

CONCLUSION

There are many unanswered questions relative to understanding the pervasiveness of the streets as an unconventional socialization institution in the African American community. For example, how do we explain the fact that most Black males who are exposed to street culture are resilient and grow up to conform to a decency orientation rather than a street orientation in terms of how they structure their daily lives (Anderson, 1999; Hunter & Davis, 1994)? What type of life events or social processes lead men to reject "the streets" at certain points in their lives and adopt a decency manhood orientation? How does street culture influence prison culture, and how does prison culture influence street culture? How does street culture influence the leisure activities of stable lower-, working-, and middle-class Blacks? What role does the streets as a socialization institution play in the social construction of womanhood identities among marginalized and nonmarginalized Black females? This is a particularly important question given the broad dissemination in many hip hop lyrics and videos of images that glorify women who present themselves as promiscuous or who are willing to do anything (legal, illegal, or die) to support their man (Morgan, 1999; Pough, 2004). Finding answers to these and other questions will enhance our understanding of the social significance of unconventional institutions such as "the streets" in facilitating socialization, sociability, and social problems in the Black community.

REFERENCES

Allen, J. (1978). *Assault with a deadly weapon: The autobiography of a street criminal*. New York: Pantheon Books.

Anderson, E. (1990). *Streetwise: Race, class, and change in an urban community*. Chicago: University of Chicago Press.

Anderson, E. (1999). *Code of the streets: Decency, violence, and the moral life of the inner city*. New York: Norton.

Best, S., & Kellner, D. (1999). Rap, Black rage, and racial difference. *Enculturation*. Retrieved from www.http://enculturation.gmu.edu/2_2best-kellner.html

Bonczar, T. P., & Beck, A. J. (1997). *Lifetime likelihood of going to state or federal prison*. Washington, DC: U.S. Department of Justice.

Clark, K. B. (1965). *Dark ghetto*. New York: Harper & Row.

Clayton, O., & Moore, J. (2003). The effects of crime and imprisonment on family formation. In O. Clayton, R. B. Mincy, & D. Blankenhorn (Eds.), *Black fathers in contemporary American society: Strengths, weaknesses, and strategies for change* (pp. 84–102). New York: Russell Sage.

Coser, L., Rhea, B., Steffan, P. A., & Nock, S. L. (1983). *Introduction to sociology*. New York: Harcourt, Brace, Jovanovich.

Dunlap, E., Johnson, B., & Rath, J. W. (1996). Aggression in the households of crack sellers and abusers. *Applied Behavioral Science Review*, *4*, 191–217.

Dyson, M. E. (1996). *Between God and gangsta rap: Bearing witness to Black culture*. New York: Oxford University Press.

Dyson, M. E. (2003, October 2). Rebirth of the pimp [Commentary]. *The Tavis Smiley show*. Washington, DC: National Public Radio.

Feagin, J. R., & Vera, H. (1995). *White racism*. New York: Routledge.

Franklin, A. J. (1999). Invisibility syndrome and racial identity development in psychotherapy and counseling African American men. *The Counseling Psychologist*, *27*, 761–793.

Freeman, R. B. (1996). Why do so many young American men commit crimes and what might we do about it? *Journal of Economic Perspectives*, *10*, 25–42.

Grandmaster Flash & the Furious Five. (1983). *The message*. Durham, NC: Sugar Hill Music.

Hannerz, U. (1969). *Soulside: Inquiries into ghetto culture*. New York: Columbia University Press.

Hare, N. (1964). The frustrated masculinity of the Negro male. *Negro Digest*, *13*, 5–9.

Hare, N., & Hare, J. (Eds.). (1989). *Crisis in Black sexual politics*. San Francisco: Black Think Tank.

Harrison, P., & Karberg, J. (2003). *Prison and jail inmates at midyear* 2002. Washington, DC: U.S. Department of Justice.

Harrison, P. M., & Beck, A. J. (2003). *Prisoners* in 2002. Washington, DC: U.S. Department of Justice.

Horton, J. (1972). Time and cool people. In T. Kochman (Ed.), *Rappin and stylin' out* (pp. 19–31). Urbana: University of Illinois Press.

Hunter, A. G., & Davis, J. E. (1994). Hidden voices of Black men: The meaning, structure, and complexity of manhood. *Journal of Black Studies*, *25*, 20–40.

Kasarda, J. D. (1990). Urban industrial transition and the underclass. *Annals of the Academy of Political and Social Sciences*, *501*, 26–47.
Kitwana, B. (2002). *The hip hop generation: Young Blacks and the crisis in African American culture*. New York: Basic Civitas Books.
Liebow, E. (1967). *Tally's corner. Boston: Little, Brown.*
Madhubuti, H. (1990). *Black men: Single, dangerous and obsolete*. Chicago: Third World Press.
Majors, R., & Mancini-Billson, J. (1992). *Coolpose: The dilemmas of Black manhood in America*. Lexington, MA: Lexington Books.
Mauer, M. (1999). *Race to incarcerate*. New York: New Press
Morgan, J. (1999). *When chicken-heads come home to roost: A hip hop feminist breaks it down*. New York: Touchstone.
Neal, M. A. (2002). *Soul babies—Black popular culture and the post-soul aesthetic.* New York: Routledge.
Oliver, W. (1998). *The violent social world of Black men*. San Francisco: Jossey-Bass.
Oliver, W. (2000). The public health and social consequences of Black male violence. *Journal of African American Men*, *5*, 71–92.
Oliver, W. (2003). The structural cultural perspective: A theory of Black male violence. In D. F. Hawkins (Ed.), *Violent crime: Assessing race & ethnic differences* (pp. 280–302). New York: Cambridge University Press.
Perkins, U. E. (1975). *Home is a dirty street: The social oppression of Black children*. Chicago: Third World Press.
Pleck, J. H., & Pleck, E. H. (1980). *The American man*. New York: Prentice Hall.
Pough, G. (2004). *Check it while I wreck it: Black womanhood, hip hop culture, and public sphere*. Boston: Northeastern University Press.
Powell, K. (2003). *Who's gonna take the weight? Manhood, race, and power in America*. New York: Three Rivers Press.
Richie, B. E. (1996). *Compelled to crime: The gender entrapment of battered Black women*. New York: Routledge.
Roberts, J. W. (1990). *From trickster to badman: The Black folk hero in slavery and freedom*. Philadelphia: University of Pennsylvania Press.
Staples, R. (1982). *Black masculinity: The Black male's role in American society*. San Francisco: Black Scholar Press.
Taylor-Gibbs, J. (Ed.). (1988). *Young, Black, and male in America: An endangered species*. Dover, MA: Auburn House.
Tucker, M. B., & Mitchell-Kernan, C. (1995). *The decline in marriage among African Americans—Causes, consequences, and policy implications*. New York: Russell Sage.
Van Haitsma, M. (1989). A contextual definition of the underclass. *Focus*, *12*, 27–31.
Welsing, F. C. (1974). The conspiracy to make Blacks inferior. *Ebony*, *29*, 84–86, 89–90, 92–95.
White, J. L., & Cones, J. H. (1999). *Black man emerging: Facing the past and seizing a future in America*. New York: Freeman.
Whitehead, T. (2000). The "epidemic" and "cultural legends" of Black male incarceration: The socialization of African American children to a life of incarceration. In J. P. May & K. R. Pitts (Eds.), *Building violence: How America's rush to incarcerate creates more violence* (pp. 82–89). Thousand Oaks, CA: Sage.

Whitehead, T., Peterson, J., & Kaljee, L. (1994). The hustle: Socioeconomic deprivation, drug trafficking, and low-income African American male gender identity. *Pediatrics, 93*, 1050–1054.

Wilson, A. N. (1992). *Understanding Black adolescent male violence—Its remediation and prevention*. New York: Afrikan World InfoSystems.

Wilson, W. J. (1987). *The truly disadvantaged*. Chicago: University of Chicago Press.

Wilson, W. J. (1996). *When work disappears: The world of the new urban poor*. New York: Alfred P. Knopf.

Wright, R., & Decker, S. H. (1997). *Armed robbers in action: Stickups and street culture*. Boston: Northeastern University Press.

Wyatt, G. (1997). *Stolen women: Reclaiming our sexuality, taking back our lives*. New York: John Wiley.

Zawitz, M. E. (1994). *Firearm injury*. Washington, DC: U.S. Department of Justice.

... Contemporary Socioeconomic Trends
An Overview of Trends in Social and Economic Well-Being, by Race

Rebecca M. Blank

QUESTIONS TO CONSIDER

In this reading, Rebecca Blank discusses seven indicators of "well-being" for various racial and ethnic groups in the United States. As you read this chapter take note of which racial groups appear to be socially disadvantaged relative to one another. How do you explain group level disparities in these quality of life indicators? Do you agree with the three explanations she provides at the end of this chapter as to why these quality of life disparities exist?

INTRODUCTION

In general, there are many signs of improvement across all racial and ethnic groups in a wide variety of measures of measures of well-being, such as educational achievement, health status, and housing quality. In some cases, disparities between different racial groups have narrowed, as all groups have experienced improvements. But in too many cases, overall improvement in well-being among all groups has brought about no lessening of racial or ethnic disparities. In a few key measures, disparities have actually widened. The primary conclusion of this paper is that race and ethnicity continue to be salient predictors of well-being in American society. To understand what is happening in America today and what will be happening in America tomorrow, one must understand the role of race.

Indicators of Well-Being

This chapter discusses trends in seven areas:

1. population/demographic change,
2. education,

3. labor markets,
4. economic status,
5. health status,
6. crime and criminal justice, and
7. housing and neighborhoods.

Wherever possible, trends over time are presented for key variables, focusing on five major population groups: non-Hispanic Whites, non-Hispanic Blacks, Hispanics, Asian and Pacific Islanders, and American Indians and Alaska Natives. These data arc taken almost entirely from U.S. government sources. In many cases, however, data for all groups are not available, or not available for the entire time period. Data available for as many groups as possible are presented in the 14 figures. The term "minority" is used to refer to a group that composes a minority of the total population. Although these five groups are currently minorities in the population, current trends project they will, together, constitute more than half the U.S. population by 2050.

This brief introduction does not attempt to provide anything like a comprehensive discussion of the available data. Provided here is an overview of some of the more interesting trends, particularly focusing on issues that introduce key topics that will be addressed in this book. One particular limitation of these data is that they present averages across very large aggregate categories of racial and ethnic classification. This hides much of the rather important information about subgroups. For instance, although data for Dominican and Cuban Americans might show very different trends, they are both combined within the Hispanic category. Similarly, Japanese and Laotian Americans are grouped together in the Asian and Pacific Islander category; Italian and Norwegian Americans are grouped together as non-Hispanic Whites.

An Increasingly Diverse Population

The U.S. population is becoming increasingly diverse. Hispanics, non-Hispanic Blacks, Asian and Pacific Islanders, and American Indians and Alaska Natives currently constitute 27 percent of the population. By 2005, Hispanics will be the largest of these groups in the United States, surpassing non-Hispanic Blacks. These changes will present this nation with a variety of social and economic opportunities and challenges.

Recent high levels of immigration are also increasing diversity within these groups. At present, 38 percent of Hispanics are foreign-born; 61 percent of Asian and Pacific Islanders are foreign-born. This raises questions of assimilation and generational change. Will the second generation among these groups show a narrowing of the disparities that distinguish their foreign-born parents from the U.S.-born population?

Where people live and who they live next to is important in determining how individuals experience racial and ethnic diversity. The population in the West is the most diverse, with more than one-third of the population composed of racial and ethnic minorities. The West is also the region where a higher percentage of Hispanics, Asian and Pacific Islanders, and American Indians and Alaska Natives reside. The South is the second most diverse region and has the largest percentage of non-Hispanic Blacks. The Midwest is the region with the least population diversity; 85 percent of its population is non-Hispanic Whites.

The household structure of these different groups varies greatly. Household structure, based on data for 1970 and 1996, correlates with a variety of other variables, particularly variables relating to economic well-being. More adults in a family means more potential earnings as well as more available adults to care for children. Single-parent households are among the poorest groups in the country. Individuals who live alone are also often more economically vulnerable than are persons who live with other family members.

All groups show significant increases in the number of people living alone or in single-parent families between 1970 and 1996, but the percentage living in single-parent families is much larger among Blacks, Hispanics, and American Indians and Alaska Natives. In fact, the biggest recent percentage of all families are in single-father families, rather than single-mother families, although single-father families continue to be a small percentage of all families. The reasons for these trends—and why some groups have much larger percentages of single-parent families in particular—are much debated.

Household structure is closely related to age distribution as well. Minority populations have a significantly larger percentage of children under the age of 17 than do non-Hispanic Whites, whereas Whites have a much larger percentage of elderly persons. The result is that the school-aged population—persons aged 5 to 17—is more racially and ethnically diverse than the population as a whole, so that today's schools reflect tomorrow's more diverse adult population—and also mirror some of the conflicts and the benefits that accompany growing diversity.

EDUCATIONAL ATTAINMENT

In a society growing increasingly complex, educational skills are key to future life opportunities. Disparities in education are fundamental because they can determine lifetime earning opportunities and influence an individual's ability to participate in civic activities as well.

The labor market of the twenty-first century will rely increasingly on computers; thus, obtaining computer skills is fundamental. Figure 1 shows how children's access to computers has changed over time, both in their schools and in their homes. Clearly, more and more children have access to computers, particularly in their schools; but there is an ongoing gap in computer use between White children versus Black and Hispanic children. Between 1984 and 1993, the years for which these data are available, this gap increased for computer use at home, leaving children in minority groups further behind.

Other more conventional measures of achievement in elementary and secondary schooling have generally shown narrowing gaps across racial groups. Mathematics

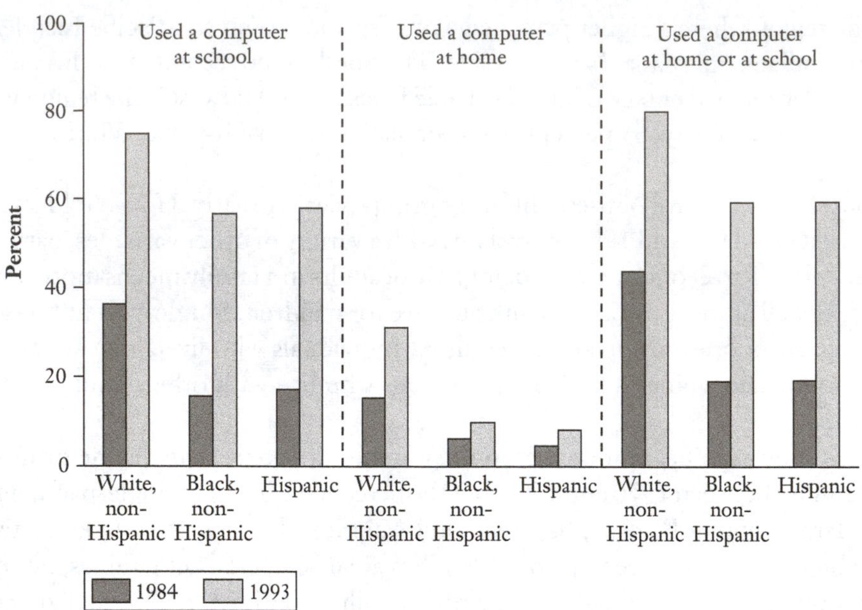

FIGURE 1 Computer Use by Children in First Through Sixth Grades. *Source:* Council of Economic Advisers (1998).

proficiency scores, as measured among children of different ages by the National Assessment of Educational Progress, have shown ongoing gains, particularly by Black children. High school completion continues to inch up among both Whites and Blacks, with substantially greater progress among Blacks; so that the White-Black high school dropout rates are slowly converging over time. Among Hispanics, high school completion has been stagnant at approximately 60 percent since the early 1980s. Hence, the gap between Hispanics and other groups in terms of educational achievement is widening.

Figure 2 shows trends in attainment of college degrees, through 1997, among Whites, Blacks, and Hispanics. Economic returns to a college education have increased dramatically in recent years, and college degrees continue to be an important credential for entry into many white-collar jobs. Although college completion has increased steeply among Whites, it has increased only modestly among Blacks, leading to a widening gap since the early 1990s. Among Hispanics, college completion rates are not much higher now than they were in the mid-1980s.

The more stagnant educational trends among Hispanics reflect, in part, the growing immigrant percentage of that population. Immigrants are less likely to hold high school or college degrees. U.S.-born Hispanics are making progress in increasing both their high school and college completion levels, but this progress is being diluted by the growing pool of less-educated immigrants. This re-emphasizes the question of how second-generation Hispanic children will fare. If they follow the trends of other U.S.-born populations, Hispanic educational attainment will start to increase over time.

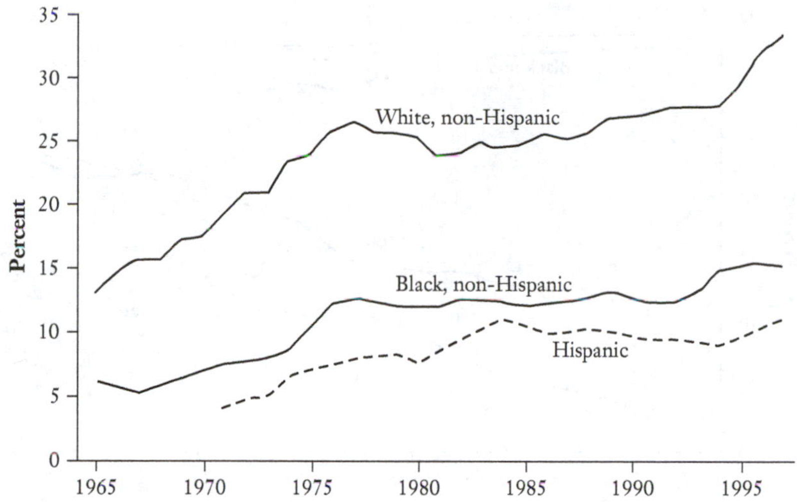

FIGURE 2 Persons Aged 25 to 29 with a Four-Year College Degree or Higher. Prior to 1971, data for Whites include Hispanic Whites, and data for Blacks include Hispanic Blacks. Data for non-Hispanic Blacks and Hispanics are three-year centered averages. Prior to 1991, data are for persons having completed four or more years of college. *Source:* Council of Economic Advisers (1998).

LABOR-MARKET INVOLVEMENT

Involvement in the labor force means integration with the mainstream U.S. economy. Earnings are the primary source of income for most persons. Although job-holding may create some stress, it also produces economic rewards. Access to jobs is key for economic progress.

Figure 3 plots the labor-force participation rates from the 1950s to 1997 for Whites, Blacks, and Hispanics, by gender. The chart shows rapidly increasing convergence in labor-force participation rates, as men's rates have slowly decreased while women's rates have increased steadily. White women, who used to be much less likely to work than Black women, are now just as likely to be in the labor force. In fact, both White women's and Black women's labor-force participation rates are rapidly converging with those of Black men, who have experienced steady decreases in work involvement.

Hispanic women also have shown increases in labor-force participation, but remain much less likely to work than other women. A major question for the Hispanic population is whether adult women will show rapid increases in labor-force participation, to the level of women from other groups. Such changes in women's labor-market involvement not only mean changes in the economic base of families—and probably in the economic security and decision-making power of husbands

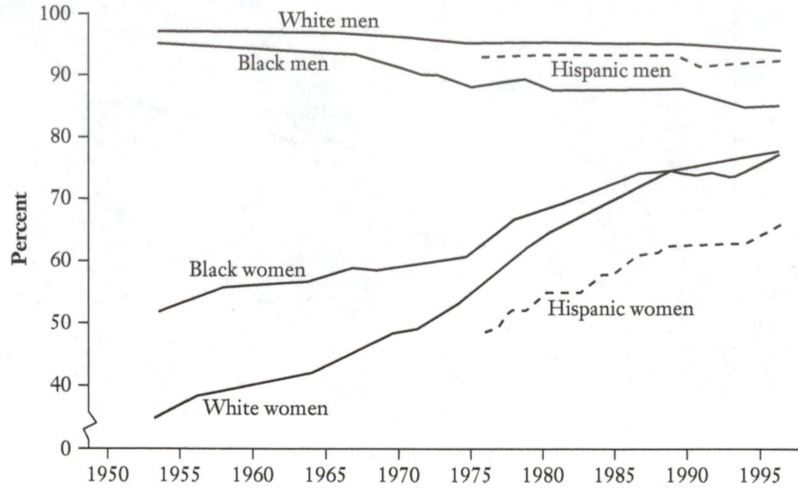

FIGURE 3 Labor Frorce Participation Rates of Persons Aged 25 to 54. Prior to 1972, data for Blacks include all non-Whites. *Source:* Council of Economic Advisers (1998).

versus wives—but may also mean substantial changes in family functioning and in child-rearing practices.

Along with labor-force participation, unemployment is another measure of access (or lack of access) to jobs. After two decades of higher unemployment rates, unemployment in the late 1990s was at 25-to-30-year lows among all groups. The differentials between groups, however, remained quite large. For instance, unemployment rates among Blacks have consistently been at least twice as high as those of Whites.

The labor-market issue that has received the most attention in recent years is wage opportunities. Figure 4 plots median weekly earnings among male and female full-time workers from 1965 through the first two quarters of 1998. Among all groups, men's wages decreased steadily from 1980 until 1995, when there was evidence of an upturn. The pay gap between White and Black men changed little, however, with no sign of relative progress in wages for Black men. Hispanic men have actually seen decreases in both absolute and relative wages, compared with White and Black men. Again, this pattern is at least partially the result of the growing percentage of less-educated immigrants in the Hispanic population.

In contrast, women have not experienced wage decreases. In fact, White women's wages have grown slowly since the 1980s, so that they now earn more than both Hispanic and Black men. Black women's wages have been largely stagnant, although they show a recent upturn; and Hispanic women's wages have decreased slightly. Thus, the wage gap between White women and both Black and Hispanic women has increased.

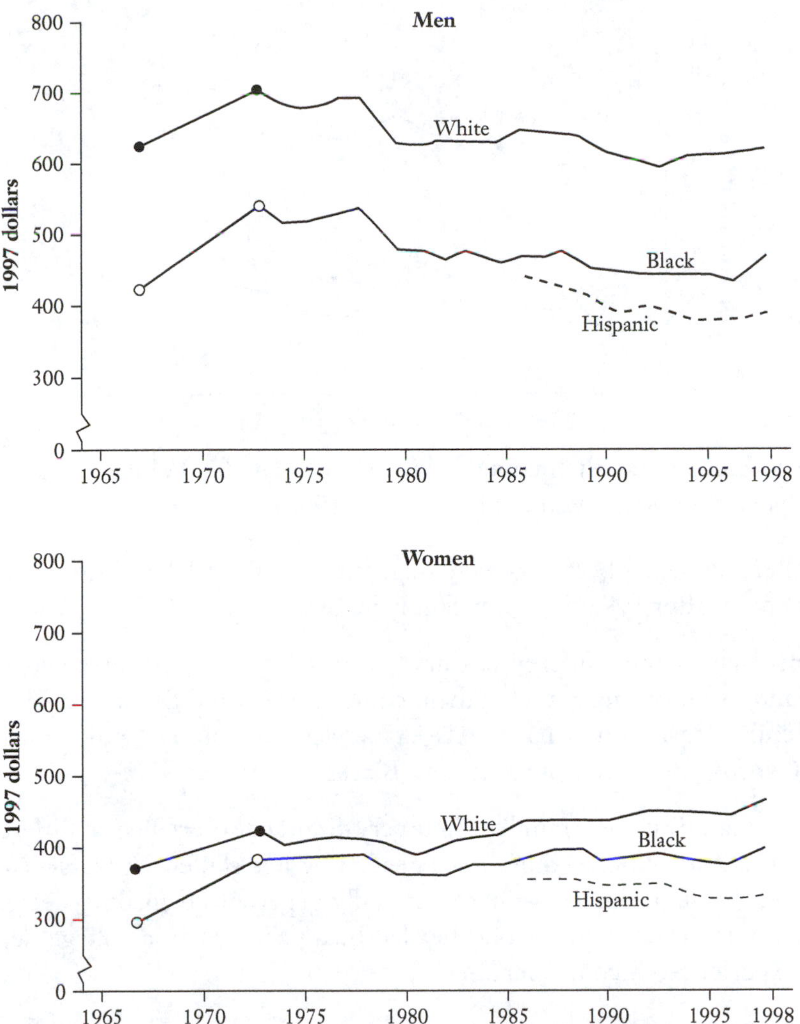

FIGURE 4 Median Weekly Earnings of Male and Female Full-Time Workers. Straight line between dots indicates data are not available for intervening years. Prior to 1979, data for Blacks include all non-Whites. Data for 1998 are from the first two quarters. *Source:* Council of Economic Advisers (1998).

ECONOMIC STATUS

Continued and even growing gaps in earnings imply that the economic situation is not improving for minority populations relative to the White population. Other measures of family economic well-being reinforce this conclusion. Figure 5 shows median family income for Asian and Pacific Islanders, non-Hispanics Whites, Hispanics, and Blacks through 1996. Family income is probably the most widely used measure of overall economic well-being. Among non-Hispanic Whites, family income has been rising steadily. Essentially, the growth in female labor-force participation and increases in White women's wages have resulted in more family income, even though men's earnings have deteriorated somewhat. Asian families earn even more than Whites.

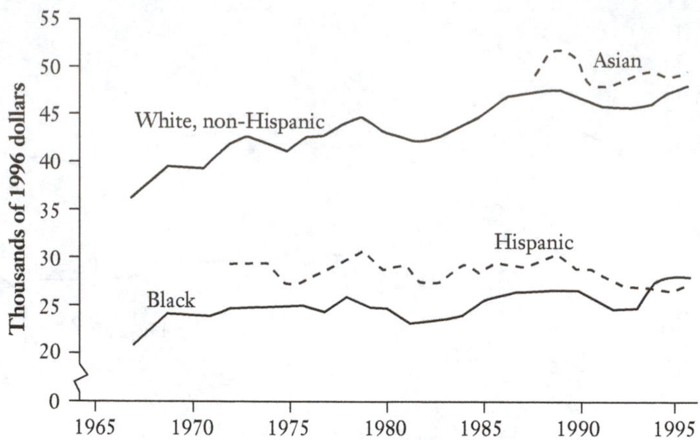

FIGURE 5 Median Family Income. Prior to 1972, data for Whites include Hispanic Whites. *Source:* Council of Economic Advisers (1998).

Black family income has been relatively stagnant since the 1970s, although there were signs of increase after 1993. Hispanic family income decreased in the 1990s.

This means that income differentials have widened between Whites and Asian and Pacific Islanders on the upper end of the income brackets and Blacks and Hispanics on the lower end. American Indians and Alaska Natives, for whom we only have data from the 1990 Census, show lower income than Blacks in that year.

These median family income numbers hide very different experiences at different points in the Income distribution. Households headed by less skilled workers—particularly those headed by single parents—have generally experienced income decreases over the past several decades. Households headed by a person with a college degree have generally experienced income increases.

One might be particularly concerned with the number of families at very low income levels. Figure 6 shows poverty rates among individuals by racial group, indicating the

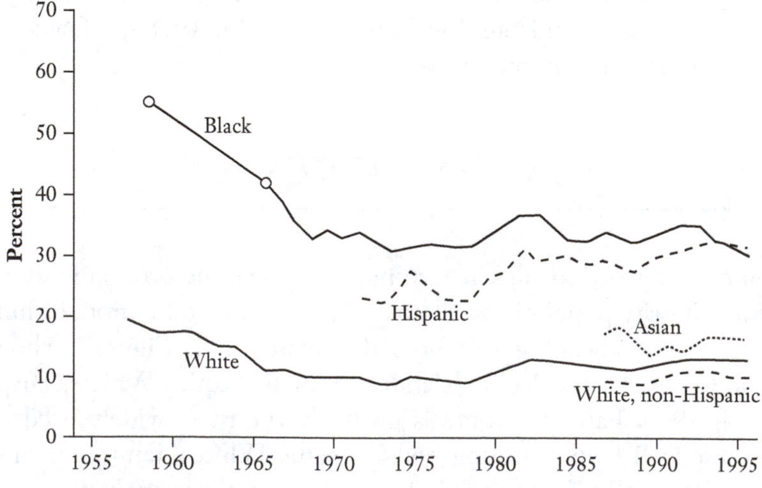

FIGURE 6 Poverty Rates for Individuals. Straight line between dots indicates data not available for intervening years. *Source:* Council of Economic Advisers (1998).

percentage of the population in each group living in families with incomes below the official U.S. poverty line, which was less than $8,000 per year in the late 1990s. In general, poverty rates have been relatively flat since the early 1970s. About 10 percent of the White population has been poor over this period. Asian and Pacific Islanders show a slightly higher poverty rate, underscoring the diversity within the Asian and Pacific Islander populations—they have both higher median incomes than Whites as well as higher poverty rates, reflecting the fact that at least some Asian groups are experiencing economic difficulties.

Black poverty has also been relatively constant, but at nearly 30 percent—three times the White poverty rate, Hispanic poverty rates are now higher than Black poverty rates. Poverty rates among subgroups, such as children or the elderly, show similar differentials between racial and ethnic groups.

HEALTH STATUS

Economic well-being is often closely linked to other aspects of well-being, such as health status. Interestingly, health differences do not necessarily show the same patterns as economic differences. Infant-mortality rates provide a primary indicator of both health status and access to health care in a population. Figure 7 plots infant-mortality rates by race from the early 1980s through 1995. Infant mortality has been steadily decreasing among all groups, indicating major health improvements within all populations. The disparities between groups, however, have remained largely constant. Black infant-mortality rates are about two-and-a-half times White rates. American Indian and Alaska Native rates have fallen a bit faster than other groups, but remain well above White rates.

Figure 7 also shows a pattern visible in much health data—namely, although Hispanics show substantial educational and economic differentials, they show far fewer

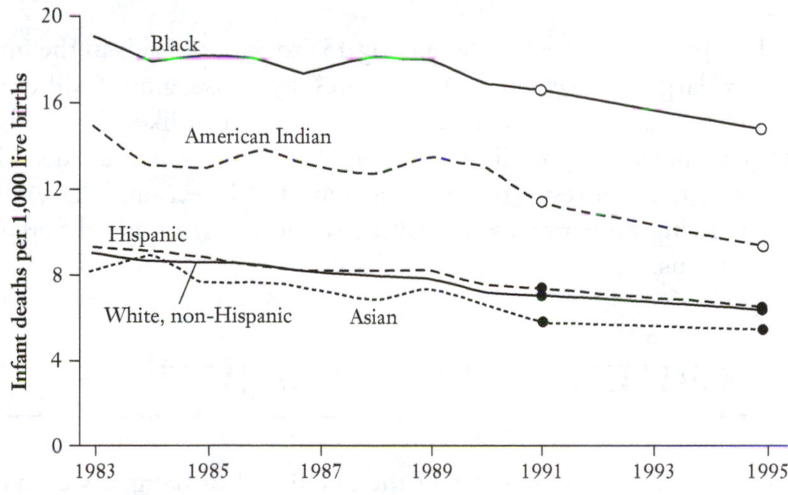

FIGURE 7 Infant Mortality Rates. Straight line between dots indicates data not available for intervening years. *Source:* Council of Economic Advisers (1998).

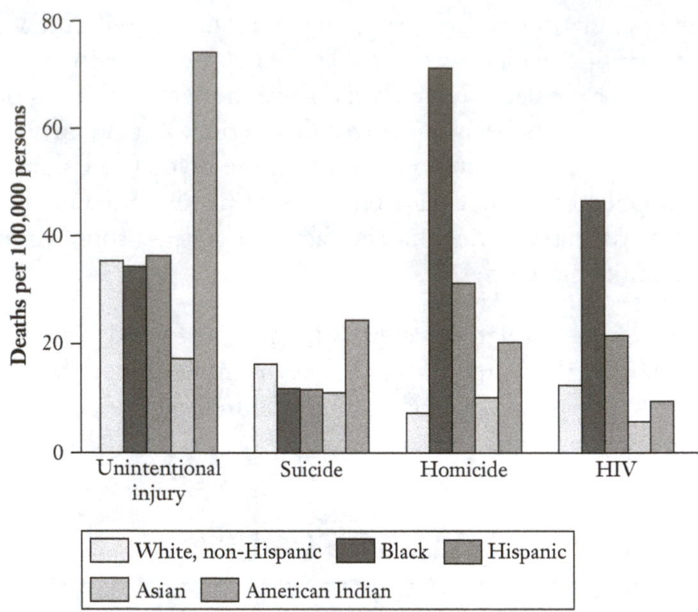

FIGURE 8 Death Rates by Cause, for Persons Aged 15 to 34, 1996 to 1995. Data for 1994 and 1995 are averaged to provide more reliable estimates. HIV data for American Indians are for 1993–1995. *Source:* Council of Economic Advisers (1998).

health differentials. Hispanic infant-mortality rates are almost identical to White and Asian and Pacific Islander infant mortality rates.

Clearly, smoking is a health issue that emerges in adolescence. Smoking is correlated with a shorter life expectancy and greater health risks. In general, smoking rates have fallen for both young women and men over the past 30 years; and this is one of the few indicators where Blacks and Hispanics do better than Whites. Black smoking rates have fallen faster than White rates, so that young Blacks, who used to be more likely to smoke than Whites, are now less likely to smoke.

In contrast, Figure 8 shows death rates among 15- to 34-year-olds in the mid-1990s. There are very large differences in death rates by cause among different racial groups. American Indians and Alaska Natives are far more likely to die as a result of unintentional injuries—typically automobile accidents—and suicide. Blacks are far more likely to die as a result of homicide and HIV infection. These differences emphasize that living conditions and health-risk factors are quite different among different populations.

CRIME AND CRIMINAL JUSTICE

There is no single aggregate measure of the likelihood of being a victim of crime. Figure 9 plots homicide rates, which constitute a small percentage of all crimes but are among the best measured crime statistics (few homicides go unnoticed or

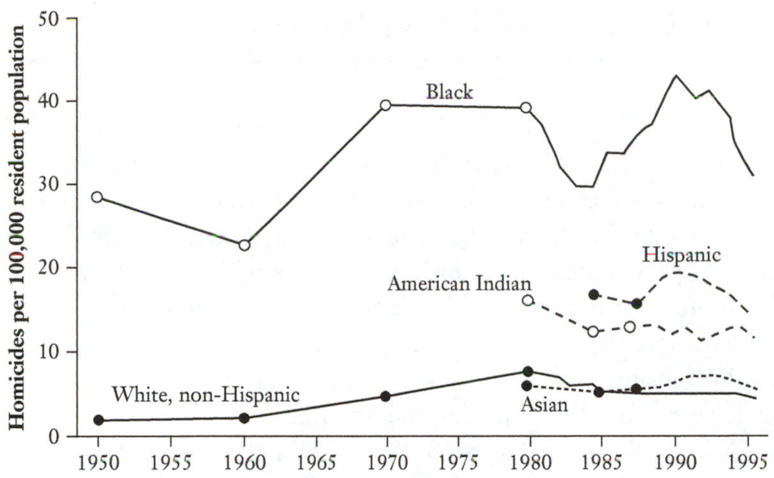

FIGURE 9 Victims of Homicide. Straight line between dots indicates data not available for intervening years. Data include deaths from "legal intervention" (use of police force). Prior to 1985, data for Whites include Hispanic Whites. Prior to 1970, data include nonresidents. *Source:* Council of Economic Advisers (1998).

unreported). Figure 9 shows that Blacks are far more likely to be homicide victims than is any other group. The homicide victimization rate of Blacks is more than twice that of Hispanics and six times that of non-Hispanic Whites and Asian and Pacific Islanders. American Indian and Alaska Native homicide rates are about twice those of Whites and Asian and Pacific Islanders, and slightly below those of Hispanics. Although public discussion often focuses on the higher likelihood that Blacks will be arrested for crimes, there is little discussion of the fact that Blacks are also much more likely to be victims. There are large disparities by race in both the likelihood of being a victim of a crime, as well as in the likelihood of being arrested and incarcerated by the criminal justice system. Although other crime statistics, such as property crimes, show smaller racial disparities, they also show higher victimization among minority groups.

Data on experience within the criminal justice system are largely tabulated only for Whites and Blacks, and hence provide less comprehensive measures across racial groups. Blacks are far more likely to be arrested and incarcerated than are Whites. Some of these differences reflect differences in the crimes for which Blacks are disproportionately arrested, and some may reflect discriminatory behavior on the part of the police and other persons within the criminal justice system. In 1995, more than 9 percent of the Black population was under correctional supervision, either on probation or parole, or in jail or prison, compared to 2 percent of the White population. Among young Black men 20 to 29 years old, more than 25 percent are under correctional supervision. Because arrests and prison stays often fracture families and reduce future labor-market opportunities, these high rates of involvement with the criminal justice system are correlated with the reduced economic opportunities of Black families.

HOUSING AND NEIGHBORHOODS

Where people live, and the housing they live in, is correlated with their health and economic status. Increasing concern among social scientists about "neighborhood effects"—the influence of peers and of neighborhood characteristics on individual health and behavior—has raised interest in housing and neighborhood issues. Figure 10 shows the percentage of populations living in housing units with physical problems, such as substandard plumbing or heating as well as electrical and other serious upkeep problems. All groups for which we have data, from the mid-1970s to the mid-1990s, show substantial improvement in housing quality; but, as in other areas, large disparities remain across groups. Non-Hispanic Blacks, Hispanics, and American Indians and Alaska Natives are far more likely to live in substandard housing than are Whites or Asian and Pacific Islanders. Other measures of housing adequacy, such as crowding, show similar trends, with overall improvement among all groups, but continuing large disparities between groups.

Information about neighborhoods raises again the question of where people live and who they live next to. The diversity of a person's neighborhood can affect his or her overall sense of national diversity and knowledge of members of other races or ethnicities.

Whites are by far the most segregated population, even more than their larger population percentage would justify. The average White person lives in a neighborhood that is more than 80 percent White. Blacks are the next most segregated, living in neighborhoods that are, on average, about 60 percent Black and 30 percent White.

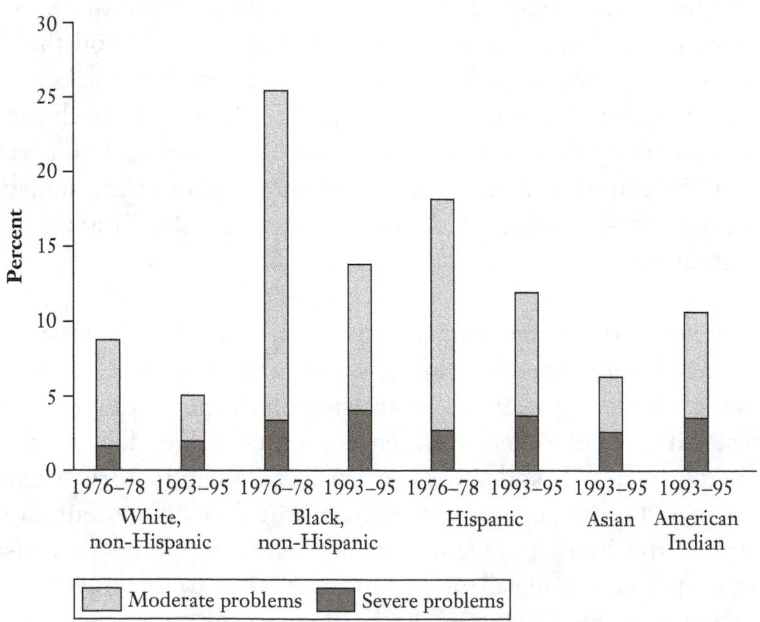

FIGURE 10 Housing Units with Physical Problems. Data for 1976 and 1978, or 1993 and 1995, are averaged to provide more reliable estimates. Data for Asians exclude Hispanic Asians, and data for American Indians exclude Hispanic American Indians. *Source:* Council of Economic Advisers (1998).

Hispanics live in neighborhoods that have close to equal amounts (about 40 percent each) of Whites and Hispanics. Asian and Pacific Islanders live in the most diverse neighborhoods, composed of a mix of Whites, Blacks, Hispanics, and other Asian and Pacific Islanders. This suggests that these two population groups are experiencing and living in the midst of diversity in this country to a much greater degree than Whites or Blacks.

WHAT DO THESE DISPARITIES MEAN?

This very quick and quite limited review of some of the key indicators of economic and social well-being underscores the ongoing importance of disparities by race and by Hispanic origin in U.S. society. Of course, there are multiple reasons behind these disparities. Many of the other chapters in this book summarize what the research literature indicates about the causes and effects of racial disparities in key areas of society. Three overarching conclusions, based on the data, are presented here.

First, race and Hispanic origin continue to be defining characteristics for many Americans. They are correlated with educational and economic opportunities, with health status, and with where people live and who they live next to. The magnitude of these differences, especially for Blacks and Hispanics, is extremely significant on average, suggesting that these disparities are widely experienced. Relative to the White and Asian populations, the Black population on average has only two-fifths as many college graduates, three-fourths as much earnings, and only slightly more than one-half as much income. The Hispanic population fares even worse. Although we do not have as much comparable information for American Indians and Alaska Natives, their data tend to be closer to those of Blacks and Hispanics than to those of Whites. Whatever their causes, these are substantial differentials; they shape our life opportunities and they shape our opinions about behavior toward each other. To repeat the point 1 started with at the beginning of this chapter, race continues to be a salient predictor of well-being in America.

Second, the growing presence of Hispanic and Asian and Pacific Islander populations is fundamentally changing the face of America. The displacement of Blacks as the largest minority group in the population in the early 2000s may cause some political and social tension. High numbers of immigrants within the Hispanic and Asian and Pacific Islander groups make questions of assimilation and second-generation progress particularly important in the years ahead. If second-generation Hispanic women behave more like other U.S.-born women, there will be many more Hispanic families with wives in the labor market two decades from now. If second-generation Hispanics acquire education at the rate of other U.S.-born populations, the education levels within the Hispanic community will rise substantially.

Third, Whites may be less aware of the changes and the challenges of growing population diversity than any other group. In part, there is often a "blindness" among the majority to the situation of other groups, because their own situation is typically taken as the norm. This "blindness" is reinforced by locational patterns and neighborhood choice. Whites are much more likely to live in the Midwest than other groups, the least diverse part of the nation; and they tend to live in the most segregated neighborhoods in the other regions. In contrast, Asian and Pacific Islanders—who do as well as Whites on many measures of well-being—live in much more diverse neighborhoods and are almost surely more aware of issues relating to diversity and difference, even when these issues do not translate into personal economic differentials. In short, the growing population of Hispanics and Asian and Pacific Islanders, as well as many Blacks, may be better prepared to address the challenges, and to take the advantage of the benefits, of an increasingly diverse population than are Whites.

REFERENCE

Council of Economic Advisers. 1998. *Changing America: Indicators of Social and Economic Well-Being by Race and Hispanic Origin.* Washington, D.C.: U.S. Government Printing Office.

Demand-Side Changes and the Relative Economic Progress of Black Men: 1940–90

Elaine Reardon

ABSTRACT

This article uses Census data from 1940 to 1990 to examine whether the hypotheses advanced for the absence of economic progress of black men relative to white men during the 1980s are consistent with the long-run trends. The findings indicate that skill-biased technological change explains more than changes in industrial composition both in the long run as well as in the 1980s. Moreover, increased competition from women and immigrants does not explain the recent slowed progress of black men; instead, the evidence suggests that middle-skilled white men may be an important source of increased competition.

I. INTRODUCTION

Many researchers have emphasized supply-side or "black-specific" explanations, such as education, migration, and affirmative action legislation, to explain the relative economic progress of black men over time.[1] However, these factors more successfully explain periods of progress than the slowdown which began in the 1970s. Other scholars, focusing on the slowdown, have emphasized demand-side factors: the effects of industrial change, technological upgrading, and falling relative wages for less-skilled workers.[2] While the study of demand-side factors shows that the 1980s were different from the 1970s, researchers have been unable to distinguish if one decade was an aberration and the other a reflection of long-run trends. One purpose of this article is

---

Reardon, Elaine. *Demand-Side Changes and the Relative Economic Progress of Black Men, 1940-1990.* Originally published in "Journal of Human Resources" 32.1 (Winter 1997): 69-97.

[1] See, for example, Freeman (1973); Smith and Welch (1989); Card and Krueger (1992).

[2] For example, Cain and Finnie (1990); Bound and Freeman (1992); Juhn, Murphy, and Pierce (1991).

to determine whether the most common demand-side explanations are consistent over a much longer time span, the 50-year period from 1940–90. The other is to advance an alternative hypothesis, that the slowed progress of black men in recent years is the result of worsening job prospects for middle-skilled white men.

Rather than focus on whether demand for certain workers declined in the 1970s and 1980s, as other researchers have done, I investigate how the 1970s and 1980s differed from previous decades in which progress was significantly faster. The data are disaggregated by race and skill level to examine both the direct effect of demand shifts on black men as well as the indirect effects of changes in the market for unskilled labor, which is disproportionately black. Another innovation, apart from using a longer time series of data, is the use of the same framework to examine whether demand shifts have favored competing groups, thereby impeding the relative progress of black men. I find little evidence to support the argument that women and immigrants are replacing black men. Black men probably have experienced increased competition for employment, but my results suggest that this has come largely from middle-skilled white men, from whom demand has also shifted away. My findings also suggest that technological change has played more of a role in the recent erosion of black progress than have shifts in the industrial composition of the economy.

This paper is organized as follows: Sections II and III describe the method and the data used to examine the demand-side explanations. Sections IV and V present the results of the analyses. I discuss the implications of the findings for both research and policy in Section VI.

II. MEASURING RELATIVE SHIFTS IN THE DEMAND FOR LABOR

Aggregate demand has played an enormous role in black progress, because growth has historically benefited those at the bottom of the wage scale disproportionately. The increased demand for labor during and after WWII enabled black men to make a great deal of relative progress during the 1940s (Wright 1986). Over the longer run, Smith and Welch (1989) estimate that 45 percent of the decline in black poverty since 1940 can be attributed to economic growth. The level of aggregate demand, however, is not sufficient to explain other black-white labor market outcomes. For example, the rise in wage inequality and the change in demand for skill over the 1980s documented by Katz and Murphy (1992) indicate that the benefits from recent growth were not distributed equally. The composition of the demand for labor not just its level, is key to understanding recent changes in the labor market. To measure such demand-side shifts, I employ employment growth measures across both industry and occupation and compare the effects of these shifts not only by race but by skill.

This is accomplished by using fixed-coefficient indexes that are essentially weighted averages of sectoral growth measures (Freeman 1975; Bound and Freeman 1992; Katz and Murphy 1992). The indexes use employment growth across industries and occupations as a proxy for shifts in output driven by international trade, shifts in final product demand, and technological change. Several assumptions are required to assert that these reduced-form indexes are meaningful estimates of demand shifts and that the sources of the demand shifts are exogenous to the phenomena being studied. These assumptions include constant returns to scale in production, a fixed cost of capital, wages equated to marginal productivity, fixed relative wages, and a small elasticity of substitution between factors. If the elasticity of substitution is high in some sectors, a small change in wages would lead to large employment shifts, making these indexes not very interesting or informative. If it is fairly low, this may not affect the indexes greatly, especially if most of the demand response to changes in relative wages operates across rather than within sectors. Even with moderate elasticities, the indexes will reflect much of the demand patterns, as long as there are large differences between groups in their distributions across sectors and large variations in employment growth across sectors. These indexes also have been used by other researchers, facilitating comparisons across studies.

Employment growth is used to measure demand shifts, thereby using changes in factor inputs as a proxy for changes in factor outputs at fixed relative prices. Growth is measured as the proportion change in industry-occupation shares of total employment (including both men and women) from one decade to the next, measured in efficiency units. For example, a sector might grow from 15 percent of employment at time t to 17 percent at time $t + 1$, so that demand growth would equal 1.13 (0.17/0.15). To estimate employment in efficiency units, aggregate hours by decade, industry, occupation, race, sex, education, and experience are multiplied by the average log hourly wage at time t for the corresponding demographic cell. Note that weighting by wages at time t means that the growth measure does not reflect changes in wages.[3]

Demand growth in an industry and occupation is then weighted by the race and skill group's employment distribution in the earlier year (measured as the proportion of total hours) to estimate whether demand tended on average to shift towards or away from that group. In other words, the demand shift index for a group is a weighted average of sectoral growth rates, in which the weights sum to 1 for each race and skill group. More compactly, the shift in demand equals

$$(1) \quad \Delta D_i = \ln (\sum_j \alpha_{ij} \Delta E_j),$$

where α equals each race and skill group i's share of total employment hours across industry and occupation cells j at the beginning of the decade (which is the equivalent of holding relative wages fixed over time). The next term is the growth in employment of an industry and occupation cell over a decade measured in efficiency units E. Trends in these indexes show changes in relative demand for a demographic group driven by increases or decreases in sectoral employment (given the assumptions stated above). The logarithm of the index is used to make the trends easier to see. If the majority of a group's employment at the beginning of a decade

[3] All workers' hours are used to calculate aggregate hours; the wage sample described in the next section and in the appendix is used to calculate average wages. Also, the results arc quite similar when the $t + 1$ wage weights are used instead.

is in expanding occupation-industry sectors, this will be reflected in a positive index number, indicating a demand shift toward the jobs that that demographic group tended to hold. Initial employment mostly in contracting occupations and industries is reflected in negative demand shift index measures.

An obvious drawback of this method is that if blacks as a group, for example, leave a declining sector for one in which they previously had no representation, this will not be captured by the index because their initial employment distribution weight will equal 0 for the new sector. This explains why the indexes might be negative in all years for all men, particularly with the growth of the service sector. When employment growth is weighted by the group's employment distribution at the end of each decade (not shown), the indexes are less negative than the ones reported below. However, overall patterns, and especially the black-white differences, are similar.

A central issue for measuring reduced-form demand shifts is identification. Changes in supply rather than in demand could be driving the changes in the indexes, as the model assumes fixed relative wages. For example, we would expect to see employment growth in industries that employ many college graduates if there were a large influx of such workers into the labor market. As their supply increased, the relative wages of college graduates would fall (holding demand constant), and so industries would use more of them. I examine whether my results are sensitive to such changes in supply by re-estimating the indexes using a correction proposed by Murphy and Welch (1993) to account for relative wage changes. My results do not change a great deal, as will be shown.

To examine the effects of industrial change and occupational upgrading separately, I estimate demand indexes by first measuring only industry growth patterns, and then both industry and occupation. The occupation-within-industry effect is calculated as the difference between these results and is interpreted as indirect evidence of technological change. As technological change increases the demand for higher-skilled workers within industries, employment will shift towards the occupations that skilled people tend to hold, given fixed relative wages. Even in manufacturing, employment is shifting away from blue-collar jobs and toward professional, technical, and managerial jobs (Murphy and Welch 1993). This measure of technological change tends to underestimate the amount of technological change occurring in occupations whose functions change greatly over the period, as it captures only across-occupation employment shifts and not within-occupation change. Moreover, it is a crude measure of technological change, necessitated by the absence of direct measures in the data.

There is also the issue of defining skill levels. The problem with using education as a measure of skill over such a long period of time is that the meaning of a particular level of schooling has changed. In 1940, a white man with a college education was considerably better educated than his peers. By 1990, when the average years of schooling for white men was 13.1 years, this was less true. In contrast, while the absolute meaning of a position in the wage distribution changes with fluctuations in economic growth, its relative meaning does not. This allows examination of relative demand shifts for different kinds of workers in a consistent manner over time (Juhn, Murphy, and Pierce 1991). Thus I use position in the wage distribution as the measure of skill.

Of course, this raises the issue of whose wage distribution to use and how to define an appropriate comparison group. For example, to contrast median hourly wages, one compares black men in the 50th percentile of the black wage distribution to white men in the 50th percentile of the white distribution. The analogous exercise here would produce skill groups with wage distributions calculated separately by race. However, the appropriate comparison is between blacks and whites who earn the same wage, who presumably are similarly skilled, not those who share a percentile ranking defined separately by race (Juhn, Murphy, and Pierce 1991). Therefore, black men in the wage sample were ranked into five equal-sized groups by their log hourly wage separately by year and state.[4] White men were then assigned a skill quintile based on their position in the black wage distribution for that year.[5]

III. DATA

The data are taken from the 1940–90 Public Use files of the decennial Census. In order to focus on areas where both blacks and whites live, only data from the 25 states with the highest black population in 1960 are retained.[6] My sample includes respondents who were at least 18 years old, with 1–40 years of potential work experience, and who were not students or in the military or living in group quarters. The sample weights provided in the 1990 Census were used in the analysis.

Two samples were constructed from these data, a count sample and a wage sample. The count sample contains all respondents described above: this sample is used to measure labor supply. The adjustments required to make the data consistent over time are described in the appendix. The wage sample is a more homogeneous group for whom

---

[4] Deciles were originally used to demarcate skill groups; aggregation into quintiles resulted in no appreciable loss of information.

[5] This adjustment makes more of a difference in the earlier decades. In 1940, a white man in my data in the lowest 20 percent of whites earned $1.52 an hour on average, whereas a black man in the lowest 20 percent of black earners earned $0.70. In the top 20 percent for each race, whites earned $8.63 and blacks $3.55 on average. In 1990, the averages in the lowest 20 percent were $3.76 for whites and $2.83 for blacks. In the top 20 percent, the averages were $21.36 for whites and $14.87 for blacks. Of course, discrimination would suppress black wages relative to whites at a given skill level, but the effect of this on skill rankings is attenuated by using quintiles.

[6] Almost all blacks are included, despite the subset of states: New York, New Jersey Pennsylvania Ohio, Indiana, Illinois, Michigan, Missouri, Delaware, Maryland, Washington, D.C., Virginia, North Carolina, South Carolina, Georgia, Florida, Kentucky, Tennessee, Alabama, Mississippi, Arkansas, Louisiana, Oklahoma, Texas, and California. Using a random sample from all states produces similar results.

hourly wages are better measured over time; this sample includes only individuals who worked at least 14 weeks in a year and at least 35 hours per week, and who earned only wage and salary income. The reasons for this are discussed in greater length in the appendix; briefly, hourly wages are necessary for comparing prices across units of labor regardless of the amount of labor provided. Using the wage sample minimizes the measurement error induced by calculating an hourly wage from annual earnings and hours data. In short, all workers are used to calculate employment growth rates in the demand indexes that follow. Wages are used only to delineate skill groups and to convert hours of work into efficiency units.[7]

The wage and employment levels for black and white men from 1940–90 are well known in the literature. They are summarized for my data in Table 1. Immediately evident in the table is the convergence in education levels that is often emphasized in the discussion of black-white wage differences. The racial gap in education levels narrowed from 3.5 years in 1940 to only 1.0 years in 1990. Relative employment rates (measured as annual weeks worked divided by 52) also fluctuated over the period. These rates reached a high in 1970 and declined thereafter, more rapidly for black men than for white men. Finally, note the wage convergence over the period. Black men earned on average 42 percent as much as white men in 1940; by 1990, this ratio was 74 percent. This relative wage growth by black men, however, was not consistent over the entire period. Between 1940 and 1950, the wage gap shrank by 43 percent (0.18/0.42) but stayed roughly constant over the 1950s. From 1960–80, the relative gains of black men were rapid but then changed little over the 1980s.

Some of this apparent relative wage progress may be due to problems with the data. First, Census Bureau undercounts of blacks, especially of men, will bias wage levels if those missed tend to be low-wage earners. We do not know, however, how this bias has changed over time and whether it is a more serious problem now than it was in 1940 when blacks were more concentrated in the rural South. Thus, it may or may not affect the time series movement of the gap in black-white wages. Second, the relative progress of blacks after 1970 may in part be due to the large number of less-skilled blacks leaving the labor force entirely. If this drain explains a fraction of the relative wage gains of blacks, how large a fraction remains an open question (Butler and Heckman 1977; Brown 1984; Smith and Welch 1989; Welch 1990). Using weights to account for men left out of the wage sample, Reardon (1994) shows that all of the meager progress of black men in the 1980s is accounted for by this selection bias.

---

[7] Using the trimmed wage sample biases the measure of efficiency units upwards, especially for black men. The indexes for black men are thus even more negative than shown in the next section. Also, the estimates by skill level would be similar even if the excluded men were included in the wage sample to calculate skill: their industry and occupation distribution looks like that of the lowest skill quintile, especially since 1970. In the earlier years, many of the excluded men were farmers, which would make the industry shift estimates somewhat more negative. Because the Census did not measure farm income, we cannot ascertain which skill quintile would be most affected.

TABLE 1 Means for Men, by Census Year and Race

	1940		1950		1960		1970		1980		1990	
	White	Black	White	Black	White	Black	White	Black	White	Black	White	Black
Education	9.0	5.5	9.9	6.6	10.7	7.9	11.6	9.7	12.6	11.3	13.1	12.1
Employment rate	79.0	74.5	86.2	80.2	90.1	81.4	92.1	86.0	88.5	78.6	88.3	78.1
Workers:												
Hourly wage	$3.85	$1.63	$5.28	$3.18	$7.09	$4.14	$8.99	$5.90	$9.24	$6.72	$9.25	$6.87
Ratio of wages		0.42		0.60		0.58		0.66		0.73		0.74
Count sample (*n*)	21,479	28,563	69,891	8,838	24,542	2,973	25,862	30,269	32,044	42,082	34,521	4,056
Wage sample (*n*)	11,361	13,846	47,979	5,804	17,819	2,094	20,326	23,622	25,078	31,875	32,347	2,917

Source: Author's calculations from 25 states in the 1940–90 decennial censuses.

Note: The hourly wages are calculated over the wage sample and equal exp (log hourly wage); all are in 1982 dollars. The 25 states used in the sample are listed in the appendix. The employment rate is measured as weeks of work divided by 52 averaged over the count sample. The count sample includes all men at least 18 years old with 1–40 years of potential work experience, and who are not students or in the military or living in group quarters; the wage sample includes only men who worked full-time, 14–52 weeks, and had no self-employment or farm income.

IV. INDUSTRIAL SHIFTS AND TECHNOLOGICAL CHANGE

The decline in manufacturing employment and the growth in service-sector employment are said to disproportionately hurt less-educated and minority workers who end up either unemployed or in poorly paid, dead-end service jobs (Bluestone and Harrison 1982; Wilson 1987; Bound and Holzer 1993). Industry-based explanations are sometimes accompanied by the argument that the pace of technological change is increasing and that less-skilled and minority workers are in danger of being left behind (Johnston and Packer 1987; Kasarda 1989). This argument posits a growing mismatch between skills demanded by jobs and those provided by workers.[8] Bound and Freeman (1992) found that part of the growing racial gap in earnings and employment since the mid-1970s could be explained by shifts in employment composition over the period that favored young white men over young black men. In their regression-based analysis, they decompose the effects of occupational and industrial change, showing large occupational effects. In their demand index analysis, however, the authors examine only industry shifts. Using similar demand indexes, my findings suggest that within-industry occupational shifts are more important than industry shifts in explaining recent trends among all black men.

If industry-based explanations are correct, that the shift away from manufacturing and toward the service sector is an important phenomenon for explaining inequality, then the industry-only demand indexes should show an increase in the demand for less-skilled/low-wage workers and high-skilled/high-wage workers. In contrast, technological change (occupational upgrading) should be reflected in skill-biased demand shifts within industries toward the most skilled workers. The combined effect of industrial and technological change on shifts in the labor demand for different demographic groups indicates the extent to which these trends reinforce or offset each other.

For such shifts, either occupational or industrial, to explain a significant part of the changes in black-white gaps in wages and employment, there must be racial differences not only across occupations and industries but also in the pattern of change over time. Table 2 presents occupation and industry distributions for black and white men at two points in time for three skill groups.[9] The differences across race and skill groups and over time are striking. For example, in 1940, almost 46 percent of blacks in the bottom quintile of the wage distribution were farmers, versus approximately 22 percent of whites in that skill group. In both 1940 and 1990, similar fractions of the highest wage whites and blacks were in manufacturing, yet high-skilled blacks were more likely to be operatives and laborers than were comparable whites in both years.

---

[8] Technological change need not leave the least-skilled behind. Technology may reduce the skill requirements for some jobs as well as upgrade the skills needed for others. This would lead to increased job opportunities for the less-skilled (Mischel and Teixeira 1991). Given that both wages and employment rates have fallen among the least-skilled, however, this effect seems more potential than actual.

[9] The data might also be divided by age; however, in the demand indexes that are the focus of this analysis I found little evidence that demand shifts across age groups were nearly as important as shifts across skill levels.

TABLE 2 Occupation and Industry Distributions for Men, by Race and Skill Rank

	1940			1990		
	Skill Group			Skill Group		
	1–20	41–60	81–100	1–20	41–60	81–100
Occupation						
White men						
Professional, managerial	5.9	9.9	30.7	15.1	27.8	59.3
Sales, clerical	14.6	19.8	23.8	18.2	19.0	18.0
Craft	9.5	21.2	26.7	20.1	24.5	13.0
Operative	20.1	29.8	13.3	21.4	17.7	6.1
Laborer	16.2	12.3	2.3	10.1	4.2	1.2
Services	11.8	6.3	3.1	13.0	6.4	2.3
Farming	21.8	0.7	0.2	2.1	0.5	0.1
Black men						
Professional, managerial	1.6	1.6	5.4	8.1	14.0	33.5
Sales, clerical	1.4	1.9	5.9	15.2	15.2	15.7
Craft	2.2	5.1	11.0	11.4	15.8	17.8
Operative	8.8	18.1	23.4	22.5	28.2	21.6
Laborer	15.5	38.8	40.4	14.3	9.4	4.3
Services	24.8	24.2	12.0	26.3	16.4	7.0
Farming	45.8	10.4	1.9	2.3	1.1	0.2
Industry						
White men						
Agriculture	24.8	3.8	4.1	4.0	2.4	2.1
Construction	7.0	7.6	7.8	12.5	11.2	8.1
Manufacturing	18.6	38.5	33.6	21.0	29.2	28.5
Transportation, utilities	6.6	13.2	15.9	7.8	8.5	7.7
Wholesale, retail	26.0	19.7	13.0	28.9	19.0	13.8
Professional services, education	5.5	6.3	13.0	16.0	17.5	31.5
Government	1.8	4.8	9.5	3.2	8.7	6.6
Miscellaneous	9.8	6.3	3.1	6.6	3.4	1.7
Black men						
Agriculture	48.5	13.1	6.6	3.4	2.2	1.3
Construction	3.5	9.5	12.5	8.5	9.3	6.4
Manufacturing	7.2	22.8	34.8	19.1	27.2	29.1
Transportation, utilities	3.0	9.3	17.7	8.1	10.4	14.2
Wholesale, retail	13.9	18.3	8.6	24.7	15.3	9.6
Professional services, education	5.2	7.5	7.9	24.1	21.5	21.6
Government	0.4	1.3	5.9	4.8	10.7	16.3
Miscellaneous	18.3	18.2	6.2	7.4	3.5	1.5

Source: Author's calculation from 25 states in the 1940 and 1990 decennial Censuses.
Note: Employment is measured in hours. Miscellaneous industry includes repairs and entertainment. Columns for race, rank, and year may not sum to 100 due to rounding.

Figure 1 displays the fixed coefficient demand indexes measuring overall relative demand shifts (combining both industry and occupation shifts).[10] The top panel shows the index numbers for white men by skill level, the middle panel shows the same for black men, and the bottom panel is the black-white difference in demand shifts. In each panel, the bar farthest to the left for each decade refers to the least-skilled and the bar on the right side refers to the most-skilled. In the top panel, the trend over time in the left-hand bars indicates that demand has always shifted away from less-skilled white men, as evidenced by the negative index numbers. Demand shifts favored more-skilled white men in the 1940s and 1950s, but by the 1970s demand was shifting away from all white men, particularly among the middle-skilled.[11] The middle panel shows that demand has always shifted away from all black men. Clearly, their relative progress since 1940 has come from the speed with which they have been able to adjust to these changes. For example, the dramatic change from the 1940s to the 1950s was due largely to their rapid movement out of Southern agriculture into the better-paying manufacturing sector. Yet until the 1980s, the demand shift away from them slowed, requiring less rapid adjustment; in the 1980s, the shift away from them accelerated, more so than was true for white men.

This can be seen in the bottom panel, which shows the black-white difference, measured as the index number for white men in a skill group minus the number for black men in the same skill group. (The difference in log points is analogous to a percentage point difference.) This panel indicates that demand shifted away from black men faster than from white men in the 1980s compared to the 1970s, especially among the more-skilled. Though by historical standards the racial gap in the 1980s is not especially large, it is also clear that in the 1980s the racial gap in relative demand shifts reversed its previous 40-year convergence, with the gap widening most dramatically between black and white men in the highest skill group.

These changes in the relative patterns among blacks and whites occurred in the context of other changes in the economy. The skill bias, or gap between most- and least-skilled workers, also shrank over time. This can be seen by comparing the bars farthest on the right and left within a decade. The top panel shows that the skill bias in demand shifts for white men in the 1940s was 27.2 log points, but only 3.1 points in the 1980s. The 1980s do not in fact demonstrate the kind of accelerated demand for high-skilled workers one might have expected given the increase in the return to education over that decade.

The trends shown in Figure 1 obscure whether the demand shifts are driven by industrial or technological change. Figure 2 shows the index numbers decomposed into these between-industry and within-industry shifts. The between-industry results for white men in the top left panel look similar to the results in Figure 1. Through the 1960s, there was a long-term skill bias in demand shifts for white men in which the composition of industrial employment shifted toward the more-skilled. This slowed

[10] These are multiplied by 100. Logarithms are used to emphasize the trends: positive numbers indicate demand growth and negative numbers indicate the reverse. To convert log points to percentage points, divide by 100, exponentiate, and subtract 1.
[11] The index numbers can all be negative because the index weights refer to time t and thereby do not pick up movement into new sectors.

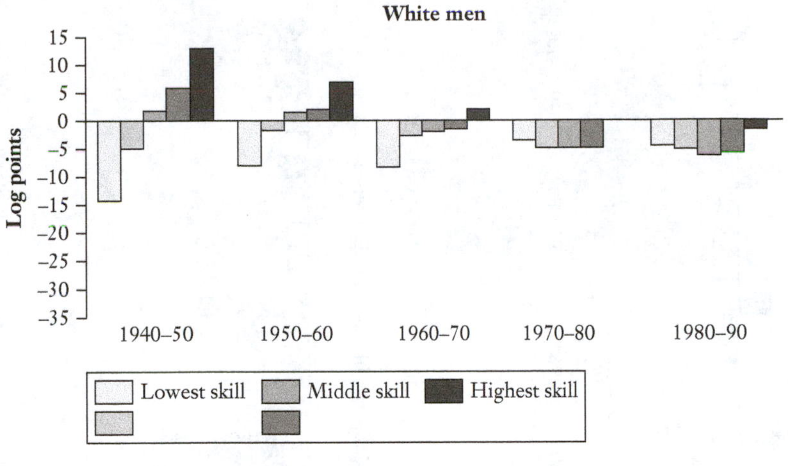
White men
15
10
5
0
-5
-10
-15
-20
-25
-30
-35
Log points
1940–50
1950–60
1960–70
1970–80
1980–90
Lowest skill
Middle skill
Highest skill

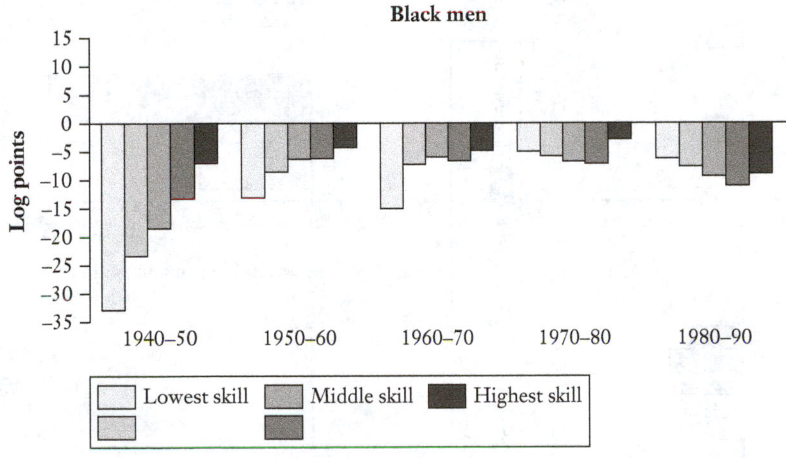
Black men
15
10
5
0
-5
-10
-15
-20
-25
-30
-35
Log points
1940–50
1950–60
1960–70
1970–80
1980–90
Lowest skill
Middle skill
Highest skill

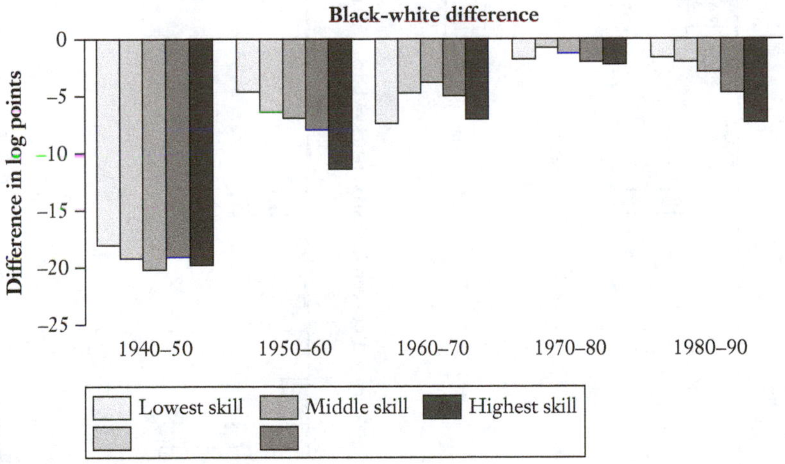
Black-white difference
0
-5
-10
-15
-20
-25
Difference in log points
1940–50
1950–60
1960–70
1970–80
1980–90
Lowest skill
Middle skill
Highest skill

FIGURE 1

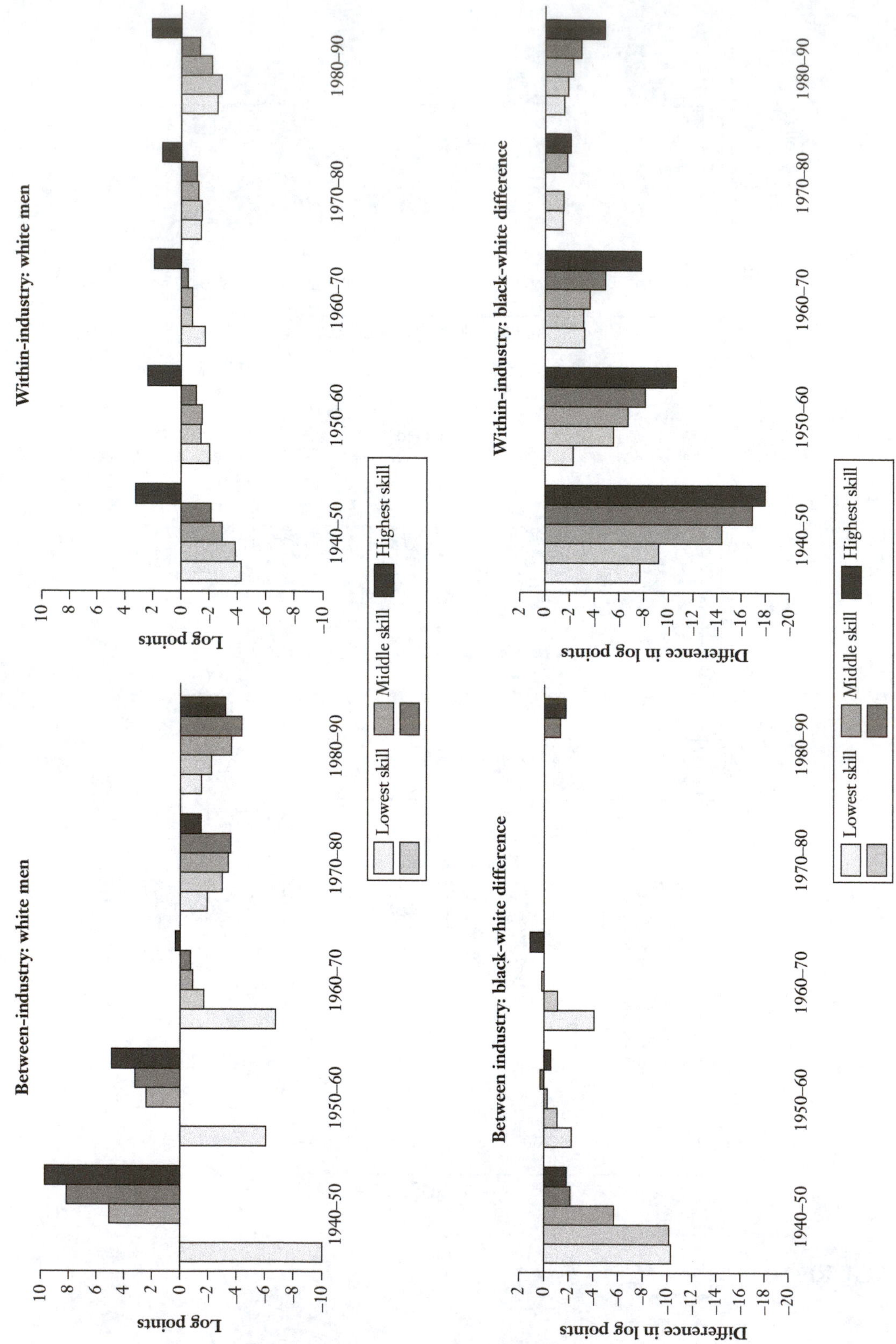

FIGURE 2 Between- and within-industry demand shifts

over time. By the 1970s demand shifted away from industries in which white men were concentrated at the beginning of the decade regardless of skill.

The bottom left panel shows the black-white difference in between-industry demand shifts. The mostly negative numbers indicate that demand has generally moved away faster from industries in which blacks tended to be employed than from those in which whites were more heavily employed. Yet the racial gap had all but disappeared by the 1970s. In the 1980s, the gap widened again among the more-skilled. However, the most interesting feature of this panel is the low numbers: Relative to previous decades, industry demand shifts did not drive black and white men apart, with the exception of the most-skilled, during the 1980s.

The trends within industry tell a somewhat different story. An interesting finding from the top right panel is that technological change has favored more-skilled white men since the 1940s, that this is not solely a 1980s phenomenon. The longer-run perspective also shows that while the skill bias in demand widened from the 1970s to the 1980s, it was not larger in the 1980s than it was three or four decades earlier. As was true of the racial gap in Figure 1, what is different about the 1980s is that the trend towards convergence reversed course. Similarly, the bottom right panel shows that while occupational employment always shifted away faster from black men than from white men, this slowed with each decade until the 1980s. Technological change plays a larger role than do industrial shifts in explaining the recent trends in relative demand for black men.

Figures 1 and 2 showed that changes in industrial composition and technological change shifted demand away from the industries and occupations in which men tended to be employed. The shifts were larger for blacks than for whites over the entire 50-year period, and the black-white gap fell over time in a pattern which suggests that demand shifts do contribute to recent black-white differences in the labor market. For example, in the 1950s, a decade in which black relative progress was nonexistent, black wages did not grow relative to those of white men, but they did grow absolutely. At the same time, the black-white gap in demand shifts continued to shrink. In contrast, not only did black wages not gain relative to whites in the 1980s; they did not grow at all. This was also the decade which saw a reversal of 40 years of convergence in the black-white gap in demand shifts, a reversal driven by skill-biased technological change. This U-turn makes it difficult to predict the potential sources of a renewed impetus toward black relative economic progress, not least because much of the convergence over time was due to demand shifting away from white men, and not because the demand shift favored black men.

The demand shift indexes in Figures 1 and 2 are biased to the extent that they do not take into account changes in relative wages which would affect the demand for labor. For example, employment growth will be fastest in sectors with falling relative wages. Thus, the falling relative wages of the least-skilled over the 1980s would increase the relative demand for labor in those sectors. Similarly, the demand shift toward the most-skilled would be countered by their rising relative price in the market. To test the sensitivity of my results to changes in relative wages, I applied a correction proposed by Murphy and Welch (1993). This sensitivity test is based on the assumption that demand has unit own-price (rather than 0) and zero cross-price elasticities. These new indexes are referred to as "elasticity-corrected," but they should be thought of as an upper bound, as 1 is too high an own-price elasticity. The indexes were recalculated by multiplying the unadjusted industry-occupation growth rate by the ratio of the cell's mean wage for men at the end of the decade and the mean for men at the beginning of the decade to weight up cells in which relative wages increased. The adjustment indicates the extent to which changes in the unadjusted index numbers were driven by changing relative wages, driven perhaps by changes in supply.

Figure 3 reports these elasticity-corrected demand shift measures for the within-occupation indexes.[12] For the 1940s and 1970s—decades in which wage inequality shrank—the adjustment reduced the skill bias in demand shifts. The adjustment had a smaller effect for the 1950s and 1960s, when overall wage inequality did not change much. In the 1980s, the correction amplifies the shift away from less-skilled men. In other words, the shift away from the least-skilled workers during the 1980s was slowed somewhat by their falling relative wages.

The elasticity-corrected index numbers do not qualitatively change any of the earlier conclusions about black-white trends and differences. On the other hand, the correction makes it unclear whether the increase in skill bias in the 1980s was large or small by historical standards. As in Figure 2, the skill bias in technological change (comparing the top and bottom skill groups in a decade) shrank from the 1940s to 1970s and widened in the 1980s. Unlike in Figure 2, however, the bias shown in Figure 3 is higher in the 1980s than in any other decade. While in either case the data show that a long-term decline in skill bias reversed direction in the 1980s, they cannot show conclusively whether skill-biased technological change was faster in the 1980s than in any other decade since the 1940s. Resolving these contradictory findings requires different data, with direct measures of technological change over a long period—data which unfortunately do not seem to exist. Nevertheless, if technological change transformed the nature of occupations more in the 1980s than in the 1940s, perhaps through computerization or firm-level changes in the organization of work, then the skill bias probably was larger in the 1980s. Census data can only measure shifts in the mix of occupations within industries and not within-occupation change, thereby understating the amount of technological change.

V. INCREASED COMPETITION FROM OTHER WORKERS

Holding skill levels constant, why would demand shifts affect blacks more than whites? Of course, a skill story might still explain why blacks are more affected by demand shifts as shown in the previous figures if we do not have a good measure of skill. Positions in a wage distribution and even educational level are crude measures of skill: wages can be artificially low because of discrimination, and a high school diploma does not certify

---

12. Skill differences across industries are smaller than those across occupations so changes in relative wages have a small effect on industrial structure. The industry results are thus excluded in the interest of brevity.

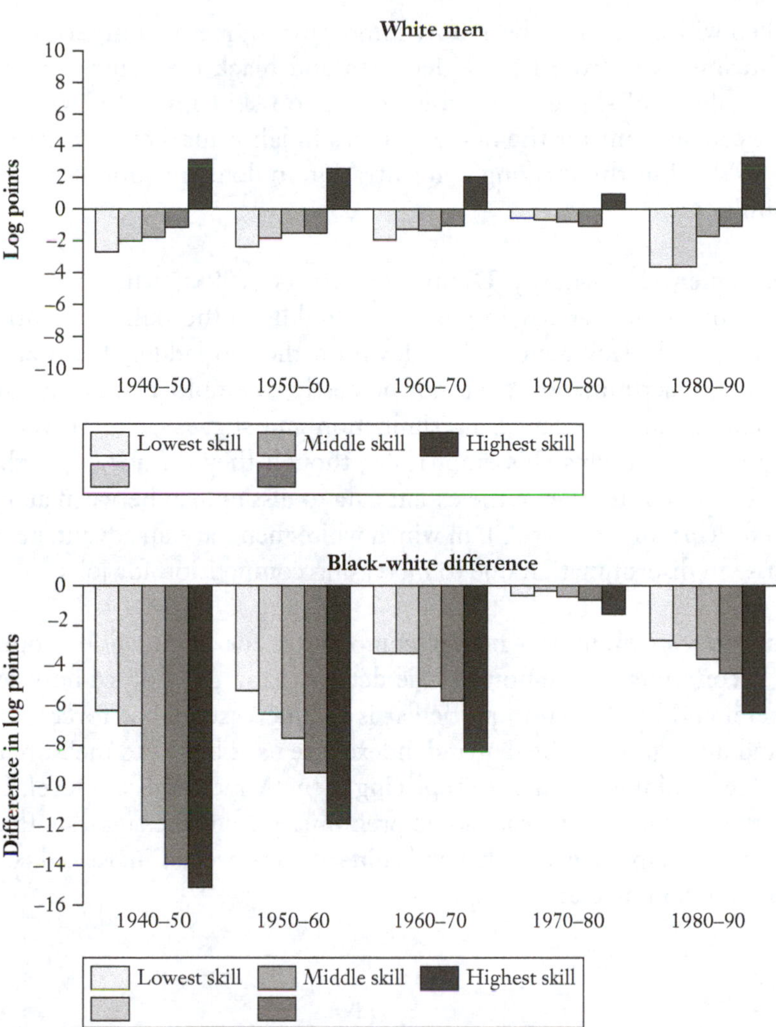

FIGURE 3 Elasticity-corrected within-industry demand shifts

that the recipient is even literate. The most prominent alternative measure of skill is the Armed Forces Qualifying Test (AFQT). Neal and Johnson (1995) shows that the gap in AFQT test scores explains all of the wage gap between young black and white men in the 1980s. Yet this cross-sectional finding does not explain why black men made such dramatic relative progress between 1950 and 1980 or why that progress ceased in the 1980s, given that the racial gap in AFQT scores between 1950 and 1980 did not change much (O'Neill 1990). O'Neill argues that the fluctuations are due to changes in the return to skill, attributing the slowdown in the 1980s to changes in the demand for skill.

Another common hypothesis is that blacks do worse because of increased competition from women and immigrants.[13] My analysis suggests instead that

---

[13] **There is also the spatial mismatch hypothesis, which posits that jobs have moved to the suburbs and to other areas where blacks are few and are less able to follow than whites (for example, Kasarda 1989). However, the evidence that the suburbs and the central cities are different labor markets for adult men is not strong (Jencks and Mayer 1990).**

middle-skilled white men may be a more important source of competition. Demand has been shifting away from less-skilled men and black men since the 1940s. Yet by the 1980s, demand shifted only toward the top skill group of white men. No single factor can account for the many changes in labor market outcomes for black men in the 1980s, but this striking concentration in demand should prove to be an important influence.

A similar argument is made by Darity and Myers (1995), who argue that rising inequality and the disappearance of jobs in the middle of the skill distribution among white men squeezed black men farther down on the job ladder. With an abundant surplus of labor, discrimination need not be costly to employers. Darity and Myers call this an endogenous model of discrimination and suggest several ways in which one might go about proving this empirically, though they do not do so themselves. Unfortunately, there is no way in the extant data to distinguish between an increase in the demand for certain kinds of skill in which white men have an advantage over black men and a rise in discrimination due to increasing competition for jobs.

Nonetheless, we can examine whether competition for certain jobs appears to be increasing. A common explanation for the deteriorating position of both less-skilled men in general and black men in particular is the increased labor force participation of women and immigrants. The demand indexes are used below to measure the extent to which women and immigrants are replacing men, by race and skill level. I find little support for this argument. Instead, some preliminary evidence suggests that middle-skilled white men facing negative demand shifts are a source of increased competition for jobs typically held by black men.

A. Women

At first glance, it does appear that women are replacing men in the labor force because their labor force participation rates have risen as those for white men have fallen somewhat and those for black men have fallen a great deal (see Table 1). The extent to which these trends should be linked is unclear. If trends in women's labor force participation are to explain black-white differences, women must be better substitutes for black men than for white men. Borjas (1986) argues that women are substitutes for black men, but his estimates of the elasticity of substitution between white men and women are just as large as those between women and black men, though not always statistically significant. Using similar cross-sectional data but a different functional form, Grant and Hamermesh (1981) find that white women are complements to white men, but so are white women and blacks (both male and female), though the estimates are insignificant. Both studies are based on cross-sectional data from 1969.

Using more recent data, Topel (1992, 1994) argues that women have increased the supply of less-skilled workers, thereby driving down the wages of less-skilled and minority men, though he considers his disconcertingly large 1994 results suggestive and not conclusive. With a similar methodology, but defining skill absolutely rather than by gender, Blau and Kahn (1994) find little evidence that increasing labor force participation by women affects the wages of less-skilled men. They suggest that their findings, as well as Topel's, indicate that skill-biased technological change has more to do with the deteriorating position of less-skilled men than does the entry of women into the labor market.

The demand indexes can be used to explore whether women are replacing men differentially by race and skill level. Growth in the fraction of women's employment in an industry-occupation is measured across decades, normalized by the industry-occupation share of total employment (the indexes are not elasticity-corrected because this formulation estimates the effect of actual replacement rather than the effect of market-wide shifts in labor demand). As before, a positive index number indicates that women moved into occupations and industries initially occupied by men of a certain skill level.

Figure 4 shows the extent to which demand has shifted away from men of a certain skill level toward women within an occupation and industry. Like Blau and Kahn, but over a longer time frame, I find that women appear to compete more with more-skilled white men than with other men, either black or white. The negative numbers in the bottom panel show that the replacement effect was smaller for black men. On the whole, however, these numbers are fairly small. In fact, the positive numbers in the top two panels show that a larger share of women entered male-dominated jobs in the 1940s and 1960s, when black men's relative wages improved a great deal. The growth in women's labor force participation is unlikely by itself to explain the slowdown of black relative progress in the 1970s and 1980s.

In fact, any story trying to explain the effect of women's labor market participation on less-skilled men would have to be a complex one, given the differences in occupational segregation even in 1990 as shown by Table 3. Entries in this table indicate the percentage of black men, by skill level, who would have had to change industry and occupation to make their employment distribution the same as the same-skilled group defined by race and sex at the top of each column. The index ranges from 0–100, with 100 indicating perfect segregation. In 1990, 29 percent of black men would have had to change industry and occupation for their employment distribution to look like that of white men. A much larger percentage would have had to change to resemble the distribution of white or black women, 47 and 40 percent respectively. Even at the lowest skill levels, the employment distributions of black men were more similar to those of white men than of women of either race. Rather than women replacing black or less-skilled men in the labor market, the positive index numbers in Figure 4 suggest that demand is shifting in ways that favor women over men in general. It is possible, though, that women have a second-order effect on less-skilled men. By entering occupations that relatively highly skilled men might have entered, women might indirectly induce the more skilled men to displace other less-skilled men further down the job distribution.

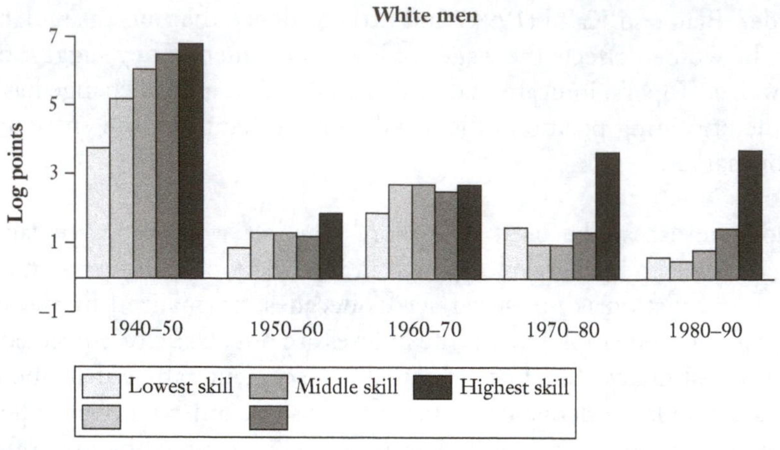
White men
Log points
7
5
3
1
–1
1940–50
1950–60
1960–70
1970–80
1980–90
Lowest skill
Middle skill
Highest skill

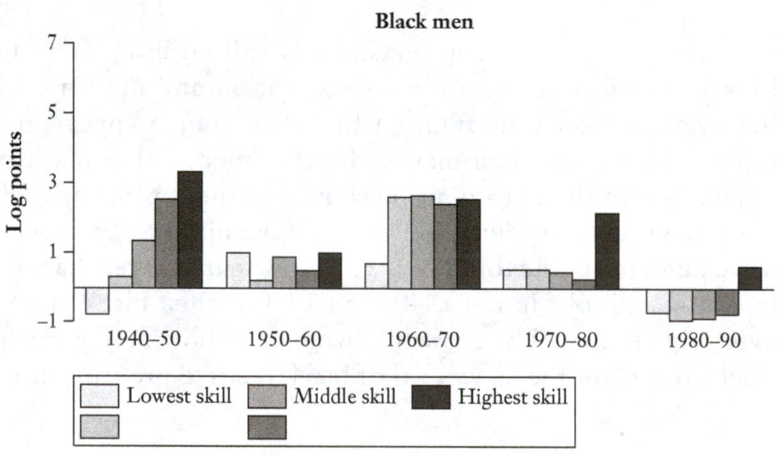
Black men
Log points
7
5
3
1
–1
1940–50
1950–60
1960–70
1970–80
1980–90
Lowest skill
Middle skill
Highest skill

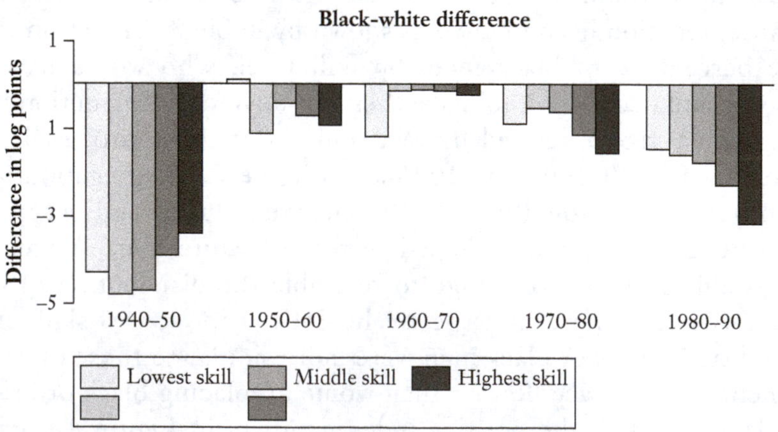
Black-white difference
Difference in log points
1
1
–3
–5
1940–50
1950–60
1960–70
1970–80
1980–90
Lowest skill
Middle skill
Highest skill

FIGURE 4

TABLE 3 Indexes of Employment Dissimilarity, by Skill Level, 1990

	White Men	White Women	Black Women
Black men			
All skill levels	29.2	46.5	40.3
By skill level			
Low 1	24.7	38.9	37.3
2	24.4	46.5	38.9
3	25.2	53.4	43.4
4	25.0	53.9	44.6
High 5	30.1	49.5	41.0

Source: See Table 2.

Note: The entries by skill level are estimated only across the wage sample, as skill is defined as position in the black men's log wage distribution. Entries are the percentage of the group defined by race, sex, and rank who would have to change occupation and industry to make the employment distribution of the group the same as that of black men. The indexes range from 0–100, with 100 indicating perfect segregation.

B. Immigrants

Immigrants are also a potential source of competition for minority or less-skilled men. In 1960, 5.4 percent of the population was foreign-born. In 1990, this had risen to 7.9 percent, before adjusting upward to account for illegal immigration (U.S. Bureau of the Census 1995). Immigrants, of course, are not distributed evenly around the country, in fact, just six cities accounted for 40 percent of all immigrants in the United States between 1970 and 1980 (LaLonde and Topel 1991). The average skill level of immigrants relative to the native-born has also declined over time, as countries with less-educated populations have become the major immigrant sources (Borjas 1992). Thus, the concern was and is that growing numbers of less-skilled immigrants flood certain local markets and displace less-educated native-born workers.

This has proven to be a difficult question to answer empirically. Cross-sectional comparisons of Standard Metropolitan Statistical Areas (SMSAs) with high versus low fractions of immigrants confound genuine effects with unobserved fixed characteristics of SMSA. Results from studies that use first differences to take these fixed effects into account suggest that while the effect of immigrants on wages and employment for minority or less-skilled U.S.-born workers has been negative, it has been small (Altonji and Card 1991; LaLonde and Topel 1991; Hamermesh 1993). In contrast, Borjas, Freeman, and Katz (1992) and Topel (1994) use national data and find that immigration has had a negative effect on the relative earnings and employment of less-skilled workers.

The demand shift indexes can also be used to study whether immigrants are replacing native-born men. This is particularly relevant for the period since 1960 when immigration rates began to rise dramatically due to the 1965 immigration law reform.

TABLE 4 Percentage Foreign-Born, by State

	1960	1970	1980	1990
New York	13.5	16.3	15.1	18.3
New Jersey	9.4	11.7	11.7	14.9
Illinois	6.4	7.8	8.5	10.4
Florida	4.6	9.0	11.4	14.7
Texas	3.5	3.9	7.0	10.9
California	8.9	12.4	17.2	25.6
National	5.3	6.6	7.4	10.2

Source: See Table 1.
Note: These fractions refer to the population age 18 or older who are not students or in the military or living in group quarters. Also, beginning with the 1980 Census, the Census Bureau allocates answers to missing values for the question regarding place of birth, making the numbers over time not strictly comparable.

Only six states are used in this analysis in order to focus on areas in which immigrants reside. Table 4 shows the growth in the fraction foreign-born in these states. In 1960, 4.6 percent of Floridians were foreign-born in my sample; by 1990, this number was 14.7 percent. In California the rise was even more dramatic: from 8.9 percent in 1960 to 25.6 percent in 1990.[14] For comparison, the national percentages were 5.3 in 1960 and 10.2 in 1990. The indexes will understate the degree of replacement to the extent that illegal immigrants are undercounted in the surveys.

I examine states rather than SMSAs in order to use a broad definition of a local labor market. This may also ameliorate the effect of the possible migratory response of the U.S.-born to recent immigration into their SMSAs, though the evidence for this migratory response is mixed. Filer (1992) finds that the native-born, especially less-skilled whites, leave cities in response to an influx of immigrants, but that native-born blacks do not, presumably because of residential segregation. Butcher and Card (1991) find that the U.S.-born and immigrants tend to move to the same cities. Furthermore, no one has yet addressed how far families move if there is a migratory response. One could imagine that whites continue to work in the same places but move to suburban areas with fewer immigrants, for example, in order to send their kids to schools with few immigrant children. Even if families do migrate, few cross state lines when they move (U.S. Bureau of the Census, various years).

Figure 5 shows that the replacement effects of immigrants are much larger than the replacement effects of women. (The indexes for immigrants were estimated in a similar fashion to those for women.) In general, recent immigrants have been

[14] These fractions are for the population older than age 14 who are not students or in the military or residing in group quarters. Published Census Bureau reports for the entire California population in 1990 indicate that roughly 20 percent were foreign-born.

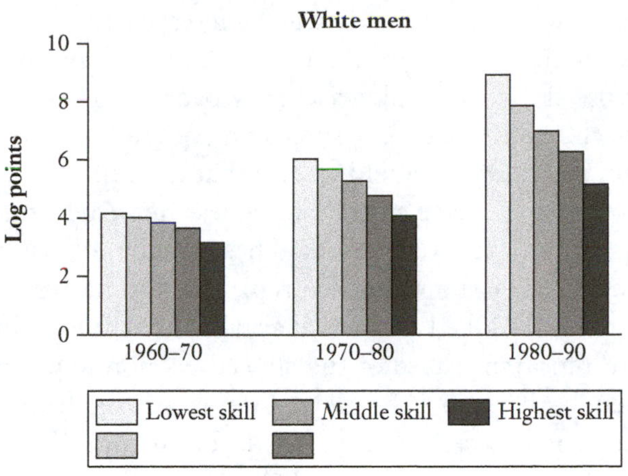

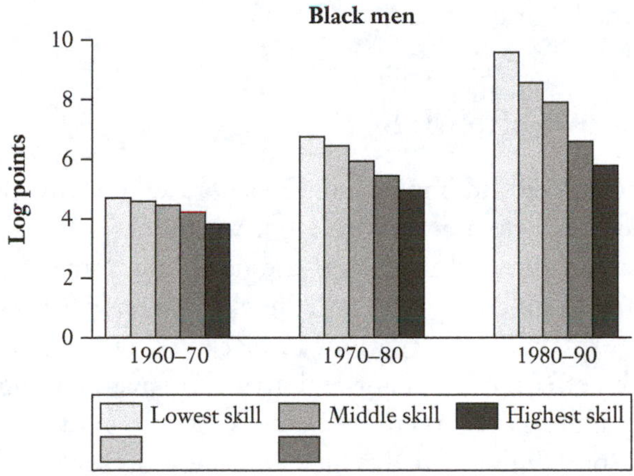

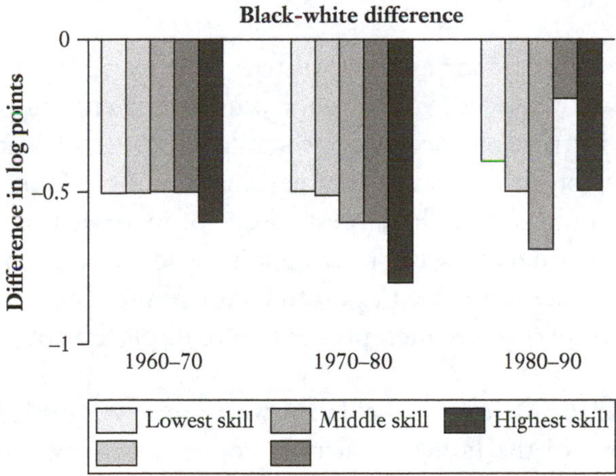

FIGURE 5 The extent to which immigrants have replaced men, by men's race and skill quintile

replacing native-born workers, and this trend increased in the 1980s. Immigrants also supplanted less-skilled men more than more-skilled men; this differential effect of immigration across skill groups likewise grew over the 1980s. Most importantly, however, the black-white differences are small and even fell some over the 1980s. The negative numbers in the bottom panel indicate that the replacement effect was only slightly larger for black men. Race appears to be less important than skill in gauging the effect of immigration on native workers. These results otherwise tend to confirm those of other researchers: immigrants are replacing the native-born in some local labor markets and the less-skilled in particular. On the whole, though, immigration is unlikely to be an important cause of the slowed economic progress of black men relative to white men, both because the racial difference is small and because the effect of immigrants is confined to certain areas. As LaLonde and Topel point out, while immigrants increased the supply of less-skilled workers in the aggregate economy in the 1970s, this inflow was much smaller than that generated by the entry of the Baby Boom cohort into the labor market.

C. Middle-Skilled White Men

If competition from women and immigrants does not explain why black men are more affected by demand shifts than are white men, what does? A striking finding from the industry-occupation demand indexes is the declining demand for middle-skilled white men. The demand shift away from middle-skilled men has been steady over time (and so this cannot explain the fluctuations in black relative economic progress), but it may exacerbate the effects of stagnant real growth in average wages and increasing wage inequality if middle-skilled men are better substitutes for less-skilled men than for more-skilled men: Middle-skilled white men may present the most formidable competition to minority and less-skilled men if downward mobility among the middle-skilled is inhibiting upward progress among those further down on the job ladder.

One way to examine this is to contrast the industries and occupations from which middle-skilled white men are displaced with those in which they end up post-displacement. If they move to industries and occupations similar to those of black men, then it is likely that they contribute to increased competition for jobs held by black men. While displaced workers would not be the largest source of increased competition, as their numbers are relatively small, they can provide some evidence that this kind of pressure exists. Dissimilarity indexes are used again to compare the employment distributions of black men with those of white men pre- and post-displacement.

The employment information for displaced white men comes from the Displaced Worker supplements of the January Current Population Survey (CPS) from 1986, 1988, 1990, and 1992. Unfortunately, data are not available for earlier years, making comparisons to the 1960s and 1970s impossible. The CPS supplements interview people who report job displacement during the previous five years and survey their pre- and post-displacement job characteristics. The sample includes men from the same 25 states analyzed above, and only those who were displaced by their employer's business failure or because the position or shift was abolished. Topel

(1990) shows that there is little evidence of recall bias for these events—unlike some other possible sources of displacement such as slack work or self-employed business failure. Men displaced in the 12 months leading up to the survey are excluded to focus on longer-run changes. The March CPS files from 1982–93 are used to create skill ranks of log weekly wages by year and state, and to calculate employment distributions for black men.[15] Displaced workers were assigned a skill group based on their pre-displacement weekly wage by year of displacement and current state of residence. (While there is no information about whether they moved out of state, 80 percent of the sample reported they did not change city or county since displacement.)

The second column of numbers (in parentheses) in Table 5 shows that 65 percent of white displaced workers were in the middle of the skill distribution before displacement.[16] The third column of numbers shows dissimilarity indexes such as those calculated for women in Table 3. Before displacement, almost 37 percent of all displaced white men would have had to change industry and occupation to have an employment distribution similar to that of black men. After displacement,

TABLE 5 Dissimilarity Indexes over Industry and Occupation: Displaced White Men versus Black Men

Pre-Displacement Rank (percent distribution)		Dissimilarity Index: Pre-Displacement	Dissimilarity Index: Post-Displacement	Percent Change
1–20	(20.5%)	35.7	25.4	29%
21–40	(25.4%)	36.7	26.1	29%
41–60	(22.2%)	41.7	30.8	26%
61–80	(17.2%)	48.5	39.8	18%
81–100	(14.8%)	60.4	53.3	12%
All quintiles	(100.0%)	36.7	27.6	25%

Source: Wage ranks are defined by the male log weekly wage distribution by year and state from the March CPS files 1982–1993. Data for the displaced white men (n = 4,230) come from the January CPS for 1986, 1988, 1990, and 1992.

Note: The distribution of displaced white men across wage quintiles appears in parentheses. The dissimilarity index is defined as the percentage of white men before and after displacement who would have to change industry and occupation to have the same employment distribution as black men. Employment distributions for black men are calculated using the March surveys. The index ranges from 0–100, with 100 indicating perfect segregation.

15. CPS sample sizes by year and state are too small to permit reweighting white men into the wage distribution of black men.

16. Although not shown in the table, almost 58 percent of displaced white men were in a lower decile after displacement than they were before, a fraction that is similar across years since displacement. Clearly, a significant fraction do worse semi-permanently, and aggregating across years since displacement to construct the indexes does not disguise important differences over time.

they find work that is more like that of black men: only 28 percent would need to change industry and occupation to have the same employment distribution. By pre-displacement wage rank, the largest changes in the index are in the bottom and middle of the distribution: The index falls by almost 30 percent in ranks 1–40 and by 26 percent in ranks 41–60. Clearly, the employment distribution of those displaced white men who found work became more similar to that of black men, suggesting that middle-skilled white men may be competing for jobs that black men tend to hold more generally.

VI. SUMMARY AND CONCLUSION

In light of the falling relative employment and the stagnant growth in the relative wages of black men since the 1970s, this study has examined the role of demand-side factors in black relative economic progress from 1940–90. Previous empirical work looking at demand-side changes has focused on data gathered since the 1970s. This analysis contributes to the debate over the causes of the slowdown by using data from a longer time period to determine whether some of the hypotheses offered for the more recent period are consistent with long-run trends. It also extends the use of fixed-coefficient demand indexes to examine the hypotheses that other workers have replaced black men in the labor market.

A simple industry decline story is not sufficiently consistent with the data to explain the recent wage and employment patterns of blacks relative to whites. The market-level demand shift measures show that black-white differences in industry shifts since the 1960s have been small.

The data also show that there is some merit to the argument that accelerated technological change during the 1980s increased the demand for skill, adversely affecting black men. It is not the case, though, that demand shifts were more equal in the past and then suddenly in the 1980s twisted in favor of highly skilled workers. Shifts in demand have consistently favored more-skilled workers since at least 1940. Yet the 1980s were different from the preceding 40 years: the skill bias in demand shifts grew rather than shrank for the first time, largely as a result of accelerating demand shifts away from the less-skilled. This perhaps explains why overall wage inequality among men increased so much in the 1980s. It also partly accounts for the slowdown in the progress of black men in the 1980s. The racial gap in demand shifts widened for the first time over the 1980s, driven by technological change.

The evidence is not consistent with the hypothesis that the entry of women and immigrants into the labor market has decreased the employment demand for black men. Instead, my analysis shows that women are replacing more-skilled men, and white men more so than black men. I do find that immigrants are replacing men and less-skilled men in particular. But I also find that the black-white difference in the effect of immigration is small and roughly constant over time: immigrants move into occupations and industries occupied by less-skilled men of both races.

Finally, there is some evidence that middle-skilled white men, facing worsening job prospects, may increase the competition for the jobs that black men tend to hold. The question, of course, is whether employers favor white men because they are more skilled or because it is easier to discriminate when there is a surplus of labor. While the 1980s witnessed an increase in the demand for skill, the increases in wage inequality were manifested even within narrowly defined education (or wage position) measures of skill, implying we do not know yet what kinds of skill are being demanded. The subjective nature of the skills thought to be important in the service sector and in more-skilled occupations (such as communication skills) also leaves room for hard-to-detect discrimination. Empirically, however, one cannot distinguish a change in the demand for unmeasured skills from a change in discrimination with the data used in this paper.

The reduced-form indexes in this study provide insight into how the structure of demand for labor has changed over a 50-year period for men, by race and by skill, thereby affecting the economic progress of black men relative to white men. To generate policy implications of these changes, future research should concentrate on developing structural models that incorporate other factors—most importantly, relative supply changes—into the analysis. Nonetheless, my analysis strongly suggests that policymakers concerned with the fortunes of black men and of less-skilled men of both races should also consider the changes occurring among those in the middle of the skill distribution.

APPENDIX 1

Data

The data for this paper are the 1940–90 Public Use files of the decennial Census. The sample includes only the 25 states with the highest black population in 1960 in order to focus on the areas in which both blacks and whites tend to live: New York, New Jersey, Pennsylvania, Ohio, Indiana, Illinois, Michigan, Missouri, Delaware, Maryland, Washington, D.C., Virginia, North Carolina, South Carolina, Georgia, Florida, Kentucky, Tennessee, Alabama, Mississippi, Arkansas, Louisiana, Oklahoma, Texas, and California. The sample also includes only respondents who were at least 18 years old with 1–40 years of potential work experience and who were not students or in the military or living in group quarters. In 1990 the Census was not self-weighting, so sample weights were used in the analysis. The education variable also changed in 1990, from one based on highest grade completed to highest degree received. We used the matched March CPS in which both education questions appear to calculate mean grade by degree received for respondents aged 27–65 separately by sex, and used these means to impute education in the Census. From these data, two samples were constructed: a count sample and a smaller wage sample.

A. The Count Sample

The count sample contains all respondents described above to measure labor supply. Some differences in the data across years cannot be reconciled. For example, in 1940, the Census Bureau converted answers to a question about weeks of work into a "full-time equivalent" measure. Other consistency problems can be dealt with. In the 1960 and 1970 Censuses, hours and weeks were coded categorically. I imputed means to the categories based on weeks of work in Current Population Survey data. Hours were imputed using the "hours worked last week" variable from the 1964–75 CPS. "Weeks of work last year" were imputed using the 1975–87 CPS; the earlier CPS years could not be used because they also coded weeks of work categorically.

In most years the Census asks about weeks of work last year, but about the hours worked during the week prior to the survey (conducted in the spring) rather than hours last year. Thus I used hours worked last week as a proxy for hours worked last year and imputed hours to men who report working last year but report zero hours last week. Otherwise, those who worked last year but not last week would be assigned zero annual hours of work. This would not be neutral across groups since unemployment is more frequent among the less-skilled, which would introduce some bias into the analysis. I imputed hours of work to respondents who were unemployed in the survey week but who worked in the prior year based on means by sex, race, education, experience, and weeks of work. Hours were not imputed to the 4.2 percent of men in work relief programs in the 1940 survey: in the official statistics of the time, these men were considered unemployed.

B. The Wage Sample

Using hourly wages is important for gauging the price of a unit of labor regardless of the amount of labor supplied to the market. Also, fluctuations in the hours worked per week and in unemployment vary over the 50-year period: the decennial Census does not always fall in the same part of the business cycle, and evidence suggests that blacks are more affected by downturns than whites.

The Census does not ask about hourly wages, so I constructed this measure by dividing annual earnings by annual hours of work. In order to take into account the measurement error induced by constructing an hourly wage, I trimmed some respondents from the wage sample. This sample includes only individuals who worked at least 14 weeks and at least 35 hours per week and who were working for wages.

I excluded farmers, farm managers, and people with self-employment income because their income data are unreliable. Non-wage-and-salary income reflects the return to capital as well as the return to labor, as evidenced by respondents who report losses. Furthermore, farm income, even for farm workers rather than farm owners, was not collected consistently over time. In 1940, only wage-and-salary earnings are available, with a binary variable indicating whether an individual earned more than 50 dollars from nonwage sources. In other words, hourly wages for farm workers could be based only on wage-and-salary earnings. To assess the effect this would have, I examined the 1950 and 1960 Censuses in which self-employment income is reported and includes farm earnings. In these years, farm workers who report self-employment income also on average earn most of their earnings in self-employment (roughly, 80 percent in 1950 and over 60 percent in 1960). They also work much more than their counterparts who report only wage earnings, meaning an hourly wage based solely on wage earnings would be far too low for this group in 1940. Thus, I included only those farm workers who report only wage earnings. In 1940, the 10.9 percent of white men who were farmers are excluded from the wage sample. In the wage sample are the 43.1 percent of the white men who were farm workers (6.1 percent of all white male workers) and the 60.6 percent of all other white male workers. Among blacks, the 18.55 percent who were farmers are excluded; 50.4 percent of the farm workers (17.5 percent of black male workers) are in the wage sample, as are 62.0 percent of the other black male workers.

Additional problems derive from the way in which hours of work are measured. In the 1940–70 Censuses, respondents were asked how many hours they worked in the week prior to the survey. Hours worked in a particular week, however, may not coincide with hours worked in a typical week. In 1980, respondents were asked both about hours worked in the prior week and usual hours worked last year. Comparing the two, men who worked part-time (1–34 hours) reported far fewer hours worked last week (on average ten fewer) than hours worked in a typical week last year, making the hourly wage construct more problematic. Based on the 1980 comparison of the two measures, full-time wages are understated by 2–3 percent for full-time, full-year men (4 percent for women), but they are far overstated for part-time men—around 40 percent. The wage sample therefore includes only full-time workers in each survey, based on hours worked last week for consistency across surveys. Another problem with the data is that the wages for men who worked 1–13 weeks also appear to be dominated by measurement error, with these men reporting an average hourly wage on par with full-time, full-year workers. Thus men who worked on 1–13 weeks in the prior year are also excluded from the wage sample. These exclusions reduce, though hardly eliminate, measurement error in wages.

Respondents' earnings in open-ended earnings intervals at the top of the earnings scale (for example, who earned "$65,000 or more") were multiplied by 1.44 to impute earnings above the top code. All dollars were then converted to 1982 dollars based on the implicit Personal Consumption Expenditure deflator. Finally, in 1990, workers earning less than $1 per hour were recoded up to $1, and those above $100 to $100. In other years, wages were recoded to the dollar amount that was the same fraction of median hourly wages (0.128 and 12.8) that $1 and $100 were of the 1990 median wage.

REFERENCES

Altonji, Joseph G., and David Card. 1991. "The Effects of Immigration on the Labor Market Outcomes of Less-Skilled Natives." In *Immigration, Trade, and the Labor Market*, eds. John M. Abowd and Richard B. Freeman, 201–34. Chicago: The University of Chicago Press.

Blau, Francine, and Lawrence Kahn. 1994. "The Impact of Wage Structure on Trends in U.S. Gender Wage Differentials: 1975–87." National Bureau of Economic Research, working paper no. 4748, Cambridge, Massachusetts.

Bluestone, Barry, and Bennett Harrison. 1982. *The Deindustrialization of America*. New York: Basic Books.

Borjas, George J. 1986. "The Demographic Determinants of the Demand for Black Labor." In *The Black Youth Unemployment Crisis*, eds. Richard B. Freeman and Harry J. Holzer, 191–232. Chicago: The University of Chicago Press.

———. 1992. "National Origin and the Skills of Immigrants in the Postwar Period." In *Immigration and the Work Force*, eds. George J. Borjas and Richard B. Freeman, 17–48 Chicago: The University of Chicago Press.

Borjas, George J., Richard B. Freeman, and Lawrence F. Katz. 1992. "On the Labor Market Effects of Immigration and Trade." In *Immigration and the Work Force*, eds. George J. Borjas and Richard B. Freeman, 213–44. Chicago: The University of Chicago Press.

Bound, John, and Richard B. Freeman. 1992. "What Went Wrong? The Erosion of Relative Earnings and Employment among Young Black Men in the 1980s." *Quarterly Journal of Economics* 107(1):201–32.

Bound, John, and Harold J. Holzer. 1993. "Industrial Shifts, Skill Levels, and the Labor Market for White and Black Males." *Review of Economics and Statistics* 75(3):387–96.

Brown, Charles. 1984. "Black-White Earnings Ratios Since the Civil Rights Act of 1964: The Importance of Labor Market Dropouts." *Quarterly Journal of Economics* 99(1):31–44.

Butcher, Kristin, and David Card. 1991. "Immigration and Wages: Evidence from the 1980s." *American Economic Review* 81(2):292–96.

Butler, Richard, and James J. Heckman. 1977. "The Government's Impact on the Labor Market Status of Black Americans: A Critical Review." In *Equal Rights and Industrial Relations*, eds. Leonard J. Hausman et al., 235–81. Madison, Wisc.: Industrial Relations Research Association.

Cain, Glen, and Ross Finnie. 1990. "The Black-White Difference in Youth Employment: Evidence for Demand-Side Factors." *Journal of Labor Economics* 8(1, part 2): S364–S395.

Card, David, and Alan B. Krueger. 1992. "School Quality and Black-White Relative Earnings: A Direct Assessment." *Quarterly Journal of Economics* 107(1):151–200.

Darity, William A., and Samuel L. Myers, Jr. 1995. "The Widening Gap: A Summary and Synthesis of the Debate on Widening Inequality." Paper prepared for the National Commission for Employment Policy.

Filer, Randall K. 1992. "The Effect of Immigrant Arrivals on Migratory Patterns of Native Workers." *In Immigration and the Work Force*, eds. George J. Borjas and Richard B. Freeman, 245–70. Chicago: The University of Chicago Press.

Freeman, Richard B. 1973. "Changes in the Labor Market for Black Americans 1948–1972." *Brookings Papers on Economic Activity* 4(1):67–120.

———. 1975. "Over Investment in College Training?" *Journal of Human Resources* 10(3):287–311.

Grant, James H., and Daniel S. Hamermesh. 1981. "Labor Market Competition among Youths, White Women, and Others." *Review of Economics and Statistics* 63(3):354–60.

Hamermesh, Daniel. 1993. *Labor Demand*. Princeton, N.J.: Princeton University Press.

Holzer, Harry. 1991. "The Spatial Mismatch Hypothesis: What Has the Evidence Shown?" *Urban Studies* 28(1):105–22.

Jencks, Christopher, and Susan Mayer. 1990. "Residential Segregation, Job Proximity, and Black Job Opportunities." In *Inner-City Poverty in the United States*, eds. Laurence E. Lynn, Jr., and Michael G. H. McGeary, 187–222. Washington, D.C.: National Academy Press.

Johnston, William B., and Arnold E. Packer. 1987. *Workforce 2000: Work and Workers for the 21st Century*. Indianapolis; Hudson Institute.

Juhn, Chinhui, Kevin M. Murphy, and Brooks Pierce. 1991. "Accounting for the Slowdown in Black White Wage Convergence." In *Workers and Their Wages: Changing Patterns in the United States*, ed. Marvin H. Kosters, 107–43. Washington, D.C.: The AEI Press.

Kasarda, John D. 1989. "Urban Industrial Transition of the Underclass." In *The Ghetto Underclass: Social Science Perspectives, The Annals of the American Academy of Political and Social Science*, special editor William J. Wilson, 26–47. Newbury Park, Calif.: Sage Publications.

Katz, Lawrence F., and Kevin M. Murphy. 1992. "Changes in Relative Wages, 1963–1987: Supply and Demand Factors." *Quarterly Journal of Economics* 107(1):35–78.

LaLonde, Robert J., and Robert H. Topel. 1991. "Labor Market Adjustments to Increased Immigration." In *Immigration, Trade, and the Labor Market*, eds. John M. Abowd and Richard B. Freeman, 167–200. Chicago: The University of Chicago Press.

Mischel, Lawrence, and Ruy A. Teixeira. 1991. *The Myth of the Coming Labor Shortage: Jobs, Skills, and Incomes of America's Workforce 2000*. Washington, D.C.: Economic Policy Institute.

Murphy, Kevin M., and Finis Welch. 1993. "Occupational Change and the Demand for Skill." *American Economic Review* 83(2):122–26.

Neal, Derek, and William Johnson. 1995. "The Role of Pre-Market Factors in Black-White Wage Differences," Paper presented at the Western Economic Association meetings in San Diego, July 1995.

O'Neill, June. 1990. "The Role of Human Capital in Earnings Differences between Black and White Men." *Journal of Economic Perspectives* 4(4):25–46.

Reardon, Elaine. 1994. "The Structure of Demand and Black Relative Economic Progress, 1940–1990." Ph.D. dissertation, University of Chicago.

Smith, James P., and Finis R. Welch. 1989. "Black Economic Progress after Myrdal." *Journal of Economic Literature* 27(2):519–64.

Topel, Robert H. 1990. "Specific Capital and Unemployment: Measuring the Costs and Consequences of Job Loss." *Carnegie-Rochester Conference Series on Public Policy* 33:181–214.

———. 1992. "Wage Inequality and Regional Labor Market Performance in the United States." Graduate School of Business, University of Chicago, June 1992.

———. 1994. "Regional Labor Markets and the Determinants of Wage Inequality." *American Economic Review* 84(2):17–22.

U.S. Bureau of the Census, Various years. *Statistical Abstract of the United States*. Washington, D.C.: GPO.

Welch, Finis. 1990. "The Employment of Black Men." *Journal of Labor Economics* 8(1): S26–S74.

Wilson, William J. 1987. *The Truly Disadvantaged: The Inner City, the Underclass, and Public Policy*. Chicago: The University of Chicago Press.

Wright, Gavin. 1986. *Old South, New South: Revolutions in the Southern Economy Since the Civil War*. New York: Basic Books.

PART 4 QUESTIONS

1. How do color complex and internalized racism impact intra-group and inter-group social relations and are there economic and political consequences?

2. What is the significance of education and religion in African American political life?

3. Given a history of unequal treatment, what economic realities do African Americans face?

4. How do gender and age factor into social and economic well-being of African Americans?

Part 5

African Americans and Africana in the 21st Century

INTRODUCTION

Lessons of the past captured in the spiritual tradition of the Black Church and evidenced in its role as the premier site of actualization of the struggle for civil rights by African Americans, is examined by Leonard Gadzekpo in "The Black Church, the Civil Rights Movement and the Future". The Black Church, apart from being a religious institution, stands as a cultural and social bulwark in face of attacks on the humanity of African Americans. In examining the strategies, successes, and failures, as well as cultural values and social mechanisms that sustain the Black Church, Gadzekpo argues that a matrix has been created that could benefit African Americans in present and future efforts to attain a more equal society in the United Sates.

In "Black versus Black: The Relationships among African, African American, and African Caribbean Persons," Jennifer V. Jackson and Mary E. Cothran examine contacts and relationships among people of African descent in America, especially continental Africans, African Americans, and African Caribbean people. Jackson and Cothran argue that because of fears and misconceptions, although African people have the same beginnings, they are perceived to be so different culturally, socially, and intellectually that they are considered completely separate people. They suggest that travel to Africa and countries with large population groups of people of African descent and African-centered education would "promote understanding about the history, origin, family structures, and social mores of Africa and the African diaspora."[1]

Femi Ojo-Ade, in "Africans and Racism in the Millenium," [LLC7]argues that African ancestry has been used by racist detractors to keep down Africans and all people of African descent. These people of Africana not only have shared experiences of colonialism but also exhibit many manifestations of a common ethos. Ojo-Ade posits that without undermining the various nationalities, Africans—that is, people of African descent—could rehabilitate the downtrodden, rehumanize them, and return value to their culture. He concludes by asking how people of African descent can survive the millennium, given the magnitude of the odds against them. Ojo-Ade's answer is that new configurations of Africanity within each nationality on an intercontinental level, exemplified in the struggle against oppression, commitment, and an ethos uncased in unwavering humanism, point the way.

Michael George Hanchard argues in "Black Transnationalism, Africana Studies, and the 21st Century" [LLC8]that because it combines various methodologies, concepts, and theories of the social sciences and humanities with which to examine Africans and African-derived people, Africana Studies has holistic and multiperspectival approaches to African and African diaspora-related topics, an intellectual advantage that other disciplines do not have. Hanchard sees contradictory effects of the relative successes of

---

[1] Jennifer V. Jackson and Mary E. Cothran, "Black versus Black: The Relationships among African, African American, and African Caribbean Persons," *Journal of Black Studies* 33, no. 5 (May, 2003): 601.

Black people to overcome oppression of earlier centuries in, on the one hand, the mass dissemination of anti-Black iconography and, on the other hand, transnational solidarity networks such as the antiapartheid movement, Garveyism, and Pan-Africanism, with all contradictory effects depending on the use of modern communication technology. He posits that the very history of Africana and its struggle to overcome oppression requires combined social scientific and humanistic methodologies and a global approach to study. Hanchard concludes that with globalization and intercontinental migration of Africans and African-derived people in the twenty-first century, the intellectual enterprise of Africana Studies is germane.

The Black Church, the Civil Rights Movement, and the Future

Leonard Gadzekpo

The recent burning of black church buildings strikes at the very heart of African-American society. The buildings themselves are not the black church, which is instead a conglomeration of several black Christian denominations. Apart from their function as places of worship, they are, however, symbols of spiritual and cultural life within black America. Burning them, therefore, is an attack on one of the cornerstones of Black communities and African-American culture. Sam Block's song, *Freedom Is a Constant Dying*, articulates the consciousness that black Christians have and that is nurtured by the black church:

> They say freedom is a constant dying.
> O Lord, we died so long
> We must be free.
> We must be free.[1]

It means the black church, along with its spiritual activities in black communities, is also the anchor of black activism in the face of the hostile conditions that these communities endure. In this social consciousness context, a look at the black church and its role in the civil rights movement of the 1960s and 1970s may act as a point of projection into the future.

The black church may be viewed as the most important black institution in the United States. It was seen during the antebellum period as the "invisible institution."[2] From the period of emancipation through the postbellum era to the present, the black church has had an enormous impact on the religious, cultural, social, and political aspects of life in America. Eric C. Lincoln and Lawrence Mamiya asserted that religion was perhaps the best prism to cultural understanding,[3] that culture was a form of religion, and

---

From The *Journal of Religious Thought, Vol. 53/54, No. 2/1 (1997)* by Leonard Gadzekpo.

[1] Eric C. Lincoln and Lawrence Mamiya, *The Black Church in the African American Experience* (Durham: Duke University Press, 1990), 371.

[2] C. Franklin Frazier, *The Negro Church in America* (New York: Schocken, 1964), 23.

[3] Lincoln and Mamiya, *The Black Church*, xi.

religion was the heart of culture.[4] One may present the black church as an institution that gives some direction to the aforementioned aspects of African-American life and influences them, particularly in American society at large.

The core values or black culture—such as freedom, justice, equality, an African heritage, and racial parity in all aspects of human life—were inherent in the black Christian ethos that gave birth to and nurtured the civil rights movement. The civil rights legislation that brought changes in the status and lives of African Americans, however, did not go far enough in addressing the wide spectrum of problems facing them. The black church, therefore, has reached the point in the last decade of the twentieth century in which searing demands are being made for a return to the tradition of self-help and agitation. Moreover, the development of new and creative approaches has become commonplace in the face of internal pressures involving changes within African-American society, external pressures involving prevalent and persistent racism, and the hostile environment in which the church exists.

CULTURAL IDENTITY

Questions arise as to the cultural identity of the black church; its function as a cultural system; and how such a system evolved, adapted, and helped cope with the problems inside and outside African-American society. The African-American religious worldview—the black sacred cosmos—was related not only to the people's African heritage, but also to their conversion to Christianity during slavery and to the developments emanating from the black experience in America. The Africans who were forcibly brought to America as slaves did not arrive in America with *tabula rasa* as some scholars such as Franklin E. Frazier or Nathan Glazer and Daniel Patrick Moynihan claimed. Glazer and Moynihan argued that "the Negro was only an American and nothing else. He has no values and culture to guard and protect."[5] While other scholars looked at the black culture as an aberrational attempt at mimicking mainstream white culture, it is clear in the face of historical facts, such as 250 years of slavery, and a hundred years of official and unofficial segregation in the South and in the North, that African Americans had an effective culture as a result of their history. The "culture is the sum of the options for creative survival."[6] Where then does the black church fit in African-American culture?

The Durkheimian concept of religion as a social phenomenon in which shared group experience shaped and influenced the cultural screens of human communication and interpretation[7] may help in the understanding of black religion and the black church. According to Emile Durkheim, the concepts of God and other religious entities

---

[4] **Ibid., 7.**

[5] **Nathan Glazer and Daniel Patrick Moynihan, *Beyond the Melting Pot* (Cambridge, MA: MIT Press and Harvard University Press. 1963), 51.**

[6] **Lincoln and Mamiya, *The Black Church*, 3.**

[7] **Emile Durkheim, *The Elementary Forms of the Religious Life* (New York: Free Press, 1965 edition), 440.**

were only symbols, and their proper reference was society because it was society that produced the individual mixture of awe and respect that was characteristic in society's attitude toward the sacred.[8] Under the given conditions of history, African Americans' symbols, therefore, would be in direct relationship to their situation; hence, the black religious cosmos was different from that of whites. Newbell Puckett wrote:

> Most of the time the Negro outwardly accepts the doctrines of Christianity and goes on living according to his own conflicting secular mores, but sometimes he enlarges upon the activities of God to explain certain phenomena not specifically dealt with in the Holy Scriptures.[9]

The Geertzian concept—which is that continuity between the form of Integration existing in the social structural ("casual-functional") dimension and the form of integration existing in the cultural ("logico-meaningful") dimension led to social and cultural integration[10]—may also be applied in the explanation of the integration of Christianity into the black sacred cosmos. While this continuity was possible, in the larger white mainstream society, a discontinuity occurred that would force the black Christians to leave and start their own churches. The schisms, the acceptance of slavery by white southern churches as "God ordained," slavery's rejection by the northern churches, and the prevalent racism of the white church indicated the discontinuity.

W. E. B. Du Bois earlier wrote:

> It was not at first by any means a Christian Church, but by the terms Obe Worship, or "Voodooism" Association and missionary effort soon gave these rites a veneer of Christianity, and gradually, after the centuries, the Church became Christian, with a simple Calvinist creed, but with many of the old customs still clinging to the services.[11]

These observations indicated (1) that the black church from the very beginning had a distinct character and was not an attempt at mimicking the white church, and (2) that it had an identity that was unequivocal and indeed intrinsically African American.

CORE VALUE: FREEDOM

The belief system of black Christians, although structurally similar to those of whites, was different in that emphasis was placed on certain particular theological views. The major aspect of black Christian belief was embodied in the word "freedom." Freedom for whites encompassed the value of American individualism, freedom "to pursue

[8] Ibid.

[9] Newbell Puckett, *Folk Beliefs of the Southern Negro* (Chapel Hill, NC: University of North Carolina Press, 1926), 545.

[10] Clifford Geertz, *The Interpretation of Cultures* (New York: Basic Books, 1973), 60.

[11] W. E. B. Du Bois, *The Negro Church* (Atlanta: Atlanta University Press, 1903), 3.

one's destiny without political or bureaucratic interference or restraint."[12] For the African in America as a slave, it meant release from bondage; after emancipation, it meant education, employment, and freedom of movement to the "Negro"; and for the past forty years, it has meant social, political, and economic justice to African Americans. At the same time, freedom to African Americans through the centuries was also communal in nature as uttered in Sam Block's song *Freedom Is a Constant Dying* and by Dr. Martin Luther King Jr. when he said, "Free at last, free at last, thank God Almighty, we are free at last."[13] Freedom for African Americans was both secular and spiritual, implying spiritually the freedom to live in obedience to God's word and will, and implying secularly a "fundamental transformation in individual and group life."[14]

The seven major historically black denominations that are the core of the black church are the African Methodist Episcopal (AME) Church, the African Methodist Episcopal Zion (AMEZ) Church, the Christian Methodist Episcopal (CME) Church, the National Baptist Convention USA Incorporated (NBC), the National Baptist Convention of America Unincorporated (NBCA), the Progressive National Baptist Convention (PNBC), and the Church of God in Christ (COGIC). All of them, except for the COGIC, grew but of the withdrawal of black Christians from white Christian denominations in the search for the attainment of spiritual and secular freedom. The withdrawals were a precursor of the fight for civil rights.

Seen in the framework of the Geertzian definition of culture, freedom was a symbol in the African-American cultural context. According to Geertz, culture

> denotes an historical transmitted pattern of meanings embodied in symbols, a system of inherited conceptions expressed in symbolic forms by means of which men communicate, perpetuate, and develop their knowledge about and attitudes towards life.[15]

The black experience in America, starting with slavery, had one critical indication of freedom that remained constant through the centuries. It was that freedom meant "the absence of any restraint which might compromise one's responsibility to God."[16] Han S. Baer and Merrill Singer claimed that while white fundamentalist or evangelical religious groups laid strong emphasis on eternal damnation, African-American Christianity stressed the joy of the afterlife.[17] The two authors failed, however, to mention the notion in black Christianity that a call to God's discipleship was a call to freedom, and that

---

[12] Lincoln and Mamiya, *The Black Church*, 5.

[13] James Melvin Washington, ed., *A Testament of Hope: The Essential Writings of Martin Luther King* (San Francisco: Harper & Row, 1986), 220.

[14] Richard King, *Civil Rights and the Idea of Freedom* (Oxford: Oxford University Press, 1992), 29.

[15] Geertz, *Interpretation of Cultures*, 89.

[16] Lincoln and Mamiya, *The Black Church*, 4.

[17] Hans A. Baer, Merrill Singer, and Hans A. Merrill, *African-American Religion in the Twentieth Century* (Knoxville, TN: University of Tennessee Press. 1992), 41.

God wants the black Christians to be free because he made them in his own image. To the black church, the Christian doctrine provided the legitimate ethical foundation that related equality directly to God's creative activities. In "God's own image" means not a white or black image but Man as a "psycho-physical unity of both a body and a soul, completely and simultaneously."[18] Many generations of white preachers tried to use theological arguments aimed at destroying this notion, but it remained the core of black Christians' faith and was etched indelibly in their psyche.[19] Again according to Geertz,

> religion is (1) a system of symbols which acts to (2) establish powerful, pervasive, and long-lasting moods and motivations in men by (3) formulating conceptions of a general order of existence and (4) clothing these conceptions with such aura of factuality that (5) the moods and motivations seem uniquely realistic.[20]

African-American religious ethos was the result of the moods and motivations generated by a system of symbols forged by the history of their presence in America. The early black Christians who founded the historic black churches did so by breaking away from white Christian denominations because "white society would not tolerate the presence of Blacks as equals in common public worship."[21] The powerful, pervasive, and long-lasting moods and motivations in the black religious ethos that caused Denmark Vescy and Nat Turner to revolt were part of the black cultural patterns that manifested themselves in Andrew Bryan and Jesse Peter when they started the Black Baptist Church. Richard Allen and Absalom Jones were founders of the African Methodist Episcopal Church. William J. Seymour founded Pentecostalism, the only black denomination started without any origin in a white denomination. Peter J. Paris affirmed black religious ethos and explained the source of black theology that these denominations presented:

> Survival theology implies neither contentment with adversity nor justification of oppression. Rather, the maintenance, preservation, and enhancement of meaningful life in community is its primary concern. The convenantal relationship between African peoples and God has empowered them to endure the pain of injustice while not affirming it. It has motivated them to do battle in one form or other against the perpetuation of injustice.[22]

One may, therefore, conclude that black theology gave the black church such conceptions as the colorblind in-God's-image of Man, which affirmed the reality of African Americans and gave them their peoplehood and personhood, or humanity, in a racist society.

---

[18] **Stuart Barton Babbage, *Man in Nature and in Grace* (Grand Rapids, MI: Eerdmans, 1957), 11.**

[19] **Lincoln and Mamiya, *The Black Church*, 4.**

[20] **Geertz, *Interpretation of Cultures*, 60.**

[21] **Columbus Salley and Ronald Behm, *What Color Is Your God?* (Downers Grove, IL: InterVarsity Press, 1981), 32.**

[22] **Peter J. Paris, *The Spirituality of African Peoples: The Search for a Common Moral Discourse* (Minneapolis: Fortress Press, 1995), 48.**

The independent church movement among blacks was the first black freedom movement and the first stage of the battle against the perpetuation of injustice.[23] Henry Highland Garnet, a fiery Presbyterian pastor, said at the 1843 National Negro Convention:

> However much you and us may desire it, there is not much hope of redemption without the shedding of blood. If you must bleed, let it all come at once—rather die freemen than live to be slaves. Let your motto be resistance! resistance! No oppressed people have ever secured their liberty without resistance.[24]

Martin R. Delany, a black physician, journalist, and theologian, anticipated and developed one of the major emphases of black theology, which was the application of the "means of Elevation," including self-effort as well as what he called "attainments" in strict conformity with the laws governing politics and economics.[25]

CIVIL RIGHTS MOVEMENT

The theme of liberation not only was supported by the intellectuals of the black church, but also was affirmed among its grassroot members. The spirituals were full of this theme. The civil rights movement of the sixties had its roots in black culture and the black church's commitment to dignity and self-determination. Du Bois, one of the black intellectuals and founders of the black protest-identity movement, wrote in 1931:

> The Church as a whole insists on a divine mission and guidance and the indisputable possession of truth. Is there anything in the record of the Church in America in regard to the Negro to prove this? There is not. If the treatment of the Negro by the Christian Church is called "divine," this is an attack on the conception of God more blasphemous than any evil the church has always been so ready and eager to punish.[26]

Du Bois's response to the stance of the white church was representative of the inner psychological responses of millions of African Americans to a white God and the hollow, hypocritical, and racist Christianity that tried to make blacks insensitive to their humanity, their political and economic deprivation, and their powerlessness caused by the system the white church supported. The black church was a symbol of freedom that had reached the point of no return in which a narrow interpretation of the Christian principle of "turning the other cheek" was no longer viable and acceptable in the face of segregation, lynchings, Jim Crow laws, and the inhumanities of the system against African Americans.

---

[23] Ibid.

[24] Gayraud S. Wilmore, *Black Religion and Black Radicalism* (Maryknoll, NY: Orbis Books, 1974), 94.

[25] Ibid., 111.

[26] Salley and Behm, *What Color Is Your God?*, 58.

Du Bois's fame was due to his brilliant articulation of black protest, which he expressed as "my role as a master of propaganda."[27] He was among a group of black intellectuals who founded the Niagara Movement. He was later a cofounder of the National Association for the Advancement of Colored People (NAACP). Secular groups such as the NAACP were filled with black Christians who took the battle for freedom and equality into the American legal arena. Black readers of *Crisis*, which Du Bois cofounded in 1910 as the official voice of the NAACP, identified with the protest in his writing:

> I am resolved to be quiet and law abiding, but refuse to cringe in body or in soul to resent deliberate insult and to assert my rights in the face of wanton aggression.[28]

The climate of protest and self-determination in which blacks "must do for themselves" was created by Du Bois and other blacks such as James Weldon Johnson, also of the NAACP; Marcus Garvey and his Universal Negro Improvement Association (UNIA) with the "one God, one aim, one destiny" motto; Charles Hamilton Houston, called "Mister Civil Rights;" and Mabel K. Stauper's leadership of the National Association of Colored Graduate Nurses (NACGN). They led the fight against racism, sexism, and segregation and prepared the ground for the civil rights movement.

The Supreme Court decision outlawing school segregation in 1954, the experience of African Americans during World War II, and the political independence movements in Africa all further heightened black consciousness in America. In the early 1940s, A. Philip Randolph's work showed signs of the coming civil rights protest. Randolph worked with the Brotherhood of Sleeping Car Porters in attacking discrimination in white-dominated labor unions.[29] He found throughout America that "Negroes did not want to shoulder a gun to fight for democracy abroad unless they got democracy at home."[30] In 1941, he threatened to march on Washington, DC, to force President Franklin D. Roosevelt to issue an executive order compelling fair employment for African Americans.[31] He told his fellow black protesters that such an approach needed persons who had developed self-control and the requisite moral and spiritual resources to meet the most trying ordeal. The black church was instrumental in developing those leadership qualities through a fervent commitment to community among African Americans. Roosevelt reluctantly issued Executive Order 8802, which was confined to the armed services. The conflict between President Roosevelt and Randolph clearly indicated African Americans' new militancy and assertiveness, which were to be characteristic of the civil rights movement.

---

[27] **Rudwick Elliot, "W. E. B. Du Bois," in *Black Leader in the Twentieth Century Black*, John Franklin and August Meter, ed. (Urbana, IL: University of Illinois Press, 1982), 63.**

[28] **Ibid., 73.**

[29] **Ibid., 158.**

[30] **Ibid., 158.**

[31] **Talcott Parsons and Kenneth B. Clark, *The Negro American* (Boston: Beacon Press, 1967), 596.**

When Rosa Parks was arrested on 1 December 1955 for violating the bus segregation ordinance in Montgomery, Alabama, the most potent catalyst for the black consciousness movement was delivered. The civil rights movement took off when blacks in Montgomery organized a bus boycott led by the Reverend Dr. Martin Luther King Jr. On 21 December 1956, after 381 days of boycott, the Montgomery buses were desegregated when the Supreme Court decreed that segregation was unconstitutional.[32] The modern civil rights movement had begun. The black church was the anchor of the movement. It provided activists, ministers, laity, and financial support through black church members. Secular civil rights groups such as the Congress of Racial Equality (CORE), the Student Nonviolent Coordinating Committee (SNCC), and the older NAACP all had many ministers as local officials who were also influenced by black religious culture. Rosa Parks was a black Christian and a member of the NAACP. "James Farmer of CORE was the son of a clergyman, and John Lewis of SNCC was a seminary student."[33] The black church also gave the movement an ideological framework through which passive attitudes were transformed into a collective consciousness supportive of collective action.[34]

The Montgomery Improvement Association at its pinnacle was made up of black Baptists and other black Christians engaged in activities of nonviolent protest. The protest spread across the South in African-American communities. The demonstrations occurred in spite of jeopardized jobs, Ku Klux Klan intimidation, police harassment, and bombs. The Southern Christian Leadership Conference (SCLC) soon became a reality. The SNCC, which was made up of mostly young black people who took up the antiracist battle, was funded by the SCLC. Both organizations supported the famous but dangerous freedom rides organized by CORE through the South in 1961, forcing the southern states to comply with federal regulations governing unsegregated interstate travel. "The Black Youth would be influenced by the new breed of activist ministers and would enter into nonviolent demonstrations by the thousands."[35] By 1957, King was being acclaimed as the leader of the movement. Sit-ins and freedom rides increased, and more liberal whites joined the protests. Southern whites became more violent in resisting desegregation and President John F. Kennedy had to call in troops in some instances, as was the case in 1962 at Oxford, Mississippi, to facilitate the registration of James Meredith at the University of Mississippi.[36] The protest that started in the cradle of the black church had become a national movement and was changing America.

Violence against nonviolent agitators and the inhumanities that continued to be perpetrated against African Americans forced civil rights leaders to accept and organize the march on Washington that A. Philip Randolph threatened earlier during World War II.

---

[32] Charles Christian, *Black Saga: The African American Experience* (New York: Houghton Mifflin Co., 1995), 391.

[33] Lincoln and Mamiya, *The Black Church*, 165.

[34] Aldon Morris, *The Origin of the Civil Rights Movement: Black Communities Organizations for Change* (New York: Free Press, 1984), 77.

[35] Rhoda Lios Blumberg, *Civil Rights: The 1960s Freedom Struggle* (Boston: Publishers, 1984), 50.

[36] Benjamin Quarles, *The Negro in the Making of America* (New York: Simon and Schuster. 1987), 281.

> A main objective was to demonstrate to Congress that public opinion was on the side of desegregation and voting rights and that considerable number of whites strongly supported these goals.[37]

During the summer of 1963, churches organized large numbers of marchers, who were joined by civil rights organizations, union locals, and others. Hundreds of thousands of blacks and whites came to Washington and held a huge rally at the Lincoln Memorial. Some of the songs of the movement, "We Shall Overcome" and "O Freedom," captured the black religious ethos inherent in the movement:

> O freedom, O freedom,
> O freedom's over me, over me,
> And before I'll be a slave
> I'll be buried in my grave,
> And go home to my Lord
> And be free.[38]

Kennedy was assassinated on 22 November 1963, before he could sign the Civil Rights Bill that he and a reluctant Congress had finally started working on.[39] Congress passed Civil Rights Act 377 U.S. in 1964.[40]

In 1965, President Lyndon B. Johnson signed into law the Voting Rights Bill.[41] On 4 April 1968, King was assassinated in Memphis, Tennessee. On 5 June of the same year, the Democratic presidential nominee and a strong proponent of civil rights, Robert Kennedy, was also assassinated.[42] The nonviolent civil rights movement was losing its momentum. King's violent death left the movement leaderless and confused. In the 1970s, the civil rights movement became overshadowed by the Vietnam War. The early 1980s and 1990s were characterized by insensitive administrations who were hostile toward civil rights causes. Nonetheless, the black church searched for new ways to uphold its tradition of self-help, freedom, and human dignity.

ANALYSIS: PHILOSOPHICAL PERSPECTIVE AND MILITANT SHIFT

The actions of Rosa Parks and those of other civil rights protesters, including Dr. King, were, in the Kantian sense of autonomy, in direct opposition to obedience. If obedience was heteronomy of the will, Kant argued, then every individual had a fundamental

---

[37] Blumberg, *Civil Rights*, 108.

[38] Ibid., 112.

[39] Blumberg, *Civil Rights*, 50–53.

[40] Christian, *Black Saga*, 420.

[41] Christian, *Black Saga*, 428.

[42] Ibid., 440.

duty to be autonomous. The protesters, therefore, made themselves authors of their actions, and they took responsibility for their actions by refusing to act to save a system on the basis of reasons they knew were good.[43] A. Philip Randolph's understanding of the qualities needed in a protester was the same as that in the Kantian concept, and Henry Highland Garnet understood the responsibility of fighting against oppression when he said, "if you must bleed, let it all come at once—rather die freemen than live to be slaves."[44] More than one and a half centuries earlier, Kant rejected the right of resistance and revolt against established government. However, Socrates, a millennium earlier "felt it was necessary to create tension from bondage of myths and half truths to the unfettered realms of creative analysis."[45] King used the Socratian concept in his argument to support nonviolent protest:

> Just as Socrates . . . we must see the need of having nonviolent gadflies to create the kind of tension in society that will help men to rise from the dark depths of prejudice and racism to the majestic heights of understanding and brotherhood.[46]

The movement's aim was not to destroy America's constitutional democracy but to make it live up to its ideals.

The nonviolent nature of the movement addressed the sense of justice of the majority, and the fundamental idea of willing social cooperation among freemen was, in the view of the community as a whole, expressed in the Constitution. By appealing to the moral basis of the public, the nonviolent protest became a political as well as a religious act although it had religious roots. The Supreme Court decision on bus segregation in 1956, the Civil Rights Commission of 1957, the Civil Rights Act, the Voting Rights of 1964, and Lyndon Johnson's Great Society Program were results of legal and political actions induced by the movement.

With James Meredith gunned down; with black and white protesters killed; with black churches bombed; and with JFK, King, Malcolm X, and Robert Kennedy assassinated, young black intellectuals and students asked themselves if nonviolence was still a viable option. The Watts rebellions of August 1965 in California showed signs of future urban conflagration and the frustration and impatience in many African-American communities.[47] On some campuses, the black studies movement started in 1966. After King's death, blacks, especially black students, asserted the validity of their own culture and their right to create and develop their own institutions, just as Jews, Poles, and

---

[43] **Robert Paul Wolff, "On Violence," in *Revolution and the Rule of Law*, Edward Kent, ed. (Englewood Cliffs, NJ: Prentice-Hall, Inc., 1971), 66–67.**

[44] **Wilmore, *Black Religion*, 94.**

[45] **Martin Luther King Jr., "Letter from Birmingham City Jail," in *Revolution and the Rule of Law*, Edward Kent, ed. (Englewood Cliffs, NJ: Prentice-Hall, Inc., 1971) 15.**

[46] **Ibid., 15.**

[47] **Christian, *Black Saga*, 429.**

Italians had done without being questioned.[48] A shift from nonviolence to a more militant approach to addressing black issues had occurred among the black youth groups.

The black power movement, cultural nationalism, and black radicalism became stronger. In the South, black armed self-defense became a necessity in the face of widespread lynching and life-threatening Ku Klux Klan activities openly supported by local white officials. Malcolm X, the spokesman of the Nation of Islam, gained a major following in the urban ghettos. Malcolm cynically referred to the 1963 event as the "Farce on Washington."[49] By the late 1960s, black youths turned their attention toward issues such as police brutality, racism, and an unfair justice system that visited daily inhumanities on African Americans.

Conflagration exploded in major urban areas as police brutality continued. At its annual conference, the Bar Association of the City of New York asked, "Is the Law Dead?" As Gideon Gottlieb put it, "This crisis of law was sharpened by a convergence of civil disobedience, riot, violence, the black revolution, and government lawlessness."[50] He argued further that the death of law from African-Americans' perspective was a misnomer because as far as they could see it had never lived long enough to die—it was stillborn.[51] Gottlieb was correct in arguing that the law enforcement system oppressed African Americans and seemed designed to protect neighboring white communities by abandoning black communities to local violence and lawlessness. Civil rights legislation attempted to remove racial barriers, but the majority of individuals of the African-American population were still left out of the community of consent as had been the case since the beginning of the United States. The 1992 riots in Los Angeles manifested the frustration and anger in African-American communities all over the nation.[52]

CONTEMPORARY CONDITIONS AND THE FUTURE

The black church was not completely ineffective when confronted with new developments and problems. At the time when the Kerner Commission affirmed that bipolarization still exists between blacks and whites and when the Voting Rights Act in 1982 came under heavy scrutiny, the Reverend Jesse Jackson appealed to all population groups, while building a strong African-American constituent base. Jackson finished second in the contest for the 1988 Democratic presidential nomination. His approach, accepted or not, showed that the black church was still the cradle of civil

48 Blumberg, *Civil Rights*, 137.

49 Malcolm X, *The Autobiography of Malcolm X* (New York; Grove Press, 1965), 281.

50 Gideon Gottlieb, "Is Law Dead?" in *Revolution and the Rule of Law*, Edward Kent, ed. (Englewood Cliffs, NJ: Prentice-Hall, Inc., 1971) 77.

51 Ibid., 77.

52 Haki R. Madhubuti, ed., *Why L. A. Happened: Implications of the '92 Los Angeles Rebellion* (Chicago: Third World Press, 1993), xii–xvi, 36.

rights activism. But the question of how it had reached the unchurched black youths is yet to be answered. Signs of future development in African-American society were manifested in secular organizations such as CORE.

The organization initially had only a small number of middle-class blacks willing to work, live, and "bleed" alongside whites in directing nonviolent protests between 1942 and 1960. After 1963, the organization was taken over by African Americans from poor, working-class, and urban ranks. A parallel development also took place, although over a longer period, in the black church. As Eric C. Lincoln wrote, "The Negro Church that Frazier wrote about no longer exists. . . . The call to full manhood, to personhood, and the call to Christian responsibility left no room for implications of being a 'Negro' in contemporary America."[53] Out of this development came the civil rights movement and the renewed attempt by the black church. Therefore, African Americans continued to address pressing issues within black communities and to attempt to reclaim more vigorously their African heritage. Such a reclamation was important to the urban youths who felt alienated by the mainstream society in their development of self-worth. But more important was the fact that the Black Church had stepped up its outreach programs to its youth.

Today, many of the prisons across America are filled with young African Americans. Another area that seems to need more attention is the African-American middle class.[54] Lincoln and Mamiya superbly summarized the future of the black church:

> If the Black Church should ask itself why it needs to be reconnected with the hard-core urban black poor, the answer is simple as it is obvious: one-third of the black population will be responsible for more than half of all black children growing up in the decade of the 1990s. The future of the Black Church in the twenty-first century will depend so much on how it responds to the poor in its midst as to the extent of racism, the abstractions of ecumenism, or the competitive threat of a resurgent Islam.[55]

The ability of the black church to motivate and encourage middle-class African Americans to participate in the rejuvenation of the society is going to be pivotal in the future, not only in African-American communities but also in society at large. Their intellectual, creative, and economic resources are going to be potent catalysts for the transformation of African-American society as shown by Du Bois and King, just to name two. Most middle-class African Americans are in one way or another already involved in both the black church and the society, and when they put in the required effort, the results are visible.

The political landscape also looks promising with more African-American mayors, governors, members of Congress, and women in public office. The black church's influence in politics grew when ministers, apart from their priestly duties as leaders,

---

[53] **Ibid., 105–6.**

[54] **Lincoln and Mamiya, *The Black Church*, 383–85.**

[55] **Ibid., 404.**

became activists during the civil rights era. Their influence, though sometimes overestimated, is very important in the African-American constituencies. The danger is that this influence could be misused by outside political manipulators as was claimed, but later recanted, by a campaign manager in the 1993 New Jersey gubernatorial elections.[56] How the black church deals with her political influence in a nation in which there is separation between church and state could affect not only the democratic process itself but also how African Americans perceive and react to such influence in the future. The question that comes to my mind is one that may be asked by those at the bottom of society: "If we did not have votes, would they have cared?"

CONCLUSION

This analysis of the civil rights movement affirms the importance of the black church in African-American culture in particular and American culture in general. But more important, the analysis presents theoretical questions on civil obedience as well as disobedience, politics, public morality, and policy. Each of the different denominations of the black church seen in the context of the theory of sovereignty may seem irrelevant in the larger American society. But because the black church is a series of culturally linked black Christian denominations, it has been influenced by each of the denominations and simultaneously has influenced them and then the larger American society. The black church has a life of its own. This argument may be supported by J. N. Figgis's discourse in *Churches in the Modern State:*

> The theory of sovereignty . . . is in reality no more than a venerable superstition. . . . As a fact, it is in a series of the groups that our social life presents itself, all having some of the qualities of public law and most of them showing clear signs of a life of their own.[57]

The civil rights movement's growth after starting in the womb of the black church is an example of the many influences that the black church has had on American society through a series of groups and black religious denominations. Showing autonomy and some degree of sovereignty, especially religious sovereignty, the black church has been able to nurture and uphold African-American society through centuries of tribulation and suffering.

African Americans bled and died to have the right to vote, and the black church was with its people all the time. The future of the black church in an information age will depend on its ability to uphold the identity, dignity, and self-reliance tradition of African Americans in the face of increasing anonymity. That future also depends on the black church's continuity and delivery of new creative and pragmatic interpretations of its spiritual and secular ethos, which have sustained it and African Americans through the adversities of the centuries and which have always given hope and leadership.

---

[56] Patrick Rogers, "Big Mouth, Big Problem," *Newsweek*, 22 November 1993, 32–34.

[57] John Neville Figgis, *Churches in the Modern State* (London, New York: Longmans, Green and Co., 1913), 23.

REFERENCES

Babbage, Stuart Barton. *Man in Nature and in Grace.* Grand Rapids, MI: Eerdmans, 1957.

Baer, Hans A., Merrill Singer, and Hans A. Merrill, *African-American Religion in the Twentieth Century.* Knoxville, TN: University of Tennessee Press, 1992.

Blumberg, Rhoda Lios. *Civil Rights: The 1960s Freedom Struggle.* Boston: Publishers, 1984.

Christian, Charles. *Black Saga: The African American Experience.* New York: Houghton Mifflin Co., 1995.

Du Bois, W. E. B. *The Negro Church.* Atlanta: Atlanta University Press, 1903.

Durkheim, Emile. *The Elementary Forms of the Religious Life.* New York: Free Press, 1965.

Elliot, Rudwick. "W. E. B. Du Bois." In *Black Leader in the Twentieth Century Black*, edited by John Franklin and August Meier. Urbana, IL: University of Illinois Press, 1982.

Figgis, John Neville. *Churches in the Modern State.* London, New York: Longmans, Green and Co., 1913.

Frazier, C. Franklin. *The Negro Church in America.* New York: Schocken, 1964.

Geertz, Clifford. *The Interpretation of Cultures.* New York: Basic Books, 1973.

Glazer, Nathan, and Daniel Patrick Moynihan. *Beyond the Melting Pot.* Cambridge, MA: MIT Press and Harvard University Press, 1963.

Kent, Edward, ed. *The Rule of Law.* Englewood Cliffs, NJ: Prentice-Hall, Inc., 1971.

King, Martin Luther Jr. "Letter from Birmingham City Jail." In *The Rule of Law*, edited by Edward Kent. Englewood Cliffs, NJ: Prentice-Hall, Inc., 1971.

King, Richard, *Civil Rights and the Idea of Freedom.* Oxford: Oxford University Press, 1992.

Lincoln, Eric C., and Lawrence Mamiya. *The Black Church in the African American Experience.* Durham, NC: Duke University Press, 1990.

Madhubuti, Haki R., ed. *Why L. A. Happened: Implications of the '92 Los Angeles Rebellion.* Chicago: Third World Press, 1993.

Morris, Aldon. *The Origin of the Civil Rights Movement: Black Communities Organizations for Change.* New York: Free Press, 1984.

Paris, Peter J. *The Spirituality of African Peoples: The Search for a Common Moral Discourse.* Minneapolis: Fortress Press, 1995.

Parsons, Talcott. and Kenneth B. Clark. *The Negro American.* Boston: Beacon Press, 1967.

Puckett, Newbell. *Folk Beliefs of the Southern Negro.* Chapel Hill, NC: University of North Carolina Press, 1926.

Quarles, Benjamin. *The Negro in the Making of America.* New York: Simon and Schuster, 1987.

Rogers, Patrick. "Big Mouth, Big Problem." *Newsweek*, 22 November 1993.

Salley, Columbus, and Ronald Behm. *What Color Is Your God?.* Downers Grove, IL: InterVarsity Press, 1981.

Washington, James Melvin, ed. *A Testament of Hope: The Essential Writings of Martin Luther King.* San Francisco: Harper & Row, 1986.

Wilmore, Gayraud S. *Black Religion and Black Radicalism.* Maryknoll, NY: Orbis Books, 1974.

Wolff, Robert Paul. "On Violence," in *Revolution and the Rule of Law*, edited by Edward Kent. Englewood Cliffs, NJ: Prentice-Hall, Inc., 1971.

X, Malcolm. *The Autobiography of Malcolm X.* New York: Grove Press, 1965.

Black versus Black

The Relationships among African, African American, and African Caribbean Persons

Jennifer V. Jackson
Mary E. Cothran

This study is based on a survey examining the relationships among continental African, African American, and African Caribbean persons. Relationships were explored in terms of contact and friendship, travel to countries of the diaspora, cross-cultural communications, thoughts and stereotypes, and education involving knowledge of the diaspora. The outcome of this survey points to the need for more Afrocentric education in the curriculum (from elementary school to college) as a means of reeducating people to have a better perspective of the African diaspora and to dispel myths and negative stereotypes about African people.

THEORETICAL BACKGROUND

As people of the African diaspora, African Americans and persons from the Caribbean region (called West Indians) share a common heritage with Africans. Palmer (2000) stressed the importance of having some common understanding of what constitutes a diaspora, and sensitivity to fundamental differences in the historical trajectory of seemingly similar peoples. Palmer also indicated that

> the very term, "African diaspora" must be used with great caution, underscoring the point that until recent times, those people who resided on the African continent defined themselves solely in accordance with their ethnic group. Furthermore, it is we who homogenize these people by characterizing them as Africans. (p. 57)

Palmer (2000) contended that "modern diasporic streams have been almost always the product of racial oppression and attendant systematic evils, and of resistance to them" (p. 58). Palmer also emphasized "that diasporic communities formed by peoples of African descent share an emotional bond with their dispersed kin, and a history

Republished from *Journal of Black Studies, Vol. 33, No. 5 (May 2003)* by Jennifer V. Jackson and Mary E. Cothran.

of racial oppression and struggle against it" (p. 58). This common bond among the African diaspora should serve as the basis for their relationship.

Lake (1995) argued that "while there are many differences among indigenous and diaspora Africans, the cultural and political dismembering of African communities on either side of the Atlantic by Europeans constitutes a bond that transgresses geographic and temporal boundaries" (p. 3). Despite a common history of slavery that led to people of African descent being separated from one another by distance and space, they are still joined by a common goal. According to E. P. Skinner (2000), "The result is that African peoples are still involved in a concerted struggle to gain total freedom and equality for themselves and the continent with which they are associated" (p. 4). There are those of the African diaspora who feel that repatriation (return to Africa) is the only way to achieve this goal. For example, in a discussion with O. Lake (1995), a repatriate said, "To me, I see that Black people have a common history and a common experience, and think it's very valuable to recognize it" (p. 19). The common experience shared by the people of African diaspora who are the focus of study is that of slavery. L. Bennett (1988) argued that European penetration and the slave trade debased much that was vital in African culture. Garvey (1925/1982), in a speech given in New York City, characterized slavery as a barbarous and brutal institution under which African descendants have suffered in this country, meaning the United States.

Waters (1999) contended that although the slaves were of African origin, there were some differences within the slavery system that continue to "shape current ideas about race, the relations between socially defined races, and the degree to which issues of slavery and race permeate day-to-day interactions in the United States and the Carribean" (p. 25). In the aftermath of slavery, African peoples are found in different countries, away from their ancestral past and cultural roots. This study sheds some light on how this has affected the relationship between the African diaspora from different geographic locations. For the purpose of this study, "Africans" are limited to two West African countries (Ghana and Nigeria) from which slaves were taken. The Africans in this study are not descendants of people taken from their countries as slaves. Therefore, it is expected that they have not experienced the same conditions associated with slavery as in the case of African Americans and Caribbean persons. However, Ghana and Nigeria share in common the English language from the British colonizers, the experience of being "colonized," and the conditions that are associated with colonization.

From a historical perspective, the work of Berry and Blassingame (1982) provides information on the effects of slavery on slaves brought to the New World from West Africa. African Americans are descendants of Africans who were brought to the United States primarily to work on cotton plantations, as a result of the slave trade, starting about 1502. The historical importance of slavery lies in its role as a major determinant of America's race relations and in the transformation of African cultural events and the creation of a unique Black culture in the Americas, especially evident in music and dance. The civil rights movement of the 1960s led to major improvements in conditions of Black Americans and an upsurge of Black nationalism, the belief that Black people share a common culture and worldview, have a common destiny, and have had a common experience of slavery, oppression, colonialism, and exploitation.

The term used to identify African people in the United States came under review after slavery was abolished, and *Negro* was replaced by *Black*, followed by *African American*. These terms are being used interchangeably, depending on the historical context.

Among the African diaspora are people who are called West Indians. This is considered a misnomer and is thought to have been based on Columbus's mistaken notion that he had landed in India, having found indigenous people resembling Indians when he stumbled on the so-called New World. West Indians are people from the Caribbean region, including islands such as Jamaica and Trinidad (and also Guyana) that have a similar history of British colonization and the English language. Due to migration, the West Indian population has grown in the United States. Waters (1999) stated that historically, as a part of survival for emancipated people, migration became a way of life in the Caribbean region. Vickerman (1994) attributed the increase in migration of West Indians to the United States because of the civil rights movement and the 1965 reform of American immigration law. After the 1960s, West Indian immigrants were no longer forced to live in neighborhoods dominated by African Americans, but Vickerman (1994) noted that

> a mixture of conflict and consensus characterized relationships between the two groups. At the heart of the conflict lay the fears of many African-Americans that West Indians would take away jobs. These fears were exacerbated by West Indians' tendency to view themselves as being set apart from African-Americans. (p. 85)

The fears and misconceptions have been perpetuated and continue to carry on the idea that although African people have the same beginnings, they are so different culturally, socially, and intellectually that they should be considered completely separate people. Thus, there is a continued rivalry for economic and social advantages among West Indians, African Americans, and Africans in the United States. This is often seen as animosity among these groups, although this is merely casual observation rather than factually established or proven. Therefore, how these groups relate to one another is of interest.

According to Patterson (1972), West Indians acquire, as their most immediate and workable heritage, a subculture that is essentially their own (based on the exigencies of tropical rural life and on surviving elements of the disintegrated cultures of West Africa brought over by their slave ancestors). Thus, the West Indians are "culturally flavored by the remnants of their half-remembered African past" (p. 34). Bryce-LaPorte (1972), referring to West Indians and Africans, expressed the view that "while black foreigners have held leadership and successful positions, and have exercised significant influence in Black life in this country [meaning the USA], their cultural impact has generally been ignored in the larger spheres of American life" (p. 31). This lack of recognition may further exacerbate the animosity that is said to exist among Black people in the United States.

There is much to be learned about the interaction and communication among people of the African diaspora. In a relationship study of Black Africans and Black Americans on a college campus, Becker (1967) contended that "there is a basic incompatibility between Africans and Black Americans that leads to mutual rejection" (p. 177). This sense of incompatibility is not only the case between Africans and Black Americans, but across the African diaspora. Lake (1995), in a study focusing on diaspora African repatriates in Ghana, found that few of the African Americans that identified themselves as African "tended to have had intellectual experiences with Africans or had become familiar with African political and historical issues while in the diaspora" (p. 12). Lake's view about barriers due to indigenous and diasporic ethnic conflicts gives merit to the idea that African people lack understanding among those of varied geographic origins.

Education may affect how people of the African diaspora relate to one another. According to Becker (1967), compared to Black Americans, African students share "a sense of both national duty and personal fulfillment and success inextricably linked with reaching their educational objective" (p. 178). Becker contended that African students' adjustment to the American educational system and the White middle-class society was judged by Black Americans as brainwashing. This made Africans disappointed by Black Americans' ignorance, apathy toward Africa, and attitudes perceived as rejection and hatred of Africans. This may be due to the Eurocentric educational system inherited from the British, which distorted the image of Africans. M. K. Asante (1991) promoted Afrocentric education to correct negative effects, such as thoughts and stereotypes that are circulated about African people.

How African people relate to one another has not received as much attention as the relationship between Black and White people. As noted by Vickerman (1994), the centrality of slavery and its aftermath in U.S. history has always meant that race relations in the United States tends to be conceived of in terms of Blacks and Whites. The dichotomization of people into Black and White does not allow for the idea that Black people are themselves a diverse group with differences to warrant examination—not issues of race relations but of getting along with one another. An article in the *Washington Post* (Fears, 2002) lends credence to this as the title itself—"A Diverse—and Divided—Black Community"—hints at the relationship among African people in the United States. Therefore, this survey examined the relationships among African, African American, and Caribbean people in terms of historical, cultural, social, and psychological forces that may affect the interaction and communication among the groups.

METHOD

Pilot Study

Because this was the first survey of its kind to be attempted, we conducted a pilot study and designed a survey instrument to explore the relationships among African, African American, and West Indian persons. The 20-item survey consisted of mainly open-ended questions. The reason was to eliminate researchers' bias and to prevent preconceived notions from influencing participants' responses. Key terms used by participants would form the basis of a more objective-type questionnaire for an expanded study. The 20-item questionnaire, called "Survey Questionnaire for Africans, African Americans, Caribbean, and Other Persons of African Descent," sought to examine some selected factors that may influence the relationships among people of the African diaspora, such as:

1. Interaction and cross-cultural communication, including travel within countries of the diaspora (items 8, 9, 10, 16, 17, and 20).
2. Thoughts about the African diaspora that may have been shaped by historical, cultural, and psychological forces (items 5, 6, 7, 12, 13a, 19a, and 19b).
3. The role of education (items 11, 13b, 14, 15, and 18).

Although this instrument was of a preliminary nature, the information gathered through its use gives insight about how African people relate with one another.

The participants who participated in the pilot study were a convenience sample of 32 persons of African descent either studying or working at one university in a metropolitan area. Because of the exploratory nature of the study, only about 60 surveys were given out. The response rate was 53% (32/60) usable and completed surveys. Participants completed the surveys anonymously and voluntarily with the assurance that individual responses would be treated with confidentiality. Results formed the basis of the major study.

MAJOR STUDY

Instrument and Participants

Based on the results of the pilot study, the instrument was redesigned with the questions having options based on responses given by the pilot participants. The revised survey questionnaire consisted of 40 questions that allowed participants to choose one or more responses in each case plus one question of a general nature requesting additional comments or suggestions (see the appendix). Items 1 to 6 collected demographic and biographic information (i.e., place of birth, ethnic classification, educational level, gender, age, professional status). Items 7 to 40 related to factors that may influence how the groups relate to each other, such as communication including contacts, friendship, among peoples of the African diaspora; travel to countries of the diaspora; thoughts about Africans, African Americans, and West Indians; and the role of education. Questions 7 to 40 had multiple responses from which participants could select whichever ones applied, with no restrictions on their choices. For example, Question 7 stated: "Under what circumstances have you come in contact with Africans, African Americans, and West Indians? (Circle all that apply) (a) fellow students, (b) students I teach/mentor, (c) community friends, (d) university colleagues, (e) friends/peers, (f) church members, (g) I have not known any personally, (h) other (specify)."

This survey questionnaire was administered to convenience samples of participants from the diaspora at a conference. Other participants were recruited from four universities located in a metropolitan area with mixed populations of students, faculty, and staff from Africa, the Caribbean, and the United States. Participants were convenience samples of African descent who participated voluntarily and anonymously to fulfill the purpose of the study. This means that results of this study must be interpreted with caution and must not be considered as representing the viewpoints of the general populations from which these participants were drawn.

RESULTS

Demographic and Biographical Data

In this section, data from items 1 to 6 are reported, based on a total of 427 persons who responded to the survey questionnaire designed to shed some light on the relationships among Africans (from Ghana and Nigeria), the United States, and the Caribbean region (mainly Jamaica, Trinidad, and Guyana). *Caribbean* persons or *West Indians* are used interchangeably.

Place of birth. Data showed that 247 (57.8%) were born in the United States, 104 (24.4%) were born in Africa, 49 (11.5%) were born in the Caribbean region, and 27 (6.3%) did not respond.

Ethnic/racial classification. Data showed that 141 (33%) identified themselves as African Americans, 134 (31.4%) as Black, 99 (23.3%) as Africans, and 53 (12.3%) did not respond.

Educational levels. Data showed that 148 (34.7%) were high school (HS) graduates, 24 (5.6%) had associate of arts (AA) degrees, 101 (23.7%) had bachelor's degrees, 69 (16.2%) had master's degrees, 23 (5.4%) had doctorate degrees, and 62 (14.4%) did not respond.

Gender. Data showed 224 (52.5%) as female, 98 (46.4%) as male, and 5 (1.1%) did not respond.

Age range. The range for 391 participants (91.6%) was 17 to 46 years and older, and 36 (8.4%) did not respond.

Professional status. Data showed 24 (5.6%) were university faculty, 25 (5.9%) university staff, 16 (3.7%) administrators, 196 (45.9%) graduate and 29 (6.8%) undergraduate students, and 137 (32.1%) did not respond.

Frequencies and cross-tabulations were computed for items 7 to 40, as applicable. To make the findings easier to follow, participants' responses are grouped in categories according to specific issues that the questions probed. The relationships among Africans, African Americans, and West Indians were examined in terms of:

1. Interaction, involving contact, friendship, travel to countries of the diaspora, and cross-cultural communication (items 7, 11 to 20, and 30 to 32).
2. Thoughts and stereotypes that may have been shaped by historical, cultural, and psychological forces (items 8 to 10, 25, and 36 to 39).
3. Role of education (items 21 to 24, 26 to 29, 34, and 35). Obstacles to understanding (item 33), how the groups can work together (item 40), and item 41 (which was open-ended) requesting additional comments are presented in the discussion.

Contact. Data (item 7) showed that 336 (78.6%) had contacts with Africans, 7 (1.6%) had no contacts, and 84 (19.7%) did not respond. Of the participants, 336 (78.7%) had contacts with African Americans, 8 (1.9%) had no contacts, and 83 (19.4%) did not respond; 297 (69.6%) had contacts with West Indians, 35 (8.2%) had no contacts, and 95 (22.2%) did not respond. The circumstances for contact were through educational institutions as fellow students, peers, mentors, teachers, and university colleagues. Contact in this context means that participants had met and interacted with others of the diaspora in face-to-face encounters.

Cross-tabulations (Cross-TABS). These were done with place of birth (POB), ethnic classification, educational levels, gender, age ranges, professional status, and relevant variables. Because the Cross-TAB results are spread out among so many variables, it was necessary to limit the report to significant responses (differences in percentages will be due to "no responses"). Cross-TABS for POB showed contacts with Africans by 74 (71.2%) of 104 Africans, 208 (84.2%) of 247 born in the United States, and 38 (77.6%) of 49 West Indians. Contact with African Americans was reported by 75 (72.1%) Africans, 207 (83.8%) U.S. participants, and 37 (75.5%) West Indians. Contacts with West Indians were reported by 49 (47.1%) Africans, 190 (76.9%) U.S. participants, and 42 (85.7%) West Indians (see Table 1).

Travel. In terms of travel to countries of the diaspora (items 16 to 20), 121 (28.3%) had visited or lived/were born in Africa; 165 (38.6%) had visited, were born, or lived in the Caribbean; and 319 (74.5%) had visited or lived/were born in the United States (participants could circle all three regions; the numbers and percentages are based on the total of 427 participants, so it is not appropriate to add them together). Some Africans visited different African and European countries, others visited or lived in the United States, and few Africans visited any Caribbean island/region. Some African Americans visited Europe, African countries (e.g., Nigeria, Egypt), Jamaica, and Mexico. Some West Indians visited Europe and/or lived in the United States, and very few visited African countries. Of the participants, 281 (65.8%) wished to visit Africa, 114 (26.7%) would visit Europe, and 32 (7.5%) did not respond; 264 (61.8%) gave reasons for choosing Africa or Europe (e.g., never been there, more knowledge of country). For visiting Africa, 154 (35.6%) selected curiosity, similar culture, heritage, and ancestry; 11 (2.5%) would visit Europe because of European influences, 351 (82.2%) would visit the Caribbean region, 47 (11%) chose Mexico, and 29 (6.8%) did not respond. For 332 (77.8%), reasons were curiosity, similar language, culture, values; 60 (14.1%) chose better vacation spot, food, and music; and 35 (8.2%) did not respond.

Friendship group. Data (items 14 and 15) showed that 24 (29%) chose friends from all three groups, 92 (21.5%) chose African American friends, 58 (13.6%) chose African American and West Indian friends, 79 (18.5%) chose African and West Indian friends, and 27 (6.3%) did not respond. Cross-TABS of POB with friendship revealed that of 104 born in Africa, 21 (20.2%) chose African friends; 10 (9.4%) chose African Americans and West Indians; 21 (20.2%) chose African and African Americans; and 48 (46.3%) chose Africans, African Americans, and West Indian friends; 4 (3.9%) did not respond. For 247 born in the United States, 11 (4.8%) chose African and West Indian friends; 87 (35.2%) chose African American; 136 (55.1%) chose African, African American, and West Indian friends; and 12 (4.9%)

TABLE 1 Contact Between Africans, African Americans, and West Indians, and Cross-Tabulations (Cross-TABS) for Place of Birth (POB) and Contacts

	Africans		African Americans		West Indians	
	n	%	n	%	n	%
Contact	336	78.7	336	78.7	297	69.6
No contact	7	1.6	8	1.9	35	8.2
No response	84	19.7	83	19.4	95	22.2
Total	427	100	427	100	427	100
	Africa		**United States**		**West Indies**	
	n	%	n	%	n	%
Contact with Africans						
Contact	74	71.2	208	84.2	38	77.6
No contact/no response	30	28.8	39	15.8	11	22.4
Subtotal	104	100	247	100	49	100
Contact with African Americans						
Contact	75	72.1	207	83.8	37	75.5
No contact/no response	29	27.9	40	16.2	12	24.5
Subtotal	104	100	247	100	49	100
Contact with West Indians						
Contact	49	47.1	190	76.9	42	85.7
No contact/no response	55	52.9	57	23.1	7	14.3
Subtotal	104	100	247	100	49	100

had no preference. For 49 West Indians, 3 (6.2%) chose African and African American friends; 11 (22.4%) chose other West Indians; 29 (59.2%) chose African, African American, and West Indian friends; and 6 (12.2%) did not respond. Of the participants, 252 (59%) gave positive reasons for choosing friends (e.g., similar background, culture, and history; positive perception); 110 (25.8%) gave negative perception for group/s not chosen, less friendly; 36 (8.4%) had no preference; and 29 (6.8%) did not respond.

Interpersonal relationships. In terms of interpersonal relationships (items 11 to 13), there were three types of responses: *positive* (e.g., good relationship through culture and heritage), *needs improving* (good in some areas, poor in others), or *negative* (e.g., they think they are superior to other Blacks; preconceived notions and myths about one another; poor, not good). For Africans and African Americans, 46 (10.8%) gave positive options, 35 (8.2%) chose needs improving, 324 (75.8%) gave negative options, and 22 (5.2%) did not respond. For Africans and West Indians, 99 (23.2%) chose good, 207 (48.5%) gave negative options, 63 (14.8%) chose needs improving, and 58 (13.6%) did not respond. For African Americans and West Indians, 74 (17.3%) chose good, 224 (52.5%) chose negative responses, 67 (15.7%) chose needs improving, and 62 (14.5%) did not respond (see Table 2).

TABLE 2 Interpersonal Relationships Among and Communication Between Africans, African Americans, and West Indians

Types of Responses	Africans and African Americans		Africans and West Indians		African Americans and West Indians	
	n	%	n	%	n	%
Items 11 to 13						
Positive (e.g., good relationship through culture and heritage)	46	10.8	99	23.2	74	17.3
Negative (e.g., poor, not good, preconceived notions and myths, superior feelings)	324	75.8	207	48.5	224	52.5
Needs improving or enhancing (e.g., good in some areas, poor in others)	35	8.2	63	14.7	67	15.7
No response/don't know	22	5.2	58	13.6	62	14.5
Total	427	100	427	100	427	100
Items 30 to 33						
Positive (e.g., good, fine, open, okay, excellent)	39	9.1	72	16.9	60	14.1
Negative (e.g., not good, lacking; myths and misconceptions; ignorance, stereotypes, communication gap)	309	72.4	177	41.5	212	49.7
No opinion, insufficient information, don't know, or no response	79	18.5	178	41.6	155	36.3
Total	427	100	427	100	427	100

Communication between Africans and African Americans (items 30 to 33). Of the participants, 39 (9.1%) chose positive options (e.g., good, open, and fine), 309 (72.4%) chose negative options (e.g., ignorance, myths, and misconceptions; stereotypes; lacking, not good), 79 (18.5%) selected no opinion and insufficient information (see Table 2). Cross-TABS with POB showed that for Africans and African Americans, 6 (5.8%) of 104 Africans, 5 (10.2%) of 49 West Indians, and 26 (10.5%) of 247 African Americans chose good communication; 88 Africans (84.7%), 172 African Americans (69.7%), and 34 West Indians (69.4%) chose negative options; 10 (9.5%) Africans, 49 African Americans (19.8%), and 10 West Indians (20.4%) had no opinion.

Communication between Africans and West Indians. This was seen as good by 72 (16.9%), negative by 177 (41.5%), and 178 (41.6%) had no opinion. Cross-TABs with POB showed that 16 (15.4%) of 104 Africans had positive responses, 50 (48%) had negative responses, and 38 (36.5%) had no opinion. Among 247 African Americans, 38 (15.4%) had positive responses, 86 (34.8%) chose negative options, and 123 (49.8%) chose no opinion. For 49 West Indians, 16 (32.7%) had positive responses, 26 (53%) chose negative options, and 7 (14.3%) gave no opinion.

Communication between African Americans and West Indians. This was seen as positive by 60 (14%), negative by 213 (49.9%), and 154 (36.1%) had no opinion. Cross-TABs with POB indicated that 12(11.5%) of 104 Africans had positive responses, 43 (41.3%) chose negative responses, and 49 (47.1%) selected no opinion. Among 247 African Americans, 36 (14.6%) had positive responses, 124 (50.2%) chose negative options, and 87 (35.2%) selected no opinion. For 49 West Indians, 9 (18.4%) chose positive responses, 36 (65.3%) chose negative options, and 8 (16.3%) selected no opinion (see Table 2).

What the groups thought about one another. This was examined in items 8 to 10. For the three groups, there were similar positive responses (e.g., proud of heritage, intelligent, courteous, and dedicated to family), and similar negative responses (e.g., feeling superior to other Blacks, distrustful), and also specific ones. Of the Africans, 146 (34.2%) selected positive responses, 243 (56.9%) selected negative responses (e.g., conniving, suffering from colonialism and war), and 38 (8.9%) did not respond. Of the African Americans, 107 (25.1%) gave positive responses (e.g., display strength and persistence against adversity), 275 (64.4%) selected negative responses (e.g., possess "slavery mentality"), and 45 (10.5%) did not respond. Of the West Indians, 138 (32.31%) chose positive responses, 214 (50.1%) selected negative responses (e.g., aggressive), and 75 (17.6%) did not respond (see Table 3).

Stereotypes. These were determined by items 36 to 38. There were similar positive ones (e.g., positive self-identity and self-image; intelligent, hard working, some are rich), similar negative ones (e.g., they think they are better than other Blacks, negative identity and self-image, many are poor), and specific ones. For Africans, 137 (32.1%) chose positive options, 222 (52%) chose negative options (e.g., pompous, reluctant to move from Third World status), and 68 (15.9%) did not respond. For African Americans, 85 (19.9%) selected positive options (e.g., kindhearted), 266 (62.3%) chose negative responses (e.g., ignorant about other Blacks, materialistic), and 76 (17.8%) did not respond. For West Indians, 132 (30.9%) chose positive options, 179 (42%) chose negative options (e.g., loud, boisterous, ambitious, and tricky), and 110 (25.8%) did not respond (see Table 3).

TABLE 3 Thoughts and Stereotypes About Africans, African Americans, and West Indians

	Africans		African Americans		West Indians	
Types of Responses	n	%	n	%	n	%
Items 8 to 10						
Positive (e.g., intelligent, courteous, friendly, proud of heritage, dedicated to family, displaying strength against adversity)	146	34.2	107	25.1	138	32.3
Negative (e.g., conniving, distrustful, aggressive, superior feelings, slavery mentality, suffering from colonialism and war)	243	56.9	275	64.4	214	50.1
No response/other	38	8.9	45	10.5	75	17.6
Total	427	100	427	100	427	100
Items 36 to 38						
Positive (e.g., self-image and identity, intelligent, hardworking, kind-hearted, some are rich)	137	32.1	85	19.9	138	32.3
Negative (e.g., self-image and identity, lazy, selfish, materialistic, ignorant about other Blacks; uneducated savages, stupid, conniving, loud, boisterous)	222	52.0	266	62.3	179	41.9
No response/other	68	15.9	76	17.8	110	25.8
Total	427	100	427	100	427	100

In terms of how stereotypes were formed (item 39), 345 (80.8%) chose Western media (e.g., television, newspapers, books, magazines, movies), European myths and system of falsification, tourist commercials, and White values; 24 (5.6%) chose personal experience and individual meetings; 14 (3.3%) chose misinformation, education, school, and history books; and 44 (10.3%) did not respond.

In terms of the most intelligent group (item 25), 39 (9.1%) selected Africans, 18 (4.2%) selected African Americans, 14 (3.3%) selected West Indians, 94 (22%) selected individual differences in intelligence, 77 (18%) selected no difference in intelligence, 69 (16.2%) selected lack of information, and 82 (19.2%) did not respond.

Education compared among Africans, African Americans, and West Indians (item 21). Of the participants, 138 (32.4%) selected individual differences, 179 (41.9%) selected one or two groups as more educated than another (e.g., Africans or West Indians or Africans and African Americans), 32 (7.5%) selected equal education among all groups, and 78 (18.3%) lacked information. In terms of participants' education (items 34 and 35), sufficient information was received by 34 (8%) about Africans; 53 (12.4%) about African Americans; 20 (4.7%) about West Indians; and 24 (5.6%) about Africans, African Americans, and West Indians; 261 (61.1%) received insufficient information; and 35 (8.2%) did not respond. Explanations were given by 297 (69.9%) as Eurocentric education through Western media and textbooks, American education excluding African and West Indian information, and learning more about British, European, and American Whites; 28 (6.6%) learned through self-education, 27 (6.3%) learned from college education, and 75 (17.6%) did not respond.

How African, African American, and West Indian parents pass a sense of history to their children (items 27 to 29). This was explored based on the total of 427 for each group. For African parents, 400 (93.6%) chose oral tradition (stories, legend), unwritten history, games, and events; 23 (5.4%) lacked information; and 4 (1%) selected school. For African American parents, 382 (89.6%) chose oral tradition, family events and reunions, family books, family pictures, experiences, and reality; 31 (7.2%) lacked information; and 14 (3.3%) chose school. For West Indian parents, 394 (92.3%) chose oral tradition, written and unwritten history, and family events; 30 (7%) lacked information; and 3 (0.7%) chose school.

Comparing civilizations and cultures (items 22 to 24). Of the participants, 162 (37.9%) chose European, 161 (37.7%) chose African civilization as more advanced, and 104 (24.4%) lacked information. For the African, African American, and West Indian cultures, 116 (27.2%) noted similarities due to common heritage, history, and family orientation; 83 (42.8%) chose negative comparisons (e.g., West Indian and African American cultures are too Eurocentric); 22 (5.2%) noted differences due to the effects of slavery on African Americans and West Indians; and 106 (24.8%) chose no comparison or lacked information. Participants chose the cultures they learned most about in their educational process (item 26) as follows: African, 126 (29.5%); African American, 90 (21.1%); West Indian, 48 (11.2%); British, 140 (32.8%); European, 226 (52.9%); and American White, 218 (51.1%) (the numbers and percentages are based on the total of 427 in each case; therefore, it is inappropriate to add the percentages together for different cultures).

DISCUSSION

This study sought to determine how people of the African diaspora born in the United States and the Caribbean region (English speaking) and those born in Africa relate with one another, and what can be done to promote better communication and understanding. The relationships among people of the African diaspora are discussed in terms of (a) interaction, contact, friendship, and travel to countries of the diaspora, and cross-cultural communication; (b) thoughts and stereotypes that may have been shaped by historical, social, cultural, and psychological forces; and (c) the role of education.

Willingness to Relate to Others of African Origin

To establish relationships (to have person-to-person interaction and cross-cultural communication), there must be contact among people of the African diaspora. Most participants had contacts with Africans, African Americans, and West Indians. For this selective group of university students, faculty, staff, and administrators, the circumstances for meeting others of the diaspora were mainly through educational institutions as fellow students, peers, mentors, teachers, and colleagues. These are the elite of their groups who have the privilege of higher education, some studying or working in the United States for African and Caribbean persons. Cross-TABs of contact information with place of birth, ethnic/racial classification, educational levels, gender, age ranges, and professional status confirmed that contact was high for Africans and African Americans but lower for Africans and West Indians.

One important way for African people to be in contact with others is through traveling to countries of the diaspora. Because most Africans traveled to the United States and some African Americans visited African countries, Africans and African Americans increased their contact with one another. Because some African Americans visited the Caribbean and most West Indians visited or lived in the United States, African Americans and West Indians had high contacts. The fact that most Africans had not visited the Caribbean (and most West Indians had not visited Africa) may explain the low contact Africans had with West Indians. Interest in visiting the Caribbean region and Africa (vs. Mexico or Europe) indicated participants' desire to have contact with others of the diaspora. The most relevant reasons to visit the "mother" country, the origin of all people, are based on similarities of language, culture, heritage, and (for Africa) ancestry. Economics may play a role in preventing travel to Africa, which tends to be more expensive than Europe; also, African people have learned about the advances of Europe in music, art, technology, renowned cities, and so forth. The same has not been true of Africa, characterized by the British system of education as "backwards, primitive, and underdeveloped." Travel offices and airlines can help make traveling affordable as a good way to learn firsthand about Africa, and build positive relationships.

Some insight into the relationships can be gained from whether there would be friendships with the different groups. Some participants desired friendships with other diasporic groups, indicating their willingness to cross boundaries of geographic places of birth. Africans seemed reluctant to have African American and West Indian friends, more African Americans would have African and West Indian friends, whereas West Indians expressed most desire for African and African American friends. Cross-TABs showed that most participants in all categories gave positive responses to justify their friendship choices. Some who preferred friendships along a Black ethnic line gave defensive reasons. For example, an African American wrote, "My social life does not bring me into contact with the other groups." West Indians justified friendship with other West Indians by invoking a cultural imperative that focused on group relationships and cultural symbols that bring people together, such as food, music, and historical experiences. Africans chose African friends as they were friendlier than West Indians and African Americans.

In terms of the interpersonal relationships, there were negative responses, such as Africans, African Americans, and West Indians have preconceived notions and myths about each other, or that the relationships needed to be improved. Some Africans and West Indians (and African Americans and West Indians) seemed to relate better than Africans and African Americans, but the general view was that the groups did not relate well. Although the groups have similar interracial struggles that create some semblance of common bonds, they fail to appreciate their common heritage. This lends credence to the divisiveness that characterizes the relationship among African people and points to the lack of understanding among them. Written responses suggested that the groups related well when they did not have to trust each other. Otherwise, the groups were cordial on the surface but suspicious that each wanted to get what was the other's just due.

In terms of cross-cultural communication, very few felt that it was good among these groups. Some took a neutral stance in claiming that it depended on the interaction or the person, or opted out of making a judgment by admitting their lack of knowledge. However, most responses indicated that communication was not good due to myths, misconceptions, ignorance, and stereotypes, thus hinting at the idea that Africans, African Americans, and West Indians did not get along. Communication problems are blamed on the history of slavery, its divisiveness, and the doctrine of divide and conquer. Black people were set up against each other and told not to associate with other Blacks because of negative attributes.

This was evident in the thoughts and stereotypes expressed by people of the African diaspora. There were few positive responses about Africans, African Americans, and West Indians, such as proud of their heritage, dedicated to family, and positive self-identity and self-image. Some expressed no preconceived notion, thus vindicating themselves from incorrectly characterizing others of the diaspora. On the positive side, written comments moderated some responses. For example, an African American wrote, "Africans are my cultural and political brothers and sisters who are in touch with their cultural roots," and professed having "great respect for them." Others reported "not stereotyping people knowing how damaging and wrong this can be." However, negative responses, such as "arrogant, and thinking they are superior to the others," indicated that the groups still harbor nonflattering thoughts and stereotypes.

Africans were seen as suffering from colonialism and war, and reluctant to move from Third World status. There were written comments from African Americans, such as: "Africans are arrogant and think they have the right to tell other Blacks what to do. Given their history, they have no right to feelings of superiority. Africans are confused about nationalism." West Indians expressed "mixed feelings about Africans; some are not trustworthy; fight among themselves, have no unity, and do not support other African countries." Africans wrote: "Centuries of oppression and colonialism left us with a void of leaders. We have come a long way toward recovery, but technologically, have a long way to go."

African Americans were characterized as possessing "slavery mentality, and sad legacy of oppression." African Americans wrote:

> We have overcome a lot of adversity and can be proud, but because we have been deprived of our heritage we still have a lot to overcome. We are having difficulties incorporating African culture with American culture, but we should build relationships with Africans and West Indians.

West Indians wrote:

> African Americans seem to have accepted defeat and have a subjective view toward Black folk of other origins. They are mostly friendly, but territorial toward immigrants, and some African Americans seem confused and disoriented. There are some rich, effective leaders who do well for others like themselves, but they do not help poor Black people.

Africans referred to the "African Americans' history of oppression as the source of their difficulties. They suggest that African Americans can concretize their objectives, by paying more attention to their family structure and learning more about their roots." West Indians were viewed as apathetic about their social, political, and economic well-being. Some qualified their stereotypes with statements such as: "West Indian identity developed differently from the others, British influence strong; less pompous than Africans, willing to share their culture more; more sympathetic about plight of African Americans than Africans." African Americans believe West Indians experienced less radical oppression than African Americans and were left in the Caribbean region in power positions. As a result, they are able to be truer to their African heritage and have a more positive self-image. Africans think West Indians are more friendly to other African people than African Americans.

There are social and psychological implications of the historical past of slavery that are evident for those whose ancestors were slaves and for those whose lands were ravaged and pillaged by the slave traders. This has resulted in African people putting other African descendants down with the view that "they have a slave mentality," especially African Americans. Bob Marley (1990), the pioneer of the Jamaican reggae music, puts it very well in his Redemption Song: "Emancipate yourself from mental slavery, none but yourselves can free your minds." This places the obligation on African people to “free themselves” from the psychological shackles of the degradation associated with the condition of being descendants of slaves. Although they have made great strides in education, African people still trail behind their White counterparts economically and look to them for employment (another form of slavery?). Socially, African people are suspicious of other Blacks who were born in different countries. They fail to recognize that they are from the same ethnic tree, the same African origin.

The European system of slavery has been blamed for creating negative myths and stereotypes about African people as a part of the strategy of “divide and conquer or rule,” which prevents Black people from recognizing their strength in unity. Western media (news, television, movies, and books) are seen as the main culprit perpetuating negative stereotypes about African people. The stereotypes are not based on true knowledge, from having firsthand information about others of the African diaspora. Therefore, African people need to learn about the diaspora themselves, and not wait on others to disseminate false information. This makes the notion of Afrocentric education relevant as a means of reeducating African people to have a better and truer perspective of others of the diaspora (see Asante, 1991). Also of relevance is Kobi K. Kambon’s (1992) view about Africentric theories, which view the basic striving in the African personality as being directed toward self-affirmation, self-determination, and self-fulfillment. In addition, Wade Nobles (1986) pointed to new ways of understanding the attitudes and behaviors Black people have toward those of different geographical origins.

In terms of intelligence, most participants did not fall into the trap of attributing higher intelligence to Africans or African Americans or West Indians, a reflection that these educated participants are willing to admit lack of knowledge, rather than accepting common notions about differences of intelligence based on race. However, there were some participants who selected no difference in intelligence among the groups, and others who pitted one or two groups against another as most intelligent (Africans vs. African Americans vs. West Indians). From a psychological perspective, Black people have been brainwashed to think that Black people have an inherent genetically induced lower level of intelligence than Whites (in studies done in the 1950s and 1960s). However, most people have moved beyond this controversy to realize that there are individual differences in intelligence in all races of people. Because intelligence is a measure of learning, it is tied in to the educational process and system to which participants were exposed, which is examined next.

Most participants acknowledged that education levels varied among individuals in all groups. However, there was a division of opinion among African Americans about American educational systems in comparison to those in West Indian and African countries. There was agreement that education levels in the United States are higher (such as Ph.D.s), but most Africans and West Indians believed that their elementary and high school education under the British system is superior to that of African Americans. If Africans, African Americans, and West Indians lack knowledge or have false perceptions about each other, it is for good reason. They learned more about British, Europeans, and White Americans than about Black people in their Eurocentric education through Western media and textbooks. No wonder Asante (1992) suggested that "the more education African Americans received, it seemed the further [they] were from their own culture, sense of identity, and their own location and sense of historical record."[1] Explanations pointed to a gross neglect of Afrocentric information in their curriculums. Afrocentric education as promoted by Asante (1991) is "the belief in the centrality of Africans in post modern history. It is our [African] history, mythology, creative motif, and ethos, exemplifying our collective will" (p. 6). There is need to incorporate information about African people in the curriculums of the educational system, particularly in the United States, throughout the year and not just during Black History Month. This issue is relevant in how African children learn their history.

Most African, African American, and West Indian parents were said to pass a sense of history to their children through oral tradition, including stories, legend, oral history, games, and family events. Because few participants selected school as the means of passing on history to children, this means that without the oral traditions, much of what is African would be lost, especially during slavery when the slaves were not encouraged to read or write. Knowledge of the history of African people would lead the diaspora to realize that there were great kingdoms in Africa (e.g., Mali and Egypt) long before Europeans claimed the glory of a more advanced civilization (see Asante, 1991; Bennett, 1988).

In comparing civilizations, one side suggested that European civilization was more advanced, technologically and academically. The other side claimed that Africa was more advanced spiritually, humanistically, and culturally; Africa is father of the Western world. If one is still in doubt about African civilization, it is relevant to call on the expertise of Asante (1991), who credits the late Senegalese activist and scientist Cheik Anta Diop (1974) for putting Egypt at the forefront of civilization. In Asante's words,

> We seek to no longer be victimized by others as to our place in the center of world history. We do this not because of arrogance but because it is necessary to place Africa at the center of our existential reality, else we will remain detached, isolated, and spiritually lonely people in societies which constantly bombard us with anti-Africa rhetoric and symbols, sometimes from Africans themselves who have been trained by the enemies of Africa. (p. x)

In terms of cultural knowledge, most participants learned most about European and American White culture, followed by British, and least about African, African American, and West Indian culture. There is agreement that the groups have a history of White domination and that the family orientation of African culture forms the basis of African American and West Indian cultures. There is consensus that formal education failed to teach about African people with whom they share cultural heritage. Na'im Akbar (1975) emphasized how critical religious and cultural beliefs are to any "constructive" understanding of Black behaviors. The cultures of Africans, African Americans, and West Indians are similar due to common heritage, history, and family orientation. However, it was noted that West Indian and African American cultures are too Eurocentric, and that there are differences due to the effects of slavery on African Americans and West Indians. H. A. Regis (1993) discussed cultural orientation, noting that the traditional cultures of African peoples tend to be collectivistic and matriarchal whereas traditional European cultures tend to be individualistic and patriarchal. Asante (1991) summarized the cultural aspect in this way: "There is first suggested the existence of an African Cultural System. Then the juxtaposition of African and American ways; and finally the values derived from the African American experience. We have one African Cultural system manifested in diversities" (p. 2). There are numerous cultural expressions of African people in music, food, religious practices, rituals, and so forth. In the Caribbean region, for example, reggae music expresses Jamaican culture, whereas calypso is the cultural form in Trinidad and Guyana. Asante (1990) noted that although the major regions of the African culture are Africa, the Caribbean, and the Americas, even within those regions there are varying degrees of cultural and technological affinity to an African world voice. One significant contributor to the cultural awareness of Black people in the United States and the Caribbean region was Marcus M. Garvey (1887—1940), a Jamaican of African descent. He gained prominence in the 1920s with his Pan-Africanism philosophy that African peoples everywhere faced common problems and should seek common solutions. This statement applies as much today as it did in Garvey's time.

CONCLUSIONS AND IMPLICATIONS

Relationships and understanding among the groups can be improved by rejecting stereotypes and developing better communication styles. There is need for a common cultural tradition for all the diaspora to embrace and more cooperation to advance their cultural, social, economic, political, and psychological welfare. African people must accept their common ancestry without putting others down by accentuating feelings of superiority. African descendants of slaves must get rid of emotional and mental baggage (from slavery and colonization) and unify themselves as one people. African people must control how their history is told and use positive and negative historical experiences to produce a stronger integrated society. There should be social, cultural, and educational exchange and joint ventures, such as scholars from Africa, the United States, and the Caribbean taking sabbatical leave to teach in each other's countries. The greatest obstacles to understanding (e.g., lack of appreciation of heritage, coordination of leadership and financial resources, education, and books) may be removed by visiting each other's countries, producing television shows and documentaries about each country, creating an annual forum for African people in the United States, and chartering low-fare trips to Africa and the Caribbean. These will promote understanding about the history, origin, family structures, and social mores of the African diaspora.

APPENDIX

Survey Questionnaire for Africans, African Americans, West Indians (Caribbean), and Other Persons of African Descent

Instructions: Please answer these questions as honestly as possible. You do not need to give your name, but your country of origin is important. This information will be used as part of the research data for a study we are conducting about people of African descent. We guarantee that this information will be treated with confidentiality, but we do plan to publish the findings. However, no individual will be identified as we do not require that you give your names. **(NB: West Indians and Caribbean persons are the same).**

1. **What is your place of birth?** (a) Africa _______ (specify which country) ________________ (b) U.S.A. _______ (c) The Caribbean _______ (specify island/country) ___________________________________

2. **What is your ethnic/racial classification?** (a) African ______ (b) Black ______ (c) African American _______ (d) Any Other _______ (Please describe) ____

3. **What is your highest educational level?** (a) High School _______ (b) Associate of Arts Degree _______ (c) Bachelor's Degree _______ (d) Master's Degree _______ (e) Ph.D. Degree _______ (f) Other_______

4. **Your gender:** Male _______ Female _______

5. **Age:** _______

6. **What is your professional status?** (a) University Faculty _______ (b) University Staff _______ (c) University Student _______ (d) Other (please specify) ____

7. Under what circumstances have you come into contact with:

(a) Africans (Check as many as apply)

1 = Fellow students
2 = Students I teach/mentor
3 = Community friends (associates)
4 = University colleagues, friends, peers
5 = Church member(s)
6 = I have not known any personally
7 = Other (please specify) ____

(b) African Americans (Check as many as apply)

1 = Fellow students
2 = Students I teach/mentor
3 = Community friends (associates)

4 = University colleagues, friends, peers
5 = Church member(s)
6 = I have not known any personally
7 = Other (please specify) ____________________

(c) West Indians or Caribbean persons (Check as many as apply)

1 = Fellow students
2 = Students I teach/mentor
3 = Community friends (associates)
4 = University colleagues, friends, peers
5 = Church member(s)
6 = I have not known any personally
7 = Other (please specify) ____________________

NOTE

1. M. K. Asante (1992), RETENTION 2000 Conference Proceedings, College Park: University of Maryland.

REFERENCES

Akbar, N. (published as Weems, L.). (1975). The rhythms of Black personality. *Southern Exposure, 3*, 14–19.

Asante, M. K. (1990). *Kemet, Afrocentricity and knowledge.* Trenton, NJ: Africa World Press.

Asante, M. K. (1991). *Afrocentricity.* Trenton, NJ: Africa World Press.

Asante, M. K. (1992). *RETENTION 2000 conference proceedings.* College Park: University of Maryland.

Becker, T. (1967). Black Africans and Black Americans on an American campus: The African view. *Sociology and Social Research, 57*(2), 168–181.

Bennett, L. (1988). *Before the Mayflower: A history of Black America* (6th ed.). New York: Penguin.

Berry, M. F., & Blassingame, J. W. (1982). *Long memory: The Black experience in America.* New York: Oxford University Press.

Bryce-Laporte, R. S. (1972, September). Black immigrants: The experience of invisibility and inequality. *Journal of Black Studies, 3*(1), 29–56.

Diop, C. A. (1974). *The African origin of civilization: Myth or reality?* Westport, CT: Lawrence Hill & Co.

Fears, D. (2002, February 24). A diverse—and divided—Black community. *Washington Post,* p. A01.

Garvey, M. (1982). *Philosophy & opinions of Marcus Garvey.* A. Jacques-Garvey (Ed.). New York: Athaneum. (Original work published 1925)

Kambon, K. K. (1992). *The African personality in America: An African-centered framework.* Tallahassee, FL: Nubian Nation Publications.

Lake, O. (1995, January). Toward a Pan-African identity: Diaspora African repatriates in Ghana. *Anthropological Quarterly, 68*(1), 21–51.

Marley, R. N. (1990). Redemption song. On *Legend* [CD]. Tuff Gong Records.

Nobles, W. W. (1986). *African psychology: Toward its reclamation, reascension, and revitalization.* Oakland, CA: Institute for Advanced Study of Black Family Life & Culture.

Palmer, C. (2000). The African diaspora. *Black Scholar, 30*(3/4), 56–59.

Patterson, O. (1972). Toward a future that has no past: Reflections on the fate of Blacks in the Americas. *Public Interest, 27,* 25–62.

Regis, H. A. (1993, May). Importation, exportation, re-exportation: African peoples and the cultural domination. *Afrocentric Scholar: The Journal of the National Council for Black Studies, 2*(1), 23–35.

Skinner, E. P. (2000). Transcending traditions: African, African-American and African diaspora studies in the 21st century—The past must be the prologue. *Black Scholar, 30*(3/4), 56–59.

Vickerman, M. (1994). The responses of West Indians to African-Americans: Distancing and identification. In D. Rutledge (Ed.), *Research in race and ethnic relations* (Vol. 7; pp. 83–128). Greenwich, CT: JAI.

Waters, M. C. (1999). *Black identities: West Indian immigrant dreams and American realities.* Cambridge, MA: Harvard University Press.

Africans and Racism in the New Millennium

Femi Ojo-Ade

Given the general excitement over the New Millennium, Femi Ojo-Ade has deemed it fit to re-visit the question of race and color with regards to Africans from the continent and the Diaspora. His intention is to determine whether humanity has made enough progress to belie the late W. E. B. Du Bois's 1903 statement on the preeminance of racism as a universal problem. The critic uses both written texts and film to assess the experiences of Africans as they encounter Euro-America and search for identity in a global village that has remained primarily Eurocentric. The article's conclusions challenge all those of African ancestry: In the face of persistent racism, a polarization of Africans along continental and national lines can only hurt the cause of all descendants of Africa, including the African Americans who are being urged to prioritize their citizenship of the United States.

> All men are born free and equal both in dignity and in rights.
>
> —4th United Nations Educational, Scientific, and Cultural Organization's Statement on Race, Paris, 1967, quoted in Ruth Benedict (1983, p. 179)

> [An African American's dream is] to be in Africa, to walk outside to see lions and leopards running around; that would have been good!
>
> —Statement in documentary film *An American Love Story* (Fox, Fleming, & Fox, 1999)

> There's a struggle between the dreamers of inclusion and the dream busters of exclusion.
>
> —Jesse Jackson, at a church in Tallahassee, Florida, in *Miami Herald*, Sept. 27, 1999, p. 1B

> When they [European immigrants] got off the boat, the second word they learned was "nigger". Every immigrant knew he would not come as the very bottom. He had to come above at least one group—and that was us.
>
> —Toni Morrison (1989, p. 120)

> A branca é mais bonita que a negra, e quem prospera troca automaticamente de carro. (The White woman is more beautiful than the Black, and whoever is prosperous automatically changes cars.)
>
> —The Brazilian historian Joel Rufino dos Santos, quoted in Pinto (1998, p. 43)

THE PAST: DEAD OR ALIVE?

Many observers of African or world history have a fixed idea of the African past and its evolution to the present: slavery, colonialism, independence, postindependence. However, those of us who know better, due to our experience in the eye of the hurricane or in the belly of the civilized monster, would make some adjustment to show that slavery and colonialism are not really dead, that independence has been nominal and superficial, and that postindependence is a euphemism for neocolonialism. The latter, concretized by the inhuman acts of military and civilian dictators, has witnessed the depletion, if not destruction, of Africa's human and natural resources to such an extent that the best minds as well as the worst are scurrying off in search of life more abundant abroad, specifically in Euramerica.

The author of this article is among the ever-growing number of these dreamers who find soon enough, to their dismay and disappointment, that the dream is very close to a nightmare and that no matter where Africans find themselves, they are faced with the problem of race and color. Yet, we Africans, wanderers of the world, resilient in our search for a better place away from home, convinced that we can shed our sufferings and shame like some past events that our masters call historical constructs, insist on reenacting the slavery of centuries past, with the distinct difference that unlike our forebears who were forcibly carried across the Atlantic into an existence worse than that of horses and dogs, the eve-of-the-new-millennium slaves are offering ourselves willingly, prepared to do anything, just to feel free. We do not care to think that this so-called freedom may be another bondage or, indeed, a continuation of that first bondage that has left an indelible and painful mark on the psyche of our people. So, here we are in civilization,[1] slaving away, contributing to the construction of citadels on top of which others perch like peacocks, while we remain at the bottom to prop up the edifice and make sure that it does not collapse.[2]

The reason for our status vis-à-vis others, including the implacable masters, is the madness called *racism.* One would not dare proffer a definitive definition here, for that is not the point. Intellectual discourse is not our objective. The incontrovertible fact is that for the African, the color of his skin and his race immediately make him less than the others. It is what Toni Morrison (1989), the African American Nobel laureate, calls "the pain of being black." We agree with Ruth Benedict (1983) that "racism stultifies the development of those who suffer from it, perverts those who apply it, divides nations within themselves, aggravates international conflict and threatens world peace" (p. 179). But in our estimation, what it does most and worst is to make everyone else feel superior to Blacks. It is the opprobrium visited upon Black people because of our race, color, and Africanity. Manifested by prejudice or discrimination, it is a question of belief or behavior, of attitude or action No matter how many theories may be propounded by "experts" who try to highlight the impact of class and economics, of culture and civilization, and of individual ignorance, racism has continued to rear its ugly head, and Blacks, including and particularly those hoodwinked into believing in their emancipation (salvation?) by material or professional success, are often urged to return to the ancestral jungle to live among the apes and chimps. This in spite of Rosa Parks and her refusal to sit at the back of the bus; Martin Luther King, the March on Washington, and the myriad achievements of the civil rights movement; W.E.B. DuBois, Kwame Nkrumah, and the glory of Pan-Africanism; Frederick Douglas and abolition and emancipation and nationhood in African countries. This in spite of General Colin Powell, son of Jamaican immigrants who rose to the very top of American military hierarchy; and Michael Jordan, the basketball megastar, symbol of deracialization, whose larger than life image on the side of Chicago skyscrapers made Louis Farrakhan, Black Muslim leader, appreciate "that process of transformation [of Black]" (Gates, 1996) and his interlocutor, Henry Louis Gates, Jr. (1996), exclaim in awe, "He's a walking phallic symbol. Here's this blackman, very dark complexion, obviously being used as a sex symbol. That wouldn't have happened when I was growing up" (p. 159).

Optimists of Black movement up the ladder could also point to Brazil, often cited as symbol of deracialized society, of the much vaunted policy of racial democracy, in essence, the epitome of "rainbow coalition." Brazil is the nation where the vast majority of Blacks have refused to see themselves as Black. Yet, one must again urge caution, because the myth of deracialization and democracy is now being debunked by those who know better (Nascimento, 1978). "The wonderful Brazilian landscape, a melange of blacks and browns and tans and taupes, of coppers and cinnamons and at least a dozen shades of beige" (Robinson, 1999, p. 10), is basically a convoluted construct of escapism, driven by the fear to face facts and the hypocrisy of a racist society: Black is at the bottom, imprisoned in the *favela* (slum or ghetto). It is only logical that given the slightest opportunity, everyone would deny his pedigree, even if it means living a lie.

It is significant that the conference at which these comments are being made is organized in Salvador-Bahia,[3] the center of African presence in Brazil and the capital of a state epitomizing the political absence of Blacks and their socioeconomic enslavement. "The question of political representation in Bahia is symbolic of the situation in the nation as a whole. In this 'antiracist' state, an African majority of close to ninety percent is governed by an all-white democratic minority" (Nasciemento, 1992, p. 112).[4] As opposed to past recidivist efforts to cover up the criminality of an establishment bent upon eradicating all African elements in Brazil by preaching deracialization, some Brazilians are now speaking out, affirming and confirming what certain observers as well as victims of the oppressive system have been condemning: Racism is a problem in Brazil.

Unfortunately, however, such intellectual gatherings as those of Salvador, organized by descendants and adherents of a Eurocentric society and visibly and almost exclusively populated by them, hardly constitute the way out for victims of racism. This critic has already commented on the peculiarities of the 1997 *congresso* (see Gates, 1996). The 1999 experience is supposed to be less scientifically oriented, that is, more popular, more open, and more committed to the cause of antiracism. Yet, as one witnesses the comings and goings of conferees, as one listens to comments from inside and outside the cavernous, definitely highbrow "Centro de Convenções da Bahia," one wonders whether much has changed. In a country where the minimum wage is about R$ 140 (reais), each participant at the conference has been asked to pay R$100. It is therefore not surprising that the very people whose lives are being discussed are largely on the outside looking in, objects of elitist notions and still instruments for promoting careers and causes far removed from the hell to which they have been banished. In essence, the Salvador congress, in a very subtle manner, reaffirms the reality of racism, derived as it does from a position of power. One would like to ask: Who is present? Whose voice is heard? Who is in control? Who oils and directs the sociopolitical machine? Who decides the nation's destiny?

DEFINING THE AFRICAN

The answer to each of the above questions would no doubt indicate that powerlessness is inextricably linked to the fact of Blackness or, more precisely, of African-ness. In other words, the closer one is to Africa, the more likely one would be victim of racism. One cannot forget that in Africa, Africans do not define themselves according to their color. The debate on color and culture has been going on for years, and no one has proffered a universally accepted solution or definition. At the 1956 First International Congress of Black Writers and Artists, Louis-Thomas Achille, from Martinique, asked whether Africans called themselves Black, "an expression that, indeed, has been imposed from outside, by the colonizing nations" (*Présence Africaine*, 1956, p. 219). In response, Alioune Diop, from Senegal, made the clarification that it is necessary to distinguish between Blacks, Arabs, and Whites. This does not lessen the import or impact of Achille's food for thought, for notwithstanding the relevance of specificity of one's Africanity, one is often mystified by certain diasporic postures on the question of Africa.

Perhaps one should not be astonished: During slavery, one major factor for determining the slaves' place in the human (civilized) hierarchy was linkage to Africa. The most recent arrivals, the *Congo*, the *African*, were at the bottom of the ladder. One recalls the story of Mag, a mulatto woman, in Harriet E. Wilson's (1859/1983) novel, *Our Nig*. Mag fell in love with a White man:

> She knew the voice of her charmer, so ravishing, sounded far above her. It seemed like an angel's, alluring her upward and onward. She thought she could ascend to him and become an equal. She surrendered to him a priceless gem, which he proudly garnered as a trophy, with those of other victims, and left her to her fate. (p. 6)

Thus abandoned and ostracized by society, the pregnant Mag goes into exile in another community. The baby soon dies. Mag is a nonentity in everyone's eyes, safe in those of "a kind-hearted African," Jim, her fuel supplier who sums up courage to ask her to marry him. For the inferior man, it is a unique opportunity at superioration. She is close to White: "He thought of the pleasing contrast between her fair face and his own dark skin. . . . 'She'd be as much of a prize to me as she'd fall short of coming up to the mark with white folks.'" So, he declares to her, "'I's black outside, I know, but I's got a white heart inside. Which you rather have, a black heart in a white skin, or a white heart in a black one?'" (pp. 11–12). When she agrees to marry the African, Mag is clear in her mind that it is not a question of love but of necessity and that she has taken one more step toward absolute ignominy: "Poor Mag. She has sundered another bond which held her to her fellows. She has descended another step down the ladder of infamy" (p. 13).

We must note here the nascent amalgamation or confusion between color and culture and, more important, the evolution of the African exiled in America into Negro-nigger-Black-colored-Afro-/African American[5] as he strives to realize the legendary American dream. With the abolition of slavery and emancipation, the process of de-Africanization continued apace. Ex-slaves and their descendants were encouraged to go back to civilize continental Africans. Even those who returned to settle back on the continent considered themselves superior for having been to the "new world"; such was the attitude of the coastal Liberians and Sierra Leoneans. Later, with the advent of Pan-Africanism, the element of superiority was notably reduced; nonetheless, there remained a condescending attitude toward the colonized Africans who were to be helped to shed their shackles.

Again, a survey of the 1956 Paris congress shows the tension between the African American and the African. James Baldwin (1985), then living in Paris, was an interested observer. He saw himself as "a black westerner." He was struck by "that gulf which yawns between the American Negro and all other men of color." He lamented,

> This is a very sad and dangerous state of affairs, for the American Negro is possibly the only man of color who can speak of the West with real authority, whose experience, painful as it is, also proves the vitality of the so transgressed western ideals. (p. 44)

In Baldwin's opinion, the Negro is fortunate to be "born in a society, which, in a way quite inconceivable for Africans, and no longer real for Europeans, was open, and, in a sense which has nothing to do with justice and injustice, was free" (p. 45). It is a society offering many more possibilities than one could ever imagine elsewhere—indeed, a superior society. For Baldwin, Africa, which he calls "a country," is "a mystery" (p. 46) with strange people and an "extremely strange language," not to forget a "hypothetical African heritage," a culture that "may simply be, after all, a history of oppression" (p. 49). Baldwin is categorical in his position that American Negroes are Americans before being anything else. In their privileged position, they can only help other Negroes because they, Americans, and the connecting link between Africa and the West know the protocol and process of climbing the mythical ladder of civilization.

Baldwin's position is supported by the objection raised by the American delegation to the following statement by one of the acclaimed fathers of Negritude, Aimé Césaire:

> This common denominator [among the conferees] is the colonial situation. And our American brothers themselves are, by the game of racial discrimination,

> placed in an artificial manner and within a great modern nation, in a situation that can be understood only in reference to a colonialism, certainly abolished, but whose consequences have continued to echo in the present (*Présence Africaine*, 1956, p. 190).

J. A. Davis makes it clear that as Americans, they are builders, "pragmatic people," working hard to achieve "equal status as citizens" and "making tremendous progress in this regard" (p. 215). Césaire is forced to apologize for daring to posit a racial and cultural unity based on African ancestry.

In Brazil, there is a unique example of racist de-Africanization, with categorization being decidedly anchored on a policy of Afrophobia. Brazil was the last country in the Americas to abolish slavery (in 1888), and when it did, something peculiar happened: The minister of finance, Ruy Barbosa, decreed in 1891 that all documents and archives related to slavery be burnt Thus began the process of trying to destroy any African presence in the country. No doubt that much success has been achieved. Even today, with the conscientizalion among Afro-Brazilian groups, such as the *Movimento Negro Unificado*, it is not unusual to find people staring at anyone wearing an African dress on the streets of Salvador, center of *Candomblé*, the Afrocentric religion, and symbol of African culture and continuity. It is not unusual to hear Blacks refusing to be called *Black*. A Black American foreign correspondent, Eugene Robinson (1999), recently recounted his experience of this racial dilemma. Individuals whom he considered Black denied being so, preferring to call themselves White. At first, he was elated by this newfound freedom to name oneself:

> I was in a world where race seemed to be indefinite, unfixed, imprecise—a world where, at least to some extent, race was what you made it. Instead of what it made you. . . . Many individuals fit into that nether region where there was no absolute racial identity, just broad categories. (pp. 10–12)

Gradually, however, he began to realize the danger in a situation where solid walls are absent. This dawns on him when he visits the *favelas*, slums, most visibly and vividly populated by Blacks, and when, at *carnaval*, he witnesses subtle but well-defined segregation, including the dehumanization of Black entertainers:

> Black was more than just a color. It was a condition. It was an identity about which some of them might have been ambivalent, that some of them might even have rejected, but that suddenly, for me, had a clarity and a pertinence that changed everything. (p. 24)

Thus, the American visitor comes to understand that Brazil, far from representing the glorious American future of a mixed society, actually symbolizes the deliberate attempt to eradicate Blackness through a process of dehumanization so that Blacks may categorically deny their color and culture and, to which one must add, their Africanness. Interestingly enough, although he indirectly made this last point, Robinson did not dwell at length on it, for a reason that we shall soon suggest. He rightly affirmed, "In Brazil, most people with some measure of African blood demand *not* to be thought of as black. . . . In Brazil, most black people do not seem to "feel themselves at all in conflict with white society" (p. 24). He noticed that the factors for naming anyone Black are usually pronounced as African features: kinky hair, flat nose, among others. Anyone fortunate to have escaped from the slums, to become empowered through education, certainly ceases to be called *Black*. Why, then, does the Black American (Robinson does not use the term *African American*) not recognize the fact of de-Africanization in the Brazilian example? From Robinson's account of life in South Carolina, what is of utmost importance is the question of Blackness, that is, the racism encountered by his people in the hands of Whites and the struggle to affirm their Americanity. In Brazil, he is an American, albeit Black, but not an American conscious of his Africanity. Therefore, it is with relief that he concluded that Brazil does not have anything to teach America and that in America, Blacks constitute a presence: "Despite all *our* [italics added] problems, I could put together a dozen magazine covers of black role models that included more than basketball players and soap opera stars" (p. 24).[6]

What is common between the American and the Brazilian realities is the refusal to recognize African heritage as a viable, positive factor in the lives of diasporic Africans; indeed, the very word *African* is foreign, strange, if not absolute anathema. Nonetheless, to this critic's mind, being African—not as a matter of citizenship or nationality, not as a question of racial or cultural imprisonment or restriction, but as a fact of an affiliation offering possibilities for affirming one's humanity—cannot but be a force and a factor in the presence and survival of those now belonging to the new world. For, after all, the European who becomes American has never forgotten his heritage. He takes it for granted, because his presence and empowerment are a matter of course, and his way of life is the standard, the mainstream. As for the Chinese, the Japanese, the Indian, and other transplanted nationalities, it is noteworthy that they also take for granted the viability of their cultures, which they live without shame or any second thought.

It is left to us Africans to find out why the hesitation, the self-hate, the self-denial. Whether we like it or not, the words of Abdias do Nascimento (1992) ring true:

> Blackness is not a question of skin color. The color of our skin, in all its varied and sundry shades, function only as a badge of our African origin, the root of our identity. *Mulato, cafuso, negro, escurinho, moreno:* all the famous euphemisms converge toward this identity, which the ruling elites in Brazil have always tried to disclaim. Therefore, when we are denied a job or shown the service entrance, it is not only our skin color that provokes the discrimination, but above all the African identity announced by the color of our skin. (pp. 71–72)

THE MALADY AND THE MADNESS: RACISM IS ALIVE AND WELL

What makes the Brazilian example particularly troubling is that descendants of Africans are so many in number but so marginalized and dehumanized that the prognosis for the future is very discouraging. The following information is supplied online by Láldert Produções Multimídia: 75% of Blacks run the risk of being arrested, 70% work in the nontechnical sector, 80% live in *favelas*, and 87% of Brazilian children who are out of school are Black. Only 15% of Blacks complete college. Among dropouts, there are 65% more among Blacks; 37.7% of Black women are illiterate, as opposed to 17.7% of White women. Of Black men, 40.25% are illiterate, as compared to 18.5% of White men. An average Black family earns R$689, whereas a White family earns R$1,440.

In such a situation, one can easily imagine how the idea of miscegenation would be widespread. The myth is that Brazilian society is a model of conviviality, cordiality, and total harmony. The reality is that Blacks, having internalized a complex of inferiority, would use the White woman as a stepping stone, a means of upward mobility, and for their offspring, life in racial paradise. Recently, an Afro-Brazilian magazine, *RAÇA* (it reminds one of *Ebony*), published an article, "Por que eles preferem as loiras?" ("Why do they [economically successful Black men] prefer blond women?") (Pinto, 1998). The thesis is quite simple and straightforward: Black men prefer White women—any White woman—to Black because White is superior and makes the man better. The magazine quotes several anthropologists and psychologists to buttress the point. Sergio Ferreira da Silva, Black psychologist, affirmed,

> Os homens negros preferem as loiras por medo de perpetuar a raça. Quando você olha o negro, vê o sujo, o piche, o macaco. É o que ele vive quando criança na escola e traz para a vida adulta. Aí, quando ele pensa em casar, sai em busca da mulher branca como objeto de negação da própria cor. (Black men prefer blondes out of fear of perpetuating the race. When you see Black, you see filth, tar, monkey. That is what he lives through at childhood and brings to adulthood. So, when he thinks of getting married, he goes out in search of the White woman as symbol of denial of his own color.) (Pinto, 1998, p. 42)

Ana Lúcia Valente, anthropologist, saw reciprocity in the relationship between a Black man and White woman and a reaffirmation of the ambiguity of racial relations in Brazil: "A loira ao lado do negro, de alguma maneira, mostra que não é racista" (The blonde by the side of the Black man, somehow, shows that she is not a racist) (Pinto, 1998, p. 42). If the affair goes bad, the woman can claim to know Black men and their behavior. Valente also quoted comments by those observing such biracial couples: "Ele deve ser rico! Senão, não conseguiria sair com uma loira dessas" (He must be rich! If not, he would not succeed in going out with such a blonde). "Ela deve estar numa pior" (She must be in dire straits). "Esse cara deve ser muito bom de cama" (That guy must be very good in bed) (Pinto, 1998, p. 42).

Joel Rufino dos Santos, a blunt, chauvinistic, and racist historian, explained why Black men lust after White women:

> A parte mais obvia da explicação é que a branca e mais bonita que a negra, e quern prospera troca automaticamente de carro. Quern me conheceu dirigindo um Fusca e hoje me vê de Monza tem certeza de que já não sou um pé-rapado: o carro, como a mulher, é um signo. (The most obvious explanation is that

> the White woman is more beautiful than the Black, and any successful person automatically changes cars. Whoever knew that I used to drive a Fusca sees me today driving a Monza is convinced that I am no longer an underdog: the car, like woman, is a symbol.) (Pinto, 1998, p. 43)

In the meantime, some of the magazine's respondents stood firm on the side of the mixed couples. According to a businessman, "Não é uma questão de preferência, é uma questão de coincidência" (It is not a question of preference, it is one of coincidence) (Pinto, 1998, p. 42). Sueli Carneiro, of the Institute of the Black Woman, saw mixed couples as representative of the ongoing universal changes in racial and social relations.

> Não são objetos de consumo, símbolo de status nem garantia de mobilidade social: são companheiros e companheiras, seres humanos, que não simbolizam êxito, mas a possibilidade do encontro, da solidariedade, do amor entre grupos étnicos e raciais diferentes. (They are neither consumer objects, symbols of status, nor guarantee of social mobility: They are companions, human beings, that do not symbolize success but the possibility of coming together, of solidarity, of love between two different ethnic and racial groups). (Pinto, 1998, p. 43)

Such a notion, one need comment, would be the ultimate ideal in a society without any racial problems, in a community where everyone's humanity was taken for granted, and in a world where skin color, social status, indeed any factor for divisions or separation, did not exist. That would be paradise, not the human society at the end of the 20th century.

The most striking aspect of the *RAÇA* article is the lack of perception in using a classic of Black revolutionary writing to support the sensationalist standpoint. The text in question is Eldridge Cleaver's (1968) *Soul on Ice* in its Portuguese edition of *Alma no Exílio*. Quoting out of context, the author, journalist Tania Regina Pinto (1998), included statements about the Black man's obsession with the White woman. For example, it is stated that he cannot help himself in craving madly for this superior flesh. He has, indeed, concluded that there can never be love between Black men and women, thus supposedly giving support and explanation for the Black Brazilian's lactifying lust. "There is no love left between a black man and a black woman" (Cleaver, 1968, p. 159): "Every time I embrace a black woman I'm embracing slavery, and when I put my arms around a white woman, well, I'm hugging freedom" (p. 160). Pinto (1998) went on to inform the reader,

> Homens negros, no tudo, ou em parte, concordam com sua analise . . . porque o branco representa realmente essa grandeza. Acho que sempre relacionei a mulher negra ao retrocesso." (Black men, wholly, or in part, agree with his [Cleaver's] analysis . . . "because White really represents that greatness. I always linked the Black woman to retrogression.) (p. 41)

Unfortunately for the reader and for the editors of the magazine, the whole article lacks focus and depth. Cleaver's (1968) text is, indeed, the confession of a sickness resulting from the experience of racism, a disease that must be cured; more important, it is a honest, blunt analysis of the malady, with the resolve to find a solution within the context of Black. It is a soul-searching journey through psychological hell toward the light provided by consciousness of one's culture, race, and humanity. Cleaver never made an absolute statement regarding the Black woman or the White. Besides, the experience of the young Cleaver is not presented as a monologue; he shared his trauma with other prisoners, and *RAÇA* fails to distinguish between the various personages in the affirmations quoted in the article.

Most significant, Cleaver found his way back home, to the Black woman, his Black Queen. The last chapter of *Soul on Ice* is a message, "To All Black Women, From All Black Men:"

> Queen-Mother-Daughter of Africa
> Sister of My Soul
> Black Pride of My Passion
> my Eternal Love. (p. 205)

Cleaver outlined the Black man's hurt and humiliation, his fear and shame, and "the naked abyss of negated masculinity," in short, the 400 years of dehumanization that left him not only impotent but also incapable of accepting responsibility toward himself and his woman. He declared, "Flower of Africa, it is only through the liberating power of your *re*-love that my manhood can be redeemed. . . . Only, only, only you and only you can condemn or set me free" (p. 207). Africa, it cannot be overemphasized, plays a major role in this process of liberation and rehabilitation. It is the past, but also the present and the path to the future.

The past is an omniscient mirror: we gaze and see reflected there ourselves and each other—what we used to be, what we are today, how we got this way, and what we are becoming. To decline to look into the Mirror of Then, my heart, is to refuse to view the face of Now. (p. 207)

Cleaver made another very thought-provoking point: that contrary to what everyone might like to believe, the abolition of slavery and the enacting of laws proclaiming equality and other human rights have not led Blacks to earthly paradise. "It's all jungle here, a wild and savage wilderness that's overrun with ruins" (p. 210). Together, Black man and Black woman are therefore called upon to build a new nation over the ruins. The Black Brazilian bourgeoisie would know nothing of such resolve; they are engaged in self-denial and self-destruction. On the streets of Salvador, the commonest sight is that of a Black man oozing some ill-defined pride in his Rastafarian dreadlocks, walking hand in hand with his elated blonde and preaching Black power while swaying to the music of Bob Marley blaring out of the giant amplifiers in a nearby bar. If and when the couple makes babies, the offspring would blend into the supposedly de-racialized society. But would they? *RAÇA*, in another recent issue (Bertlolino, 1998), raises the question of the experience and behavior of siblings of different color shades, "Irmãos de sangue, porém com tom de pele diferente" ("Blood Siblings, but with Different Skin Color"). Implication: There does exist difficulty in paradise.[7]

In the United States, in spite of declarations of tremendous progress made in regard to racial relations, everyone remains obsessed with race and with good reason: Racism is endemic to the system; it is embedded in the culture; it is entrenched in the air we breathe. In fact, race remains the issue, and precisely, it is the dichotomy between Black and White. As Morrison (1989) asserted, "Black people have always been used as a buffer in this country between powers to prevent class war, to prevent other kinds of real conflagrations" (p. 120) Everyday, in every major-city newspaper—*The New York Times*, *The Washington Post*, *Los Angeles Times*—some outrageous, racist act is reported, with Black as victim of White. At the end of the century that has witnessed a move beyond modern to postmodern, civilized savages are on the prowl, more daring than ever before, more barbaric in their actions.

In Bryant, Texas, a Black man is tied to the back of a truck by two White supremacists, who then go on a joy ride on the town's dirt road, dragging along their innocent victim. His body is shredded to pieces. In New York, an African immigrant is arrested and sodomized almost to death by a White police officer in the presence of other unprotesting officers. Two pipe bombs are detonated at Black Florida A. & M. University (FAMU) in Tallahassee, after many Black churches have been victims of similar hate crimes. Racial profiling is a daily fixture on public roads, and DWB (Driving While Black) has become a theme of discussion in bars and bistros, with Black men finding themselves, as usual, categorized as irresponsible criminals culpable for being Black. A police officer said with conviction, "To be honest, my sense of suspicion is greater towards black males than any other race of people" (*The Washington Post*, Sept. 26, 1999, p. A1). The Ku Klux Klan, hiding behind constitutional provisions, marches with impunity on main streets. And one remembers O. J. Simpson and Rodney King and the racial divide defining their cases. And one recalls that this is not the early 20th century, not the times when Blacks were lynched for having the audacity to look at a White woman; not the 1950s or 1960s, when Blacks were fighting to ride in front of a bus or obtain service in a bar. This is the postmodern era, when Blacks are supposed to be free: free to walk tall, to sit where they want, to use any toilet, to attend any school of their choice, and to date any person they want. And, indeed, they are doing all that; however, somewhere, someone, by an act of hate, supported by a system that allows such madness to thrive, reminds us that we are living in a fool's paradise.

AFRICANS AND RACISM: A QUESTION OF INCLUSION OR EXCLUSION?

One is fascinated by how easily we Africans—and here we are including all those on the continent and in the diaspora—overlook the reality of our lives to gravitate toward *Eldorado*, a dreamland that allows us peace of mind but not much else. The individualism encouraged by capitalism contributes to this spurious search for peace and prosperity. The West has taught us that attachment to community is the bane of primitive society and that the hallmark of modern society is the ability and desire to compete, to assert oneself, to be oneself, to set one's goals, and to be the best that one can be in a setting that rewards the outstanding individual willing and able to beat the competition. So the goal of the progressive Black is to get out of the ghetto by all means necessary. As for the leaders, their objective is to lead the followers into the melting pot of American mainstream to attain the almighty American dream.

Talking of leadership, one finds a certain confusion among those of the diaspora. On the continent, leaders are afflicted by decadence. First, the diasporic leadership: One observation made by Baldwin (1985) resonates with relevance and cogency: Black leaders, the new bourgeoisie, have a special relationship to the West, a relationship that they must deal with, with honesty and sincerity of purpose; otherwise, they will have difficulty leading their people in the right direction. Frantz Fanon (1952, 1961) called these leaders "men of culture," that is, those who have "penetrated into the heart of the great wilderness which was Europe and stolen the sacred fire" (Baldwin, 1985, p. 54).

In the case of the African American, there is a tendency to eschew Black nationalism and opt for American nationalism. Note that it is an element peculiar to the Black struggle to consider everything in phases of progression, delineating and distinguishing movements, generations, and personalities as historical constructs so that the past is forgotten as the present welcomes something better that is closer to and more acceptable by the mainstream. Several questions arise: Is it true that racism has been eradicated? What should Blacks do in a society that considers them inferior and liable to return to the level of their cousins living on trees in Africa? Is it wrong to proclaim one's Blackness, to promote it, to protect it, and to live one's culture based on values extant in the motherland? For Blacks to survive in the West, correct answers must be found to these questions. In the United States, not only is there lack of leadership interested in such questions, but those standing out among the crowd are too often engaged in bickering among themselves, struggling to be the most visible and vocal, the most viable candidate for whatever is available because, rather than think of the people's destiny, they are busy thinking of their image (individualism) and the so-called larger society (American nationalism).

One of the most prominent leaders of the Black community is the Reverend Jesse Jackson. At a gathering used to express support and encouragement for the students and faculty of the Florida university where those bombs exploded, the good reverend stated,

> There is a struggle between the dreamers of inclusion and the dream busters of exclusion. . . . This is not racists, this is fascists. This is shooting children in Los Angeles. . . . This is not black and white, it's wrong and right. Whether it's Jews in Los Angeles or FAMU in Florida, people of conscience know none of us are safe until all of us are safe. . . . Black and white together, that's power. When we register to vote, that's power, and when we pray, that's power. (*The Miami Herald*, Sept. 27, 1999, pp. 1B-2B)

Of course, one easily notices the preacher's rhetoric and the rousing style of the civil rights era: relevant, one might say, but also confusing and confused. Perhaps one mistake committed then and continued now is to link the Black struggle to others, thus diluting it, making it commonplace, hoodwinking the people, and giving them a false notion of their condition. Fascists, anti-Semitic bigots, child killers, and ethnic cleansers are all criminal monsters, yes; but although their crimes may be categorized in the general construct that would include racism against Blacks, it must not be forgotten that being Black is indeed considered to be a crime, at birth. Jackson and others are often more engaged in assimilationist politics than in combating racism. Precisely, Jackson's Rainbow Coalition, in its attempt to be all embracing to cut across the color and other lines, so as to be all-American, compels one to note that after all, Black is not a color of the rainbow.

Another Black leader whose actions leave one in doubt of a clear understanding of the Black condition and his commitment to the community is the Black Muslim Louis Farrakhan. His whole organization is, to a certain extent, representative of a misunderstanding of culture and heritage; for, if Christianity has been the bane of Africans, Islam has been no less of an instrument of imperialism. To reject one and embrace the other, therefore, might be regarded as a matter of jumping from the frying pan into the fire. But, then, how can one sincerely blame the Black Muslim or the Baptist in the United States when continental Africans are engaged in religious zealotry and bigotry as servants of messiahs and masters from abroad while they continue to condemn their own original beliefs as paganism? Farrakhan would appear to think first and foremost in terms of maligning and embarrassing the oppressive system in his country and cooperating with whoever stands against the system, without paying much attention to issues of major concern to his culture and community. This would explain, for instance, his visit to the late Nigerian dictator, Abacha.

A quick look at the situation in Brazil confirms the kind of confusion and lack of focus noticeable in the American setting. Only there the situation is worsened by the deliberate lack of opportunity made available to the Afro-Brazilian. At least the United States does throw up umpteen possibilities if there is a concerted effort to avail oneself of them. By successfully promoting a faceless brand of nationalism, Brazilian establishment has reduced the level of militancy among Blacks. And within the rank of the militant minority, engagement is dissipated in sectional struggles when not mired in the mysterious myopia of religious mysticism. Ironically, unlike in the United States, the vast majority of Afro-Brazilians (one could actually say most Brazilians) admit adherence to African religion, which holds the potential for self-determination, affirmation, and progress within the society. The problem is that the faith favors resignation, an acceptance of the status quo, and an inertia that imprisons the acolytes in the shrine, even as the leaders corner socioeconomic power.

Black ambiguity is exacerbated by the machinations of an establishment that discourages communal action. Elements of solidarity are definitely more noticeable among African Americans than their counterparts in Brazil. Nonetheless, both countries have their share of mongrelization. If Brazil's racial democracy has effectively reduced to a minimum adherence to one's Blackness, American individualism is continually arousing thoughts of biracial and bicultural egalitarianism. Thus, miscegenation, more and more visible, appears to be a fad, a way of showing the great possibilities of a society accepting Black and White on the same level. Stories of biracial couples abound in books and articles and, most recently, a documentary, *An American Love Story* (Fox et al., 1999), which was broadcast on public television. The film raises questions about the whole process of Americanization. Rather than level the playing field, as it were, the outcome seems to be de-conscientization. At best, the offspring of interracial marriage would be human beings, neither Black nor White; at worst, they could be simply mad. Of the many themes addressed in the documentary—which, by the way, reminds this viewer of an earlier docudrama *Roots*—the one on the African-ness of a biracial child is of most interest to us here.

Cicily Wilson, daughter of a Black blues musician and a White corporate manager, is a student at Colgate University in upstate New York. She travels for a summer semester in Nigeria in company of other students: 7 White, 7 Black, and 2 mixed blood (she and her only friend in the group, Nicole). The sojourn reveals the tension and latent hate between mulatto and Black Americans. It also reveals the tension between African Americans and Africans, not to forget the mutual ignorance of both American and African Blacks.

Cicily's trip is a fulfillment of sorts of her father Bill's dream of going to Africa and waking up "to walk outside to see lions and leopards running around." His daughter does not see lions and leopards but visits a zoo and sees chimpanzees as well as human beings. Her opinion evolves from ignorance through confusion to some acceptance of her African-ness. She falls in love with a young Nigerian, Tony, who, significantly, cannot hide his yearning for the American dream. Indeed, his fawning and cringing toward the American woman is reminiscent of many an African prepared to do anything to become part of the human cargo of the postmodern slave ship.

The relationship between Cicily and her African American colleagues is sad, because it takes the trip to Africa to bring both sides to live together. On the other hand, it is symbolic that by going back to the ancestral continent, both sides come face to face with their color and, particularly, their culture. Perhaps, back home in the United States, Cicily, now a working woman, would convince her parents that it is important to live and understand her "Black side," a side that, subconsciously, she and her family have downplayed or denied.

According to Census Bureau statistics, since 1990, the annual number of marriages between Blacks and Whites has nearly doubled: In 1997, it was 13% of all weddings (311,000). "They offer an intriguing lens through which to look at the ever-perplexing role of race in America" (*The Washington Post*, Sept. 9, 1999, p. C9). The thrust of the American love story would seem to be the potential to create a cocoon of humanity or humanism, precisely American, with no thoughts of another place or presence, so that lovers may live their life in this earthly paradise. Unfortunately, the truth is otherwise. The very fact that the two children of this all-American family bear different surnames—the first takes the mother's name, Wilson, whereas the younger takes the father's, Sims—constitutes a loud comment on the spuriousness of such a sense of family. And when Bill Sims visits his extended family, one cannot help thinking of the African concept of community, with family as nucleus of a well-grounded unity, complementarity, and continuity. Such elemental configurations are hardly accorded importance in American society.

Cicily's visit to Nigeria also underscores the way Africans contribute to the racist perception and misrepresentation perpetrated by the West. The Americana mannerisms of the young men and women around her make the perplexed student remark, "I didn't think I was going to see people striving to be like Americans!" If one condemns American media for their Afrophobic propaganda, as they emphasize only and always the negative (violence, misery, death, official corruption, lack of material development, with the jungle as symbol), one must also condemn Africans for aiding and abetting the propaganda: There are innumerable Tonys approving of any negative statement on Africa and serving as mouthpiece for American state departments by warning the foreigner to steer clear of "the dark continent." Moreover, if one feels nauseated by Western officialdom for failing to recognize Africa as part of the world—the world that for them seems to begin and end between United States and Europe, with outposts in Asia and Latin America—one must simultaneously feel outraged by the actions of African dictators, money-mongering monsters with designs at self-perpetuation in power and the patriotic objective of reducing their countries to rubble. Meanwhile, it is conveniently forgotten that past colonizers and present imperialists are also culpable in this art of debauchery and destruction; they prop up the abominable dictators who readily serve as pimps in the prostitution of Africans. The West cannot claim innocence from the tragedies exemplified by Angola, Burundi, the Congo, Liberia, Rwanda, Sierra Leone, Somalia, and Nigeria.

For the African American or Afro-Brazilian or Afro-Cuban or any descendant of Africans returning to the continent, there is the need to know Africa's history, not from the perspective of the invaders who exploited the land and peoples and are now collaborating with internal colonizers but from the point of view of Africans, aware of their past and how it has led to the present and committed to using those experiences to genuinely liberate the beleaguered culture and civilization. Such visitors from abroad would come to understand that Africa is not just the land of safari, not the jungles depicted on television and postcards, not the land of filth and corruption and coups d'état. They would find out that Africa has a culture and a civilization from which others borrowed and stole without making any acknowledgment. They would learn that that culture represents a continuity in their new homelands and that they would do best to recognize and draw from that living culture for their own benefits.

CONCLUSION: A MILLENNIAL PAN-AFRICANISM

If this sounds like another call for a return to roots, that would be an unfortunate misunderstanding, because no one in their right mind would tell citizens of other countries, with the commitment of nationalism and patriotism, to reject their nations for other habitats that in reality are geographical conglomerations concocted by vainglorious exploiters. The coming together being proposed here is based on not only the shared experiences of colonialism but many manifestations of a common ethos. In addition, this article has proved that African ancestry has been used by racist detractors to keep down Africans. It is therefore only logical to rehabilitate the downtrodden by returning value to their culture and rehumanizing them.

As Morrison (1989) has asserted in disgust, "One black person is all black people" (p. 120)—that is, when the particular individual has perpetrated something considered negative, evil. On the contrary, when a Black person does good, shows signs of brilliance, or affirms his or her genius, then he or she is an exception to the rule. Our proposal here is that we reject the ruse of individualism while reviewing and revamping our cherished ethos of community: To begin with, we must perceive the bad egg as an exception to be rehabilitated and the exceptional talent as representing the potential for widespread excellence. In other words, we must reject the habit of having others write our history. To date, we have allowed them to make our history not even on our behalf but over our dead bodies, using us as objects to promote their various agendas. In the new millennium, the image of Africa has to change: Africa, the most exploited, the most expendable, the least aided, and the most afflicted by the AIDS virus has to give way to another Africa, conscious of its values and its humanism; prepared to make sacrifices to make its people survive; clean again, as it used to be in generations past, when dignity, probity, and honor were essential aspects of commitment; and committed, not to oneself, but to all. An Africa of achievers, with research institutions where foreigners went to study; an Africa that contributed immensely to human development. That is the Africa of which every son and daughter can be proud. It is the Africa to which the mentally enslaved and the socially deprived will not hesitate to return to drink from its well of wisdom and its source of strength and to continue the struggle against racism.

In the face of this persistent racism, the worst that could happen is polarization of Africans along continental and national lines. And the temptation is very strong, what with the United States' emergence as the "only world superpower" and the African Americans' tendency to prioritize their adhesion to this superior society to the detriment of their Africanity. That worst scenario can only hurt, not help, the cause of all descendants of Africa, including the African American. It would constitute the apotheosis of determined efforts at de-Africanization (call it "civilizing the savage") begun centuries ago. In this process of dispersal, dilution, and dissipation, diasporic Africans have come to believe that "the best and brightest" were saved from the motherland.[8]

There appears to be a growing support for the theory that Africans themselves must bear the blame for slavery and that Euramericans were only exercising their God-given right to free trade. As outrageous as it may sound, such an idea was expressed back in 1966 by a Brazilian, Clarival do Prado Valladares, who after the First World Festival of Negro Art in Dakar, Senegal, declared, "Whites did not hunt blacks in Africa, but bought them peacefully from black tyrants" (Nascimento, 1992, p. 114). Thus, whereas reparations are being paid in multimillion dollars to Jews for the Holocaust, Africans are being compelled to engage in another set of arguments about their culpability in the heinous crimes committed against them.[9]

Indeed, it is only with us Africans that people dare suggest that the past be doctored or buried and forgotten, either because of shame or because, we are told, the very thought of it is too painful to bear. Yet, other pogroms, at best comparable in bestiality to our enslavement, are constantly kept on the front burner, so that the perpetrators of the evils may continually ponder the past and pay for it—so that any potential monsters may think a million times before rearing their ugly heads.

How can we as Africans become self-sufficient and self-fulfilled to survive in the new millennium, given all the odds against us? How can we thrive in a so-called global village where Black has not ceased to be globally marginalized and dehumanized? Where others are aware and proud of their past, which they have used to carve out their niche in the present, without denying or being ashamed of their heritage? Why are we always apologetic and afraid? Why do we need anyone's permission to propagate programs that will promote our culture and affirm our humanity? To this writer's mind, the most appropriate action must be based on the complementarity among the various African communities spread across the world. Each nationality would evolve new configurations of self, taking cognizance of Africa as an essential presence. After all, the qualifier—*Afro* or *African*—already admits such a presence. The increasing number of continental immigrants also attests to the rising possibilities for new formations. Contrary to the widespread stereotype of the African as vagrant, drug courier, credit-card defrauder, and con artist, most Africans in the diaspora are hardworking professionals and artisans engaged in constructive rather than destructive enterprises. It would be worthwhile, for instance, to provide data on these responsible citizens. Apart from debunking certain myths, the exercise would, it is hoped, make for well-deserved respect and open the door toward solidarity among all of Africa's children.

The Yoruba, one of the major nations to which diasporic Africans can trace their roots, affirmed, "*Àpàpò ówó l'afí só àyà*" (We use the whole hand, with all the fingers together, to beat our chest). And "*Ènìkán k'ĩ jé àwà dé*" (An individual cannot be called the community). The notion of community, serving as underpinning for communality, has been successfully used in great kingdoms on the continent and in the diaspora. It was, indeed, an essential aspect of maroon societies (Colombia, Cuba, Haiti, Jamaica, Venezuela), and the Republic of Palmares in Brazil[10] remains a symbol of pride for all African descendants who know their history. Such solidarity has remained our source of strength, even in this age of selfishness and individualism. If we return to our ethos based on the cycle of life, we would be able to forge a new ideology. We would thus synthesize the best elements of the cultural nationalism of Quilom-bismo, Negritude, and Indigenism; the pride and zeal of Harlem's New Negro; the commitment to freedom of the original Pan-Africanism; the militancy of Black Power; the artistic and socio-cultural return to roots of Black Aesthetics—all anchored on Mother Africa's unwavering humanism.

To anyone who might wish to condemn this as proof of retrogression, let us respond, with conviction, that a call to go back to understand, appreciate, and live one's culture—a constant in human existence—cannot but be the height of progressiveness, particularly because our experience of dehumanization was actually precipitated upon a systematic alienation from that culture. In essence, to become human again, to combat and conquer the ills of oppression, exploitation, and racism, we have to find our way back home. Let us note that when, years ago, such a call was made, the proponents were imbued with a mixture of superiority complex vis-à-vis Africa and a sense of inferiority in their relationship with America. And those who heeded the call, the reputed leaders of Africa's struggle for independence, stood a chance to lead their countries out of bondage; but confused in their colonized minds, they soon became collaborators with our oppressors and murderers of their own people. Today's call comes from those who realize the deep confusion and lack of commitment raging in the community. With this perspicacity, all Africans can come together and walk through the tunnel into the light of a new day.

NOTES

1. The word *civilization* is used ironically throughout this article to connote a society that purports to epitomize the zenith of humanism while, in reality, actualizing savagery and dehumanizing fellow human beings.
2. Years ago, in 1939, the Haitian writer Jacques Roumain (1972) captured this image of African slaves in his poetry, "Bois d'ébène."
3. Congresso Mundial Sobre Racismo, September 28 to October 1, 1999. An earlier gathering (August 17-20, 1997) took place in the same city: V Congresso Afro-Brasileiro, which addressed several sociocultural issues, including racism. From that congress emanated a book, edited by Jeferson Bacelar and Carlos Caroso (1999), *Brasil: Urn Pais de negros?*. See Femi Ojo-Ade's (1999) chapter in the book.
4. See also Ojo-Ade (1996a, pp. 228–260).
5. For comments on this evolution in nomenclature and psyche, see Ojo-Ade (1996b, pp. 181–186), "Afterword: What's in a Name?"
6. Robinson's (1999) *we* is defined as all Americans, Black and White. Of course, one can easily contest his statement with other facts. The truth about Black Brazilian role models is hardly different for their American counterparts. Michael Jordan, Oprah Winfrey, Bill Cosby, and Quincy Jones, all entertainers, are at the top of any list of role models.
7. It is noteworthy that several of the issues being lately addressed in Brazil have caught the attention of people in the United States. Indeed, the tendency is to think that America has already dealt with and resolved such problems. On the contrary, one finds that what America does is deal cursorily with many problems without finding solutions or with superficial ones. Legislation, a historical marker, records official action but not the beliefs and actions of human beings. Furthermore, it is amazing how easily the establishment as well as the marginalized also forget. Group amnesia attends many seminal works by Blacks, including Cleaver's (1968). Often enough, personalities themselves suffer from the disease: Cleaver metamorphosed from revolutionary to reactionary, a Republican propagandist and a conservative Christian whose words and works came to belie the position held in *Soul on Ice*. Chester Himes's (1972) novel *The Third Generation* analyzes the problem of color shades among siblings. Spike Lee's movie *School Daze* does a similar analysis of students at an all-Black college. The film certainly ruffled many a complacent, contented feather.
8. One vividly remembers the nighttime television talk show hosted by Arsenio Hall. His guest was another popular African American personality, Bryant Gumbel, host of the morning-time *Today* show. It was 1990, the year Nelson Mandela was freed from his 27-year incarceration by South Africa's apartheid government, and Gumbel was planning to take his show on the road to South Africa. He and Hall were having fun talking of the past and present and were visibly enthralled by the notion that the best and brightest had crossed the Atlantic during slavery.
9. A present source of controversy is the public television documentary by Henry Louis Gates, Jr., of Harvard University and one of the officially recognized voices of the African American community. *Wonders of the African World* is the

subject of ongoing e-mail exchanges and a collection of essays to be published by Africa World Press. This author intends to be a contributor.

10. Zumbi was the king of this Afro-Brazilian nation, *quilombo*. The republic of Palmares resisted armed colonizers for more than a century (1594–1696).

REFERENCES

Bacelar, J., & Caroso, C. (1999). *Brasil: Um País de negros?* [Brazil: A Black country?]. Rio de Janeiro, Brazil: Pallas.

Baldwin, J. (1985). *The price of the ticket.* New York: St. Martin's.

Benedict, R. (1983). *Race and racism* (2nd ed.). London: Routledge & Kegan Paul.

Bertlolino, É. (1998). Irmãos de sangue, porém com tom de pele diferente. *RAÇA, 3*(28), 52–56.

Cleaver, E. (1968). *Soul on ice.* New York: Dell.

Fanon, F. (1952). *Peau noire, masques blancs.* Paris: Eds. Du Seuil.

Fanon, F. (1961). *Les damnes de la terre.* Paris: Maspero.

Fox, J., & Fleming, J. (Producers), & Fox, J. (Producer). (1999). *An American love story* [Documentary film]. London: BBC2.

Gates, H. L., Jr. (1996). Farrakhan speaks. *Transition, 70,* 159.

Himes, C. (1972). *The third generation.* New York: World Publishing.

Morrison, T. (1989, May 22). The pain of being Black. *Time,* pp. 120–122.

Nascimento, A. (1978). *O genocídio do negro brasileiro* [The genocide of the Brazilian Negro]. Rio de Janeiro, Brazil: Editora Paz e Terra.

Nascimento, A. (1992). *Africans in Brazil.* Trenton, NJ: Africa World Press.

Newspaper article. (1999, September 9). *The Washington Post,* p. C9.

Newspaper article. (1999, September 26). *The Washington Post,* p. A1.

Newspaper article. (1999, September 27). *The Miami Herald,* pp. 1B-2B.

Ojo-Ade, F. (1996a). *Being Black, being human.* Ile-Ife, Nigeria: Obafemi Awolowo University Press.

Ojo-Ade, F. (Ed.). (1996b). *Of dreams deferred, dead, or alive: African perspectives on African American writers.* Westport, CT: Greenwood Press.

Ojo-Ade, F. (1999). *O Brasil, Paraíso ou Inferno para o Negro? Subsídios para uma Nova Negritude* [Brazil, paradise, or hell for Blacks?: Towards a new negritude]. In J. Bacelar & C. Caroso (Eds.), *Brasil: Um País de negros?* (pp. 35-50). Rio de Janeiro, Brazil: Pallas.

Pinto, T R. (1998). Por que eles preferem as loiras? *RAÇA, 3*(26), 40–43.

Présence Africaine. (1956). Le ler Congrès International des Ecrivains et Artistes Noirs [First International Congress of Black Writers and Artists]. In *Présence Africaine,* Issue 8-9-10. Présence Africaine: Paris, France.

Robinson, E. (1999, August 1). On the beach at Ipanema. *The Washington Post Magazine,* pp. 8-13/21-24.

Roumain, J. (1972). Bois d'ébÈne. In *La Montagne ensorcelée* (pp. 229-235). Paris: Les Editeurs Français Réunis.

Wilson, H. E. (Ed.). (1983). *Our nig.* London: Allison & Busby. (Original work published 1859)

Black Transnationalism, Africana Studies, and the 21st Century

Michael George Hanchard

The renewed interest in diaspora studies, intcrdisciplinarity, and transnationalism has long been a feature of African American, Africana, and Black studies. African American studies combines two modalities of knowledge formation that have been common to Western academia throughout the 20th century; the disciplines (the categorization of the social and natural sciences as well as the humanities) and area or regional studies. It combines various methodologies, concepts, and theories of the social sciences and humanities to examine specific groups of people (African and African derived) from specific territories and regions of the world (Africa and the Americas). Its unusual intellectual foundations continue to be an advantage in relation to the conventional disciplines in terms of multimethod, multiperspectival approaches to African and African diaspora related topics. The debates about area studies and their relevance for social science research have not generated much commentary or debate within African American studies. Nevertheless, these debates have profound implications for the direction and future of African American studies as a discipline, its scholarly direction, and its relation to a world beyond the academy.

Keywords: *Black internationalism; African American studies; globalization*

I would like to thank Tukufu Zuberi and the staff and faculty of the Africana Studies department at the University of Pennsylvania for inviting me to participate in their 30th-anniversary commemoration of African American Studies. The name change of the department is emblematic in some ways of the shifts among the constellation of departments and programs focusing on the study of African-descended populations across spatial, temporal, linguistic, cultural, and historical boundaries that do not always correspond to the borders of nation-states nor to the borders of academic disciplines. Africana and African American studies have played a unique role in the U.S. academy. Foisted on many institutions of higher learning in the United States due to the struggles and gains of civil rights and Black nationalism, African American studies, lest we forget, was often treated as the child of an illicit relationship between social struggle and the conventional disciplines. Its existence in many ways highlighted both the importance of political struggle and alternative intellectual traditions to the development of African American studies and Africana studies and interdisciplinary departments and programs. At elite U.S. academic institutions, African American studies departments often lurked in basements and neglected buildings on the spatial and administrative margins of many well-endowed research institutions.

By the late 1990s, African American studies in the United States gained increasing visibility as a site for disciplinary and pedagogical innovation, with an episteme that is interconnected but relatively autonomous from other disciplines. As a comparativist scholar in political science at the intersection of comparative politics and social theory, I have watched the transformation of the profile of African American and Africana studies with keen interest. The increased visibility of African American studies emerged at a moment in U.S. history when polemics and innovations involving concepts and practices of multiculturalism, diversity, and subsequently globalization drew increased attention in U.S. society as a whole. Depending on one's perspective, African American and indeed Africana studies could be viewed as part of an increasingly pluralized society and community of scholars, or as anachronisms fostering increased racial segregation in both the academy and broader society. I believe that part of the pedagogical task of any Africana studies program is to address both perspectives head on, by reminding its students and audiences outside the classroom that the best teaching and scholarship in African American and Africana studies has made profound contributions to the study of global history, and not just the study of U.S. African Americans.

As a site of knowledge production, neither Africana nor African American studies fit neatly within the borders of the United States, the Americas, or even the Western hemisphere. Although this point may be obvious to many long-time students, readers, and practitioners within these scholarly enterprises, this simple fact is not known to many outside the U.S. academy, much less within its domain. Given the circumstances of their birth on major college campuses, Africana and African American studies have often provided a unique combination of philosophical skepticism, community involvement, and political practice, activities in which academic departments, colleges, and universities as a whole are invariably engaged.

The globalized dimensions of anti-Black racisms, African-derived cultural dissemination, and transnational Black politics are just three of the foci to be found in top programs and departments in the country. I will emphasize some of the contemporary implications of these three foci in African American studies. Recent polemics and scholarship criticizing the seemingly "parochial" cast of African American studies often ignore the intellectual traditions of both African American and Africana studies in the United States that have emphasized the African-derived and descended, not just the U.S. dimension of the African American. I believe it is important to provide a brief account of the historical and contemporary elements of African American studies' "global vision," to use Robin Kelley's phrasing, to allow readers to contextualize the evolution of African American, Africana, and even African studies in relation to developments in the U.S. academy as well as national and world politics.

The renewed interest in diaspora studies, interdisciplinarity, and transnationalism in various disciplines and area studies concentrations has long been a feature of African American, Africana, and Black studies. African American studies combines two modalities of knowledge formation that have been common to Western academia throughout the 20th century: the disciplines (the categorization of the social and natural sciences, as well as the humanities) and area or regional studies. It combines various methodologies, concepts, and theories of the social sciences and humanities to examine specific groups of people (African and African-derived) from specific territories and regions of the world (Africa and the Americas). For this reason, neither Africana nor African American studies is limited by the singular perspective or paradigm of any single discipline. Its unusual intellectual foundations continue to be an advantage in relation to the conventional disciplines in terms of multimethod, multiperspectival approaches to African- and African diaspora-related topics.

The global character of Black struggle in the United States is well documented over the course of at least 2 centuries, in such scholarship as the work of Robin Kelley (1999), Tiffany Patterson and Robin Kelley (2000), and Cedric Robinson (1983), among others, to comprehend what many stateside and elsewhere have long understood, that many individuals and organizations in U.S. African American history have had a very distinct understanding of their relation to the U.S. state, its political culture, and more broadly, other peoples and nation-states in the world.

The abolitionist and emigrationist movements in the New World spawned the first generations of Black transnational political actors from the United States and the Caribbean who would travel to Europe and elsewhere to decry the evils of the slave trade and bondage of African peoples. Afro-New World missionaries who traveled to Africa, specifically U.S. African Americans traveling to West Africa, developed contacts with West African proto-nationalists who often looked to Black communities in the New World, particularly in the United States, as sources of political inspiration. The dissatisfaction with limited political, economic, and cultural opportunities for human development in the United States has invariably led scholars, activists, and common folk outside the boundaries of the United States, whether to Liberia in the founding of a nation-state by former slaves, or to Ghana during the period of national independence to help build the first independent, Pan-Africanist nation-state (Painter, 1977).

The well-documented linkages between West African and African-descended populations since the 18th century (da Cunha, 1985), the transnational political genealogies of the abolitionist, emigrationist, and Pan-Africanist movements of the 19th and first half of the 20th century, and the mass migration and movement of African populations to the metropolitan centers of former imperial and postcolonial powers in the post-World War II period all evidence an interplay of peoples, ideas, and cultural and economic practices that do not fit neatly under the disciplinary and regional studies rubrics of African, African American, or even Africa-New World studies.

ONGOING CHALLENGES FOR AFRICAN AMERICAN AND AFRICANA STUDIES

In the 1960s, advocates for African American studies, Africana studies, and Black studies on predominantly White college campuses were faced with three distinct challenges. The first challenge was undoubtedly political: to make persuasive arguments about the necessity of African American studies in institutions of learning in the United States, or at the very least, make political demands for the inclusion of African American studies in the conventional disciplines. Their second challenge was to provide intellectual justification for African American studies' unique position in the academy—not quite a discipline, national, or regional studies paradigm. This entailed the development of *transdisciplinary* approaches to the study of U.S. African American peoples, cultures, artifacts, politics, belief systems, and norms that did not fit within single disciplinary paradigms. *The Souls of Black Folk*, now considered a seminal, foundational text for African American studies, is a paradigmatic example of a transdisciplinary approach that melds sociological, historical, and literary methods to convey the singularity of the U.S. African American experience. The unique history of this particular text's reception also resonates with the unique history of African American studies as a whole; once marginalized, it is now considered essential to a well-rounded liberal arts education in most of the United States. *The Souls of Black Folk* has become required reading for many disciplines, including area and regional studies concentrations (American studies and sociology, for example). The incorporation of these and other previously neglected texts into more mainstream disciplines, however, allows the third challenge met by students of African American studies to remain ignored.

The third challenge to practitioners of African American studies was and continues to be epistemological, not only to study experiences of Black life that were neglected by social scientists and humanists in the conventional disciplines but to demonstrate how students and approaches of African American studies could successfully alter how the politics, history, and cultures of U.S. African Americans were taught in the conventional disciplines. Thus, rather than simply incorporate texts and "raw data," disciplines such as English and sociology broadened their own interpretive schemes for analyzing both U.S. African American and national experience. Within sociology, for example, the modern civil rights movement has proven to be a valuable resource for the elaboration and expansion of the study of social movements, in the United States and in comparative perspective (McAdam, Tarrow, & Tilly, 2001). In the study and production of African American literature, the critical insights of scholars such as Houston Baker, Wahneema Lubiano, and Toni Morrison have fundamentally transformed how texts and authors seemingly unrelated to African American studies have been taught.

I would like to identify the ways in which African American studies can continue to meet the epistemological challenge first posed by the creation of African American as well as Africana and Black studies on college campuses, specifically in relation to (a) ongoing debates about the continued relevance of area studies in relation to the social sciences and (b) the renewed emphasis on globalization.

AFRICAN AMERICAN STUDIES, AREA STUDIES, AND THE NEW MODES OF GLOBALIZATION

The recent consolidation of African and African American studies programs under the rubric of Africana Studies at the University of Pennsylvania is in some ways part of a larger trend of the late 1990s. As was the case for several scholarly units of major research institutions that did not evolve from one of the conventional disciplines, the epistemic terrain of African American studies has increasingly been encroached by disciplines within the social sciences and the humanities. As disciplines have broadened and expanded to encompass new methods of research and phenomena (the Internet, for example), African American, gender, and feminist studies literatures have wended their way into multiple disciplines. Though hotly contested by specialists in both fields, the boundaries of African and African American studies have come in closer proximity to one another due, in part, to the resurgence of African diaspora studies.

During the same era, debates between prominent social scientists occurred within specific disciplines and subfields, as well as in major funding institutions, about the continued relevance of area studies, language training, and qualitative methods of research to the social sciences. These debates extended into departments, disciplines, and journals over the scholarly direction and shortcomings of disciplines such as political science.

At first glance, these two processes of questioning and reconfiguration might seem to have little to do with one another. Yet, scholarly and intrainstitutional debate about these distinct processes of reconfiguration share at least two common features. Both processes necessarily entailed an examination of the direction of a particular discipline, field, and/or subfield, their continued relevance for scholarly inquiry, and the appropriateness of research methods and objects of inquiry. Second, the actual reorganization of area, regional, and population-specific studies programs at major research institutions, coupled with the gradual or sudden phasing out of area studies foci in major funding institutions such as the Ford and MacArthur foundations, generated considerable discussion and reflection about the relationship between funding sources and the direction of scholarly research, as well as the relationship between a particular field or discipline and the larger world.

The debates about area studies and their relevance for social science research have not generated much commentary within African American studies. Nevertheless, these debates have profound implications for the direction and future of African American studies as a discipline, its scholarly direction, and its relation to a world beyond the academy. What follows is an attempt to synthesize the themes of the two processes outlined above in order to highlight their significance for African American studies.

Postcolonial immigration policies in metropolitan centers have in some cases exacerbated and accelerated migration patterns between metropolitan countries and African nation-states. Thus, demographic shifts have led to new migratory patterns within the continent and between continental populations and metropolitan countries. National, ethnic, and even familial networks and identities are often reconstituted as a result of these processes. In the case of populations migrating to nation-states such as Britain, Canada, France, and Germany, as well as the United States, the overwhelming majority of African migrants assimilate and often modify extant racial and ethnic dynamics. These migrants are often transformed from Nigerian, Senegambian, or Angolan into "African" or "Black." What are the consequences of such transformations for these host countries, their "indigenous" populations, and the newly arrived populations themselves? How does the presence of such "foreigners" change existing racial and ethnic dynamics? To what extent does Blackness, rather than economic necessity, undergird the exchanges between African-descended populations within cities such as New York, which has seen a visible increase in the number and variety of African and African-descended populations over the last decade? More specifically, on 125th Street, the presence of West African immigrants engaged in labor ranging from selling trinkets to braiding hair of U.S. African American, West Indian, and other members of African and African diaspora communities begs for anthropological, sociological, and ultimately political examination. By the early 20th century, Harlem was viewed as the metropolitan center of the Black world, both as an established home and locale for Blacks from the West Indies and Africa (see Johnson, 1969; Watkins-Owens, 1996). These more recent African and African diaspora networks and linkages continue this phenomena, this time in a more highly interconnected world of travel, exodus, and migration. Phenomena such as these require tools of analysis that combine social scientific and humanistic methodologies to ascertain the various forms of significance of these phenomena.

To what field or area studies paradigm does this particular phenomenon belong? For the Africana Studies program at this university, this question is a significant one. If Africana Studies is to avoid the trap of intellectually conservative variants of regional studies approaches, the study of African and African-descended populations and their contributions also entails understanding these populations and their contributions in movement and circulation, in other words, how African-descended peoples and their contributions interact with other peoples and parts of the world.

One of my long-standing concerns for U.S. African Americans and African American studies is the tendency to equate U.S. African American experience with the entirety of the American experience (see Hanchard, 1990). To the extent that African American studies curricula, scholarship, methods, and training only concern themselves with the United States, African American studies as a scholarly enterprise will certainly be diminished and betray a more global legacy left by previous generations of scholars within the field. My hope is that the evolution of Africana studies at Penn (or anywhere else) does not devolve into a preoccupation with U.S. African American perspectives on Africa and African-descended peoples without first interrogating "African Americanness" as a settled category of racial and cultural identification.

Ongoing immigration patterns from other parts of the world also serve as reminders of African American studies' unique legacy in this regard. Immigration from Latin America and the Caribbean to the United States, for example, not only complicates the United States–centric notion of America but also challenges extant racial categories. How does one, for example, categorize an African-derived Dominican, Brazilian, or Jamaican in the United States: Latino, Black, Caribbean, or Hispanic? As the work of Mary Waters, Reuel Rogers, Phil Kasinitz, and others have shown, the processes of immigration have not only changed the ethnic and racial identities of immigrants, but they have often forced U.S. African Americans, Whites, Latinos, and incoming immigrants to interrogate, reconsider, and renegotiate U.S racial categories. It has also led many African-descended immigrants to acknowledge, often for the first time in their lives, anti-Black racism. The implications of such migratory phenomena for African American studies are potentially enormous. They may affect political, cultural and economic patterns for U.S. African Americans and for the society as a whole.

The conventional disciplines have at least one epistemological advantage in relation to ethnic and regional studies programs: the focus on concepts and multiple methods, rather than phenomena and places. One of the presumptions and critiques of area studies in the 1990s was the seeming hyperparochialism of a so-called area studies paradigm and a relative inability to situate the trends and phenomena of a particular region to more global, cross-regional trends. The emphasis on analytic abstraction, typicity, and generalization has often been presented as a comparative advantage in relation to regional and area studies. The fall of the Berlin Wall, the implosion of the Soviet bloc, and more recently, 9/11, has at the very least highlighted the continued need—rather than planned obsolescence—of ethnographic, historically and culturally nuanced research and interpretive methods.

Perhaps one of the positive outcomes of contemporary debates in political science over the continued viability of area studies in the post-Cold War era is a renewed emphasis on methodologically and conceptually driven explanations of political phenomena across nation-states and cultures, rather than region- or country-specific studies that isolate local or national politics from global political and economic phenomena. The resurgence and, in some cases, emergence of diaspora studies has not occurred in isolation. The implosion of the Soviet bloc, radical transformations of Pacific Rim economies, and structural shifts in global economies and markets have generated a variety of human consequences: wars based on ethno-political conflict; new concentrations of wealth, labor, and poverty; and unprecedented patterns of transmigration. Recent study of various diaspora populations (Jewish, Armenian, Chinese, etc.) in the disciplines of sociology, anthropology, and comparative literature has been precipitated, in part, by these new phenomena as war, famine, and bleak life opportunities have forced very specific populations to transport and adapt themselves to new societies, economies, and cultural traditions.

To what extent are African and African-descended populations part of these processes? This is just one of many research questions that a more globally focused African American and/or Africana studies can undertake. The work of scholars such as Colin Palmer, Carole Boyce-Davies, Robin D. G. Kelley, Brent Edwards, and Tiffany Patterson to further refine and elaborate research methods and design suitable for African American and Africana studies projects and programs has enabled students and scholars of African American and Africana studies to conduct more rigorous research designs and more sophisticated research questions. In addition, it allows for students of both projects to develop a more self-conscious relationship to the same or clustered set of methods, concepts, and theories of the social sciences and humanities that drive the conventional disciplines, with the advantage of remaining focused on a specific cluster of populations: their literature, aspirations, dilemmas, pathos, cultural practices and production, sense of technologies and community, even their politics. Unlike disciplines such as philosophy, political science, and economics, which have increasingly moved toward formal methods and mathematical models and away from more ethnographic research design, interdisciplinary programs and projects such as African American, African, and Africana studies can undertake scholarly investigation laden with all sorts of conceptual, theoretical, and methodological implications, only beginning with a specific population or research site rather than a discipline.

The seeming divide between the conventional disciplines and projects such as African American and Africana studies gets blurred when one considers the fact that area studies programs such as Latin American studies or African studies, or even population- or territory-specific programs such as African American or Africana studies are abstractions in the same manner as the conventional disciplines. They are analytic categories within which highly divergent populations, regions, and economic, cultural, political, and linguistic practices are organized for the purpose of scholarly identification and investigation.

For example, the operative distinctions between African American studies, Latin American studies, and American studies are largely based on presumptions of national/regional difference. There is considerable overlap, however, in the origins, cultural practices, and political dilemmas of peoples and societies of the New World. As with the conventional disciplines, these programs are defined not only by their research focus but also by what they generally do not study, the margins or neglected aspects of their research foci. Thus, Latin American studies, for example, until recently could be defined in part by the fact that most Latin Americanists did not study racisms in Latin American countries, which was often considered the obsession of the "other America," the United States. Students of the Caribbean have often had to distinguish their region and scholarship from the work of Latin American studies. To give yet another example of the arbitrary nature of area studies paradigms which often do not coincide with topographical and geographical distinctions, why is coastal Columbian or Cuban literature often categorized as Latin American literature and not part of the corpus of Caribbean literary production? Why is Guyanese literature generally read and examined under the rubric of Caribbean and not Latin American literatures? Although language, in this case Spanish, is one obvious form of categorical demarcation distinguishing one home for literature from another, these examples nonetheless point to the tensions and contradiction inherent in area studies categorization. Literatures, peoples, territories, languages, influences, and ideologies rarely line up in the way that area studies paradigms do. In their encounters with disparate ideas, histories, languages, cultures, politics, economics, and people (not to mention research methods), African American studies is not entirely African American, African studies is not entirely African, and Africana studies could not possibly be solely about the investigation of African-descended peoples and related phenomena.

What requires further study is the relationship between African American studies, African studies, and other discipline-, area-, and population-specific epistemes. Until recently, these issues have lurked at the borders of African American studies and African studies (as well as Latin-American and American studies). Shifts in demography, culture, and economy, however, have forced an encounter with these issues within the aforementioned knowledge formations. Whereas much attention has been paid to the impact of post-Cold War politics on European geo-politics, less attention has been paid to the impact of world realignment on transnational Black politics and cultures. With increased immigration to the United States from others parts of the Americas and Africa, as well as the increased fluidity of movement of populations, technologies, and information, African, Afro-Caribbean, and U.S. African Americans (not to mention people of African descent in other parts of the world) have increasingly engaged in dialogue concerning political, cultural, and economic cooperation that transcends the boundaries of national and regional distinctions while underscoring the tensions and differences between them.

This leads to the final thematic that could be further examined by students of African American and Africana studies: the relationship between these two knowledge formations and globalization as a defining phenomenon of our age. Viewed historically, Africana and African American studies provides an opportunity to connect contemporary globalization to its antecedents in global history. The middle passage and racial slavery generated two distinct but deeply intertwined modes of globalization affecting African and African-derived populations: the circulation and dissemination of ideologies of race and racism, and the scattering of various African peoples, technologies, cosmological systems, and cultural practices throughout the world. The middle passage, symbol of the forced migration of peoples across the Atlantic and their enslaved labor in multiple colonial and imperial societies, constitutes a moment of globalization. The dissemination of racist ideologies justifying African enslavement, from the 16th century onward, was also made transnational during this period. These two processes were distinct from the slave trade across the Indian Ocean, or connections between peoples from the African continent prior to the middle passage, because they did not entail racialization processes that situated African-descended subjects at or near the bottom of a hierarchy of humanity.

The legacy of these two processes through the postemancipation, colonial, nationalist, and postcolonial eras in the New World and on the African continent have had different, contradictory effects. On one hand, the mass dissemination of anti-Black iconography could have occurred only in an era in which mass media and transportation networks and technologies were placed in the service of colonialism, imperialism, and the evolution of the nation-state system. At the same time, movements against enslavement, negative imagery of Africa, and African and African-descended peoples, as well as transnational solidarity networks such as the antiapartheid movement, Garveyism, and Pan-Africanism, are equally inconceivable in the absence of the technological, organizational, and socioeconomic features of the modern era. How do we make sense of these tensions between these two very distinct but interrelated features of modernity?

Current forms of globalization, ranging from flexible production, regional consolidation of national-state economies (NAFTA, EU, and Mercosur), and new technological applications, are all unprecedented features of this era and no other. These phenomena and processes have generated new patterns of migration, regimes and demands of production, and increasing tensions between national sovereignty and new formations of capital. One possible area for scholarly investigation would be to study certain aspects of the political economy of contemporary globalization to an examination of how African-descended populations have migrated and shifted in response to new employment opportunities, or conversely, in response to limited economic opportunities in response to shifts in production regimes from one region to another. The influx of African-descended populations from places such as Honduras, Belize, Haiti, Nicaragua, and elsewhere in Central America, the Caribbean, and Latin America, has increasingly pluralized the notion of what it means to be an African American in the United States (see, e.g., Hintzen & Rahier, 2003; Kasinitz, 1992; and Gordon, 1998). The circulation of toxic wastes and other polluted substances, recycled clothing from the overdeveloped world to the underdeveloped world could be another research opportunity for students of African American and Africana studies.

Phenomena such as the aforementioned require that students of African American studies (less so for Africana studies) have to problematize the logical series of easy assumptions of population/culture/nation-state/territory intrinsic to the idea of African American studies as the study of African-descended populations born and raised in the territorial dominion of the United States, with certain recognizable cultural, linguistic, political, and other patterns to readily identify them. The more plural U.S. African American communities become, the more African American studies has to elaborate methods and a vision of U.S. African American studies as part of a broader configuration of disciplines, methods, and foci aimed at expanding a knowledge base for understanding how African-descended populations in the United States interact with the entire world.

REFERENCES

Cunha. M. C. da. (1985). *Negros estrangeiros* [Foreign Blacks]. Sao Paulo, Brazil: Brasiliense.

Gordon, T. (1998). *Disparate diasporas: An African-Nicaraguan community on the coast of Nicaragua.* Austin: University of Texas Press.

Hanchard, M. (1990). Identity, meaning and the African-American. *Social Text*, *8*(24), 31–42.

Hintzen, P., & Rahier, J. (2003). *Problematizing Blackness*. New York: Routledge.

Johnson, J. W. (1969). *Black Manhattan*. New York: Athenuem.

Kasinitz, P. (1992). *Caribbean New York*. Ithaca, NY: Cornell University Press.

Kelley, R. (1999, December). Problem: Black history's global vision, 1883–1950. *Journal of American History*, 1045–1077.

McAdam, D., Tarrow, S., & Tilly, C. (2001). *Dynamics of contention.* New York: Cambridge University Press.

Painter, N. I. (1977). *Exodusters: Black migration to Kansas after Reconstruction.* New York: Knopf.

Patterson, T., & Kelley, R. (2000). Unfinished migrations: Reflections on the African diaspora and the making of the modern world. *African Studies Review*, *43*(1), 11–46.

Watkins-Owens, I. (1996). *Blood relations: Caribbean immigrants and the Harlem community*, 1900–1930. Bloomington: Indiana University Press.

PART 5 QUESTIONS

1. How significant is the Black Church in the political experience of African Americans, given constitutional separation of church and state?

2. How do African Americans and others of African descent interact and view each other across nationality and multiplicity of identities boundaries?

3. Do racism and oppression emanating from identity boundaries [LLC9]still impact African American reality in the present?

4. What are the lessons of the African American struggle, and what do Africana Studies offer in understanding the struggle in the twenty-first century?

CPSIA information can be obtained
at www.ICGtesting.com
Printed in the USA
LVHW021143040822
725060LV00001B/1